Thomas Hare

The Election of Representatives, Parliamentary and Municipal

Thomas Hare

The Election of Representatives, Parliamentary and Municipal

ISBN/EAN: 9783337152284

Printed in Europe, USA, Canada, Australia, Japan

Cover: Foto ©Suzi / pixelio.de

More available books at **www.hansebooks.com**

THE

ELECTION OF REPRESENTATIVES,

PARLIAMENTARY AND MUNICIPAL.

A Treatise.

By THOMAS HARE,

BARRISTER-AT-LAW.

FOURTH EDITION.

ADAPTING THE PROPOSED LAW TO THE BALLOT, WITH APPENDICES ON THE
PREFERENTIAL AND THE CUMULATIVE VOTE.

LONDON:

LONGMANS, GREEN, READER, AND DYER.

1873.

PREFACE TO THE FOURTH EDITION.

THE issue of another edition has become necessary, not only to introduce such alterations as shall adapt the proposed electoral law to the Ballot Act, but also to make known the progress of the representative principle in actual practice, and in theoretical development. In both, the greatest advances have been made in the United States. The experiments in Harvard College, Massachusetts, and in the Technological Institute at Boston, show that a preferential choice from competing claims to distinction, may form a highly instructive part of the historical and political education in our schools ; while the recent election in Illinois, of the Upper House by the old, and the Lower by a proportional system, contrasts their results.

In our own country the preferential and proportional method of election has been twice brought before the House of Commons: first on Mr. Mill's amendment to the Reform Bill (29th May, 1867), and again on the motion for the second reading of Mr. Morrison's Bill (10th July, 1872).

When in 1869 the House of Commons appointed a Committee to inquire into the modes of conducting elections, with a view to provide further guarantees for their purity, tranquillity, and freedom, the event was hailed as an opportunity of subjecting the proposed method to an exhaustive inquiry, and bringing prominently forward the anticipated results. Evidence was therefore tendered to the Committee for the purpose of showing how greatly the temptations to corruption

*

a 2

would be reduced, tranquillity assured, and electoral freedom extended by proportional representation. The Committee, however, requested their chairman to reply that the object of their inquiry did not extend to a consideration of the subject under any other than the existing conditions, and they declined to accept the evidence. It is greatly to be regretted that at a period of transition in the history of representative government they should have considered that so comprehensive a reference was satisfied by an inquiry thus superficial, and thought that the evils of corruption, violent manifestations of discontent, and restricted power of selection, had no deeper sources than the imperfect machinery of the polling booth. It would be scarcely thought compatible with scientific investigation if one charged to inquire how the public health in a city might be best promoted, should decline to look into the sources and purity of the water or the completeness of the drainage, and regard himself as confined to the "existing conditions," assume the existing diseases to be inevitable, and try to discover nothing more than the medicines that could be resorted to as antidotes.

The Ballot Act, whether it be regarded as a fruit of the inquiry of the Committee, or as the result of a foregone conclusion, has now become law; and all the rules and forms heretofore proposed as to voting, which were in any respect incompatible with it, have been altered or expunged.[1] The author has not, however, thought it necessary to withdraw any of the speculative observations which he ventured to make in former editions with regard to secrecy in political action. Secrecy is no obstacle to any part of the scheme; on the contrary, in many points of view it may render its adoption still more desirable or even necessary; but a frank manifestation of all opinions is more in conformity with the ideal of healthy national life.

[1] A few words implying arrangements inconsistent with secrecy, which escaped attention, are pointed out in the *errata*.

PREFACE TO THE THIRD EDITION.

THE criticism of seven years on this method of relieving electors from the artificial restraints which impede the freedom of action in representative institutions may be summed up in a few words,—that it is too complicated to be practical, —that it is hostile to our local system,—and that it would admit of abuse from party organization. If the first objection were true it would be insurmountable: the second would be an obstacle to the adoption of the method. If the last had any foundation, in its exposure to party influence it would still deserve a comparison with our present system. Apart from these supposed objections,—a system which would bring home to every elector the feeling of actual and personal responsibility,—convert what are now only majorities into unanimous constituencies, and mischievous and demoralizing contests into efforts of honourable emulation,—in which all moral and intellectual elements would have their direct expression and just force, and the corruption that remained would be confined within such natural and inevitable limits as to take from it nearly all its political and most of its personal evil,—has met with very general approbation.

First, as to the alleged complexity. The system, while it gives to every elector the most ample choice of candidates, makes a vote effectual in the election of one only. It is therefore necessary to provide for the probability that men of great popularity and eminence will have a large number of

votes, many of which would be thrown away, if means were
not given to the electors of transferring them to another
candidate, in case the first they have named be elected without their aid. Accordingly, the form of the voting-paper,[1]
without making it compulsory on the voter to name more
than one candidate, yet permits him to insert a second name
under the first, a third under the second, and so on,—at
his discretion, and according to the measure of his sympathy,
his desire to show a concurrence of opinion, or to manifest his
respect or appreciation. Those who come to the examination
of this scheme for the first time will probably be amazed to
learn, that—so far as there is anything to be done by the
voter—this is the whole extent of the complexity from which
so many politicians have shrunk.

Many of the epithets used in describing this proposal
would appear intended less to invite attention than to turn
away inquiry. Legal phraseology has been borrowed to
cloud with its abstractions the simple act of writing the
name of one candidate under another,—that the vote may
be transferred to the second, if the candidate named first
should have votes enough without it. It has been called a
" contingent remainder," and an " estate tail " in a vote! It
may be left to the electors of the kingdom to judge between
those who seek for them this vast augmentation of their
electoral power, and those who tell them that a vote for a
second person to be used on the contingency of the first not
requiring it, is beyond their understanding. I would remark,
however, that if any voter can be found to whom it is not
intelligible,—the use of the contingent vote by others will do
him no harm. Every power which he has under the present
system is scrupulously reserved to him, except that (which
may indeed have its value in the eyes of those who are skilful
in wielding ignorance) of drowning the voices of other people.

A vote is to be given to the candidate placed second on

[1] Page 124.

the paper, if the first has enough votes without it,—but how many are enough?—and how is that to be known? The simple course is to ascertain how many persons vote, and to try how many votes each member to be elected would have if the votes were equally divided. On the morning which follows the election day, the entire number of votes would be known. If 658,000 people had voted, and there were 658 members, 1000 would be enough (or be the quotient or quota) for each member; and if any candidate had more than 1000, the excess beyond that number would be transferred to the successive candidates named on the voting-papers. I suppose that no inspector of a national school would allow a child of ten years old to be reckoned as entitling it to head-money out of the public grant who is not able to divide the number of the voters by 658, and thus obtain the quota. But even this achievement in arithmetic is not required from any elector. It is an operation to be performed by registrars, to whom the numbers are reported.

It is then necessary to determine which of the voting-papers shall be taken to make up the member's quota, and which shall go to the next candidates. It is of little importance to the voters, but may be of much consequence to the candidates placed lower on the papers. The papers might be drawn by lot, but I have preferred a series of simple rules, in which the appropriation is made to depend on locality, and on the number of alternatives the voting-paper displays. These rules are to be applied by the registrars, and any voter to whom they might appear perplexing need not trouble himself with them. It is only necessary to satisfy him that the rule is impartial and just. The voter has nothing to do necessarily but to look to his own voting-paper. It will be deposited in his town. He may at any time refer to it, and see by the endorsement to which of his favourite candidates it has been appropriated. This will be proved by his name being found among the constituency of

that candidate ; and the fidelity of the disposition will be
tested by tables showing that the votes severally appropriated
make up the total polled. The telegraph and the railway are
not of less public utility because few who use them are
masters of the science of mechanics and the laws of electricity.

The alleged impracticability of the method has recently met
with an unexpected and conclusive refutation. Mr. Lytton,
Secretary of Legation at Copenhagen, judging that there
was no subject of internal polity, which the inquiries of our
ministers abroad could elucidate, so fraught with consequences deeply affecting the public prosperity, and none,
moreover, in which the institutions of free states had gathered
such small improvement in the progress of civilization—in
July, 1863, laid before the government at home a paper on
the mode of electing the Rigsraad, or Supreme Legislative
Council of what was then the United Kingdom of Denmark
and the Duchies.[1] This method, which was first adopted in
1855, at the instance of Mr. Andræ, Minister of Finance,
Mr. Lytton discovered to be almost identical with that which,
after several more imperfect embodiments of the same leading
idea, has been propounded in this Treatise. He regarded
the existence and operation, for eight years, of an electoral
system, which had theretofore been considered in England as
a theory only, to be a very remarkable event in the history of
representative institutions. " If," Mr. Lytton says, " the question, ' Will it work ?' can be eliminated, the more important
question, ' What will be the result of its working ?' will be
entitled to increased attention." With a rare appreciation
of the essential elements of the scheme, and of their bearing
under different political conditions, Mr. Lytton explains the
extent to which it was capable of application in the election
of the Rigsraad. Of the eighty members which composed

[1] *Reports of Her Majesty's Secretaries of Embassy and Legation on the
Manufactures, Commerce, &c., of the Countries in which they reside.* No. 7.
Presented to both Houses by Command. 1864.

that body twenty were nominated by the Crown for twelve years, and the remaining sixty were elected for eight years; thirty being chosen indirectly by the provincial assemblies, and thirty directly by the people. The system of quotas was adopted in both, the popular vote extending to the thirty elected directly. This limited application of the method, moreover, was for the election of an assembly whose ordinary sittings were only two months in every second year, and the membership of which conferred no great accession of dignity or influence, and opened but a very small, if any, field for political rivalry or effort. A seat in it had so little to invite activity or tempt ambition, that Mr. Andræ found it necessary to provide in his law for the case of a candidate who, after having been duly elected, should decline the seat. Even a simple declaration of candidature, it was said, would be distasteful; and it is the practice for those who desire the election of a particular person, to ascertain privately beforehand that he will not disappoint the electors. This condition of the national mind, and the antipathies of race in the Duchies, which were all the time on the point of breaking out into open war, together with the restricted measure in which the popular voice would be thus collected, caused the experiment to be made under circumstances as unfavourable as can well be conceived. A part of the kingdom repudiated the constitution, not owing to any opinion as to the mode of election, but from hatred of the union; and this reduced the directly elected representatives to twenty-two. A scheme, therefore, devised to abate the fierceness of electoral conflicts among people of great political activity, to moderate the bitterness of struggles by which parties labour for the extinction of each other, and to regulate and hold within reasonable bounds the force of passions that, pursuing with intense desire objects of personal and party ambition, too often threaten to sweep away in their resistless torrent the virtues, the moralities, and even the decencies of life, came thus, in

a partial degree, into use amongst a people in whom the
common current of political feeling and effort is so sluggish
that an artificial stimulus must be employed to overcome
its inert character. Yet, notwithstanding these hindrances,
election by this method is effected without difficulty; it has
facilitated the introduction to the national legislature of men
of the highest character and intelligence, and is working out
a corresponding improvement in the constituent bodies.

Secondly,—of the effect of the method on local elections.
The system which really destroys the wholesome influences of
locality is that which has long been, and still seems to be,
most in favour with popular reformers,—grouping some
boroughs, disfranchising others, here severing cities and
counties, and there adding a score of villages to some small
borough. The component parts are rather repelled than
attracted by such undesired combinations. It is proposed to
amend this anomalous patchwork, and allow the country
spontaneously and without any arbitrary rule, to recover its
natural subdivisions,—to recognize no right to any monopoly of
electoral privilege, and in the place of disfranchisement to en-
franchise not less than four hundred towns which are now
shut out from any local action; and the proposed amendment
is alleged to be destructive of the local character of our electoral system! To give the widest scope and inducement for
local combination is to delocalize!

The apprehension of a disregard to localities is probably
owing to the fact that the first step in the method is to add
together all the votes given in the kingdom in order to compute the quota. Thence it is imagined that the whole kingdom is in some manner made one electorate, whereas, in
truth, the computation is nothing more than a momentary
operation to arrive at a common measure of the constituencies
without any purpose of blending them together.

A doubt has, indeed, been expressed by one who has given
much attention to the plan,—whether it is consistent with

the maintenance of local distinctions, or with the identification of particular representatives with particular groups of voters. In the present edition, the eighth chapter, which treats of the duties of the returning officers, has been considerably expanded,[1] in order that it may be better seen that none of the legal subdivisions of the constituency are effaced, nor any of the visible landmarks of the electoral field swept away; and that, on the contrary, as the surge of our national life rolls deeper and wider, such legal subdivisions will be multiplied, and many new landmarks added to the old. It will be seen that the identification of particular representatives with particular groups of voters is promoted and secured to an extent and with a completeness hitherto unknown.

A London merchant, on the register in Devonshire, may vote for a candidate for the City, and a Scotch merchant in London may vote for a candidate for Glasgow,—how is that consistent with the integrity of localities? It is true that any elector, however humble in rank, or feeble in influence, may pass by the candidates for his own constituency, and propose, instead of them, any other candidate he might prefer, but this is nothing more than his ancient common-law right. Every elector may now propose and vote for whom he pleases. This method enables him, however, to do much more,—and it is to this additional power that some of our politicians object, and against which they raise the cry that "localities are in danger." It enables the elector to put his vote in writing, and makes it possible that the vote, although without effect in his own constituency, may help the return in some other place of the candidate for whom it is given. Yet it does this without any control over or interference with the voters of such other constituency. There may not be enough voters in it to make up the quota, or not enough given for that candidate, and the distant vote may therefore serve to complete it,—not impeding but assisting everywhere the majority,

[1] Pages 164–174.

—the greatest number that can agree together,—in the work of electing their local member. Without such a power, it would be commonly useless, and even absurd, for an ordinary elector to propose a new candidate against the nominee of the clique or caucus of the borough ; but this power, which vindicates his individual right, most of our politicians shrink from giving him. It would, they fear, make the voter too free. He is not to be trusted without the bridle and the bit. Extend the suffrage,—make the constituency more numerous,—but do not trust them out of harness. " All our schemes of election management may be defeated, if every voter had such extensive means of comparison and choice, and if no small cabal could affect the general result."

With the integral political rights of counties, cities, boroughs, and corporate bodies, the constitution of this kingdom, and the public life and habits of its people, are inseparably interwoven. This method of election contains very much which would promote the development of such centres of action, and impart to them a purer and nobler spirit,— nothing that would weaken their force. Can it be supposed that the moment the electors are allowed a freedom of choice they will all immediately be seized with a desire to vote for some distant candidates with whom they are unacquainted, rather than for those whom they know,—who are near to them, whose addresses they have heard, and who have personal recommendations to the favour and respect of the town and neighbourhood ? Local and corporate associations are highly and justly prized. From them the state derives benefits analogous to those which the close fellowship and community of the domestic and family relation afford to the individual. These natural ties are not so fragile that they disappear as soon as they cease to be forcibly kept alive by positive law. It argues but a small belief in the regard of our people for local action to suppose that they must be imprisoned within their constituency to be kept true to it.

If we consider the mental effect on the observers, of nearly every kind of competition the result of which is doubtful, we shall find there is every reason to conclude that local interest, activity, and effort will be stimulated by an election in this form to a greater degree than heretofore, and will be of a far more wholesome character. Many more candidates will be everywhere put in nomination. The measure of local regard for each candidate the votes will display,—the anticipated evolution of varieties of preference,—the desire of the more public-spirited inhabitants that the choice of the majority may light on the best, or on him they think so,—will " present the situation of suspense and pleasurable engrossment " [1] in great force. This aspect of the subject has been treated in another place,[2] and, interesting as it is, I forbear to dwell upon it.

The third objection,—that a party " ticket " would be used, and party organization become omnipotent,—is scarcely more than an offset of the last,—that the method delocalizes. If, indeed, it created one electorate,—if every member were chosen for the whole kingdom, and by no county or town in particular,—each party might safely produce a printed ticket for its own followers, and be certain that, to the extent to which they adhered to that ticket, the candidates named upon it, one after the other, would make up their quotas or majorities, until the whole strength of the party is exhausted, and it can elect no more. Supposing, also, party devotion to be thus blind and indiscriminate,—that every voter chose to be either a Tory, a Whig, or a Radical, they might vote either for the T., W., or the R. ticket in blank, and leave it to the leaders of their parties to fill up the names according to the number of quotas which each could muster. Yet see how alien all this management is to our habitual action,—how irreconcileable with our forms of political life! Our pro-

---

[1] *Bain, The Emotions and the Will.*

[2] Representation of every Locality and Intelligence. *Fraser's Magazine,* April, 1860, p. 536.

vinces are not the merely passive and stolid reflex of the opinions of the capital. The people of Liverpool or of Manchester would not set aside their eminent merchants or manufacturers for the nominees of a London club; nor would the inhabitants of Devon, or Warwick, or Edinburgh, or Glasgow, submit to such dictation. No county or borough would consent to use such tickets if they had not been consulted in the selection of any of the names. Even if the kingdom were a single electorate (voting by quotas) no party would dare to ignore,—on the contrary, each party would invite the co-operation of local eminence and the power which it carries with it.

A single electorate, voting by this method, and using party tickets, would still have no resemblance whatever to the "American ticket." That "ticket" is got up to enable the numerical majority to hold together in one unbroken, compact mass, and crush the minority. It is politically a life-and-death struggle:—it admits of no balancing, no wavering,—no hesitating or half support. The stronger party will emerge in safety,—the weaker will perish.

A single electorate and the use of tickets by party supporters, voting in quotas, by the contingent method, would, alone, be a vast improvement. The strength of each party would be measured by the popularity of its principles,—each party would place its best men foremost in a gradation of supposed merit,—and each would select and nominate its very best to attract the support of the independent electors, while the latter would have before them a choice of the superior men of every party.

The proposed method, however, is not that of a single electorate. The representatives of the United Kingdom would be chosen by seven or eight hundred distinct constituencies, acting separately and apart, and it would become the endeavour of the most intelligent persons of every constituency to prevent it from being stultified by giving the major part of its votes to a candidate who would throw discredit upon it. The voting paper in every constituency would be different, and *no uniform ticket could be safely used.* Every candidate will require his name to be placed first, or first after some one certain of being elected,—or it will probably be of no use to him. The intercalation of any candidate who fails would prevent the vote from being used for any lower name, and may deprive it of any influence on the election. Parties may, indeed, adopt the use of printed voting papers, leaving blanks at the head, or near it, for the local candidates, and inserting below the names of other principal candidates of their side. The extent of the use of these papers, or "tickets," would measure the popular sympathy with the party whose opinions it expressed, and would give them the moral weight of such adherence. It is a mode of gathering a knowledge of popular opinion and sentiment which is every way desirable; and it would have no other than a salutary effect on the particular election.

In an earlier stage of the method it was proposed to re-duce the number of candidates, and arrive at an equal quota for those who were elected, by giving a proportionate value to every contingent vote, and computing the total of such values as the measure of support each candidate had received. This was open to the objection that it gave inordinate weight to numbers acting by means of party papers or tickets, and the suggestion was for that reason withdrawn.[1] The plan proposed for the city of Frankfort[2] is liable to the same objection.

The principle always kept in view has been that in form-ing the representative assembly of the nation, full play should be given to the expression of all opinions and sentiments, that they may be admitted to the test and scrutiny of discussion. The electors are the dispersed inhabitants of an extensive and

---

[1] Pages 187, 188. See also Appendix C. This is the difficulty alluded to by Mr. Mill in his *Considerations on Representative Government,* p. 158 2nd ed. It has been obviated by excluding a contingent vote from any effect *on the election,* until it is taken to make up a quota or comparative majority.   [2] Appendix B., p. 299.

b

populous kingdom, possessing knowledge and powers of thought infinitely varied and diffused; and to expect that the electoral forms of a rude and illiterate age will gather for the national benefit the fruit of this expanded intelligence, is as reasonable as to suppose that the vast manufacturing results of this day could be produced by the primitive loom and the hammer. To succeed in this work it is indispensable that every elector should have the widest field of choice, and the most extensive sphere for co-operation. It is by comparison that the standard of excellence is raised. " As we eliminate comparison we fall into dead acquiescence." It is by the co-operation of kindred and sympathetic minds that great ends are accomplished. In the kingdom there is a range wide enough for that accord which can be rarely obtained in any single constituency. " The essence of liberty is the simultaneous manifestation and action of all rights, all interests, all social elements and forces." We follow the true guiding of experience when we found our conclusions of the probable actions of men from the motives by which they are commonly guided: it is thus that the science of political economy has been evolved; and in the improvement of representative institutions we must pursue the same method.

As electoral action is freed, most of the evils which now accompany it will disappear. A seat in Parliament, as an avenue to social estimation, as well as to political power and rank, will still be an object of intense ambition; and the rich candidate will as surely use his money to bribe, as the crafty and fluent candidate will use his tongue to delude. Penal laws cannot reach the latter, and only aggravate the demoralization occasioned by the former. But in casting off the legal shackles, this moral disorder is dealt with as physical maladies are encountered. Its virulence is abated,—as many of its causes as are capable of removal are got rid of; and, above all, the contagion is prevented from spreading to those who are in health.[1] Personal representation equalizes the pecuni-

[1] See pp. 106–109, n.

ary value of every vote, and reduces it to its minimum. Three fourths of the temptation is thus swept away, and, what is even far better, no man can sell more than his own vote: he cannot at the same time, by turning the scale, sell his town, or affect the representation of the rest of his constituency. Nor would any candidate thenceforward be driven to call evil good, and praise conduct as virtuous and patriotic which he knows to have been selfish and corrupt.

Personal representation encourages every man to do the best that is in him, and leaves him without excuse if he does not; and it therefore in the highest degree tends to promote individual effort. "The general public opinion is formed and modified by what the mind of each individual contributes towards it: it represents the sum or balance of the abstract moral principles of the persons forming the community. The state can only hear advice, or yield to suasion, or imbibe the spirit of genuine improvement through the medium of the individuals of whom it is composed."[1] It was a remark of De Tocqueville that the rulers of our time sought only how to use men in order to effect great things. "I wish," he said, "they would try a little more to make great men,—that they would set less value upon the work, and more upon the workman." Every detail of this scheme converges to one central point,—that of making the exercise of the suffrage a step in the elevation of the individual character, whether it be found in a majority or a minority. I disclaim for it, therefore, the title of a representation of minorities. M. Morin, to whose labours in Geneva I refer elsewhere,[2] has better comprehended its object, and I presume to quote his description of it. "Il est vrai que M. Hare poursuit un but plus élevé que la représentation des minorités et que si celle-ci est obtenue, dans son système, ce n'est qu'indirectement. En conséquence, ce qui paraît une défectuosité, considéré au point de vue des minorités, peut n'en être pas une, lorsqu'on se place à celui de l'auteur. M. Hare se propose avant tout

[1] Gladstone.   [2] Appendix A. p. 295; and see p. 255, n.

d'affranchir l'électeur du joug des partis et de le relever à ses propres yeux. Pour cela, il le place en face de lui-même pendant l'acte important qu'il est appelé à accomplir et le rend partiellement responsable de la composition de la législature. Ce n'est donc pas sans motifs plausibles que M. Hare se présente comme fauteur de la représentation personnelle, plutôt que de celle des minorités. La lecture de son traité conduit facilement à la persuasion que le pays qui façonnerait son organisation électorale, d'après de telles idées, s'assurerait les bienfaits d'un corps législatif, composé d'hommes capables et estimés, en même temps qu'il élèverait le niveau moral de la population."[1]

The political education afforded to our people by the occasional opportunity of concurring in or opposing the election of one or two representatives, has been compared with that conferred by the town autonomy of the Greek cities—as of Athens, where the Demos met at short intervals, and exercised the office both of parliament and government, and questions of foreign policy and domestic administration were constantly argued.[2] Certainly, with our present system the comparison is humiliating enough; but if the constitution would open to every voter a scope for thought and reflection as wide as his intellectual and moral horizon,—if it gave him a choice from among all who by their candidature show that they aspire to public distinction,—the political school of the "every-day Englishman" would surpass in value that of the citizen of Athens in its proudest time. The long procession of history, and the phenomena of a progressive civilization,—the accumulated records of human action,—the influence of Christianity,—the opening portals of natural science, afford endless themes for instruction, bearing on the policy and complicate arrangements of social life in modern times, of which the Greek orators or statesmen could not dream. The subjection of a theorem, moreover, to the calm

[1] Page 17.   [2] *Freeman's History of Federal Government*, p. 40.

deliberation of the closet is a more instructive process than its reception from lips however eloquent.[1]

After all, the end is "good government,"—but that includes the moral and intellectual development of the men and women to be governed. Institutions are good which call them habitually to perform such public functions as tend to awaken a true conception of their real interests and duties in respect to their households, their neighbourhood, the state, and the brotherhood of nations ; and lead them to realize their endowments of conscience and intellect, the gifts by which God has fixed their high place in the order of creation, and in the great inheritance of humanity. But a government is not good which, as to numbers of its people, contemplates no more than protection from an external violence,—which allows them no voice in the choice of their legislators, or in framing the laws by which they are to be ruled, and which disdains any appeal to them in its consultations on the public welfare. Such a government differs from natural society only inasmuch as the individual is guarded by the civil power instead of his own strong arm. It fails to cultivate the higher qualities of his nature, to foster a love of country, a regard for public duty, or even a just self-respect. What it bestows is but the attention of the kind master to his horse or his dog. It misses even the poor end at which it aims. The classes usurping all power cannot confer even the physical and material comfort of which they boast. Where the right is absent, the corresponding duty or responsibility will not be felt. The classes treated as inferior beings, will discard the higher obligations of civil life and throw upon those who have assumed the charge of their destinies, the blame, if not the consequences, of their moral weakness and degradation,—thence our load of pauperism, our catalogue of crime. The wise parent admits his children to his counsels, and makes them partners of his labours and his hopes, not from caprice or by fits and starts,

[1] See pp. 253, 254.

but gradually and impartially, as education bears its fruit, and intellect is matured. The nation is but a greater family.

If the choice be wide and free, the examination of the list of candidates, by an intelligent elector, with the practical object of placing on his voting paper the names of the most worthy of a seat in Parliament, would be an intellectual exercise of no mean value, bringing home to him important truths and noble aims. The thoughts it is calculated to awaken in his mind, and the discussion among his family and friends to which it is likely to give rise, would be sources of more than transitory benefit. He may give effectual support to the local candidate, and at the same time render a moral tribute to others. Few exercises would be more instructive than that of gathering information and forming an estimate of the character of candidate after candidate,—weighing their labours,—their public claims from achieved service, or the hopes inspired by youthful promise,—with the looked for pleasure of being able to offer an unsolicited testimony to merit and an unexpected homage to worth. This is no visionary expectation. Experience teaches us that it is an ordinary impulse, when the mind is not distorted by prejudice. "The judgment and criticism we pass freely upon our fellow-creatures, and their ways and performances, are a common gratification, partaking of the freedom of thought itself. Whatever good qualities strike our minds, or impress the community we live in, are sure to be sought after with especial ardour, whilst those that are in bad odour are kept in subjection. The contemplation of superior greatness is a fund of delight."[1] Aspiration is generally higher than knowledge, and multitudes of less education and narrower intelligence will gladly associate their votes with those of the more eminent and distinguished of their age.

It would probably become habitual with intelligent voters, to preserve a copy of the voting paper, making in it, from

[1] *Bain, The Emotions and the Will.*

time to time, such alterations as the withdrawal of old and
the introduction of new candidates, the progress of opinion
and of events, might occasion. It will thus be a political
register, and the act of framing it anew at each election will
be an instructive lesson. The admission or rejection of every
name may involve a conclusion on the domestic, social, or
international questions of which he may be the type or
exponent. The precipitancy with which the mind approves
or rejects the claims which are put before it, and the caution
it uses in sifting, weighing, and examining them, is the touch-
stone of the order of intelligence. "Where the consciousness
is not awake except under a very broad difference, we consider
the mental constitution the opposite of intellectual. In
whatever department of impressions the nicest sensibility to
difference prevails, in that department will reside, in all probability, the intellectual aptitude of the individual."[1] The
mere act of voting may thus be made the basis of a study
widely diffusing a knowledge of the principles of social
polity. "If the human mind grow dwarfish and enfeebled,
it is ordinarily because it is left to deal with commonplace
facts, and never summoned to the effort of taking the span
and altitude of broad and lofty disclosures. The understanding will gradually bring itself down to the dimensions
of the matters with which alone it is familiarized, till having
long been accustomed to contract its powers, it shall lose well-
nigh the ability to expand. The laws of the body are those
of the mind. Exercise and excitement strengthen and ener-
gize—indolence and habits of insensitiveness, contract, debili-
tate, and at length kill."[2]

Everything which in political life liberates and increases
the scope and influence of enlightened judgment and cultivated reason, is of inestimable service also to those who
occupy the higher places in social rank, and possess in the
greatest measure the advantages of education and leisure.

[1] Id.   [2] Id.

It is to the state "that sovereign intellect naturally betakes,
and here that it unfolds itself: not only does it give scope
and space to the highest energies of the human understanding,
it is also directly the parent, and the object, of some of the
noblest feelings which belong to our nature, and, these too,
such as operate on the most comprehensive scale."[1] It was
long ago said that "the main thing which social changes can
do for the improvement of the higher classes is gradually to
put an end to all unearned distinction, that the only road
open to honour and ascendancy be that of personal qualities."[2]
Rank and wealth set out with the most favourable auspices,
and stand on the vantage-ground of competition. They will
more certainly retain their position in the race, as they
themselves eschew, and endeavour to purge political life of
all that is vile and base ; put forward their highest order of
minds for public duties and public honours, and do their
utmost to prevent seats in Parliament, or great offices or
functions, from being made the appanage of triflers or
weak men. It is not wise to stand contentedly by, as
some would seem to advise, and wait the behest of public
opinion to be communicated by the newspapers. Such apathy
is perilous. It is true, as Lord Grey has said, that "to be
in constant conflict with evil in some shape or other is
obviously the condition appointed by Providence for men
and nations, and the moment that struggles for improvement
cease, corruption and decay commence."[3] Society, notwithstanding the wider diffusion of material prosperity, has yet a
vast accumulation of political, moral, and physical evils to
vanquish and sweep away. " Civilization is yet very young ;
the world is very far from having measured the extent of the
career which is before it." The great embodiment of the
national life, the State itself, should be, in its popular action,
like the awful seat of justice, as far as possible free from

    ‥   ¹ Gladstone.   ² Mill.
        ³ *Parliamentary Government*, &c., by Earl Grey, p. 113, n.

every corrupting taint, and every degrading element, that it may attract to its service and duties the most enlightened and the purest minds. Instead of excluding large classes from the franchise, they should rather be invited to its exercise; but the invitation should be accompanied with the inseparable condition that every elector shall, in the act of voting, show both his capacity and his worth, and be enabled gradually to rise to the importance and dignity of the function with which he is intrusted.

I have collected in an Appendix to this edition, extracts showing the efforts that have been made to introduce this system in different parts of the world, and the large degree of support they have met with, notwithstanding its novelty. The progress of the idea among the more profound writers on political subjects is not less remarkable. If it has yet been adopted only in one northern kingdom,—if in the other free states of Europe, and the great Anglo-Saxon communities of the Southern Seas and the New World it has been hitherto a subject of barren discusssion, it must be remembered that the powers of statesmen are limited; whilst effort for improvement is still the duty of all who possess any portion of political power. "A great ruler cannot shape the world after his own pattern. He is condemned to work in the direction of existing and spontaneous tendencies, and has only the discretion of singling out the most beneficial of these. Yet though a pilot cannot steer in opposition to wind and tide, the difference is great between a skilful pilot and none at all. Improvements of the very first order, and for which society is completely prepared, which lie in the natural course and tendency of human events, and are the next stage through which mankind will pass, may be retarded indefinitely for want of a great man, to throw the weight of his individual will and faculties into the trembling scale."

February, 1865.

THE subject of political representation now assumes an aspect entirely different from that which it presented in the discussions that preceded the Act of 1832. The question was then between a partial representation, the inequalities of which were in their general effects balanced by many compensating influences, and a scheme which, dispensing with most of such influences, made the representation more direct and real, and established it on a wider basis. That Act, which was the offspring of a political compromise, extended the application of the representative principle, without excluding, and not intending to exclude, many imperfections and irregularities. The anomalies which remained were chiefly owing to the attempt to give effect to two principles which the arrangements of our electoral system made it impossible to reconcile,—the representation of interests and the representation of persons. Some constituencies were retained, framed or modified, upon the supposition that they would, in all circumstances, support what were conceived to be special interests. The idea of the constituency as the constituted exponent of an interest having been once received, excluded the idea of personal representation within that constituency, and therefore led to the consequence,—that if persons not governed by the prevailing interest found their way within the prescribed limits, it was necessary, in pursuit of the representation of interest, to exclude such intruders, as far as it could be done, from the electoral power. As the law, however, did not, and could not, adopt, as an electoral qualification, a test of fidelity to the special interest contemplated, it is not found possible to exclude from the constituency some who are guided by other motives, and form an antagonistic class. The electoral bodies which are regarded as the exponents of special interests are thus exposed to internal conflicts, which render their action more or less uncertain.

In the mobile and susceptible condition of population and society at this day, it is impossible not to observe the purely speculative character of all conclusions founded upon what the permanent interests of the inhabitants of a particular district may be,—upon what they will themselves consider them to be, or upon what their majority may resolve. In a revision of our electoral system, all those who would found the Parliamentary strength of interests or classes upon the basis of constituencies formed for their support, should consider with what degree of safety they can rely upon a body of electors within any certain area remaining permanently faithful to the principles by which they may be at present guided. So long as any definite or indefinite number of persons shall be attached to those principles by the force of mental association or material interest, their support may be reckoned upon ; but if it be a further condition of rendering this support, that such persons shall be so numerous within any geographical limit as to preponderate and overpower all opposing forces within it,—the security to be derived from their attachment is certainly not strengthened. The sources of permanent support are weakened by the introduction of a condition which does not increase sympathy,—which may be impracticable,— and which is of no value unless it can be used as a means of disregarding or setting at defiance the opinions of a minority. The territorial condition must be one of two things,—a source of strife if it succeeds,—or a cause of weakness if it fails. It is deserving of the most profound consideration of all who desire to perpetuate any definite political principle, whether it is possible to insure it for a geographical ascendancy; and whether there are any means of promoting its maintenance so certain and lasting as would be found in a consistent adoption of the sole and simple principle of personal representation.

In framing the constitution, there has been little of that kind of aid which physical science derives from experiment. Government is necessarily established before the question of circumscribing its powers can arise,—and powers once possessed are not often willingly given up. Every step by which a class has been admitted to a new participation in power has been either a concession or a conquest; and the moment of gaining it has been a time of action, and not of speculation. It may have been so far experimental as to have arisen from the sense of some prominent defect in the existing institutions calling for amendment. "Many minds, long ages, and various events have contributed to the advance" of our representative institutions. The successive labourers worked under the unconscious influence of the idea of representation, —though "only seeking to remedy the injustice of some particular case, or prevent the recurrence of some particular evil." But, "when the idea of any institution becomes distinctly apprehended, we may proceed with a firmer step and more assured success towards its full development. We have the guidance of a principle; we have the clue to what had appeared a tangled maze. Our notions may be termed theoretical, but the theory is a condensation of all the practicality of the past."[1] The full display of the principle of representation "is as much the function of the future, as the origination and progress of the principle has been the achievement of the past. We have here our test of the venerable and the obsolete; of the use and the abuse; of

---

[1] *Westminster Review*, vol. i., p. 10, N.S.

what is to be abolished, and what retained. We have a guiding star for the work of reformation."[1]

In considering the process of interesting greater numbers in the constitution by investing them with political rights, we meet with the fact that the proportionate interest felt by the constituency appears to diminish as the numbers of the constituency increase. It is found that in the larger constituencies about fifty-five per cent., and in the smaller ones about ninety-two per cent., of the electors recorded their votes on the occasion of contests at the same general election.[2] This divergence from representation is still more apparent when the active elements,—the fifty-five per cent.,—are further reduced by taking from them the minority,—the voice of which is extinguished, and which consists of about two-thirds,—leaving the numbers actually represented in the larger constituency as about thirty-three per cent. The unrepresented portion is not only great in numbers; but there is no doubt that in many populous boroughs it also contains the largest portion of the educated classes, of those to which, in every view of representative institutions, it is desirable that full weight should be given. It is therefore of paramount importance to discover, and if possible remove, the causes which tend practically to exclude from representation so extensive and valuable a part of the electoral element; and this is now of especial urgency, as every step in the extension of political privileges, whilst it has the effect of changing the class in which power resides, increases at the same time the disturbing causes that interfere with and are evidently obstacles to true representation.

A perfect *representation* is plainly inconsistent with the exclusion of minorities; but the subject of representation would be very inadequately conceived, if it were regarded as a mere question between majorities and minorities. The formation of electoral majorities and minorities is no more the

---

[1] Id., p. 17.   [2] *Edinburgh Review*, vol xcv., pp. 279, 280.

natural means of arriving at political representation than it would be a natural result of any other association that it should be divided into two parties, one perpetually labouring to counteract the wishes of the other. The order and the occupations of mankind,—the distribution of population, and the supply of its necessities, are all provided for by physical and moral laws operating on the diversities of nature and of character which are found amongst men. These differences preserve the harmony and the vitality of social life. In political sentiment there is not less variety than in the other motives of human conduct; and abstractedly it would be no more likely that the political opinions of the electors of a borough should fall into two or three antagonistic divisions, than that they should be composed of twenty, fifty, or a hundred distinct views or conceptions. The dissimilarity would be much more probable than the similarity. Opinion and action in politics would be as various as opinion and action in other sciences, if there were not causes that enter into political bodies, and create a disturbed and unhealthy movement, provoking antagonistic divisions.

On the occasion of adverse desires in a society composed of many free agents, the majority *must* necessarily decide; but in the formation of a representative body, the purpose is that the body thus to be created, and not the constituent body, is to be intrusted with the power of decision. If that were the function of the constituent body, there would be no necessity for appointing the representative. It is, consequently, by the majority of the representative body that the decision must be pronounced. It is that majority which speaks for the whole, and is irresistible. It may be likened to an engine of enormous power which crushes all opposing forces. The election is the process by which this engine is constructed; but it is not necessary to the efficiency of the engine that the same overpowering force should have been employed in the process of its construction. It is when the engine is formed that we require its power to be exercised;—whilst the engine is being made,—it is the engine we want, and not the power.

The conduct of men may be actuated by two different motives, one, the desire to do that which is believed to be right,—the other, the desire to do that which shall be attended with direct success. A parliamentary representative is to be chosen by two or three thousand electors, and opinions and interests are greatly divided;—two questions may present themselves to every elector,—the one,—who is the person best fitted by character and talent to fill an office in the duties of which the interests of the nation, to an incalculable extent, may be involved,—and the other, who will my co-electors be most likely to choose? In other words,—what is right, and what will succeed?

It may be answered, that abstract right, when considered by a prudent man, resolves itself into a question of expediency and practicability,—that it is a case of compromise;—and that, therefore, the second question is that which such a man is justified in asking. It is true that in all political action we must consider what is expedient and practicable. This is the well-known and just defence of party action. Singly, one man can do little, and yet, by combining his efforts with others having similar objects, he may accomplish much. But it is necessary to consider under what conditions an individual is placed when he is called upon to yield up his own opinions of rectitude and prudence. To what extent is the will at liberty? That which is a free concession amongst persons who have associated voluntarily, to pursue the same objects and the same means,—as the partners or shareholders in a company, or the members of a particular society, may be, and most commonly is, entirely different, when the persons collected together are infinitely various in character, disposition and object, and their association is compulsory and not voluntary. In such a case the question ceases to be of the nature of a compromise, and becomes one of mastery. Instead of yielding to the opinion of others with whom the elector has been led to associate by the existence of some mutual basis of sympathy or harmony, he is, in the case supposed, obliged, in order to succeed, to give up his own opinions to those who form the most numerous portion of his co-electors, the greater number being, as one of the conditions of nature, the lower in capacity, and he is obliged also to take into account all the disturbing and corrupting influences which may prevail. He is,—to refer again to the analogy of party,—in the position that a member of Parliament would be in,—if, instead of attaching himself to the party with which he sympathises and is content to act,—he found himself indissolubly bound to a section,—say of fifty other members whom he has had no part in selecting,—and unable to take any step in which he cannot persuade the majority of the fifty to concur. If he does not remain inactive, his objects must be lowered to, and measured by, theirs. This condition is parallel to that of the elector who is forced to act on the answer to the second question, instead of the first and true one.

The necessity of obtaining a majority involves the necessity of creating a party, adopting a party name, and putting forward some party tenet, or dogma, to all of which the majority must lend itself. It is not usually the political tenet which has caused the party, but the party which has created the tenet. In none of these things, any more than in the choice of their representative, can the members of the majority usefully ask themselves what they ought to do,—the only practical question is, what will be successful? Thus, the process of creating the majority demoralises most of those who compose it: it demoralises them in this sense, that it excludes the action of their higher moral attributes, and brings into operation the lower motives. They are compelled to disregard all individuality, and, therefore, all genuine earnestness of opinion, to discard their political knowledge,—their deliberate judgment,—their calm and conscientious reflection,—

all must be withdrawn or brought down to a conformity with those who possess the least of these qualities.[1]   The same injurious influences, in a measure, operate on the minorities, whenever they make a decided stand for the purpose of contesting a seat.   The most intelligent will have submitted to the most numerous, except that, in the minorities, the greater apprehension of defeat may have led the more numerous classes within it to raise their standard of choice in order to increase their hopes of success.

Whilst this process of deterioration is going on throughout those who compose the *active* parties, a result even more fatal to the design of true representation is produced on another large, intelligent, and more scrupulous class of persons, who feel no disposition to make themselves the instruments of giving effect to the views of others with whom they have no common object or sympathy.   These, therefore, take no part in the business of choosing those who are nominally to represent them.   We find, as it has been observed, that, in the large constituencies, nearly half of the electors are, for all useful purposes, in the same position as if they were disfranchised.

A system which forms the electoral body into adverse parties,—arrayed under formal names which are themselves exaggerations calculated to excite hostility where none really exists,—has thus the effect of preventing the expression of the true and individual opinions of the members who compose either party.   It lowers the force of thought and conscience, reduces the most valuable electoral elements to inaction,—and converts the better motives of those who act, into an effort for success and a mere calculation of the means of accomplishing it.   It is not therefore surprising that we hear of the infirmities of representative institutions, and that many persons should be unable to look forward without terror to the aggra-

---

[1] It is by no means uncommon to hear persons state that they vote for a particular candidate, not from any appreciation of his merits, but to exclude some other candidate to whom they are more averse.

vation of their more obvious evils by any large extension of some of the causes which produce them.

If these consequences be inevitable,—if in the progress of constitutional government we are exposed to the danger of excluding from their just share in representation the more educated and intelligent classes, — and of paralysing in political life the action of the infinite varieties of disposition and sentiment which are found in society,—if there be no means of making representation a reality,—the infirmity of the institution must be borne. It is useless to lament that for which no remedy can be found. It must be accepted as the lot, and part of the discipline, of humanity. But, at least, every effort of the understanding should be brought to bear on the question, whether the representative system be not capable of more perfect development than it has yet received. No time perhaps was ever more favourable to the inquiry. The inconsistencies and anomalies of the existing system have been long felt, and successive governments have addressed themselves to its improvement. The patriotism of every class has been challenged, and at no former period has so general a disposition been evinced to abandon long-cherished traditions and opinions, and adopt such a revision of the representative system as may appear most likely to be conducive to the public good.

If, after the construction of the representative body shall have received the aid of all that thought which the importance of the subject imperatively demands, it be held impossible to render it a perfect expression of the sense of the people, or more than of the will of a multitude of detached majorities, *that* should be recorded as a fact, and received as a distinct constitutional principle. If it be a necessity of government that a multitude of petty majorities,—for petty they must be compared with the nation,—shall exclusively elect the representative assembly, let it be the declared and acknowledged form of the constitution. It is due to the more thoughtful and scrupulous of the electoral body, as well as to the minorities, and not more to them than to the precepts of truth and justice, that the principle should be distinctly propounded,—and it is very different from the principle of true representation,—that not the representatives of the people or of all those who possess the suffrage,—but, representatives chosen by the resolved and active majorities of certain arbitrarily-formed electoral bodies,—are to be consulted in making the laws. The whole people may be bound to obey the laws thus made, but that does not make the nominees of a part the representatives of all. It may be claimed as a homage to what is just and true, that it be not falsely imputed to any class of persons that they are represented by men whose views and opinions are utterly repugnant to their own. The member elected in every constituency may be returned as representing so many as shall vote for him, but not as representing those who do not vote for him, or who oppose him. The democracies of former times asserted their power, but did not assert an untruth. The necessity of obedience to the law, wherever the power of making it may reside, is easily seen: if it be concluded that there is a necessity for depositing the power in the combined majorities, the nation must bow to that authority,—but there can be no necessity that our institutions should be founded on an untruth or a fiction. They should stand on substance and reality. Let the representation be declared to be what it truly is, and not what it is not.

: It will be observed, that the causes which operate to render the franchise valueless or ineffectual to large and intelligent classes, are causes peculiar to an advanced state of civilisation ; and we may properly seek, in the increased knowledge which accompanies social progress, the means of removing the impediments to representation which it discovers. Representation itself is a matter of daily occurrence, and common necessity. It is the vicarious performance of duties which cannot be personally executed. It intervenes in commerce, in jurisprudence, in education, and in a thousand other forms. In a multitude of circumstances people are compelled to place themselves and their interests in the hands of others. The exercise of individual judgment and deliberation suffices for all these purposes; and if, in the choice of their parliamentary representatives, the electors were freed from the embarrassing restrictions by which their action is incumbered, there is no reason to doubt that they would employ the same care and caution as that with which they select persons to fill other fiduciary or vicarious offices.

The object of this Treatise[1] is to show that the attainment of a perfect system of personal representation is not opposed by any difficulties inherent in the subject; and that such a system is not only consistent with the due and just representation of every class and interest in the kingdom, as well as of the public which comprises all, but that it affords the most permanent and certain mode of representing and expressing the special views and opinions of all interests and classes; and that it also goes very far to remove, even if it does not entirely obviate, all the sinister influences which have been hitherto found to prevail in the collection of the suffrages of the electors. It will be seen that personal representation, to be perfectly carried out, must be founded upon the basis of individual independence; that such independence

[1] The author first published the principle of the suggestions contained in this Treatise soon after the general election of 1857, in a pamphlet intituled *The Machinery of Representation* (Maxwell, Bell Yard). A note to the same pamphlet, and, subsequently, a second edition, was published in the same year, the details being materially altered, and brought much nearer their present shape. The communications which the author from time to time received, led him to believe that the scheme had excited interest in the minds of many who had given much thought to this and kindred subjects; and that it was generally considered to stand in need of development more in the way of showing its practicability, than of proving the value of the objects which it was directed to attain.

may be obtained without departing from any of our traditional forms of electoral incorporation,—and that it even affords peculiar facilities for giving greater scope and expansion to such local and traditional combinations. The electoral arrangements which are proposed require no operation that cannot readily be executed by instruments which the administrator will always have at his command ; and they prescribe no duty, which any person of ordinary capacity is not competent to perform. It is only necessary to resort to those common aids which education and science now afford,—the knowledge of letters, which was not implied in times when the election was made by a show of hands,—and the means of rapid conveyance and transport, which were not possessed by former generations.

With a view to avoid any expressions which might be vague or indeterminate, to render the proposal definite and precise, and enable its practicability to be readily and distinctly considered, the whole scheme has been wrought into the form of a supposed electoral law, the clauses of which are distributed amongst the several chapters,—following the respective branches of the subjects to which they relate, and in which are explanations of the principle, the purpose, and the operation of every clause. A table has also been introduced, showing the entire law, and referring to the pages in which every clause will be severally found.

If, by the means which are here proposed, or by any which are better and wiser, an electoral system can be established, which, in the work of forming a representative body, shall succeed in calling into action all the thought and intellect of the nation, the effect would be to create a new object of inquiry and study, extending over a field of which we know not the bounds. All attempts to engage society in political conflicts for abstract principles would be thenceforth vain, and statesmen would seek to build their fame on something more

solid and durable than party triumphs. A representation of
all intelligences, founded upon a wisely-regulated franchise,
cannot be dangerous; it would contain within it breadth,
symmetry, cohesion, and durability,—all the elements of
strength and safety, and would possess, moreover, a capacity
and a disposition for social improvement, without any limit
but that of the human faculties.

Gosbury Hill, Kingston-on-Thames,
January, 1859.

TABLE OF CONTENTS.

CHAPTER I.

THE REPRESENTATION OF MAJORITIES, MINORITIES, AND INDIVIDUALS.

Foundation of the power, *page* 1—and definition of majority, 2—Composition, 3—Burke, 1, 6—Guizot, 2, 7, 12—Calhoun, 3, 5, 19, 20—Conventional character, 3—Absolute government of numerical majority, 3—Its abuse, 6, 20—Suffrage insufficient to form constitutional government, 4—Distinction of numerical from concurrent or constitutional majority, 5—Extinction in the representative body of the less popular parties by the detached action of local majorities, 7—Minorities in this country, 8—Supposed compensative representation, 9—Its injustice, impolicy, and danger, 10—Collection of the diversities of opinion of many, instead of the record of the preponderance of one of two or three opinions, 12—National loss in excluding the intelligence of all the minorities, 12—Three-cornered constituencies, or restricted vote, 12—Cumulative Vote, 13—Objections, 15—Ancient powers of knights and burgesses, and analogy of the jury, 16—Speeches of Mr. Bright, 17—Protection to Minorities and individuals in the power to form other new constituencies, 21—Free interchange of political force, 21, 22.

CHAPTER II.

CONSTITUENCIES BY VOLUNTARY ASSOCIATION AND UNANIMITY.

Association of individual electors of different constituencies, *page* 23—Its basis a community of sentiment, 24—Registrars, 24, 25—Relative magnitude of voluntary constituencies, 25—Average number of electors, 26—Mode of ascertaining the quota, 25, 26—Extent of the field for collecting kindred opinions, 27, 28—Facilities of intercourse, 27—Educational franchise, 28—Defects of the form suggested, 29—Unsuitableness of the

geographical principle, 30—Increased scope for electoral action, 31—
Representation of interest, 32—Inadequacy of the county representation,
33—The agricultural interest, 34—Manufactures, shipping, trade, 35—
Absence of representation of the working classes, 36, 37—Contrast of the
system of personal representation with its opposite, 30, 40.

CHAPTER III.

GEOGRAPHICAL, LOCAL, AND CORPORATE DIVISIONS OF ELECTORS.

Reform Act of 1832, page 41—Double process of giving representation to
boroughs and creating boroughs for the purpose of representation, 41—
Natural order in forming communities, 42—Artificial divisions, 43, 47,
48—Burke, 42, 48—Projected reform by grouping some boroughs and
disfranchising others, 44—Disposition to voluntary association in guilds,
fraternities, companies, &c., 46, 47—Its operation to be encouraged in
forming electoral divisions, 47—The Crown the essential basis of legislative construction, 49—Provision for such reconstruction from time to
time, 50—Immediate need of it, 52—Effect on the public spirit and
emulation of majorities, 54—Guizot, 53—Early access to political life of
men of talent, 56.

CHAPTER IV.

NUMERICAL DIVISIONS OF ELECTORS.

Duke of Richmond's plan in 1780, page 58—Reform Act of 1832, 59—Examples of Electoral districts, Ayr, Finsbury, Exeter, 59—Equality or
permanency of geographical divisions impossible, 61—All involve the
extinction of minorities, 62—Establishment of a self-acting scale, 62—
Apportionment of representatives to the several states in America, 63—
"Gerrymandering," 64—Proportional system, 65—Geographical equality
of this system, 65—Compared with that of contributory boroughs, 66—
Efforts to pack the constituencies anticipated, 67—Majorities pronouncing
on questions of peace or war, 68—Examples, 70—Comparison of classes
likely to be represented in voluntary constituencies and in the smaller
boroughs, 71, 73.

CHAPTER V.

THE SELECTION OF REPRESENTATIVES.

Vastness of political science, page 74—Traditional method of selecting
legislators now unsuitable, 75—Legal and practical obstacles to candidates, 76—Contrast between the former and present mode of choice, 77
—Traditional responsibility, 77—The Reform Bill and its necessity, 79—

Change of leaders, 80—Montesquieu, 80—Principle of order to be sought and evolved, 81—State of Society, 81—Activity and combination of the vicious elements, and misleading of the rest, 83—Helplessness of the more upright and intelligent electors, 85—Demoralizing character of election contests, 87—National and individual deterioration under the new system, 88—Absence of volition and responsibility, 90, 92—The individual conscience must be aided and invoked, 92—Restoration of personal responsibility, 93—A corporate conscience non-existent, 94—Individuality needed, 94—Announcement of candidature and deposit, 95—Example of a gazetted list of candidates, 97—Expiring traditions to which the House is indebted, 98.

CHAPTER VI.

THE OBSTACLES WHICH DIMINISH THE NUMBER OF CANDIDATES.

Necessity and right of electors to the most extensive range of choice, *page* 99—Principle of the Commons' resolution of 1769, relating to Wilkes, 100—Impediments to candidates, 100.
I. Expense of elections, 101—Educated classes not necessarily wealthy, 101 —National disposition for public labours, 102—Contemporaneous labours in Parliament and in professions, 102—Wealth not a security for character, ability, or conscientious action, 103—Its demagogism, 104—Burke, 104—The selection of the worthiest the interest of all, 105—Limit of necessary expense, 105—Bribery, 106—Causes of its prevalence, 107—Hardship of exposing to it the poorer voters, 108—Reduced to its minimum, 109—Voluntary and disinterested support, 111.
II. Introduction to constituents, 112—Canvassing, 112—Its demoralizing character, 113—A concurrence of sympathies contrasted, 113.
III. Incapabilities created by law, official persons, 114—Debate on the Indian Council, 114—Exceptional exclusions only justified by necessity, 115—Persons in holy orders, 116—The injustice and mischief of their exclusion, 117—Returning officers, 119—Presumptuous legislation on matters of individual judgment, 119.

CHAPTER VII.

THE ACT OF VOTING.

Documentary voting substituted for oral, *page* 121—Option of voting for one, or contingently for one of several candidates, 121—No single vote for more than one representative, 123—Voting paper, 124—The act necessarily deliberate, 126—Grote, 126—Burke, 126—Nature and sources of knowledge of candidates by electors, 128—Personal and public information, 129—Encouragement to inquiry, 130—Manifestation and recognition of superiorities, 132—Nurture of love of country, 134—Contact of intelligences, 135—Attraction of sympathy, 137—The ballot compared with this system, 139—Practical difficulty of effectual concealment without falsehood, 143—Necessity of faith or trust, 146—Christian principle of individuality, 148—Special consecration of the national act of electing representatives, 149.

CHAPTER VIII.

DUTIES AND POWERS OF RETURNING OFFICERS.

General duties, *page* 152—Number and distribution of polling-places, 153—Residential registration, 153—Poll-clerks and polling-places, 154—Tendering, receiving, and entering votes, 155—Tabular book of the poll-clerk, 156—and of the Registrars, 156—Appropriation of votes, 159—Where a candidate has more than the quota, 160—One candidate for several constituencies, 163—Certificate and transmission to the registrars of the unappropriated voting papers, 164—Example in a supposed Aberdeen case, 164—Ashburton, 166—Return of candidates having local majorities, 167—Computation of local majorities, 168—Supposed Norwich case, 169—Appropriation of votes *from* other constituencies, 170—*to* other constituencies, 172—Subsequent disposition of unappropriated votes, 173.

CHAPTER IX.

THE DUTIES OF THE REGISTRARS.

General functions, *page* 175—Registrars' fund, 176—Officers and clerks of registrars, 177—Appropriation of votes polled for the same candidates in different constituencies, 180—Preservation of family, territorial and traditional connection, 182—Process when no more quotas can be made up, 183—by eliminating the candidates having the smallest number of first and contingent votes, 185—or on unappropriated votes only, 185—or those having votes of less relative value computed by their position, 186—or by selecting comparative majorities, 187—Method of selection adopted, 188—Suggested alternative of transfer, 189—no candidate having a quota and no local majority, 192—Mr. Morrison's Bill, 193, 196—Quota applicable to a system rigidly local, 197, 200—Occasional vacancies, 200.

CHAPTER X.

THE DESIGNATION OF MEMBERS AND CONSTITUENCIES.

Several constituencies represented by one member, *page* 201—Multiple return of titular member for any number of constituencies, 203—Operation of such law, 204—Distribution of members to constituencies, 204—

Personal representation independent of the extent of the suffrage, 204—
Tests of electoral capacity, 204—Guizot, 205—Capacity independent of
place, 206—Town and country inhabitants, 206—Difficulties in asserting
the rights of the latter, 207—Burke, 207—Conduct of proprietary classes,
208—Mr. Bright, 207, 208—Imaginary antagonism, 208—Importance of a
just county representation, 209—Metropolitan constituencies, 210—Their
failure in representation, 213—Remedy, 214—Effect of individual electoral
independence, 215—Defective judgment drawn off, 215—Scotch, Irish,
county, and local preferences of some voters in metropolitan and other
constituencies, 218—Individual independence consistent with local and
territorial interests, but not è converso, 217—Distinct action of localities
preserved, 218—Examples of Liverpool and North Cheshire, 219.

CHAPTER XI.

THE HOUSE OF COMMONS AND THE IMPERIAL GOVERNMENT.

Relation of constitution to government, page 221—Calhoun, 222—Pascal,
222—Guizot, 223—Burke, 223—Inevitable abuse of a sole depository of
power, 224—Despotism of a multitude, 226—Concurrent consent, 228—
British constitution, 228—Appeal to conscience and necessity, 229—Constitutional principle as opposed to mere physical power, 231—Concurrent
interests and opinions in representative constitution, 232—Party government, 235—Means of perpetuating it, 237—Result, 238—Public opinion,
239—Its imperfect, false, or delusive declaration, 241—Public meetings,
241—Illustration in April, 1848, 242—The press, 244—Its function in
forming public opinion or expressing it, 248—The House of Commons
its proper exponent, 250—Ancient democratic law to ascertain public
opinion, 251—Importance of decision, 253—Oratory less effectual than
reading, 253—Stability of the position of individual statesmen, and of
the general government, 254—Operation in political life of an enlarged
range of causes, 256—Frequent elections with convenience and safety,
257.

CHAPTER XII.

THE SUFFRAGE.

Personal representation a subject apart from the suffrage, page 258—Qualification dependent on locality is unjust, 258—Principle of Mr. Locke King's
Bill, 258—Equality of county and borough suffrage necessary, 259—
Natural rights, 260—Burke, 260—Tests of electoral capacity, 263—Manhood; its legal, physiological, and statistical definitions, 263—Other
qualifications or tests, 265—Proper conditions of such tests, 266—Accessi-
bility, universality, and practicability of application, 266—Indirect

election, 267, 270—Suffrage to be treated as a valuable right, 271—
Amendment of the registration system, 272—Removal of disfranchise-
ments in respect of office, 273—Special facilities for voting by deposit of
voting papers in special cases, 274—Voting by seamen, travellers, &c.,
274—by British subjects in the colonies, 275—Women's suffrage, 275.

CHAPTER XIII.

LOCAL GOVERNMENT.

Reasons for increasing the functions and powers of local governing bodies
277, 279—Defects of the Municipal Corporation Act, 279—Arbitrary
restriction of voters to particular wards, 279—" Gerrymandering," 279—
Impolicy of arbitrary qualifications of candidates, 280–282—Elections
of a third every third year, 282—Absence of direct representation of
property, 283–285 — Form of proprietary voting-paper, 285—Indirect
election of the Board of Works, 286—A metropolitan corporation, 286–289
—Conclusion, 290.

APPENDIX A.

Switzerland: Association Réformiste, Geneva.   MM. Ernest Naville,
Roget, and Morin, 292—Classification of Systèmes Empiriques, 293—
and Systèmes rationnels, 294—La liste libre, 295.

APPENDIX B.

Method proposed in 1863 in Frankfort, *page* 298.

APPENDIX C.

Valuation of first and contingent votes, formerly proposed, but subsequently
withdrawn (see p. 186), *page* 301.

APPENDIX D.

Report of Mr. Lytton of the application of the system in Denmark,
page 302.

APPENDIX E.

Mr. Droop's method of reducing the dividend and thereby the quota, *page*
305.

APPENDIX F.

Parliament of New South Wales—Report of the Committee of the Legislative Council on the Bill for the election of the Upper House, *page* 307 —Debate on the Bill in the Council, 310—in the Legislative Assembly, 317.

APPENDIX G.

Parliament of Victoria—Debate on cumulative voting when more than two members, *page* 323.

APPENDIX H.

Discussions in Frankfort in 1861, 1863, 1864, *page* 328.

APPENDIX I.

France—M. Louis Blanc, *page* 340.

APPENDIX K.

Holland and Belgium—International Social Science Congress, Amsterdam— M. Robin-Jacquemyns, *page* 344.

APPENDIX L.

United States of America, page 347—Senate report, 349—Illinois constitution, 349—Mr. Sterne, 350—New York Charter, 350.

APPENDIX M.

The preferential and proportional vote, *page* 351—Experiment in the Technological Institute, Boston, 351—in the nomination of Overseers of Harvard College, 355.

APPENDIX N.

Memorandum of the history, working, and results of the cumulative vote, *page* 359—Birmingham School Board Election, 363—Marylebone, Lambeth, and Sheffield, 364.

APPENDIX O.

Progress of the study of the representative principle, *page* 372—Italy 374-5—Experience in . Illinois, 375—Practical contrast of majority representation, in the Upper, and proportional, in the Lower House, 376-379.

TABLE OF THE CLAUSES

PROPOSED ELECTORAL LAW.*

I. For the computation by the General Registrars of the aggregate number of votes polled at every general election, and of the number which form the quota .. .. *page* 25

III. For publication of the quota, and for certifying the same to the returning officers 25

IV. For the return of every candidate for whom a quota of votes shall be given 31

V. For creating and reconstructing electoral divisions from time to time, by Order in Council 50

VI. For making a quota or comparative majority of votes necessary for the return of every member 65

VII. For the entry of the names of all candidates, and making the prescribed deposit, with the Registrars in London, Edinburgh, or Dublin 95

VIII. For the publication of the names of all candidates in the London, Edinburgh, and Dublin Gazettes 96

IX. For regulating the order in which the names of candidates shall be inserted in the Gazettes 96

X. For abolishing the liability of the candidates, for booths, clerks, and election expenses 106

XI. For abolishing disabilities in respect of any office held at the time of election 116

XII. For repealing the statutes excluding priests and deacons 118

XIII. For enabling returning officers to appoint substitutes 119

XIV. For regulating the form of the vote 124

XV. For securing uniformity in the day of election 153

XVI. For empowering the returning officers to take and hire parochial and other buildings for the purpose and day of the election 154

* Clauses II., XXVII., XXIX., XXX., and XXXI. have been withdrawn.

XVII. For certifying to the Registrars the aggregate number of votes polled in every constituency, and for determining the cases in which the returning officer may make an immediate return 161

XVIII. For directing the order of appropriation of the voting papers . 161

XIX. For regulating the order of appropriating the excess of votes beyond those required for any candidate 161

XX. For the transmission of the remaining voting papers to the Registrars 162

XXI. Nor prescribing the duties of the returning officers in cases where one person is a candidate for several constituencies 163

XXII. For the deferred return of members by the returning officers upon receiving the Registrars' certificates, and for the computation of the local majorities 166

XXIII. For the certifying by the Registrars to the returning officers, of the quota having been completed 179

XXIV. For defining the rules, and the order, of appropriation of votes polled for the same candidate in different constituencies 180

XXV. For ascertaining and declaring the number of votes polled for every candidate having less than the quota,—for certifying to the returning officers the names of candidates having the comparative majorities, and for the return of such candidates as members.. 188

XXVI. For the appropriation of every remaining voting paper to the candidate having a quota or comparative majority, who shall stand highest thereon respectively 194

XXVIII. For admitting, by a resolution of the House, a member elected by a quota, or comparative majority, and not returned 192

XXXII. For admitting an additional return of titular representatives 203

XXXIII. For regulating the number of members to be returned by every constituency 216

ERRATA.

Preface, p. ix, *dele*, 4 lines from the bottom, from " It will," to " candidate,"
    p. x.

P. 73, last line, *for* natural, *read* national.

   85, line 21, *for* selected, *read* suspected.

  162, line 4, *for* endorsed, *read* shown by the number.

  168, line 5, from bottom, *for* unsuccessful, *read* successful.

  176, last line but one, *dele* " Clauses XXIX., XXX., XXXI."

ELECTION OF REPRESENTATIVES, &c.

CHAPTER I.

THE REPRESENTATION OF MAJORITIES, MINORITIES, AND INDIVIDUALS.

THE position which majorities and minorities of the people should respectively occupy in representative government has, within a few years past, been frequently considered. The title or claim of majorities to be exclusively regarded and obeyed must have its foundation either in agreement or in force. The power of acting by a majority, so far as it depends on an agreement, Mr. Burke observes, "must be grounded on two assumptions, first, that of an incorporation produced by unanimity; and, secondly, an unanimous agreement that the act of a mere majority (say of one) shall pass, with them and with others, as the act of the whole."[1] He adds: "If men dissolve their ancient incorporation, in order to regenerate their community, in that state of things each man has a right, if he pleases, to remain an individual. Any number of individuals, who can agree upon it, have an undoubted right to form themselves into a state apart and wholly independent. If any of these is forced into the fellowship of another, this is conquest, and not compact. On every principle which supposes society to be in virtue of a free covenant, this compulsive incorporation must be null and void."[2] M. Guizot, treating of the same subject, points

[1] *Appeal from the New to the Old Whigs.* 3rd ed., p. 103. [2] *Id.*, p. 105.

out the inconsistency of the claim of the majority to absolute power, with another principle, sometimes asserted, which affirms a right in every individual to be governed only by those laws to which he has given his assent,[1] unless the latter be accompanied with a right in the minority to withdraw themselves from the state. He adds, " dans l'idée de majorité entrent deux éléments très différents; l'idée d'une opinion qui est accréditée, et celle d'une force qui est prépondérante. Comme force, la majorité n'a aucun droit que celui de la force même qui ne peut être, à ce titre seul, la souveraineté légitime. Comme opinion la majorité est-elle infaillible ? Sait-elle et veut-elle toujours la raison, la justice, qui sont la vraie loi et confèrent seules la souveraineté légitime ? L'expérience dé- pose du contraire. La majorité en tant que majorité, c'est-à- dire en tant que nombre, ne possède donc la souveraineté légi- time, ni en vertu de la force qui ne la confère jamais, ni en vertu de l'infaillibilité qu'elle n'a point." [2]

The majority in the sense which expresses the major or greater power has ever been purely conventional, some civil institutions requiring it to be composed of a greater and some of a less number of voices. It may be, either a majority con- sisting of the more numerous of two bodies supporting respectively two contrary propositions, or of the more numer- ous of several bodies supporting respectively several distinct propositions. If ten propositions, or, which is the same thing, ten candidates be offered to the choice of fifty persons, that they may select one of the ten, six of the fifty persons might form the majority, and the voices of forty-four have no

---

[1] *Histoire des Origines du Gouvernement Représentatif*, vol. i., p. 106. Paris, 1851.

[2] Id., p. 107. Sir George Cornewall Lewis has collected the reasons given for the rule that the decision of the majority shall govern, and re- marks that they are exhausted in Barbeyrac's translation of *Puffendorf*, in which the rule is simply founded on this ;—" parce qu'il n'y a presque point d'autre expédient pour terminer les affaires."—*Essay on the Influence of Authority in Matters of Opinion*, § 246, new ed. London, Parker, 1849.

weight. If there be no law—as in our electoral system there is no law—which requires a moiety, or any definite proportion of the entire body, including both the present or active and the absent or inactive members to form an effectual majority, the six must prevail, and yet the excluded candidates, or propositions, might perfectly express the sentiments of those who put them forward ; and, moreover, may even be in harmony with the opinions of the most part of the fifty voters, and who are thus silenced by the six. An attempt has been made in a few recent borough elections to prevent the division of parties or interests amongst several candidates, by subjecting them to the difficult, cumbrous, and often illusory trial of a preliminary ballot. Under the prevailing systems, some means of giving unity to party action becomes, indeed, indispensable unless the result be abandoned to accident or chance. In America it has led to that species of political movement known by the appellation of the "caucus." [1] It is, in fact, the method by which a few clever and adroit persons substitute their dictation for that of the leadership which, in earlier times, was conceded to territorial power, high birth, or natures fitted to command. The misfortune is that the qualities which are best adapted to succeed by intrigue, cajolery, and pandering to mean desires and appetites are far more common and degrading than those which formerly compelled submission, if they did not always inspire confidence.

With regard to the character of government by a numerical majority, where there is no constitutional provision for giving due weight to the minority, it is useful to listen to republican statesmen. Mr. Calhoun, who occupied at different times some of the highest offices in the government of the United States, and who studied American institutions with

---

[1] For the origin of this word, see *Pickering's Vocabulary*, Boston, 1816; *Webster's Dictionary*, New York, 1828. On the operation of the caucus, *Tremenheere, Constitution of the United States*, p. 223.

the aid of long experience, employed his latest hours and his
most elaborate efforts, in a work designed as a warning
against the dangers of that absolutism which would result
from committing the destinies of the country to the uncontrolled government of the numerical majority. The right of
suffrage, he says, is, indeed, the indispensable and primary
principle; "but it would be a great and dangerous mistake
to suppose, as many do, that it is of itself sufficient to form
constitutional governments."[1] "To this erroneous opinion,"
he adds, "may be traced one of the causes why so few
attempts to form constitutional governments have succeeded;
and why, of the few which have, so small a number have had
a durable existence. It has led not only to mistakes in the
attempt to form such governments, but to their overthrow,
when they have, by some good fortune, been correctly formed.
So far from being of itself sufficient—however well guarded
it might be, and however enlightened the people—it would,
unaided by other provisions, leave the government as absolute
as it would be in the hands of irresponsible rulers, and with
a tendency, at least as strong, towards oppression and abuse
of its powers."[2] "The more extensive and populous the
country, the more diversified the condition and pursuits of
its population; and the richer, more luxurious, and dissimilar
the people, the more difficult it is to equalise the action of
the government, and the more easy for one portion of the
community to pervert its powers to oppress and plunder the
other."[3] "The dominant majority for the time," he repeats,
"would have the same tendency to oppression and abuse of
power, which, without the right of suffrage, irresponsible
rulers would have. No reason, indeed, can be assigned why
the latter would abuse their power, which would not apply

---

[1] *A Disquisition on Government, and a Discourse on the Constitution and
Government of the United States, by John C. Calhoun.* Edited by R. C.
Cralle, p. 13. Charleston, 1851.
　　　[2] Id., p. 13.　　　　　　　　　[3] Id., p. 16.

with equal force to the former. The dominant majority for the time would, in reality, through the right of suffrage, be the rulers—the controlling, governing, and irresponsible power,—and those who make and execute the laws would, for the time, in reality be but their representatives and agents."[1] And he proceeds to show that the abuse of the power which would thus be acquired, could only be counteracted by giving to each division, or interest, through its appropriate organ, a concurrent voice.[2] The majority which is formed by this concurrence he calls the constitutional majority, in contradistinction to that which is obtained by treating the whole community as a unit, having but one common interest. "The first and leading error," he says, "which naturally arises from overlooking the distinction referred to, is to confound the numerical majority with the people, and this so completely as to regard them as identical. This is a consequence that necessarily results from considering the numerical as the only majority. All admit, that a popular government, or democracy, is the government of the people; for the terms imply this. A perfect government of the kind would be one which would embrace the consent of every citizen, or member, of the community; but as this is impracticable, in the opinion of those who regard the numerical as the only majority, and who can perceive no other way by which the sense of the people can be taken, they are compelled to adopt this as the only true basis of popular government, in contradistinction to governments of the aristocratical or monarchical form. Being thus constrained, they are, in the next place, forced to regard the numerical majority as, in effect, the entire people; that is, the greater part as the whole; and the government of the greater part as the government of the whole."[3]

The work being adapted to a republican form of government, contains observations on a political organism, by the

---

[1] Id., p. 22.   [2] Id., p. 25.   [3] Id., p. 27.

concurrence and veto of different bodies, which happily is, in this country, provided for by a different constitution ; but all the remarks on the error of so dealing with numbers as to extinguish interests, is equally applicable to the constitution of the House of Commons. The danger of a popular body, unbalanced by the introduction of elements other than those which have their origin in a triumphant numerical force, is stated, with equal confidence, by Mr. Burke. He says,— " Of this I am certain, that, in a democracy, the majority of the citizens is capable of exercising the most cruel oppressions upon the minority, whenever strong divisions prevail in that kind of polity, as they often must; and that oppression of the minority will extend to far greater numbers, and will be carried on with much greater fury, than can almost ever be apprehended from the dominion of a single sceptre." [1]

Those who contend that neither good government nor individual liberty is necessarily secured by a suffrage which commits the government absolutely to the numerical majority, do not, therefore, argue that there must not be a resort to arithmetic. It is impossible to suppose a popular form of government in which the votes must not be counted. The problem of constitutional organism is, in what manner the individuals composing the entire community are to be classed so that no opinions or interests shall be unheard, or extinguished, in representation.

Most of the advocates for the amendment of our system of representation seem content with, or to despair of obtaining anything better than, a division of the country into certain districts or localities.[2]

[1] *Reflections on the French Revolution,* &c., p. 186. See *Mill, Considerations on Representative Government,* c. vi. (Note to 3rd ed.)

[2] Lord Grey, in the last edition of his work on *Parliamentary Government* (pp. 209—213), has suggested that the votes of graduates of colleges and universities, and of workmen in trades, to be incorporated for the purpose, might be taken without regard to localities, but still, as I gather, by majorities, and not in unanimity, as here proposed. (Note to 3rd ed.)

If it were not a low and unbecoming view of political parties to liken them to enemies in a hostile camp, a case might be imagined of the division of the electors generally into two classes: one satisfied with the condition of things, apprehensive of the consequences of change, and ready to oppose all experiments the utility of which is not manifest; and the other uneasy in their position, imagining that social alterations might be made which would ameliorate their condition, and who are not deterred by the apprehension of consequences which they do not see or admit. Supposing there were a contest between these classes, a struggle, not of arms, but of the peaceable forces which are brought to bear in the operation of representative institutions, and the proportion in which these classes is found in every locality be, for the purpose of argument, taken as two to three, the majority of every constituency would, of course, elect a representative of the more numerous class. If five constituencies be taken as the entire number, there would be in the representative assembly five members for the party of progress and *none* for the party of preservation; whilst, in justice, the majority and minority ought to stand in the constituted assembly in the same proportion as in their constituents, that is, three against two. It is clear, as a matter of strategy, that by the defeat in every constituency of the detached minorities, the less numerous class have no means of meeting their adversaries in the representative council, but are previously cut off in detail.

"Le but du gouvernement représentatif est de mettre publiquement en présence et aux prises les grands intérêts, les opinions diverses, qui se partagent la société et s'en disputent l'empire, dans la juste confiance que, de leurs débats, sortiront la connaissance et l'adoption des lois et des mesures qui conviennent le mieux aux pays en général. Ce but n'est atteint que par le triomphe de la vraie majorité, la minorité constamment présente et entendue. Si la majorité est déplacée par artifice il y a mensonge. Si la minorité est d'avance hors de combat, il y a oppression. Dans l'un ou l'autre cas, le gouvernement représentatif est corrompu."[1]

In the general election of 1852, the aggregate number of votes polled by the majorities where the seats were contested was 291,118, whilst the minorities polled 199,994. These numbers may, with sufficient accuracy, be treated as represented by three and two; and if the same calculation be extended to the whole of the constituencies, and taken as expressing the silent and suppressed differences of opinion where no contest was attempted, it would appear that 500,000 electors are not represented, except, by a sort of fiction of law, their opinions are supposed to be expressed by other means. If liberalism be triumphant in one constituency, conservatism, it is answered, is triumphant in another. The argument is as untenable as the principle is dangerous. It is not the fact that the opinions suppressed by the electoral voice at one place are expressed in those of another. It has been truly said that "the separation of parties according to localities does not even approach completeness. The number of localities in which any given opinions prevail are not proportioned to the general prevalence of those opinions. Large political parties are widely scattered and intermixed throughout the country."[2] This supposed system of balances and counteractions is the *ignis fatuus* of the politicians of this century, and the source of jealousies and wranglings without end. It recedes as they pursue it. No sooner do they imagine that its elements are caught and fixed upon their canvas than they are gone like a dissolving view. The discovery or the opening up of some unexpected mineral wealth creates a town on a barren moor. Commerce establishes a thriving port where stood the hovels of a few fishermen. A rapidly-increasing population overflows the boundaries of the city. The case and rapidity of

---

[1] *Guizot, Gouvernement Représentatif,* vol. ii., p. 259.
[2] *Edinburgh Review,* vol. c., p. 229.

locomotion open to the middle classes of the towns the advantages and the pleasures of rural life. The more agreeable sites of a country, rich in natural beauties, are being covered with the dwellings of classes who were formerly a town population. On the shores of our island coast, wherever they can be approached, on every hill-side and in every valley from which can be beheld

" The many-twinkling smile of ocean,"

the builder is constantly engaged in the construction of dwellings replete with comfort, if not remarkable for architectural beauty. Numerous residences, many almost of palatial character, have in several places, in less than half a century, formed, what in earlier times would have deserved and received the name of cities, but are now hardly recognised as municipalities. The rate of progress of the first forty years of that period was as nothing to that of the last ten years ; and probably the progress of the last ten years will be inconceivably outstripped by that of the ten which are to come. Industry, education, the progress of civilisation, and the diffusion of higher tastes and enjoyments, all contribute to defeat every attempt to attach special interests or objects to specific districts. The lines of distinction between the town and country population become more and more faint, and are constantly shifting their places. To form a constitution on such a foundation is to build on sand.

Let it be supposed, however, that it were possible to succeed in accomplishing that which the changes in society forbid, the system would be founded upon injustice, and, therefore, could not be permanent. To contend that, although the opinion and sympathies of a minority are set at defiance in one place, it is a sufficient justification for this state of things that persons, whose opinions correspond with those of that minority, may form a majority in some other place, and that they then succeed in suppressing the voices of those whose opinions are in harmony with the victorious party elsewhere, is to set up one great evil as a compensation for another. " Can it," inquires the writer last quoted, " be seriously argued that to balance one great mischief against another, is as well and as safe a mode of proceeding as an endeavour to avert both?" Political action, instead of being the result of a steady and legitimate adaptation of means to an end, is converted into a game of chance, a speculation in which the failure upon one card is to be compensated by success upon another, and, by the sacrifice of the active and cordial assistance and adherence of two-thirds of the people, we even profess to gain no more than the same relative power for each of two or more parties, which they may have obtained without such sacrifice. Assuming, however, that the equivalent result, as a matter of party warfare, were in this manner obtained, the purpose of constitutional and representative government would be as far off as ever. The purpose of such a government is not satisfied by dividing the nation into two parties, and converting the area of legislation into a battle-field. It is not necessary here to discuss the merits of party government, it is enough to say, that in the vast field of modern legislation, in the adaptation of our ancient institutions to a new state of society, and in providing for new emergencies, a multitude of political and social problems come to be solved with which party has nothing to do, and into which the introduction of party elements and considerations is not only useless, but is absolutely pernicious. It is obvious that the tendency of a system of government founded on numerical majorities alone, is to absorb all differences into one issue—a contest for power. The extension of knowledge and the progress of civilization open the door of inquiry, prompt activity of thought, encourage diversities of opinion, and thus lead the way to social improvement; but the benefit of this progress in the composition of a representative assembly is excluded when every variety of opinion and shadow of thought is expurgated—thrown aside as so much lumber, in order that both sides may come unencumbered to the trial of strength which is to determine the single issue—the possession of power. Such a result would be impossible if full play were given to the partialities which arise from individual character and sympathy, for these would be in constant rebellion against the tyranny of faction, and would moderate its influence even amongst those who might be subject to it. Every man, according to the degree in which he is intellectual, and possesses public spirit, would bring his talent and weight to the public aid, in the business of concentrating in the representative assembly a selection of the best minds of the nation, and the statesmen who shall have been proved by experience to be trustworthy; and the deposit of official power, from time to time, would be safely left to an assembly thus constituted, under the conditions which our parliamentary system imposes.

In the selection or choice of representatives we require the aid of the multitude of electors whose votes are rendered useless, and whose judgment is thus rejected. Instead of damping and extinguishing their patriotic zeal by destroying that hope of the utility of exertion which can alone keep it alive, every disposition to political action on the part of every worthy and sensible citizen should be encouraged and assisted. By making elections nothing but a question of adhesion to one of two or three parties, the standard of merit and qualification in the candidate is lowered to a bare question of party tests.

It has been seen that about half a million of voters are in this country incapable of securing a representation by any act of their own. The public loss is surely not trifling. To what a multitude of subjects of public and private interest have the thoughts and studies of large numbers amongst that half million of voters been directed! If we go through many of the streets and squares of the metropolitan boroughs, and form our conclusions of the intellectual rank of the inhabitants from their probable education and means of acquiring knowledge, and when we know that of these thousands would in vain approach the hustings to give expression to their views or opinions, it is impossible to look on the nominal representation of the metropolis as other than a mockery of the name. Yet the House of Commons has been truly described as " a place where minorities, heresies, oppositions, remonstrances, and protests of all sorts are to be represented and entitled to a hearing, and it is intended to comprehend, and not to exclude them."

"Le but du système représentatif, dans ses éléments généraux, comme dans tous les détails de son organisation, est de recueillir, de concentrer toute la raison qui existe éparse dans la société, et de l'appliquer à son gouvernement." [1]

If our present method of obtaining this concentration of the national reason be considered with analogy to operations connected with the material world, the comparison at once displays its unscientific character. Two-fifths of the intelligence of the country is lost in the process: It is a waste of material which would have been a reproach to any operation in physical science in its rudest day; even if the material so lost were only of the average value of that of which the constituencies are composed; but it is far more lamentable : it is considered that the material thus lost comprises a very large proportion of the best moral and intellectual elements of society, whilst the process of local condensation to which the numerical majorities owe their success has done much to extinguish independent thought, convert men into machines, and thereby deteriorate the result of the votes by which the supposed representative assembly has been actually chosen.

The first and greatest practical attempt which was made, at least in this country, to remedy this defect in representative institutions was the provision introduced by Lord John Russell in the bill of 1854. It was proposed that, in cities

---

[1] *Guizot, Gouvernement Représentatif*, vol. ii., p. 253.

and boroughs returning three members, no elector should vote for more than two, which would have the effect of permitting a minority of two-fifths of the constituency to return one member. This, called the " restricted vote," is said to have been suggested by Mr. Praed in 1832. It admits, and indeed requires in most cases, an organisation of parties. Suppose eighty-four voters, of whom, say, fifty-one are supporters of the ministry, and thirty-three of the opposition, and that there are four candidates, A, B, and C, of the ministerial party, and D of the opposition. It might be supposed that the minority would succeed in returning D; but this would be prevented by the majority dividing themselves into three distinct bodies of seventeen each, one of which shall vote for A and B, another for B and C, and the third for A and C. The consequence would be, that each of the three ministerial candidates would have thirty-four votes, and all would be returned, and the thirty-three voices of the minority would be silenced.[1] In the discussions in the House of Commons on the Reform Bill, in 1867, the cumulative vote, originally suggested by Mr. Marshall in 1857, was proposed for adoption by Mr. Lowe,[2] but was rejected by a large majority. Subsequently, in the House of Lords, the restricted vote was adopted by a majority in proportion nearly the same as that which opposed the cumulative vote in the Commons.[3] On the return of the bill to the Lower House the amendment was accepted,[4] and the principle was thus embodied in the Reform Act of that year. Three years later the principle received a further practical extension by the introduction of the cumulative vote for the election of the School Boards.[5] In the sessions of 1870 and 1871 attempts

[1] See Appendix N.
[2] Hansard, *Parl. Deb.*, vol. clxxxviii., pp. 1068–1120.
[3] The speech of Lord Stratford de Redcliffe (Hansard, clxxxix., p. 465) refers to the abuse of the power of majorities in remarkable examples.
[4] Hansard, Id., pp. 1125–1179.
[5] Appendix N.

were made to repeal these provisions, and thus put an end to the opportunities they give for a better representation of the various sentiments and opinions of the electoral body. In the former year the restricted vote, simply on the ground of the justice of the basis on which it stands, although it has practically less to recommend it than any of the other methods by which the extinction of minorities is sought to be averted, was retained by the vote of 183 members in a House of 358, notwithstanding the weight of the Government was thrown into the opposite scale. On a motion in the latter year for the second reading of a bill that proposed to withdraw the clause as to the cumulative voting, of nine members who took part in the debate, only one, besides the mover, supported the second reading, and he stated that he did so because " our ancestors had always been content with the old clumsy system of representation by majorities; and he believed proportional representation was contrary to the habits and sentiments of the people." It was rejected without a division.

Nothing is perhaps more remarkable than that the attempts to retrace the steps that have been made towards rendering the representative bodies comprehensive and not exclusive in their character, should all emanate from members of the Liberal party, which is understood to insist upon equality in political freedom, without partiality in favour of person or of place. The abolition of the restricted vote was put forward as a pretended vindication of electoral rights,[1] while by delivering the electoral power of every community over to the majority, it would practically disfranchise a third or more of the electors. Its promoters argue that if two members, say for Manchester or Birmingham, vote with one party, and one with the other, those great towns have not their due weight in the government, but are partially neutralised, and reduced in parliamentary force to a level with the smallest borough. This, however, is to forget the people who form the aggregate

[1] Appendix N, p. 361 (§ 8).

or corporate bodies known as Birmingham or Manchester, and to require that the individual interests and wishes of a third or more of them shall be sacrificed to the name by which the community is designated,—to an abstract conception which has no existence apart from the living beings whom it describes or indicates. The true way of reconciling the corporate influence of these great centres of industry with that of the individuals who inhabit them, is a fair distribution of seats, no longer assuming, as the present arrangement practically does, that one voter in Bury St. Edmunds is to be recognised as worth ten voters in Birmingham, or that the Irish and Scotch constituencies are reasonably treated, when "the inhabitants of Portarlington have 132 times as much representation as the inhabitants of Glasgow."[1] It will be well to compare the result upon the electoral power which Birmingham, for example, could gain by the reactionary efforts in favour of exclusive majority representation, supposing they were successful, with that which it would acquire by a just system of proportional representation.[2] In the meantime it is surely desirable to secure the means of gathering the fullest expression possible of the views of all the inhabitants of our greater cities and districts, trusting that thereby their corporate interest and dignity will be best served and sustained.

It is possible that some of those who desire the repeal of the restrictive and the cumulative vote may be less offended by their effect on reducing the nominal power of the city or county than by their attack on the exclusive dominion of the local majority. In this light it is a painful symptom of the arbitrary and intolerant character of majorities. It affords an illustration of the principle which has been quoted from the work of Mr. Calhoun, a principle which all history corroborates, that government by numbers is not less insatiable of power, and certainly not more scrupulous of the claims

---

[1] "Proportional Representation," by Milicent Garrett Fawcett, *Macmillan's Magazine*, Sept., 1870, p. 376.   [2] See Mr. Morrison's Bill, *infra*, p. 196, n.

of those who are without its pale, than any other absolute, uncontrolled, and irresponsible authority. Looking at the place which representative institutions are apparently destined to fill in the government of mankind, it becomes of the highest importance to consider whether means cannot be found to eradicate the vice in their constitution which deprives the state of the benefit of the judgment—it is to be feared of a large number—of the most calm and dispassionate, as well as of the most instructed and thoughtful of its people. The problem is, how to render representation in fact what it is in name,—to make it universally truthful, and to give to the best elements in every constituency their best and most perfect expression.

The founders of our parliamentary system,—if that appellation can be justly conferred upon any particular men in any age,—did not contemplate, and could not provide, for the difference of political opinion to be evolved in the progress of civilisation. Yet, on the other hand, they certainly did not contemplate a state of things in which the will of a vast proportion of those whom they entrusted with the franchise would be wholly disregarded. It is remarkable that the writs require the returning officers to send the knights and burgesses to Parliament "with full and sufficient powers;"[1]—a form of expression which students of common law know is inconsistent with the existence of a body some of whom repudiate the person whom the others have nominated, and refuse to concur in investing him with such powers. It is probable that the idea of the constitution and unanimity of the jury entered into the conception of its framers.

The restricted vote, in the Reform Act of 1867, is, no doubt, open to several objections. It operates very partially in reaching only a few constituencies; in the far greater number it leaves the evil untouched. Whilst the law recognises, in a measure,

---

[1] *Brady, Histor. Treat.*, Lond., 1777, p. 54. *Hallam's Middle Ages, Eng. Const.*, c. 8, part 3.

the injustice of extinguishing the opinions of minorities, it at the same time declares to the minorities in most constituencies that, however entitled to respect they might be from their intelligence or their aggregate numbers, still they are not, individually, large enough to be protected.   Even in the constituencies to which it applies a minority considerably more in number than one-third of the entire constituency may, it has been seen, be defeated by a skilful organisation of the majority.   The cumulative system is also susceptible of organisation, and in its present unguarded form is open to great uncertainty, and subject to a vast waste and fruitless expenditure of electoral energy, as is hereafter shown.[1]   Both belong to what M. Ernest Naville has, in his examination of the several methods of electoral action, styled the "empirical," as distinguished from the "scientific" systems.[2]   It is indeed impossible to know how much of the hostility to the restricted vote in these discussions, has been really owing to objections entertained to the principle of proportional representation, and how much to the partial extent, and the infirmity of the remedies that have been chosen.   That these are the main causes of the opposition instinctively suggest itself on considering the language of Mr. Bright, its most eminent opponent in the debate on the Lord's amendment.   He studiously admonished his hearers that the restricted vote was no "portion of a grand scheme to give to every person in the country, whether one of a minority or one of a majority, a representation in this House."   He cautioned those who did not value it as a correction of a democratic measure, not to be misled by supposing it to "approximate to or be an admission of the principle of a plan in which everybody would be represented, and such things as majorities and minorities never known."[3]   A description more truly characteristic of what is

---

[1] See Appendix N, *infra*, pp. 359–372.

[2] Appendix A, *infra*, p. 293.

[3] Hansard's *Parl. Deb.*, vol. clxxxix., pp. 1126, 1127.

here proposed had not proceeded from any pen or tongue, and not a word implies that the speaker thought it undesirable if it were possible; not the smallest intimation that he was adverse to giving every considerable section of opinion in the nation, whether it be more or less centred in any particular locality, its just expression in the national council. On the contrary there are to be found in Mr. Bright's speeches the most powerful arguments for the necessity and duty of exercising individual thought, the strongest appeals to the intellect and conscience of every elector, addressed to them as persons capable of meditation in silence, and not to conglomerate masses who can only act upon one another through external signs. To the people of Birmingham, on the eve of the election, he says:—"Bear in mind that you are now going to make a machine more important than any that is made in the manufactories of Birmingham—you are going to make a parliament that shall legislate directly for the United Kingdom, and indirectly for two hundred millions of men—a parliament that will levy taxes in the United Kingdom, and in India, to the amount of £110,000,000, and a parliament that, when it once takes its seat in Westminster, is all-important for all these things; and every member you send is a part of that grand machine, and every elector throughout the United Kingdom who shall vote at the coming contest is partly the manufacturer of that stupendous machine whose power no man could measure." The force of this exhortation is lost if it fails to lead those whom it reaches to recall facts, and thereupon to awaken reflection in their minds—that faculty which is the exclusive possession of each individual brain. In this process everyone must work alone; though the physical force of a hundred or a thousand arms may be combined to accomplish a mechanical result, there can be no common cerebral action of so many heads to solve a problem in moral science, any more than to invent a steam engine or write ' Paradise Lost.' Those who thus address the people know that if their advice be fruitful it must be through its influence in leading every voter at the election to do what in his own judgment he shall conclude to be best and wisest. The counsel is not to find out what the majority will do and blindly follow it. Everyone would feel that it would be of small use to ponder over any solution of social or economical problems, in order to select, for the business of government, those in whom he could most perfectly trust, if after all his study his conclusion could not be acted upon unless more than half of his constituency, by something in the nature of a miracle, arrived at precisely the same conclusion. When we would stimulate thought and inquiry as a guide to action, we intend the action to be directed by the thought, and not by some accident independent of it.

All systems by which hundreds or thousands of persons who are not associated by any pervading harmony of mind or feeling, but are gathered together by the mere accident of living in the same district or town, are led or forced, on pain of political extinction, always to agree in the choice of their representatives, are inconsistent with the free exercise of individual will, guided by those diversities of thought and sentiment upon which men form their various estimates of character; and their subjection to such compulsion tends to the mental and moral deterioration both of the electors and the elected. They degrade men from the rank of living and individually thinking and responsible beings, and treat them only as so many mechanical units making up a certain party. "I always feel," says Dr. Walker, in his election sermon, "when I put my hand into the ballot box, that I am being *used* by somebody, I know not whom, for some purpose I know not what."[1] "The principle," says Mr. Calhoun, "by which constitutional governments are upheld, is *compromise*, that of absolute governments is *force*." By giving full, and

---

[1] "Machinery of Politics," &c., *American Law Review*, Jan., 1872. Boston.

no more than full weight to opposing and conflicting interests, a salutary check is interposed to all precipitate resolutions. ' They render deliberation a matter not of choice but of necessity; they make all change a subject of compromise, which materially begets moderation: they produce temperaments preventing the sore evil of harsh, crude, unqualified reformations, and rendering all the headlong exertions of arbitrary power for ever impracticable." How are those who form their opinions upon considerations which the majority do not appreciate,—to bring about this compromise? They must have the power of exercising a volition of their own. Without this, neither reason, entreaty, nor persuasion, can be relied upon. The basis of union and permanence, in the ordinary partnerships by which the commercial transactions of the world are carried on, is the necessity of mutual attention, forbearance, and respect. If this be not rendered by one to the other, the partnership is dissolved. That it is not so dissolved, is because the feebler judgment yields to the stronger, the cautious is encouraged by the more impetuous, the more impetuous is tempered by the cautious, and each character and person derives improvement and profit from the combination. The progress of physical science has advanced by observation of the laws which apply to things under our sight, and the application of the same laws to bodies of greater magnitude which are otherwise beyond our vision and comprehension. It reasons from the lesser to the greater. So in political life; an element which is potent, and preserves harmony in the smaller sections of society, may be brought to bear on its larger combinations. Let electors, whether they consist only of the " tens or twenties scattered in vast communities, and whose votes are now utterly without influence in any one place,"[1] or whether they com-

---

[1] *Parl. Hist.*, vol. cxxii., p. 1184. This claim on behalf of voters of the learned professions distributed throughout the country was put forward in a petition presented by Lord Harrowby.

pose any of the various sections of society who look to moral, rather than to purely political doctrines; or, whatever may be their causes of dissent, be permitted, when occasion arises, to dissolve the union which the place of residence or some other accident has created between them and the other members of the constituency on which their votes are registered, and let them add their votes, if they desire, to those of some other constituency, but so as not to interfere in the smallest degree with the just weight of the majority in such other constituency. They may thus become partners with other electors with whom they have more sympathy. Eminent judges, in administering the law, have, when they looked at the losses and evils which commonly accrue to partners from suddenly and angrily severing the connection, considered the union as having some analogy to another,—for better and for worse. There is, however, no such indissoluble bond uniting together the dwellers in every borough. They may be told to be, if they can, unanimous in the choice of a representative; but if an elector cannot agree with the majority on one side of a parish boundary, there would be no necessary breach of the order, or even of the courtesies of society, if he be permitted to unite himself with a number of his fellow-countrymen on the other side. He is not precluded from choosing his friends or associates beyond the boundaries of his own borough, and there does not seem to be any sound reason why he should not be allowed, with a like freedom, to seek elsewhere his fellow-constituents. If the legal obstacles in the way of this exercise of individual volition were removed, and the elector were enabled to add his vote to the votes of any other of his countrymen, agreeing with him in sympathy and opinion, and sufficient to form a constituency, it is obvious that, so far as representation is concerned, the question as to minorities would cease, for the minorities would be absorbed. An age which has achieved the freedom of commercial intercourse in spite of the pretensions of local protection and monopoly, may not unreasonably hope to find advocates for the free interchange and communication, as well of political action as of political thought, against the far less plausible and more insolent claims of dominant inhabitants of arbitrarily selected and privileged boroughs and districts to a monopoly of the great right of national representation.

The purpose of this work is to show how practically small in form is the change that would suffice to liberate the elector from the bonds that now tie him to the other voters of the borough in which he happens to dwell, whereby his action is absolutely fettered to theirs, however weak, ignorant, or corrupt they may be,—how perfectly such a change would be in accordance with the letter and spirit of our constitution, and how trivial are the arguments against it, when thoroughly weighed. By such means, the unrepresented minority would be reduced to the smallest limits, and include only those impracticable tempers, for whose satisfaction it is neither possible nor desirable to provide.

CHAPTER II.

OF CONSTITUENCIES BY VOLUNTARY ASSOCIATION AND
UNANIMITY.

IN the last chapter every constituency or electoral college has been regarded in the light of a partnership, the members of which are engaged in a great undertaking that requires all their individual as well as their joint skill and energy, and in which none should be even sleeping partners, much less partners repudiating and protesting against the acts of the rest, and yet unable to extricate themselves. It has been said that, in order to express the various opinions of those who form minorities, they should be permitted, not by dissent to impede the free action of the majority of the society or partnership with which the accidents of life, and the frame of our electoral system, has connected them ; but, leaving all such free action of the majority untouched, to come out of that society or partnership, and form another society and another partnership, with the members of which they entertain opinions in common. The hypothesis, that they can thus for the time sever their connection with the constituency in which they are registered, is necessarily founded upon the assumption that they are able to find kindred opinions elsewhere than with the majority of that constituency. If such kindred opinions, held by sufficient numbers, cannot be found, the severance would be useless, and their voices, as at present, are necessarily extinguished.

The severance, it is to be observed, is only for the time. The partnership may begin and end with the election. The objections to concurrence with the majority of the constituency which are strong at one election may have no existence at the next. The very circumstance that every elector is free, will tend to procure respect for his opinions from every other elector, and will therefore be a motive for attempting the selection of a representative who shall command the general respect.

The election of a representative by a combination of minorities supposes a community of sentiment in those who combine, or, in other words, unanimity of choice in such a constituency. In order to render this arrangement possible, it is necessary to prescribe what shall be the extent or numbers of the new constituency which is thus to be created, and to ascertain in what manner its members can be enabled to coalesce.

An electoral body, formed of the detached members of various constituencies, ought to correspond in magnitude with the average of such other constituencies; and this is obtained by taking as the basis the number of votes polled at each general election.

It is proposed that a registrar of voters be appointed for each of the three kingdoms, who may not only superintend the business of local registration, but be charged with the duty of collecting and computing the number and quotient of voters, and—where votes from more than one constituency are contributed towards the election of the same candidate—the arrangement of the votes according to the names of the candidates indicated in the voting papers. At the conclusion of the poll in the several constituencies, a telegraphic despatch from every returning officer might communicate to the general registrar of the kingdom the number of voters that had polled; and these numbers being added together and the aggregate number divided by the number of epresentatives to be chosen,[1] the product or quotient will be he maximum number of the constituency sufficient to secure he election of a member.

It will be convenient at this point to begin the draft of the proposed ELECTORAL LAW, with the clauses which specify he manner in which the quota or number of votes sufficient or the election of a member is to be ascertained and made mown at every general election. They point out portions of he duties of the returning officers and registrars, and would all within that part of the Treatise which describes those luties, but they are necessary in this place for the elucidation of that which follows. It may be assumed that at this stage of the election the registrars and their clerks assemble ogether, for a few days, at a central point—for which some own in Derbyshire, or the south of Yorkshire, may be more suitable than London.

Section I. The registrars at every general election, as soon as they shall ave received the reports of the returning officers of the various constituencies a England, Scotland, and Ireland (to be transmitted to them as hereinafter mentioned), showing the number of votes polled in every constituency, shall ompute and ascertain the total number of votes polled at such election, nd shall divide such total number by 654, rejecting any fraction of the ividend which may appear after such division, and the number of the said quotient found by such division shall be the quota or number of votes ntitling the candidates respectively, for whom such quota shall be iven, to be returned at the said general election as members to serve in 'arliament.

III. The registrars, as soon as practicable after the said quota has been ound as aforesaid, shall make and jointly sign a declaration setting forth he total number of votes forming the aforesaid dividend, and the quotient

---

[1] Instead of forming this quotient by taking the total number of votes as he dividend, the dividend may be formed by adding together only the otes polled by so many of the candidates highest on the poll as shall be ufficient to fill the House. The effect of this variation, which by diminish-ing the quota would be in many respects an improvement, is shown in a ote to Chapter IX., in the remarks on Clause XXV. of the proposed lectoral law.

of the same, and shall thereby certify that the said quotient is, by virtue of this Act, the quota of electors at the general election for the   Parliament of the United Kingdom of Great Britain and Ireland (specifying the Parliament then summoned, and for which such election is made); and shall also, with all practicable speed, transmit a copy of such certificate to every returning officer, and cause the same to be ˙published in the London, Edinburgh, and Dublin Gazettes, respectively.[1]

The registries of the United Kingdom contained, in the year 1857, the names of 1,227,274 voters. This may afford a datum for estimating a probable quotient. When the sympathies of all who are disposed to employ any measure of thought on political duties shall be so strongly appealed to, the number of voters exercising their franchise will doubtless exceed anything we have hitherto known. Still the votes polled will fall considerably short of the votes registered. To explain the calculation, the voters who poll at a general election, under this system, are supposed to be equal to the number on the registry in 1857, and this total is supposed to be divided by 654, the number of members in the House,[2] and the quotient is 1876. The quotient necessarily varies as the numbers of the voters vary, and the quotient, so varying, will be always the number of voters, who, belonging to what constituencies they may, but being unanimous in their choice, may be permitted to elect a representative.

The difficulties which will immediately suggest themselves are,—how this unanimity is to be obtained amongst persons of infinite variety of character and temperament, and how a scheme of such a nature is to be worked out? Doubtless, if there were but one or two, or a few of these bodies of 1876 voters, or whatever may be from time to time the number of the quota, it would be impossible to secure unanimity; but the difficulty vanishes when the minorities amount to half a

[1] The above laws, I. and III., are substituted for laws I., II., and III. in the first edition.

[2] It has since been restored to 658, but it is not necessary to alter the original calculation.

million, and not only half a million, but when they far exceed the entire number of any minorities now existing, by the operation of numberless affinities and repulsions, which, in a state of liberation, will dissolve the present majorities. Opinions which approve themselves, and sympathies which are common to any considerable number of minds,—and it is chiefly these with which we have to deal,—will form round different centres, whilst the parts, or atoms, actually incapable of cohesion, would be reduced to their minimum.

It will be found, upon consideration, that it is not more difficult for the State to provide for its people the means of combining, for the purpose of representation, all the elements which make up its intelligence and judgment, infinitely dispersed and varied as these appear to be,—than it is by the simple mechanism of the Post-Office, that vast contrivance, at once a cause and an effect of civilization, to perform its wondrous daily task of interchanging knowledge and thought, and thereby instructing and enriching society. In our own day, the facilities of intercourse have brought almost into contact with one another those who dwell at opposite quarters of the empire, and have produced effects which our ancestors could never have anticipated or imagined. Full of interest are those inquiries, which show the connection between external things and mental progress, and trace the influence on human institutions, of literature and its allied and hand-maid arts. The amazement of Atahualpa, when he saw that a few mysterious lines, without speech, conveyed, from one to another of his stern conquerors, their words and thoughts, exhibits the untaught condition of a perishing race. In other regions, and more cultivated minds, letters had long sown the seeds of enterprise and freedom, but had not always preserved its fruits. They afforded to the world but a twilight gleam. The brighter rays shone but in a few solitary or isolated spots, until a student-artisan taught to stamp by one block or type many repetitions of the same thought, and thereby opened wide the doors of knowledge. It remains, still, instead of the signs by voice and hand,—the means of expression in the rude assemblies of old, in which writing was an unusual accomplishment even for the noble, to substitute the vehicle of letters, and by them to transport and concentrate, in the choice of legislators, the stores of wisdom and virtue that are scattered throughout the land, extracting them, like the precious ore from quartz or sand, by the powerful sympathies and affections which God has implanted in our nature, and which it is for man either to let die, or call into healthy or baneful luxuriance. In gathering the electoral will, we seek for the expression of every thoughtful and earnest mind, and of all pure, lofty, and patriotic resolves,—

" Warm from the soul, and faithful to its fires."

In the following pages it will be shown that this is no vain hope, and that, to render the exercise of the parliamentary franchise an act in which the highest moral and intellectual power of every elector may be excited and employed, is no impracticable attempt.

In treating of the representation of minorities, on a principle of unanimity amongst those who are so represented, it will be observed that the course proposed is very different from, and almost the opposite to, that suggested in the address presented to Lord Palmerston, towards the end of the year 1857, on the subject of making an educational franchise a part of the anticipated Reform Bill. The address was entitled to high respect, as bearing the signature of many eminent men; but it is believed that the greater number of those who signed it, intended to express nothing more than their adherence to the principle of giving a just weight to education, and that they did not intend to intimate any adoption of, or preference for, the details of the scheme adverted to in the address. The form in which it was proposed that the educational franchise should be conferred was, indeed, unfortunate; and, perhaps, in that respect, a great cause was never more unhappily marred by injudicious advocacy. An educational franchise must be considered in two phases,—first, the suffrage; secondly, the combinations to give effect to the suffrage. The justice of the claim of suffrage on the ground of scientific and literary distinction,—not for any special advantage to those who claim it, but that the people at large may have the aid of all contemporary knowledge in the business of their government,—will be adverted to in a subsequent chapter. The electoral combinations for giving effect to the suffrage, appear to have been the main subject of the address; and these, it was proposed, should be territorial, to avoid, as it was said, the danger of subjecting them to the influences of any particular class or profession. The apprehension that the learned bodies, if left to themselves, unfettered by territorial limitations, might make an improper choice, or, perhaps, submit to sinister influences, evinced less confidence than might have been expected in the discretion of those whose claim rested on the ground that they were more discreet than the general members of constituencies of which they formed a part. But the very apprehension was, in truth, one of little depth. If one of any of the learned professions were chosen by the members of his profession, he would, probably, be amongst the most distinguished of their number; and he who is a master in one science, as a general rule, approaches with more care and circumspection those departments of knowledge which he has not made his study than the man whose mind has never received any such special direction. Profound knowledge of one branch of science is no unfit preparation for the study of others, whilst it is a guard against that superficiality which is the bane of political discussion.

Passing from the reason assigned for the arrangement, to the territorial constitution which was proposed, it is difficult to avoid the conclusion that a division of electors throughout the kingdom into two classes, the learned and the unlearned, would place the classes which assumed the pre-eminence in a position impossible to be maintained. An institution which might too often have the misfortune of exhibiting to mankind the practical distinction between learning and wisdom, would be little calculated to promote either. It would be always exposed to the most powerful engine of assault which can exist in a civilised age,—that of ridicule. It is not, however, on such objections that it is useful here to dwell. A territorial arrangement must operate by majorities. But the circumstance that the educated classes formed the minorities in the detached constituencies, was the cause of the application for a separate representation; and yet the minorities of the electors, thus permitted to sever themselves from the majorities, would, in their turn, be extinguished; and the very inconvenience which led to the severance would, at the utmost, be but little more than half cured. Indeed, if the educated classes to be thus formed into distinct territorial constituencies, should, be composed of men of independent minds, taking their own distinct and varied views of public affairs, and determined to act for themselves, instead of being led by a few of their number,—they would be likely to bring forward more candidates than appear in a borough in which differences are suppressed. This would be the natural tendency of a highly-instructed constituency; and in such an event, it might happen that a small part of the aggregate number of the educated electors within the territorial division would impose their views upon the rest.

The adoption of the principle that a quota of electors, by unanimity in their choice, may return a representative, would, with the aid of other arrangements of a mechanical kind, and of no difficulty, enable every individual elector,—who shall consider the choice that the majority of the constituency in which he happens to be registered is disposed to make, as the result of corruption or of intrigue to which he will not lend himself, or who shall entertain opinions with which those of their favourite candidate do not harmonise, or who shall consider that a better or a wiser selection can be made, and that with such a belief it is his duty to make it,—to exercise his vote according to his own judgment. The principle might be embodied in and made effectual by the following law :—

IV. Every candidate, whose name is contained in the list of candidates hereinafter mentioned, for whom the full quota of votes shall be polled (subject to any qualification or disqualification otherwise imposed by law), shall be returned as a member to serve in Parliament, in manner hereinafter mentioned.

It will, of course, be immediately perceived, that this law would have consequences far more extensive even than the admission of the voices and opinions of an aggregate of minorities, numbering half a million of electors, great as those consequences would be. The admission and concentration of all those whom the numerical majorities, when dominant, exclude, in truth involves the representation of all opinions. It is because the simple expression of the numerical majority, under a system of equality in suffrage and district, would deprive all classes, except the most numerous, of any weight in the House of Commons, that the framers of our representative system exhaust themselves in ingenious contrivances to parcel the electors into such divisions that some may neutralise others, and thus reduce to its minimum the evil which they apprehend. More than to diminish the evil effects which must result from the extinction of all political power, except that of the poorer classes, they seem scarcely to hope. The object should rather be, to exclude no legitimate influences, and to give such a scope and direction to all political energy, that every elector, in his sphere, and according to his knowledge, may labour to obtain the maximum of good. If every elector be made to see and feel that he is personally responsible for what he does, what he attempts, or what he omits to do, something will be done, at least, to make him deliberate before he acts ; and when a man begins seriously to reflect on what he is to do, much is already gained.

The same machinery which permits the minorities in every constituency to exercise their franchise, by uniting their votes with those of others wherever they find sympathy, will also accomplish other objects, of no less importance.   It will permit all the smaller boroughs and constituencies, or any portion of them, to form similar unions, and will put an end to all questions of disfranchisement ; and it˜will, moreover, afford to every class, and every interest, in the country, the means of being adequately represented in the Legislature.

The subject of the representation of counties, cities, and boroughs, will be considered in subsequent chapters.[1]   On the representation of distinct classes and interests, something may be said in this place.

All those who deem it of paramount importance that the great interests of the country should be adequately represented,—whatever their different views may be as to those interests being homogeneous or antagonistic,—should seriously address themselves to the consideration whether there is any geographical distribution of seats which can hereafter, with anything approaching to accuracy, or with a probability of duration, procure for any distinct interest an effectual representation ; a representation which, if it be obtained at all, will not be overwhelmed by a majority of representatives from other adverse—or, at least, unsympathetic—constituencies.   In examining this question, they should consider, not only the present parliamentary system, but what it is likely to become in the progress of events, which, even if amongst us it went no further than the operation of existing causes, will increase the electoral body under the present law, by adding to the lower and less instructed voters, in a far greater propor-

[1] Ch. III., IV., and X.

tion than to the classes who have greater opportunities of knowledge, and more leisure for thought. They might then usefully proceed to consider whether any machinery exists, or has been proposed to them, which can so effectually secure the protection of every interest, as by giving to those who are attached to every species of property and industry the power of voluntary association. The distinctive interests commonly regarded as the broadest, are those of the landed and commercial classes. The county constituencies were supposed to be the strongholds of the former, and the borough constituencies of the latter. The ulterior view of the general subject of representation—by which the county franchise is regarded as intended to provide, not so much for the representation of the inhabitants of the counties, or of places not within the limits of boroughs, as for the purpose of giving weight to the landed and agricultural interest, has shorn the county population of two-thirds of its political weight. The hypothesis that the county electors did not represent themselves, but were the agents, or retainers, of the landowners, has placed them in such a position of inferiority as to give to 66,000 electors in the county no more weight in the State than 22,000 electors in a borough.[1] In the last chapter, mention has been made of the social changes which have opened the country to the population of the towns, and of the amount of the intelligence and wealth which has thus been transferred from the cities and boroughs to the counties. If, in pursuit of the fancied, but most mistaken, interests of the landowners, the attempt to keep up the geographical distinction between the representation of the boroughs and counties be obstinately persevered in, and be successful, the electoral

[1] In an article in *Fraser's Magazine*, in April 1860, entitled "Representation of every Locality and Intelligence," I have gathered from a valuable paper by Mr. Newmarch, a summary of the Statistics showing this disparity. In counties each member represents also £730,000 of annual income; in the boroughs there is a member to every £280,000.—*Fraser's Magazine*, 1860, p. 540.

elements that might be derived from a population which thus partakes both of the rural and the urban character,—elements not surpassed in value by that of any class in the country,—would be, for the most part, sacrificed. They would be lost to the boroughs, and not gained by the counties. To secure, or preserve, a selfish and an invidious power—which, after all, will escape their grasp,—the landowners, if they were betrayed into such a course, would have excluded from the representation a conservative force of great value, daily augmented in strength and importance, and to the growth of which there is no conceivable limit.

The more extensive, the more numerous and varied the ramifications of any interest, the less should it trust, and the less does it need to trust, to any geographical limitations, and the more may it safely rely on its inherent strength. The landed interest under a free system could not be dependent on the county constituencies. It has its branches in every city and borough in the kingdom. Its interests are identified with those of large numbers of the inhabitants of London. Not only in Belgravia, or Tyburnia, or May-fair, but with the clergy, the lawyers, with Westminster, with Finsbury, with many of the professional classes, the wealthy manufacturers, the principal merchants, the chief tradesmen. Again, in the census of 1851, about 300,000 persons are returned as farmers, nearly all of whom would probably be voters under a system which recognised their equality with the voters in the boroughs. The numbers who reside in cities and boroughs, and who have connections and interests with the same great class, are incalculable by any data which these tables afford, but their numbers must be enormous. In the place of a fatal policy, which seeks—through geographical limits and arbitrary distinctions, by unequal apportionments of political power, and by creating or adhering to unreasonable and invidious inequalities of capacity and franchise,—to secure some remnants of their preponderance, the landowners and the agricultural interest might safely rely, under a free and equal system of representation, on the elements of their just, and legitimate, and unquestionable strength. A distribution of electoral bodies, which would give to every voter the power of adding his vote to those of other electors, with whom he might more perfectly agree in interest and opinion, would, it may be safely predicated, give to the agricultural interest a weight and influence greater than can be attained by the most ingeniously-constructed territorial system they can devise. It would be a weight and influence obtained without any sacrifice of the claims of others. In principle and practice it would be perfectly unassailable, inasmuch as it would be determined, like that of all other bodies, by the measure of the numbers, intelligence, and property which it comprehends.

A similar reasoning will apply to every other class of interest, great or small. The various manufacturing, the mining, the shipping interests, might severally be the framers of their own constituencies, and be thoroughly and satisfactorily represented in the national councils. The population of the manufacturing, commercial, or maritime towns, in which the operations of any of these departments of industry are chiefly carried on, is too miscellaneous to be the organ of any common principle having relation to such special interests. There might have been a time when Norwich or Exeter was ready to advocate, above all others, the real or supposed interests of the woollen, and Newcastle or Liverpool those of the shipping trades; but these times have passed. In the present century, although especial interests may accidentally obtain an exponent of their views in the persons of some of their body who have chanced to find their way into the House, they cannot generally obtain any such representation except by tampering with and corrupting the voters of limited constituencies. No interest, in truth, is provided with any proper or legitimate means of securing at all times its due weight and representation in the legislature. The possession of such weight, or the existence of such representation, are matters left to the determination of chance or accident. This is surely not a basis on which a great representative system should rest.

Another interest remains—and which, not less than any, if not more than all, deserves consideration—the interest of the working classes. To the honour of the age be it said, that the history of the world does not present a time in which the labours of the wise, the great, and the wealthy, were directed with more persevering energy to promote the social benefit of the great masses who are engaged in the manual occupations of life. Some there are in the House of Commons who address themselves to such questions in the spirit of an enlightened philanthropy. But neither science nor philanthropy can reach the depths of the knowledge painfully won in the daily life and experience of the man or woman. It is unnecessary to advert to the cases in which the doctrines of political economy and considerations of morality and duty, when their several provinces are not sufficiently distinguished, seem to conflict. " The want," says the economist, " will produce the supply." " What," replies the moralist, " if the want be not felt, but is yet one which it is a proof of the degradation of our nature not to feel ? The wants which tend to produce a supply are of two kinds—instinctive and artificial. The former seeks after that, a desire of which has been implanted in us by nature,—the latter, after that which we have been taught to desire by experience. The light must enter into the darkness, ere the darkness can know that is without light, and open its heart to desire and embrace it."[1] The questions in which the working, or, as it has been proposed to call them, the wage classes, are deeply interested, become daily more and more developed, as the increase of the population and the progress of material wealth and civilizing influences render the condition of society more complicated.

[1] *Guesses at Truth*, 2nd series, p. 351.

New subjects for consideration incessantly arise. Legislation has dealt at different times more or less superficially and partially with the hours of female and infantine labour, the education of children, the application of endowments for the aid or relief of poverty; the imposition of public taxes to avert destitution; with sanitary necessities, with friendly societies, and the investment of savings; and there is still probably none of these subjects on which the existing legislation is not capable of great amendment. The laws that govern the tenure and conveyance of interests of smaller value in real property, especially of cottages, and of the dwellings of the labouring classes in towns, require extensive modification and improvement; and open a large field of civil reformation, in which the wealthier proprietors may have no sympathy, even if it be not altogether opposed to their prejudices. There is much that touches the condition of the poorer classes which persons in a different social sphere can hardly feel or know. Subjects of still deeper permanent importance appear in the distance. The progress of the co-operative movement is likely to affect extensively the condition of labour, and the relations between the employer and the employed. A consideration of what is due to the vast masses of the working population leads inevitably to the conclusion that they ought to have the power of placing in the House some persons in whom they have confidence, and who are able to view all such questions from *their* side, who have been brought up with them, and know experimentally where and how their condition needs amelioration. A representative assembly of the Commons, without this element, is grossly defective.

Nothing exemplifies more clearly the maxim, that all injustice rebounds upon its authors, than the claims of the working classes for representation in times of popular excitement. Their class having been unwisely and improperly excluded, they then demand such a construction of the fran-

chise, and of electoral divisions, as will tend to throw all
power into their hands, every class but their own being
numerically overpowered. It may be hoped that the friends
of good government will avail themselves of a period of tranquillity to place the representation on such a basis of justice
as shall make it thenceforth unassailable.

In the state of society at which we have arrived, the vesting in every elector of a power to act, if such be his will,
without any trammel created by the particular section of
voters to which he is nominally annexed, is the keystone of
parliamentary reform. It is by this means that the utmost
facility and inducement will be afforded to every elector to
exercise his judgment in making the best and wisest choice.
"That the service of our country is no chimerical, but a real
duty," are the words of a great constitutional philosopher.
When a political system promotes and encourages the association of minds having common pursuits and common sympathies, and when these associations are necessarily so extensive that they can be governed by no narrow or selfish motives,
and by nothing less comprehensive than a desire to further
the moral or material welfare of large numbers of men, the
union becomes necessarily the occasion of exciting generous
sentiments, and to the degree in which the object of the
association is pure and wise, to that degree are its members
elevated above all ignoble and selfish objects. All good
influences will be aided and all evil ones discouraged, not as
results directly aimed at, but as the indirect and natural
consequence of a wholesome state of political existence; just
as the cultivation of a pure mind, and application to honest
objects, is a better protection for virtue than all the repressive
laws that can be made to extirpate vice. Full scope will be
given to every generous sentiment by which men may be drawn
together. Devotion to a great principle—regard for an
illustrious name—affection for an ancient house—admiration
of worthy deeds—attachment to a particular neighbourhood—

love of country or of class—community of feeling—harmony of
taste—may all form so many occasions of concord, and create
innumerable circles, binding together in society all varieties of
rank and station, with an attraction of such power that malig-
nant influences will find no place, and the occupation of the
demagogue will be gone.   Inclination will thus be brought to
the aid of duty.   When no elector can, by the reflection that
any exertion on his part would be vain, if not mischievous, as
injuring the cause he desires to support, excuse his inaction to
his conscience, he will then be sensible of the obligation which
the service of his country imposes upon him.   It is beyond
the power of law to compel men to unite for a common purpose, and labour in it with energy of will, unless it be one in
which their nature prompts them to agree.   An electoral
body, composed of the most heterogeneous and antagonistic
materials, bound together by law, and told that they must
act together, and find one person who can reflect the most
dissimilar things, can be compared to nothing better than the
melancholy spectacle of subdued and torpid natures, which is
sometimes exhibited by the animal showman, in a cage, in the
streets.   With equal truth, or irony, one is called the "happy
family," where every instinct is quelled; and the other the
"independent constituency," where every man's action depends,
not upon himself, but in most cases on those to whom, of all
others, he would be least willing to trust either his honour
or his purse.   The indifference of hopelessness, and the
languor of debility, are occasionally varied by fits of spasmodic
animation when they are roused by those who extract a
miserable profit from the exhibition.   Is it too much to say,
that instead of on one side constructing schemes which shall
perpetuate a stereotyped expression of political sentiment, and,
on another, contriving how it may be counteracted, by secret
voting that may shroud every elector in a veil of obscurity,
statesmen might more wisely employ themselves in discover-
ing, in that great laboratory of science in which we find all we

know of man's nature and of the elements of his moral health, the means of dissipating the unwholesome miasma, and clearing the tainted atmosphere which now envelop political life?

The two following chapters will explain the position in which majorities would be placed, in relation with unanimous constituencies—the respective provinces of the two principles, and their essential harmony.

CHAPTER III.

GEOGRAPHICAL, LOCAL, AND CORPORATE DIVISIONS OF
ELECTORS.

IN the ancient and historical form of our constitutional system, the right, or privilege of nominating representatives in
Parliament, was given,—or, it may be more correct to say,
accrued—to the various detached and distinct communities in
the then existing divisions of counties, cities, or boroughs, in
consequence and as an incident of that previous existence. In
the remodelling of the electoral system in 1832, a course in
many respects the reverse of this was pursued. Districts, or
boroughs, were then created, or unions of such communities
formed, without any other basis of connection than that of
electing representatives. The representation was not given
to the town simply because it was a town containing inhabitants who ought to be represented, for the Reform Bill recognised no such right; but the borough was created, or its
limits extended to the surrounding parishes,—a union of
boroughs formed,—or counties divided into sections, in order
to create an artificial basis of representation. We are now,
it may be hoped, unembarrassed by many of the difficulties
which impeded the labours of 1832, and enabled to view the
entire subject in different aspects. The experience of a
quarter of a century does not encourage the extension of a
system of arbitrary divisions, constructed entirely for electoral
purposes. A representative system, resting on such a basis,

can scarcely be otherwise than a source of discord. It is without landmarks. It has not its origin in that stream of events which has disposed material things in an order wherein all are the more inclined to acquiesce because they have not seen it disturbed or controlled by any visible hand. The example of other countries, as well as of our own, teaches us that, if an arbitrary division for electoral or other purposes is formed to-day, there will not be wanting reasons for its reconstruction to-morrow. On the other hand, these political incorporations which grow out of the constantly operating causes by which all human associations, like material things, are dissolved and reorganised, are found to have the deepest roots. "By preserving the method of nature in the conduct of the State, in what we improve, we are never wholly new ; in what we retain, we are never wholly obsolete. By adhering in this manner, and on those principles, to our forefathers, we are guided, not by the superstition of antiquarians, but by the spirit of philosophic analogy."[1] "Our political system is placed in a just correspondence and symmetry with the order of the world, and with the mode of existence decreed to a permanent body composed of transitory parts, wherein, by the disposition of a stupendous wisdom, moulding together the great mysterious incorporation of the human race, the whole at one time is never old, or middle-aged, or young, but in a condition of unchangeable constancy,—moves on through the varied tenor of perpetual decay, fall, renovation, and progression."[2]

The people of this country have always evinced great reluctance to be arbitrarily parcelled out, formed into sections, and divided by metes and bounds, to correspond with a theory, and they have commonly cast aside, at the first opportunity, such artificial limits. The advocates of equal electoral divisions, who look to a new geographical distribution as the only means of accomplishing their object, will have to surmount

---

[1] *Burke, Reflections*, &c., p. 49.   [2] Id., p. 48.

great prejudices before they succeed in dividing the country like a chess-board. Many of these prejudices are deeply rooted in historical causes, and deserve the respect, rather than the contempt, of the legislator. " To be attached to the sub-division,—to love the little platoon we belong to in society, is the first principle,—the germ, as it were, of public affections. It is the first link in the series by which we proceed towards a love to our country and to mankind." " We begin our public affections in our families. No cold relation is a zealous citizen. We pass on to our neighbourhoods, and our habitual provincial connections. These are inns and resting-places; such divisions of our country as have been formed by habit, and not by a sudden jerk of authority, are so many little images of the great country in which the heart finds something which it can fill. The love to the whole is not extinguished by this subordinate partiality. Perhaps it is a sort of elemental training to those higher and more large regards, by which alone men come to be affected, as with their own concern, in the prosperity of a kingdom." " But no man ever was attached by a sense of pride, partiality, or real affection, to a description of square measurement. He will never glory in belonging to the Chequer, No. 71, or to any other badge ticket."[1] Few, probably, have been known to manifest any degree of pride from their political incorporation with Marylebone, Finsbury, or any other arbitrary metropolitan section.

The glaring anomalies and inconsistencies of a system which enables a great number of the members of the House of Commons to be elected by towns insignificant in wealth and population when compared with other places, often in their immediate neighbourhood, which are without such powers—a system which cannot now be defended on the grounds which were formerly urged in its support—renders some extensive alteration indispensable, if the representation

[1] Id., p. 290.

is to be placed on a rational or satisfactory basis. It has been a common thing for the representatives of such places, and the advocates of the system under which they hold their privileges, to refer to the smaller boroughs, as favourably contrasted with the metropolitan and other larger constituencies, by the more independent tone which their members are able to assume. Those who know they are indebted for their seats to influences which personally affect themselves and the electors, and in which any public principles enter but in a very small degree, are of course more free in their public conduct. They know that they have other securities for their seats than a servile adoption of any popular cry. The preservation of the last remnant of political independence in France, in the early part of the eighteenth century, was the vested interest of the principal members of the provincial parliaments in their offices, and which was due to such offices being vendible, and therefore partaking of the security of individual property. It is stated to have been once somewhat coarsely said by an independent member—that what he had bought he would also sell. It must be allowed, however, that so far as regards the national interests, even the effects of this independence are often to be preferred to the slavish subserviency of the delegate of some of the more numerous electoral divisions.

In order to raise the more populous of the unrepresented and inadequately represented towns to their just position, two plans have been suggested—first, the combination of several of the smaller boroughs into single electoral districts, or as it is called, the formation of groups of contributory boroughs ; and, secondly, and which with many writers seems to be the favourite course, the disfranchisement of many of the smaller towns at present represented. The latter course, the disfranchisement of boroughs at present in the possession of the electoral privilege, all forming parts of the great body of the people, in their degree equally valuable and necessary to the national life, in order to render the representation of that body more perfect, would appear to be a strange kind of progress towards the political perfection at which reformers profess to aim. You have, by your artificial restraints, prevented the blood from freely circulating, and caused in one part of the body a diseased or unhealthy action—and the remedy of these physicians is, to amputate the limb! Surely, instead of this mutilation, instead of leaving the body politic a maimed, a disfigured, and dismembered frame, the physician of the State should rather seek to restore and give strength and vigour to that free circulation, to the want of which the peccant humours owe their origin.

In favour of the formation of groups of contributory boroughs, there is much more to be said. The consideration of this subject is reserved to the next chapter, which treats of the method by which the electors of small towns or districts may contribute with other electors to form a constituency. For the present it is sufficient to suggest the question, whether the advocates of the system of contributory boroughs connected together by reason of their contiguity, and acting by the aggregate majority of their electors, have satisfied themselves that it is impossible to leave the question of incorporation to the voluntary choice of the individual electors? This impossibility should, in common justice, be proved, before any group is permanently incorporated without any regard to the will of the electors, from time to time, within it. It must be asked,—what insurmountable necessity arises from the circumstance that the town A. is half a dozen miles, or an hour's ride, from the town B., that the towns A. and B. must necessarily agree together in the choice of a representative; whilst it is at least equally possible that there may be less sympathy between many of the electors of A. and the electors of B. than between them and others in distant towns, or in the metropolis? If the accident of geographical propinquity, or any other cause, creates this necessity,—whether for moral or physical reasons,—it must be submitted to; but if there be no moral or physical necessity for such a combination, it certainly cannot be the duty of a wise legislator artificially to create it. It is not his province to raise legal or technical obstacles, having no foundation in natural causes, to the free action of mankind.

Nothing is more remarkable in the early history of this country than the disposition to form guilds and associations. Our archives contain records of these forms of political existence. The association produced strength. It was the threefold cord which withstood oppression, and was too stubborn to be easily broken. These societies became an offence to arbitrary princes. Sir Francis Palgrave has remarked, that so early as the reign of Richard the Second, when that monarch was asked by the Commons to restrain alienations of land to ecclesiastics, he went still further than the petition demanded, and extended the restriction to lay guilds and fraternities. The king, he observes, was jealous of the strength and independence of such voluntary bodies, and they were ordered to make returns into Chancery of their regulations and bye-laws. He says, that there are now in the Tower a great number of these returns, and that the Statute of Mortmain, of the 15th of Richard II. (cap. 5), was intended to hold in check the guilds and corporations,—which included all the ancient trading companies, — who were acquiring that political influence which not long afterwards deprived the king of his crown.[1]

In later times, the guilds and fraternities assumed a mixed character, and became partly civil and partly ecclesiastical. They sought to combine the objects of mutual assistance and support in temporal necessities with the consolations of religion. If the rolls of some of these city fraternities were perused, they would astonish many who regard the want of

---

[1] *Evid. Report on Mortmain*, July 1844, p. 10.   *Lucas, Secularia*, pp. 18, 19.

sympathy between different classes, at this day, as a necessary state of things. In them, high and noble names are combined, in one society, with the citizen and the artificer. They afford examples of the manner in which the claims of the great brotherhood of humanity were understood by many of the proudest of other days. The property of many of these bodies, which had always been looked upon with favour by the Crown, was brought within the Acts which gave to the king the property of other fraternities at the Reformation; but it was, probably, felt to be of a secular character, and much of it was granted either freely, or on easy terms, to several of the London parishes which now hold it. All these are proofs of the prevalent spirit of association. This spirit has taken a different direction, according to the hue of the age. It was the same spirit which led the larger communities, the cities and boroughs, to solicit and obtain incorporation, and its attendant powers. It has been always active amongst us, from that time to the present. Witness the great undertakings which have been accomplished by the combination of individual power, without other aid from the State than that which sanctions and adopts the proceeding. Nothing has been too great, or too small, to be beyond its reach—from making a road leading only to a poor hamlet, to gaining, in other realms, an imperial dominion, which the proudest conqueror might have envied.

It is to this voluntary and natural disposition to associate, to which full scope should be given in forming our electoral divisions. It is thus that, when we amend, we build in the old style. If this be permitted, the huge agglomerations of voters combined in some modern boroughs, the wide expanse of acres added to some ancient ones, and the legal bonds by which many boroughs, having otherwise no connexion with each other, are tied together, will be gradually dissolved; and the communities will assume, without any legislative interference, their natural and convenient form. It has been pertinently asked,—" Why Islington, with its hundred thousand inhabitants, should covet a junction with Saffron-hill and Hatton-garden, Ely-rents, or Glasshouse-yard?—why Bloomsbury and Lincoln's-inn should court the alliance of Clerkenwell, or Clerkenwell hang on to Finsbury?" The electoral amendment which would be most in accordance with the historical forms of social progress in this country, would be that which would enable every locality, every community, and every great or ancient association having a distinct corporate existence, and the ordinary conditions that imply permanency, to form a constituency, or electoral nucleus, capable of being represented in Parliament. It will be only necessary to provide, by a general law, that the relative weight of every new constituency in the representative assembly shall be precisely that of its relative magnitude and importance.

In the mode of effecting,—in the construction of the representative branch of our constitution,—such necessary amendments as are from time to time called for by the expanding force of population, wealth, and social changes, every step should have a reference to, and connection with, the other branches of that constitution. It should flow naturally from, and be consonant with, a monarchical form of government. Upon this point it is useful again to listen to the authority so often cited in these pages.

" Mr. Burke was represented as arguing in a manner which implied that the British constitution could not be defended, but by abusing all republics, ancient and modern. He said nothing to give the least ground for such a censure. He never abused all republics. He has never professed himself a friend or an enemy to republics or monarchies in the abstract. He thought that the circumstances and habits of every country, which it is always perilous, and productive of the greatest calamities, to force, are to decide upon the form of its government. There is nothing in his nature, his temper, or his faculties, which should make him an enemy to any republic, modern or ancient. Far from it. He has studied the form and spirit of republics very early in life; he has studied them with great attention, and with a mind undisturbed by affection or prejudice. He is indeed convinced that the science of government would be poorly cultivated without that study. But the result in his mind from that investigation has been and is, that neither England nor France, without infinite detriment to them, as well in the event as in the experiment, could be brought into a republican form; but that everything republican, which can be introduced with safety into either of them, must be built upon a monarchy; built upon a real, not a nominal monarchy, *as its essential basis;* that all such institutions, whether aristocratic or democratic, must originate from the Crown, and in all their proceedings must refer to it; that by the energy of that mainspring alone those republican parts must be set in action, and from thence must derive their whole legal effect (as amongst us they actually do), or the whole will fall into confusion. These republican members have no other point but the Crown in which they can possibly unite. This is the opinion expressed in Mr. Burke's book. He has never varied in that opinion since he came to years of discretion."[1]

It is through the constant exercise of the authority of the Crown, to the prerogative of which it belongs to confer corporate powers—that the creation of electoral bodies can most effectually keep pace with the rapidity of internal changes. The census of 1851 is, in many places, no guide to the state of the country, or of its population in 1858. It is only in the localities where these alterations in the face of society, and in the condition of the neighbourhood, are actually going on, that their extent can be fully appreciated. It is from the people who are themselves affected by such alterations, that any application for separate or local incorporation should emanate. It is not the business of a central power to

[1] *Appeal from the New to the Old Whigs,* p. 46. 3rd ed. 1791.

E

initiate, on their behalf, the proceedings necessary to obtain a new constitution. It would be, moreover, highly inconvenient, that the Parliament should be required to interpose its powers on every occasion. The principle by which such local divisions are to be constituted, separated, or reconstructed, should be settled once for all, and then applied through the constitutional exercise of the royal prerogative, as the established laws are administered through the judicial authority of the Crown.

A law under which new electoral divisions might be formed, as occasion should require, is suggested in the following outline of the fifth clause of the proposed electoral law :—

V. Any borough, and any parish or district or division of a parish or other parochial division, and any ward or other division of a city, town, or borough, and any hundred, wapentake, or other division of a county, and any body, college, or society incorporate, may, in pursuance of a resolution agreed to by a majority of the electors in such community, at a meeting convened and held after due notice, apply to her Majesty in Council, by petition, signed by the chairman of such meeting, praying that such borough, parish, division, or body, may be empowered to return a member to represent the same in Parliament, and that a writ for such purpose may be issued accordingly at future general elections; and such petition shall state who it is proposed shall be the returning officer, and where it is proposed that such election shall take place, and what hall or public building it is proposed to provide for the same, and the situation of the other polling-places, if any, which it is proposed to provide, and in what manner it is proposed that the expenses of such elections, and of the registration and record of voters, and other the incidental expenses of such separate representation shall be borne; and upon the hearing of the said petition, of which not less than three months' notice shall be given in the London, Edinburgh, and Dublin Gazettes respectively; and also upon the hearing of any person or persons, who may apply and be admitted to be heard in opposition to the petition, under such regulations as shall be made in that behalf,—if it shall appear to Her Majesty in Council to be proper to accede to the prayer of the petition, and to grant to such borough, parish, division, or body, a charter of incorporation (if the same be not already incorporated), it shall be lawful for Her Majesty in Council to order that at all future general elections a writ shall be issued for the summoning of such borough, parish, division, or body, to return a member to serve in Parliament, and to prescribe who shall be the returning officer, and any other special rules which may appear to be necessary for the due exercise of such powers; and the said borough, parish, division, or body shall thereupon be empowered to make such return accordingly; but no such order shall confer any right of suffrage on any person who would not, by the general laws affecting the suffrage, be entitled to the same; and a copy of the petition, and of any counter-petition, and of the order made thereupon, shall, within three months after the making thereof, respectively, be laid before Parliament if then sitting, or if not, within the same time after the commencement of their ensuing session.

In explanation of the foregoing clause, it will be observed, that—

It leaves the initiative of all proceedings to obtain a separate representation, to the local or provincial divisions or corporate bodies, themselves.

It must be taken in connection with the clause,—the principal subject of the ensuing chapter,—which would equalise the number of electors necessary for all constituencies, and give to all their due and appropriate weight, and it would not, therefore, affect the number of members.

It does not confer on any person the suffrage, but assumes the right of suffrage, in every case, to be previously settled by law.

It is also assumed, that, in acting under this power, rules for the guidance of the proceedings would be prescribed by an Order in Council, and that they would be such as would guard against any decision upon an application, on which every party really interested had not been heard. The Council, it is assumed, would consider the circumstances of the locality, or of the body making the application; the extent to which the objects of any incorporated institution, which might so apply, were of a public character; competency to provide for the distinct expenses of the registrations, elections, and returns, which would be cast upon them; and generally, whether any public or national object, or any advantage affecting any considerable class or section, would be gained by acceding to the prayer of the petition. The bias would, probably, be to confer the power of making a distinct return, where it is desired by any sufficient body of electors, and where it could be granted without prejudice to others. The Council would lay before Parliament their rules of proceeding, the applications made to them, and the decisions thereon, with the grounds of such decisions. In administering this law, the Council would have the aid of, and would safely be guided by, public opinion, as it might be elicited by any discussion of their proceedings. The question would always be one purely of an administrative character, not affecting any political party, and one in which party feelings could hardly enter.

A corresponding provision should be made for relieving any constituency, local or corporate, of the necessity of making a separate return,—and thereby exonerating them from the additional charges which it would occasion,—upon a petition to her Majesty in Council, setting forth the decay or diminution of the numbers of such constituency, or other sufficient cause.

A self-acting law, of the kind which has been proposed, or some other of an equivalent effect, is absolutely necessary to provide for the fluctuations that are a consequence of the immense activity of modern life, unless Parliament is to be constantly engaged in the labour, and embarrassed by the jealousies, of a reformation of its own constitution.[1]

---

[1] In a note to the pamphlet in which the scheme of personal representation was first rudely suggested, the author referred to upwards of a hundred English towns, every one of which contained at the last census more than 4000 inhabitants. They were: *Bedfordshire*—Leighton-Buzzard, Luton *Berks*—Newbury. *Cambridgeshire*—Ely, March, Whittlesea. *Cheshire*—Altringham, Birkenhead, Congleton, Crowe, Nantwich, Runcorn, Tranmere. *Cornwall*—Camborne, Falmouth, Penzance, Redruth. *Cumberland*—Maryport, Penrith, Wigton, Workington. *Derbyshire*—Belper, Chesterfield. *Devon* Bideford, Brixham, Exmouth, Teignmouth, Torquay. *Durham*—Barnard Castle, Bishop Auckland, Darlington, Hartlepool. *Essex*—Barking, Chelmsford, Halstead, Stratford. *Hampshire*—Cowes, Gosport. *Hertfordshire*—Bishop Stortford, Hitchin, Ware. *Kent*—Ashford, Dartford, Deal, Margate, Ramsgate, Sheerness, Tunbridge Wells. *Lancashire*—Accrington, Burnley, Chorley, Colne, Eccles, Haslingden, Leigh, Middleton, Ormskirk, Over Darwen, Prescot, Southport, Stalcybridge, St. Helen's, Todmorden, Ulverstone.

" Toute institution immobile est vicieuse, parce qu'elle finit par constituer un privilége en contradiction avec l'état réel de la société."[1]   " Si au lieu d'attribuer nominément et à jamais les droits électoraux à tel ou tel bourg, les lois Anglaises les avaient confiés à toute ville dont la population s'élèverait à telle limite (ou dont le revenu serait de tel taux), la représentation, au lieu de se corrompre, aurait suivi les déplacements et les progrès de la véritable capacité politique. Nous pourrions multiplier les exemples, et prouver de mille manières, qu'il n'est bon, ni d'avoir un seul signe légal de la capa-

---

Leicestershire—Hinckley, Loughborough, Melton-Mowbray. *Lincolnshire*— Gainsborough, Horncastle, Louth, Spalding. *Middlesex*—Brentford, Chelsea. Kensington. *Monmouthshire*—Chepstow, Tredegar. *Northamptonshire*— Daventry, Kettering, Wellingborough. *Northumberland*—Alnwick, Hexham. *Notts*—Mansfield, Worksop. *Salop*—Oswestry, Wellington. *Somerset*— Yeovil. *Staffordshire*—Burton-on-Trent, Leek, Wednesbury. *Suffolk*— Beccles, Lowestoft, Woodbridge. *Surrey*—Croydon, Kingston, Richmond. *Sussex*—Worthing. *Warwickshire*—Leamington, Nuneaton, Rugby. *Wilts*— Bradford, Trowbridge, Warminster. *Worcestershire*—Bromsgrove, Stourbridge. *Yorkshire*—Barnsley, Bingley, Dewsbury, Doncaster, Goole, Keightley, Otley, Rotherham, Selby, Skipton, Sowerby-bridge. There is, however, no reason for excluding towns containing less than 4000 inhabitants.

In a note in the *Star* newspaper, relating to South Durham, the writer observes, that " by far the largest town community in that county not separately represented in Parliament, is the seaport town of Hartlepool. A portion of this town is an ancient municipal borough, with a population of between 9,000 and 10,000 persons. Another portion of the seaport, commonly called ' West Hartlepool,' is under the local government of a Town Improvement Commission, incorporated by a private Act, obtained in the year 1854. The present population of the entire community is estimated at between 24,000 and 25,000,—that of Darlington, at between 12,000 and 13,000. In the year 1851, when the census of the municipal borough of Stockton was taken, the borough boundaries inclosed only a group of buildings in the centre of the town. By an Act passed in the following year (1852), the boundaries were made coextensive with the town, and the result has been to inclose a town's population superior to Darlington, by at least 1000 persons." These facts illustrate the impracticability of founding a durable representative constitution upon any present geographical divisions. It is only preparing the occasion for a new struggle.

[1] *Guizot, Gouv. Rep.*, vol. ii., p. 214.

cité électorale, ni de mettre ce signe hors de l'atteinte des vicissitudes de la société." [1]

It would be necessary to fix the numbers of the population, or the rated value of property, or some other measure, on attaining which any borough or local division should be entitled to elect a representative, if such election were to add an additional member to the representative body ; but when, under the operation of another rule, the aggregate number of members can never be exceeded, and the relative and proportionate weight of every constituency is preserved, whatever may be its mutations, the constitution is relieved from the necessity of prescribing any measure, whether of number, or value, or other denomination.   It may then be left wholly to the option of any body of electors proposing to form themselves into a separate constituency, and having reasonable grounds for doing so, to take proceedings for that purpose. The application for the privilege would be some evidence that the constituency deserved it ; for nothing would be gained but the power of being represented in their corporate character by some man chosen by the majority, and between whom and the electoral body the connection of member and constituent may be a source of mutual gratification.

With our present experience of the apathy which is commonly manifested in political matters by great multitudes of the most intelligent classes—especially in their own particular districts—it is difficult to realise the expansion of individual energy and corporate spirit which a free political system would be likely to call forth ; or to estimate the amount of the beneficial influence it would be calculated to exercise both on the character of the electors and the elected.   It would bring out in all its force that spirit of zealous endeavour, honourable emulation, and just pride, which both creates majorities and renders them beneficial to society.   Instead of extinguishing all but themselves, they stimulate the exertions

[1] *Guizot, Gouv. Rep.*, vol. ii., pp. 236, 237.

of the minorities. They do not quench, but fan the generous flame. In the successful struggle of the majority to elect the man whom they regard as the most distinguished of the competitors, the minority may be vanquished without disgrace, and retire with all the honours of a capitulation, the terms of which they have been able to dictate. It is an Isthmian triumph. It has brought out what is vigorous and powerful, and encouraged or provoked to some effort even the weaker and the more feeble, and the nation rises stronger and purer from the contest.

The effect of the free action of every member of an electoral division, in elevating the motives and objects which govern the general choice, is no vain imagination, unless all those feelings by which men were formerly attached, or were supposed to be attached to their country,—to their native or adopted town,—to their place of education,—or to the special society of which they form a part, are now extinct, and that we are reduced to a miserable personality, in which no man regards aught but himself. But the feeling is not extinct. The man, whose virtue or whose genius has conferred honour upon his country and his age, is still thought to shed some reflected ray upon the persons and places he was more nearly connected with. Universities claim a merit from having given to the world men of exalted worth. There is still a pride in companionship with the good and great. To give full scope to these better sentiments in political life, the electors of the kingdom must be extricated from the ties which indissolubly bind together the instructed with the ignorant, the pure with the corrupt, the good with the evil, those morally living with those morally dead, and which swamp all high hopes, and almost all high desires, in "that great Serbonian bog," where all are confounded together. Once set free, all the better elements existing in this great people would be brought into action, and encouraged to employ their most earnest thoughts and energies in assisting to gather and surround the throne with the best and wisest counsellors which their times afford. When the present rude and undiscriminating method of election has ceased, and the names of the most distinguished men in every walk of life are laid before the electors, it will not be easy to make even the humblest voter turn aside to the inferior claims of more obscure men, unless they are brought before him with better recommendations than now suffice to determine his choice.

It has been a subject of great and just regret, that one consequence of the abolition of the close boroughs has been, in a great measure, to impede the access to parliament of a class of able men, who by their aid were enabled to devote themselves, and were gradually disciplined, to political labours. The complaint is admitted to have some foundation, even by those who had no confidence in the proprietors of the close boroughs as the examiners of rising ability or the arbiters of political success. The law which is here proposed would enable every University and College, every Inn of Court, and every collection of learned or professional men, having a corporate union, to be distinctly represented. It will open to all such bodies an honourable rivalry in an object which will at once confer dignity on themselves, and promote the public good. It will be their especial office and laudable pride to bring forward the men in whom they observe the highest qualifications. They will supply in at least an equally effectual, and, in a far more satisfactory manner, that avenue for talent, which the existing system has closed. The judgment of small and highly-qualified bodies of men, in selecting as candidates for public life those amongst themselves, or within the range of their observation, who have displayed remarkable abilities or qualities of mind, is more to be relied on than the operation of the uncontrolled will of any single individual, especially when the choice so made, in order to be effectual, requires the confirmation and approval of a considerable number of their countrymen. We may hesitate to give credit to the opinion of the patron of a borough as to the eminent talents which recommend his nominee. The choice is apt to be attributed less to ability than to favour. When, however, we find the members of a college, or of a learned or other distinguished association putting forward, if not unanimously, yet with a very general concurrence of opinion, a man of whom they have personal knowledge, and whose character has made a powerful impression upon them, and confidently seeking a confirmation of their verdict from a large body of voters, it will not be unreasonable to place some reliance on the merits of him to whom such testimony is borne. The desire of success will afford the strongest inducement to the introduction of the best competitor. The increase of the number of constituencies, especially of constituencies numerically small, and having peculiar qualifications, would in many cases facilitate the entry into public life of men able and willing to employ themselves in the political service of their country, but whose merits are not widely known. Such an one might thus address himself at first to a comparatively small body of electors, perhaps favourably disposed towards him by companionship, appreciation of character or effort, by neighbourhood or traditional respect, and through the judgment and discrimination of this narrower circle, he may ultimately acquire that reputation which will secure for him the suffrages of larger constituencies or a national fame.

CHAPTER IV.

THE formation of electoral districts has been a subject of discussion from almost the earliest time at which the question of parliamentary reform began to be agitated. Various plans have been suggested for forming such districts or divisions. In the year 1780, the Duke of Richmond propounded, in the House of Lords, a comprehensive scheme of reform, in a bill which the brief record of that day states occupied an hour and a half in reading. This measure, after declaring the right of suffrage to be in male persons of twenty-one, went on to prescribe that a list should be taken in every parish of the number of voters, and returns of them made to the Lord Chancellor. "The numbers to be told-up, and divided by 558 (the number of members then in the house), and the quotient to be the number by which one member of parliament was to be elected. Every county to be divided into as many districts as they contain quotients of this nature, and these districts to be called boroughs."[1]

The course adopted in the Reform Act of 1832, is so well known that it will be unnecessary to do more than refer to a few of its features. As an alternative to avoid the disfranchisement of some small boroughs, the area of such boroughs for parliamentary purposes was extended to much of the surrounding country,—embracing, in some cases, a circuit of

[1] *Parl. Hist.*, vol. xxi., p. 687.

NUMERICAL DIVISIONS OF ELECTORS.

many miles. Of this the borough of Shaftesbury may be taken as an example, which was made to include thirteen surrounding parishes. In other cases, several towns, sometimes with their adjoining parishes, contributed to form a district of boroughs, and were empowered to return one member. In the Ayr district, for example,—Ayr, with portions of two adjoining parishes, having, in 1851, 17,624 inhabitants,— Campbeltown, 6880 inhabitants,—Inverary, 1064 inhabitants,—Irvine, and part of an adjoining parish, 7534 inhabitants,—and Oban, with part of an adjoining parish, 1742 inhabitants, were formed into such a constituency. In the case of a very large population, as in the metropolis, a district was formed by combining groups of contiguous parishes into a borough returning two members, as Finsbury. In other cases, where the neighbourhood of an ancient borough had become populous, the surrounding population was taken within the precincts of the parliamentary borough, as Exeter, a city of 34,317 inhabitants, which, for parliamentary purposes, was made to include parts of the parishes of Topsham, Heavitree, St. Thomas, and Alphington, containing together 6371 inhabitants. The principles involved in these forms of division or annexation exhaust all that has been proposed by reformers in this country. The plan of the Duke of Richmond is perhaps the nearest approach to that which was adopted in France by the National Assembly, and there founded on the several bases of territory, population, and contribution ; the territorial basis being created by a division into departments, communes, and cantons.

The annexation of several agricultural parishes to a borough in their centre, as in the case of Shaftesbury, would seem to be a recognition of the fact that the alleged distinction between the interests of the borough and the county electors is but imaginary ; for, if any real distinction existed, injury would have been done to one or the other. It would have been an injustice to hamper the action of either set of electors by

attaching them to the other. It may possibly be said that
the borough electors are, in the cases of towns situated like
Shaftesbury, only another class of county electors, and that the
addition of the county electors to the borough was of no other
importance than that of giving them another polling-place,
and a larger share in the election of a member. All such
considerations are in truth but solemn trifling. The parade of
distinct interests and distinct objects in the country and the
town it is to be feared is now rarely used, except to blind
the eyes of the public, and perplex the question of representation.

The addition of populous suburbs to the constituency of a
city or borough, already possessing no more than its share in
the general representation, is certainly a mode of removing the
discrepancy between the electoral privileges of the inhabitants
of the city and the suburb; but when a suburb, containing a
thousand voters, is added to a city which already contains four
thousand, it is very difficult to say in what sense the representation is improved. If anything be gained by the thousand
new electors,—any power of infusing their opinions into the
representative body,—it must be so much taken from the four
thousand old electors. The representation must have been
made less a reflex of their opinions. "Au lieu de dénaturer
les droits politiques en les exténuant, sous prétexte de les
répandre, qu'il y ait partout des libertés locales, garanties par
des droits réels."[1]

Such annexations to boroughs, or extensions of the franchise
to surrounding districts, are, however, still gravely proposed
as amendments. They may remove an inequality between
the inhabitants of two contiguous places, leaving the greater
anomalies and inequalities which extend over the kingdom
untouched; but this is to divert the amendment which
pretends to make, and should make, the representation more
perfect, to another, a distinct, and a far inferior, object,—the

---

[1] *Guizot, Gouv. Rep.*, vol. ii., p. 263.

mere abolition of a local discrepancy,—an alteration which, it is seen, may even render the actual representation less perfect. Instead of resting satisfied with the removal of mere local irregularities, or inequalities, the object should be to create a general congruity, in which every part of the political edifice is adapted to its true purpose.

There are insurmountable objections to an electoral division founded solely on a geographical or territorial basis, and not corrected by some balancing movement, which answers to the fluctuations of society. In addition to the difficulty of arriving, even in the outset, at anything like equality in such a division, it has constantly to be reconstructed. The shifting centres of population and industry will every year disarrange and disturb it. No session of Parliament would ever pass without claims being urged for a new Reform Bill,—claims which, upon the principle of the divisions supposed to have been already made, are necessarily well founded, and entitled to attention. No one who duly estimates the importance of the ordinary labours of the Legislature, will be inclined to interrupt them by sowing the seeds of such perennial contests.

It is sometimes said, that merely a proximate, and not a mathematical, equality is sought for. Political justice is not so rigid as to demand the same measure of constitutional right for every corner of the kingdom. It is not like the law of nature, inflexible and impartial. It admits of inequality and injustice, on the condition that it be not too great, or too glaring. But who are to be the victims; and will they or ought they to be content with their fate? Would not such contentment, on the principles upon which the reform is carried out, be the mark of a servile disposition? A foundation adopted on the supposition that it is just, and which, after all, proves to be only an approximation towards justice, will render any settlement that rests upon it necessarily transitory and short-lived. If we begin with perfect accuracy, it secures, at least, a longer period before the scheme will require material alteration ; but if we set out with a system loosely and unfairly constructed, we begin with that which is already condemned, and has advanced some steps towards its end.

A defect in all geographical or territorial systems, from that of the Duke of Richmond downwards,—greater in its practical consequences than all the other inconveniences which attend them, great as some of the latter are—is that they, in their result, separate every part of the kingdom into two main divisions, one somewhat more, and the other somewhat less numerous ; and they not only do not provide for, but they absolutely exclude from the Legislature, the representation of the opinions, feelings, or desires, of the less numerous of these divisions.   It destroys the minorities, and in so doing seriously weakens and deteriorates the representation, even of the majorities.   " Un système électoral qui, d'avance, annulerait, quant à la formation de l'assemblée délibérante, l'influence et la participation de la minorité, détruirait le gouvernement représentatif, et serait aussi fatal à la majorité elle-même qu'une loi qui, dans l'assemblée délibérante, condamnerait la minorité à se taire."[1]

In the establishment of what may be called a sliding or self-acting scale,—by which the additions to population that constantly occur, and the new communities that grow up, silently enter and take their place in the constitution, and for whose admission the communities that are stationary or decay, as silently make room, by a general and fundamental law, operating without any jerk or effort, preserving all parts without repletion and without void,—we are instructed by the experience of the United States, a people from whose institutions we have much to learn, both for example and for warning.   It is that one part of their system which has never failed to work harmoniously and well.

If the American constitution had not fixed, as a funda-

---

[1] *Guizot, Gouv. Rep.*, vol. ii., p. 260.

mental law, the proportion of every state in the House of Representatives, and had not made that proportion to vary with the relative population of the several states, without the necessity of recurring from time to time to the federal legislature, it would have left the constitution open to internal contests, dangerous to the Union. The number of members in the House of Representatives was fixed at one for every 228th part of the population, to be determined at the census which is taken every ten years, a fractional number in any state exceeding one-half of the quotient entitling that state to an additional member. The federal law of the 5th June, 1842 (c. 47), requires the division for electoral purposes of every state into so many parcels of contiguous territory as shall be equal to the number of representatives. This method of distribution is the temptation of the party which happens to be in power to form the districts in the manner which shall be most useful in consolidating their votes and diminishing the electoral power of the opposite party. In the United States this has become an art, and is known as "gerrymandering."[1] The name is peculiar to America, but the contrivance itself is a familiar one in France, and it is not unknown in England.[2] In this country, indeed, the inequalities of representative distribution surpass the art of the "gerrymander." Statistics collected by late writers and speakers are absolutely startling in what they reveal. Mrs. Fawcett remarks that "at the general election of 1868 ten successful candidates polled 159,650 votes; ten other successful candidates were returned by 1873 votes; and ten *unsuccessful* candidates polled 83,217 votes."[3] Mr. Blennerhasset observes that "there are eight constituencies, *viz.* Portarlington, Dungarvan, Mallow, Downpatrick, Ennis-

---

[1] See an article in the *American Law Review*, Boston, January, 1872. "The Machinery of Politics and Proportional Representation." Reprinted by the Representative Reform Association, 27, Villiers Street.

[2] See Mr. Morrison's Speech, House of Commons, 10 July, 1872.

[3] *Macmillan's Magazine*, Sept., 1870, p. 376.

killen, Kinsale, New Ross, and Youghal, with about 2000 electors between them, and a population under 40,000, which have together the same amount of representation as the four greatest constituencies in Ireland—Cork County, Dublin City, Down, and Mayo, with their 40,000 registered voters and 1,200,000 of population."[1] It is idle to speak of such a state of things as a mere anomaly of historical growth, and to dismiss it as of no importance. It is offensive to the common understanding, and to uphold it as tolerable, and as something which it is not worth while to disturb or correct, is essentially demoralizing to the public conscience. It is to treat all government as a game of chance, having no stable ground or sound foundation on which to rest, but ever dependent on the chapter of accidents. It saps the foundation of effort for political or social improvement, by depriving it of all logical hope of success through constitutional action. The late explanation of an eminent speaker, that "the nation has outgrown the state," has doubtless much truth; but it cannot be wise, even if it were long possible, thus to ignore the national growth. The only safe course is to render the political weight of every local constituency dependent upon and variable according to the number of the registered electors within it who go to the poll. We thus adopt a rule of mathematical precision, which is self-correcting, and yields to no party exigencies. It is found by dividing the number of votes given in the three kingdoms, at the general election, by the number of members required to constitute the House, the quotient forming a quota of votes entitling every candidate for whom that number shall be given to be returned as a member.[2] Different methods of supplying the numbers which are then wanting, from the candidates standing next on the voting papers, are pointed out later,[3] and a method of selection when the quotas cease, has been embodied in Clause XXV.

---

[1] Speech, House of Commons, 10 July, 1872.
Clause IV., p. 31.   [3] See Chap. IX.

of the proposed electoral law, for the direction of the Registrars in appropriating the remainder of the voting papers.

The fourth clause of the proposed electoral law has prescribed the number of votes which shall be sufficient for the return of any member,—and the following clause defines the number which shall be insufficient. .

VI. No person shall be returned as a member to serve in Parliament, at any general election, for whom there shall not be polled the full quota or number of votes, to be ascertained from time to time as hereinbefore prescribed, or one of the comparative majorities of votes to be determined from time to time as hereinafter directed.

In effecting the greatest moral object that society is called upon to undertake,—the formation of a legislative assembly, —a rational standard of association is thus substituted for a traditional one. Instead of an arbitrary geographical division, which the migrations of population will constantly disturb, the proposed equality of division would be affected by no commercial or social changes which the face of the country might undergo. It affords the means of giving to the counties, and to all the larger, as well as to the smaller towns, their due weight in the Legislature, by a rule at all times arithmetically correct, and admitting of no invidious distinctions between the inhabitants of the metropolis, or of the provinces. It places upon an equality the gentleman in Devonshire with the gentleman in Yorkshire, the merchant in Liverpool with the merchant in Yarmouth, the tradesman in Cornhill and in Calne, the artizans on the Trent and on the Tees. The relative weight of the larger, as well as of the smaller constituencies, is accurately measured and reconciled with the general representative system.

The operation of a system of electoral divisions composed of an unanimous quota of votes, may be compared with the operation of a system of contributory burghs, founded on

F

the principle of election by majorities, according to the existing law.　Take the Ayr district, and suppose that there are
1039 voters, viz.,—

In Ayr	500
„ Campbeltown	200
„ Invernry	35
„ Irvine	230
„ Oban	74

It is possible that a majority of the electors of Ayr, or
even every elector of Ayr, may be entirely unrepresented.
The inhabitants of the four other towns may form the majority, and leave the town of Ayr without any share or voice in
the representation.　The same may, of course, happen to
Campbeltown, Irvine, or any of the other towns.　Nothing
but securing a majority of the electors of the five towns can
assure to any of the towns, or any of the electors in them,
the election of their representative.　If an unanimous quota
of votes, wherever found, be made sufficient to return a representative, not one of the towns, or one of the electors in any
town, could be, owing to the votes of the rest, without a
representative.　The member for Ayr would be elected by
the majority of the electors of Ayr.　Instead of being restricted to the other four towns, and compelled to consult
their respective local prejudices, or succumb to their jealousies
or intrigues, every burgh in the district might look for the
residue of the ʼ quota required by the candidate whom they
chose, throughout the entire kingdom of Scotland ; and if
that be not enough, throughout the United Kingdom.　Their
position may be likened to that of a merchant, to whom the
facility of locomotion has opened all the great marts of commerce ; and who is no more confined, as he had previously
been, to the scantily-furnished stores of three or four neighbouring market-towns.

It is a necessary part of the proposed system that the quota

of votes must be made up, or if not, that at least a comparative majority must be attained; but that is nothing more than
a necessary consequence of the principle, that towns of small
importance, or containing comparatively few electors, cannot
have the same corporate weight in the public councils as those
which are inhabited by more numerous constituencies. Besides
the relative corporate weight of the borough, there will be
the uniformity of the individual weight of every vote, which
becomes the same, whether the elector reside in Campbeltown
or Camberwell.

Many objections will, no doubt, be raised to a scheme which
insures success to every candidate who receives a certain quota
of votes. There are parties, and leaders of parties, who have
other plans and other objects. They appear to consider it
their interest, or the interest of their class, that the electors
should, in some constituencies, be counted by thousands, and
in others by hundreds, or tens,—here huddled together in
mobs,—there made up of a narrow clique,—here in huge
masses,—there in petty clusters,—masses which may be led
by clamour, clusters which may be bought for money. A
system which is merely rational and consistent, and treats the
franchise and its exercise as sacred things, is likely to find
many opponents and little favour. The discourses which
have been heard since the amendment of the Reform Act has
been agitated, lead to the suspicion that in constructing any
future measure there will be attempts on all sides to frame a
system which shall pack the electors, so as to expose them
especially to the operation of such forces as each party
imagines that it has most at its command.

A highly-gifted member of the lower house has recently, as
the firsts fruits offered—and no unfit tribute—for the blessing
of restored health, again devoted his political efforts to that
cause which he has always advocated,—the cause of peace.
There is no greater or nobler mission. In such a theme the
language of indignation at the follies and the crimes of men

may well be pardoned. It is a repetition of the sad story
which foretold that—

> "Might only shall be admired,
> And valour and heroic virtue called.
> To overcome in battle, and subdue
> Nations, and bring home spoils with infinite
> Man-slaughter, shall be held the highest pitch
> Of human glory."

It is possible that since war has originated in cabinets and
been sustained by loans, its true causes would often appear
more deserving of contempt and reprobation from having lost
that glow of heroism shed upon the deeds of those who personally executed what they planned, and shared in the suffer-
ings and privations caused by the struggle. It cannot be
doubted that low and selfish motives have entered into
the business of government, and led to great calamities.
Parties in this country have not been backward in exposing
the faults of each other, but to regard such mean objects as
the especial inheritance of any particular class is unjust. The
proportions of good and evil existing in one class differ probably very little from those of all the rest. The class in
which the government of this country has been chiefly vested
may point with some confidence to records proving that if
they have not been superior, they have at least been equal to
the rulers of any other land, and that they have never been
wanting in the full measure of the virtues of their race and
age.

Where, however, in history, where in modern experience, is
there ground for the belief that if the kingdom were parcelled
into equal electoral divisions, and the majority in every division called upon to pronounce for peace or war—that it would
follow that peace would be more certainly preserved? Let us
recall the latest impressions, which, as individuals, we have
all gathered of the opinions of the more numerous classes in
recent times, and reflect whether war with Russia or war with

China would not have been entered upon with equal readiness, applauded with equal vehemence, and probably prolonged even more vindictively and more fiercely, if it had been left to a ballot of such electoral districts. It is said that this would not be so, for the poorer classes are those from which our soldiers and sailors are taken,—it is they who suffer in the conflict, and it is they who are still more impoverished by the prostration of industry which attends it. It is, indeed, true that they are the victims; but to suppose that, therefore, their passions will be restrained, that they will learn forbearance, that they will resist the specious arguments of men who know how to make the worse appear the better cause, that they will foresee the retroactive efforts of extravagant expenditure, the exhaustion which is to succeed unprofitable effort, the economical consequences which follow a vast outlay in destruction—is to suppose that the majorities have suddenly risen to the height of this great argument, and have become temperate, moderate, and wise. That such a consummation is the wish and hope of some who desire to place all political power in the hands of the greater number is not to be doubted ; but is the expectation reasonable—is there the shadow of a hope of its realisation? Are the numerical majorities which govern the United States remarkable for their concern at the horrors of war,—for their solicitude to avoid national quarrels,—for their anxiety to preserve peace, —for their forbearance towards other countries,—for their respect of the claims of weaker neighbours,—for their tenderness of all aggression ?[1]

[1] These pages were published before the beginning of the American civil war, but the Author cannot now let them pass without protesting against the injustice of attributing to the American form of popular government, either the severities of the war or the persistence with which it is prosecuted. There has been no act of cruelty, however deplorable, which is not equalled and surpassed in the exploits of the armies of Europe; and notwithstanding the evidences of indomitable spirit displayed by the South, if the Federal government had not engaged in a struggle,

It will be remembered, that the general election of 1857 afforded the advocates of the Chinese war a signal triumph. It was not alone the voice of small constituencies; some of the largest were even more remarkable for the manner in which they received and rewarded peaceful counsels. Whether in the late war with Russia the vital and material treasures of the nation have been vainly spent to sustain upon a throne an effete dynasty, to uphold the symbol of a cruel and intolerant creed, and perpetuate a social condition inimical to civilization; or whether it was the act of that deep and profound wisdom—that insight which is foresight—that study of history, which is philosophy teaching by example—that long experience of the dealings of nation with nation, which in humbler stations is gathered from the conduct of man to man, and which may enable statesmen of the highest order to gaze almost with prophetic eye into the future, and see to guard against other, perhaps distant, but more fatal evils—are questions which this age will scarcely solve; but there is no doubt that in this country the multitude, so far as they were heard, approved the sacrifice. Whether that sacrifice was made to the balance of power, to national interests, national pride or rivalry, or whether to the genius of war, there is no denying that the holocaust was freely offered, and that the altar was thronged with votive worshippers. A discourse in which peace and justice were displayed as the true wisdom of nations as of men, might have been heard with delight and applauded with enthusiasm, but that temporary emotion affords only slender reason for the hope that the lesson is the more deeply engraved on the popular mind.

> "'Hosanna' now—to-morrow, 'crucify,'
> The changeful burden still of their rude lawless cry."

---

however long and bitter, rather than yield up so large a portion of the territory of the Union, it would have set an example of political moderation which neither monarchies nor aristocracies have hitherto displayed.—[Note to 3rd Ed.]

Some misgiving may well be felt even in the mind of the orator and teacher himself, whether there will in electoral majorities be any sure anchorage for the doctrines that lead to peace and tranquillity, when he observes that of the many assemblies which have since met, all ready to grasp the electoral power he would give them, how few have accepted its higher and holier uses.

It is by a concentration of the political strength of the advocates of peace—of all those who believe it to be inconsistent neither with the dignity nor the security of a great people, and that it may be safely built on a policy—open, frank, and just towards all, that they will acquire their due weight. They may rely on that theory which has, "if any theory has —borne the wear of time, and seen empires rise and set, the eternal theory that Truth is better than Falsehold, and that man was made to be upright."[1] This kingdom contains forty thousand ministers of the gospel of peace; perhaps, of all these, not a hundred have had in the existing system any opportunity of giving such votes as expressed their abhorrence of unjust wars—perhaps not one has by his vote produced the smallest effect on the result of any election—nor would their votes have any more weight in the most perfect system of geographical divisions which any Reform Bill has put forward.

On the other hand, there are many who, rejecting all electoral divisions, desire to preserve some of the small boroughs as the avenues for the representation of special interests. In a tabular statement, showing the population of the represented boroughs, beginning at the most, and ending at the least populous, the twelve last places are :—Arundel, Honiton, Ashburton, Lyme Regis, Thetford, Totnes, Harwich, Dartmouth, Evesham, Wells, Reigate, and Richmond, which may be taken as fair examples. What classes, it may be asked, do the electors of these boroughs represent, of what opinions are they the exponents, what interests do they

---

[1] *Westminster Review,* vol. xiii., N.S., p. 417.

protect ? What have these unfortunate voters done, that they should be put forward in so prominent a place as the few men whose judgment in the choice of legislators may be more safely trusted than that of the great body of their country-men ? It is a position which is almost certain to expose their wisdom to doubt, and their virtue to danger. In several of these towns, so far as they appear to have any decided opinions, the majority appear favourable to the ballot, as, perhaps, might naturally be expected. All the representatives of those boroughs who are deserving of their high trust, would, no doubt, be elected under a different system. High rank, accompanied by character, talent, industry, and patriot-ism, is sure to be esteemed and welcomed. People look to an aristocracy of some kind for those whom they are ready to regard as their natural leaders.[1] But it is difficult to see in what respect any particular class or interest in the nation would suffer, if the twelve boroughs above named ceased as such to exist. It would be a curious speculation to take the political history of any of the smaller boroughs, and, following the votes of its representatives for the last half century, to ascertain what distinctive opinions or feelings the action of its electors has been the means of imparting to the legislature.

If it be the object of any party to preserve the small boroughs, either with or without the ballot, for the purpose of securing what they may deem the advantage of reserving some seats which shall be accessible to pecuniary influences, a more honest, and a not less effectual course, would be at once to propose that a certain number of seats should be put up to auction, and that the State should have the benefit of the purchase-money.

It is not, however, any part of the system now proposed, to deprive any of these boroughs of their just weight in the political system of the country. On the contrary, as in the case of the contributory boroughs before referred to, every

[1] See *Westminster Review*, vol. i., N.S., p. 26.

elector they contain will have his electoral privileges for every good purpose largely extended. Like the other electors of the kingdom, instead of being confined within the narrow boundaries of their respective boroughs, they will be enabled to seek for concurrent views and opinions in the kingdom at large. Modern facilities and habits of locomotion have gone far " to remove national and provincial antipathies, and bind together all the branches of the human family. In the seventeenth century, the inhabitants of London were, for almost every practical purpose, farther from Reading than they now are from Edinburgh, and farther from Edinburgh than they now are from Vienna." [1] It is probable that many, if not most of the voters, will add their votes to those of their townsmen and neighbours, especially when the chief causes of jealousy and discord are taken away. Contiguity of place produces a tendency to union. It will always assert its influence. It is certain to affect more or less the conduct, and control the ties of social and political life,—but it is not, therefore, necessary that it should tyrannize over them. The destruction of a city in China affects us less than a broken limb happening before our eyes. It is a happy provision that our sympathies are most excited where they are most useful. But in the wider relations of national life, it is desirable that we should be governed less by impulse and more by reason— less by merely proximate, and more by general and universal causes. It is better to trust to the qualities of the person, than to the contiguity of place. Geographical limits, made the sole basis of political action and association, is not the development of a power, but the aggravation of a natural incapacity.

[1] *Macaulay, Hist. of England,* vol. i., p. 379.

CHAPTER V.

THE SELECTION OF REPRESENTATIVES.

In forming the representative body, to which, co-ordinately with the other branches of Parliament, is committed the power of government and legislation, it is undeniable that it would be wise to invite by every suitable inducement, and to gather together with every possible diligence and care, such minds as are by constitution, experience, or study, the best fitted to deal with the subjects which, at this day, come within the range of political action. The election confers no quality that the elected did not before possess—none other than "nature and education, and their habits of life, have made them. Capacities beyond these the people have not to give. Virtue and wisdom may be the objects of their choice, but their choice confers neither the one nor the other on those upon whom they lay their ordaining hands. They have not the engagement of nature—they have not the promise of revelation—for any such powers."

·· Political science is, perhaps, of all studies, the most difficult, from the boundless variety of its phenomena. The apparent simplicity of much that is upon the surface leads us to think that we comprehend it; and the depth and complexity of what is beneath and behind, which eludes our sight, seem to mock our attempts to penetrate its secrets. "If there be not a true understanding of what constitutes social development, there must necessarily be grave mistakes made in checking these changes and fostering those. If there be lack of insight respecting the mutual dependence of many functions, which, taken together, make up the national life, unforeseen disasters will ensue from not perceiving how an interference with one will affect the rest. If there be no knowledge of the natural *consensus* at any time subsisting in the social organism, there will, of course, be impossible attempts to achieve ends which do not consist with its passing phase of organisation. Clearly, before any effort to regulate the myriad multiform changes going on throughout society can be rationally made, there must be an adequate comprehension of how these changes are really caused, and in what way they are related to each other, how this perplexed web of phenomena hangs together, how it came thus, and what it is becoming. That is to say, there must be an adequate acquaintance with social science,—the science involving all others,—the science standing above all others in subtlety and complexity,—the science which the highest intelligence alone can master."[1]

It is but too obvious that the traditional method of filling the House of Commons,—suitable as it was in earlier times, when a few master minds directed all public affairs, and the people came together, not to reason, but simply to confirm what their leaders had done, or proposed to do, is unsuited to this day. The subjects which now arise, and in which the public both feel and take the deepest interest, are almost infinitely various, and require to be approached with great preparatory knowledge. The growth of populous cities—the conquests of science in the material world,—the activity of commercial intercourse,—the progress of mental development,—all tend to create, daily, new questions and new problems, which it requires more than merely empirical knowledge to solve. On one side, it is proposed that political science should be systematically taught, and a measure of

---

[1] *Westminster Review*, vol. xii., N.S., p. 469.

proficiency distinguished by a diploma.[1] Others turn from the task in despair, and conclude that the vast range of the study places it, as a whole, beyond the intellectual grasp of any single mind, and that it is, therefore, vain to seek for greater qualities than we find in our daily path.[2] All, however, will probably agree that the country should collect the best materials which it possesses in the construction of its great representative assembly. Instead of this being attempted, the House of Commons, though nominally open to every subject, is yet surrounded by barriers, practical and legal, which tend, in their general character, to exclude the greatest number of those whose aid it would, upon that principle, be desirable to invite, and to facilitate the admission of those whom it would be desirable to exclude.

The obstacles are of a character which may be described as both practical and legal; practical, inasmuch as the cost and manner of elections impose difficulties which many, probably far the largest number, of those who possess the highest qualifications, are unable to overcome, and conditions to which they are naturally unwilling to submit; legal, inasmuch as large numbers of persons are disqualified by the arbitrary restrictions of positive law.

It is proposed in this chapter, after pointing out the circumstances in which our present methods of selection differ from those of former times, and remarking on the necessity of introducing a governing principle of a better nature, to treat of the increased facilities which may be provided, for obtaining in the House of Commons the services of the most highly qualified persons, and thereby giving effect to such better principle; and in the next chapter, to suggest the abolition of the practical and legal obstacles in the way of all such persons, of whatever class.

The difference, or rather, as it may not incorrectly be

---

[1] *Journal of the Statistical Society*, vol. xx., p. 121.

[2] *Blakey, History of Political Literature*, vol. i., p. 299. Lond., 1855.

termed, the contrast between the position of the country, with reference to the election of members of the House of Commons at the present time, and that in which it formerly stood, ought to be considered with much attention.

The natural process in a rude age would be the selection in every borough of persons in the town or neighbourhood, known to the burgesses, and willing to undertake a business which usually involved, of necessity, much expense and inconvenience. It is found, in fact, to have been very frequently avoided. As the institution advanced in importance, the great men of the county or locality became accustomed to point out to the freeholders and burgesses the persons whom they should choose, and their recommendations were commonly attended to. These leading men were themselves a part of, or intimately connected with, the higher aristocracy. They felt a personal responsibility in making the selection,— a responsibility which increased with the importance of the office. It was not a responsibility to the people, but to the party, or perhaps the faction, in the country with which they were connected or identified. They were answerable for the judicious exercise of this, as of all other influences which they possessed. Unwise or unskilful conduct in the business of his party would then, as now, cost a man more or less of its respect. Responsibility is not less real, because its sanctions are conventional. In pointing out to the freeholders or the burgesses the members whom they were to choose, they were under an obligation to select men fitted for the purpose, whatever that purpose might be. It might not then have been thought a duty to select men who were qualified to make laws or to act for themselves, or to discuss political questions. The questions for discussion were few, and such as they were, the leaders of the party or the faction probably intended to decide for themselves; but whatever interests, great or small, they thought it their duty to consider in the matter of selection, that duty they performed. The great rebellion, it has been well observed, did not so much divide the country in support of any antagonistic and abstract principles, as range the contending forces on the side of the great leaders whose influence prevailed in the different parts of the kingdom.

The revolution brought a vast addition of earnestness into the business of choosing representatives. The great parties in the State began then to assume modern forms. The struggle for power became more intense, and electioneering was converted into an art. But throughout the whole of this period, it must not be forgotten that all elections were governed by persons acting under a sense of the importance and responsibility of their work. By importance, it is not meant that they necessarily felt the serious public interests which the task involved. The importance and responsibility were regarded with a view to party strength and party confidence. Upon the management of these forces appeared to depend, at one time, the overthrow of a dynasty; at other times, certainly depended the overthrow of a minister. The objects of the leaders in any part of the country, in labouring in either cause, might have been their own profit or aggrandisement; but in order to succeed in these objects, however selfish, they were obliged to select the best instruments to strengthen and concentrate their power. Their own relative importance in the court and the country might depend on the success with which they brought up the combatants in the great field of political warfare. The growing activity of the press, the general diffusion of information, made it necessary, in later times, to collect a different class of men. The necessities of debate called for talent. Those who influenced the elections, whether for counties or boroughs, gave their attention more and more to this species of political action. Whether a borough was owned or governed by a whig or a tory,—whether bought to support an East Indian or a West Indian interest,—or whatever special or general object its patron had in view, in order to succeed in that object he was compelled to choose the most suitable instrument which could be had. The result of this competitive pursuit, possibly more of selfish than of national objects, was yet to produce an assembly composed, for the most part, of superior men. It was the sure operation of those adequate causes, which, to use the words of Mr. Burke, filled the House of Commons with much of that which the country possessed,—"illustrious in rank, in descent, in hereditary and in acquired opulence, in cultivated talent, in military, civil, naval, and politic distinction."

The state of society silently underwent a change. The system which produced these results had fulfilled its purpose. It could not be perpetuated, the middle classes which grew up were not prepared to yield unreasoning obedience to hereditary leaders or ancient names. If the few possessed a sacred and prescriptive right to speak and act for the many, it was a right not easy of proof, and not to be admitted without proof. They bore about them no marks indicative of the divine origin of their claim, and no muniments were found to support their pretensions. The old chronicles of the people told that their forefathers, while yet in the German forests, had used to be consulted by their chiefs,—that the Plantagenets had summoned their ancestors to the royal councils,—and that the haughtiest of the succeeding monarchs had then found no security but in laws which the deputies of the people had confirmed. They demanded that the representation should be what it professed to be. They were not satisfied that the government had attained, or was in the road to, perfection. They were acute and severe critics of its evils and anomalies, and were not content with arriving occasionally, and by indirect courses, at objects which they insisted should be sought for incessantly and directly. In forming a representative assembly they preferred a homely and clumsy reality to a splendid and not unsuccessful show. Their demands

were conceded, and the vessel of the state has been borne
safely through a period which has seen the wreck of many
other constitutions.

The picture unfortunately has another side. The powerful
patron,—the guiding hand that ruled the election, and suppressed all other influences,—could form no part of a system
in which the representation is to be personal. But with the
indicating mind is gone all sense of responsibility for ·the
choice which is made. There is no obligation on any voter to
bow to the choice of another. Every man is as well entitled
as another to be the leader; and where every man is equally
entitled to be chief, there can be no usurpation and no rebellion. A community so situated is reduced to a state of
natural society so far as relates to duty or function. They
remain in a state of civil society in all other respects, for the
laws are present to· enforce its obligations; but, as to the
right of voting for parliamentary representatives, the principle
is,—that every man shall do what is right in his own eyes.
Viewed on this side, the electoral principle is anarchic. In
this diffusion of forces which were heretofore concentrated, it
becomes of paramount importance to purify the sources from
whence they derive their energy.

"Il ne faut pas beaucoup de probité pour qu'un gouvernement monarchique ou un gouvernement despotique se main-
tiennent ou se soutiennent. La force des lois dans l'un, le bras
du prince toujours levé dans l'autre, règlent et contiennent tout.·
Mais, dans un État populaire, il faut un ressort de plus, qui est
la VERTU.

"Les politiques grecs, qui vivoient dans le gouvernement
populaire, ne reconnoissoient d'autre force qui pût le soutenir,
que celle de la vertu. Ceux d'aujourd'hui ne nous parlent
que de manufactures, de commerce, de finances, de richesses,
et de luxe même.

"Lorsque cette vertu cesse, l'ambition entre dans les cœurs
qui peuvent la recevoir, et l'avarice entre dans tous. Les

désirs changent d'objets; ce qu'on aimoit, on ne l'aime plus; on étoit libre avec les lois, on veut être libre contre elles; chaque citoyen est comme un esclave échappé de la maison de son maitre; ce qui étoit *maxime*, on l'appelle *rigueur;* ce qui étoit *règle*, on l'appelle *gêne;* ce qui étoit *attention*, on l'appelle *crainte*."[1]

It is necessary to examine closely the operation of the principle of representation under the system now inaugurated, and if it be possible, to discover in what guidance, wisdom and safety are to be found. This inquiry involves some investigation of the state of popular life and manners amongst us.

The natural tendency to association, common to society, has been the subject of remark in a former page. The places in which people meet, and their habits and employments, form the features of social life. At the present time it is impossible not to remark the great number of public-houses and beer-shops.[2] There is no doubt, that these houses of entertainment are places of great resort. It must not be thought that this is mentioned as a social reproach. It is due to many causes: much to the uninviting character of the vast number of dwellings in cities and towns, not of the labourers alone, but even of the smaller tradesmen. The mind yearns for some relief from sights and sounds ever sordid and ever discordant. Much, also, is due to climate, which permits little social intercourse of any prolonged kind, except under the protection of warmed and covered buildings. An eminent statesman, in one of his addresses on national subjects, lately remarked upon the difference between our modern life and public life in Greece and Rome, where the people conversed

---

[1] *De l'Esprit des Lois*, liv. iii., chap. 3.

[2] In one borough, Kidderminster, in 1852, of 494 parliamentary voters, 109 were publicans and beer retailers, and the licensed houses of this kind in the town were 150. Of these establishments it would therefore appear, that about forty were not of sufficient value to place their occupants on the register.—*Times*, April 15, 1857.

G

in the open air, and under more favoured skies. With us it is unquestionable, that much of the time which the lower classes can spare from daily toil and necessary rest is spent in seeking ease and enjoyment in the houses which are thus provided for their use. It is there that they meet society of congenial habits and tastes. Another feature of English life, especially, is its domestic character. This feature is predominant in the classes somewhat above the lower, and is more and more brought out as the depressing conditions of existence are removed. As a man advances in his pecuniary circumstances, he gradually becomes less gregarious,—his house assumes an air of comfort,—furniture of mean appearance is exchanged for what is more elegant,—his rooms are embellished with engravings or paintings that bring before his eyes some scene or tale touching a hidden chord, and awakening thoughts, deeper and higher than the counter, the workshop, or the desk has ever prompted ; he loves his home, as his home becomes lovely,—his enjoyments, though intensified, are brought more within the narrow circle of his family and select friends. The refining process of society thus proceeds, and the coarser elements are left behind. They are left behind, because their capacity for better enjoyments has not been cultivated, and perhaps even the desire for them has in many been chilled and extinguished by adverse circumstances.

There are also many clubs and associations. Of these are the numerous benefit clubs—the Odd Fellows, Foresters, and other societies, embodied under various names and rules, and having many good purposes. In all these bodies there are some men who have gained an influence over others, to which they consciously or unconsciously, more or less, submit. The multitude thus form innumerable knots, linked and tied by the countless affinities and tastes which attract men to their fellows.

In every borough, in every electoral district, in every community, some men will be found with penetration enough to discover the weaknesses, the follies, and the vices of their neighbours, and who are both skilful and unscrupulous enough to make them subservient to their own ends. These men are keen in the discovery of fit companions and tools for their purposes. "Noscitur a sociis" is a proverb. They form connecting links with another class of men which had grown up before the time of the Reform Bill, and has since ripened and increased with great fecundity—a class of election agents. The election agent is in habitual communication with the cleverest and the most unscrupulous of those who are either themselves leaders, or know how to tempt or cajole the most influential members of the various little knots or clubs which meet in the parlours and tap-rooms of every public-house in the borough or district. The intercourse between the agents and the intermediate parties is kept up by many reciprocal services, by assistance in business, introduction to offices and employments, under railway companies, in municipal and parish offices, and in other occupations in life, loans of small sums of money, and in infinite variety of favours of greater or less value. By this connection a machinery is ready at all times to cast a web over a very considerable number of the voters of the borough or district, including, of course, a large number of the inhabitants who have no votes. It is time enough to make a distinction between the two classes when the net is to be drawn.

We now come to the candidate. A general election is anticipated, and the aspirants for parliamentary distinction are brought into communication with the local agents. The candidate may be the director of a joint-stock bank, having a large credit given him by his brother directors; he may be an embarrassed man, seeking, by a desperate effort, to retrieve his affairs; he may be a roué requiring a change in his method of dissipation; he may be a second or third-rate lawyer, hoping that the chances of parliamentary subserviency may open a road to promotion which the legitimate labours of his profession are unlikely to afford ; or he may be a wealthy man, moved by " a wish to garnish an acquired fortune with a little bit of ornamental dignity, or to lay the foundation of a successful career of tuft hunting." [1]   Money, however, finds its way to the hands of the agents—money which has apparently nothing to do with the expenses of the election, and does not even come, by any direct or traceable means, from the candidate.   It happens, however, that the parlours and tap-rooms become wonderfully animated.   More refreshments are consumed ; and less is said about the payment.   These convivialities have ostensibly nothing to do with the election. There is no mention of any such thing ; they are all in the way of good-fellowship, and are matters into which nobody has any business to inquire.   The time comes when the signal is to be given, and the curtain drawn.   The election is at hand : the approach of a first-rate liberal or a conservative of the purest water has been darkly announced.   Perhaps an address, inviting the distinguished individual to offer himself for the representation of the electoral district, is got up, presented, and graciously responded to ; but whatever be the course adopted, when the word is given by the chief agents to their inferior auxiliaries, a simultaneous concert bursts forth in praise of the candidate elect, and if the game has been played with anything like skill and liberality, he has already made such progress towards success as to render it very difficult for any adversary to displace him.   The various steps have been taken silently, and apparently without any plan or contrivance.   Nobody knows how the candidate first came to be thought of.   Nobody knows, of course, how the mantle happened to fall upon him, but the remarkable concurrence of opinion amongst so many persons, having no visible connection one with another, is to the simple-minded electors no small proof of his merits.   It is easy to purchase the needful quantity of laudation and bluster.   The hidden

---

[1] *Quarterly Review*, vol. cii., p. 58.

source of all this activity is known only to two or three, or at most a few of the initiated, who convert other men into their unconscious tools. "The corrupt lead the blind, and the blind lead one another." The candidate is instructed in what he should say, and more perfectly still in what he must not say. The proper insignia of party, whether liberal or conservative, the popular shibboleth, are settled and made the most of; and, unless the candidate be encountered by an adversary with more funds or better tactics, he embarks with every chance of success. In a general scramble for votes, with no trusted leader, it is not surprising that the most cunning and the most impudent should gather the greatest share.[1]

If, it may be asked, any of the electors, especially the more intelligent, be not satisfied with the candidates who have presented themselves, why do they not bring forward others? Why do they suffer themselves to be led or cajoled by a section or clique? To this question there are many answers: first, the machinery by which the candidates have been placed where they are, has been carefully concealed. The foul play may be selected, but it is not known, and cannot be proved. Secondly, it is well known, that when the ground is once occupied, all attempts to introduce other candidates are nearly hopeless, and, if made, are sure to cover him who makes them with obloquy. He is branded as a traitor to the cause of his party. He is told that it will divide the interest, and let in an opponent. It is clear, in fact, that every additional candidate—every step which would thus appear to afford a wider field for the choice of the electors—actually tends to defeat its own purpose, and more

---

[1] "Better the Whartons and Delavals," is indignantly said, "than mediocrity and meanness returned by jobbery and machinery." Id., p. 42. The description given by an American writer of the arts of electioneering practised under their institutions, and quoted by Mr. Tremenheere (Constitution of the United States, p. 130), shows that they are of an analogous kind under similar circumstances.

and more to extinguish the voices of the electoral body, by
throwing the election into the hands of the few who, by the
absence of all scruples, are held most compactly together.
Thirdly, if he persisted in bringing forward another candidate, he would probably be met with the proposals of the
fairest aspect; he would be invited to submit his candidate
to a preliminary ballot, in which not only his more formidable adversary, but some others, should also be submitted for
the choice of the party, and in which the phalanx of his chief
opponents are, by their previous arrangements, assured of an
easy victory. Fourthly, if he still persisted in bringing
another candidate to the poll, the language of invective
would be exhausted to stigmatize the conduct of one who
should thus, instead of submitting to party, think fit to act
for himself. His personal quiet and repose would be destroyed, and the neighbourhood, for a year or two at the
least, would be too hot to hold him. And, fifthly, not only
is the business of leading an opposition at an election one for
which few men have at once time, talent, and disposition;
but no man can bring forward an opposing candidate without
subjecting him to considerable expense; and, before a man
will undertake such charges, there must be more hope of
ultimate success than the possession of senatorial qualities, of
ever so high an order, would in such a case give. It is
obvious, that the practical difficulties in the way of the
escape of individual electors, by any efforts of their own,
from the power of an organised network of corruption, are
insuperable.

There have been, since as well as before 1832, some
boroughs, in which other means of direction and guidance
have been preserved,[1]—as there were before that time, as well

[1] See *Parliamentary Government*, &c., by Earl Grey, p. 19. The
question of adhesion to the landlord is in these boroughs generally not a
question merely of a little more or less rent, but whether the tenant is to
abandon the business in which he has been brought up, and the connection

as since, counties and boroughs in which elections were scenes of moral degradation more disgusting than any of the metropolitan fairs which, within the last few years, have been put down as intolerable. The political leaders of those days had prepared the way for a system of corruption, which is now less open and barefaced, but more extensive, systematic, and effectual. Poets and painters have given permanence to the memory of the orgies of former times, which sapped the foundations of morality, by showing that persons of the highest station were ready to sacrifice morals to expediency. It was a maxim then, as now, that all is fair in electioneering,—the result being, that people whose probity was unquestionable, lost all their strictness on the occasion of a dissolution. " Men," says Southey, "who at other times regard it as a duty to speak truth, and think their honour implicated in their word, scruple not at asserting the grossest and most impudent falsehoods, if thereby they can obtain a momentary advantage over the hostile party."[1] The system was only a fit accompaniment of the age of drinking, duelling, cock-fighting, and like brutalising habits. To it was sacrificed as well female delicacy as manly truth and honour. An idiot laugh was echoed by the crowd, as a high-born dame, in rank of the noblest, in beauty glorious as a vision, profaned the heavenly gift, cast aside the modesty of her sex, and yielded to a filthy caress, to buy a vote.

The effect of electoral contests before 1832, which, from the number of close boroughs, were, of course, much less numerous, tended to demoralise a portion of the constituency, and the inhabitants of the places where they occurred ; but, at the same time, they generally ended by placing in the House the most eminent men of the day. The system since

---

which he has formed, for some new and untried sphere or avocation. It is one of vital importance, and no secrecy would give the voter independence. They would be held responsible for one another to the patron.

[1] *Quarterly Review*, vol. cii., pp. 43, 46.

1832 vastly increases the number of electors who are subjected to moral or mental degradation, or both, and at the same time, with a few exceptions, fills the representative assembly with an inferior class of men,—men who have not been compelled to pass through the tests which, in the former period, were generally effectual barriers in the way of those who had nothing to recommend them but the command of ready money or audacity. Extending the suffrage under the present system, extends the demoralising influences, as it increases the necessity for a skilful organisation. The price of a vote, or the inducement to vote, may become very small; it may be no more than suffices for a day's debauch; but the organisation must then be more perfect, as more complicated management is necessary in the government of a large manufactory, than in the conduct of a single workshop. This may be confidently predicted,—that if our electoral bodies are to be all concluded by the votes of their majorities, and if the ballot is to be introduced, whereby the profit of the managers and club-leaders can be made dependent on their success, all means of punishing or detecting bribery being abandoned,—wealth and luxury increasing, and the power and influence of the House of Commons also at the same time increasing,—we have not yet sounded anything approaching to that depth of corruption, and consequent degradation, which we shall surely reach.

The reformers of 1832 cannot be supposed to have been ignorant of the disposition of the mass of mankind, a disposition amounting to a law of nature, to follow where it is led, whether the way be good or evil. It is the few who will always conduct the many. "An immense majority of men must always remain in a middle state, neither very foolish nor very able, neither very virtuous nor very vicious, but slumbering on in a peaceful and decent mediocrity, adopting without much difficulty the current opinions of the day, making no inquiry, exciting no scandal, causing no wonder,

just holding themselves on a level with their generation, and
noiselessly conforming to the standard of morals and knowledge common to the age and country in which they live." [1]
Left to themselves they will willingly—every one according
to the tendencies created by his moral or physical condition
—adopt as their guide and model him whom they may
happen to regard as the most distinguished or the most
admirable.   There is not the shadow of doubt that, other ·
things being the same, the man of high rank or noble descent
would be chosen by the vast majority; and, probably, the
same grounds of pre-eminence would eclipse in their eyes
many other virtues and qualities which they are less able to
appreciate.   This is not necessarily sycophancy.   There is
nothing to deprecate in the habit of yielding respect to a
nobility which bears the stamp of the highest authority of
the State in which we live—the recognised fountain of
honour.   "It is, indeed, one sign of a liberal and benevolent mind to incline to it with some sort of partial propensity.
He feels no ennobling principle in his own heart who wishes
to level all the artificial institutions which have been adopted
for giving a body to opinion and permanence to fugitive
esteem."   Of this result we may at least be certain, that a
leader will appear, and if he be not discovered in the palace,
he will issue from some lower degree of life, and if no better
be found, he will be taken even from the beer-shop.   The
reformers of 1832 might not unreasonably have hoped that
in the future public action for the public good, the better
influences would appear and assert their power; but it was
not possible for the Reform Bill to set up other leaders in
the place of those it dethroned.   The oligarchical spirit was
expelled from the temple dedicated to the use of a free
people; but no sooner was it cleansed than it became the
habitation of a legion of other spirits, more vile than those
which were cast out.   It behoves the Legislature, while

[1] *Buckle's History of Civilisation*, vol. i., p. 162.

there is yet time, to commence the purification of the temple which has been thus defiled, lest we realise the other part of the Gospel parallel, and our last state be worse than our first.

There is not at present one legal or practical security, that the so-called representative of any borough or district shall possess a single quality fitting him for the high trust committed to his care. He has not been chosen for any special attainments, for there has been no test or examination; or for his superiority to others, for there has been no comparison. Much value has of late been attributed to administrative talent, and much importance has been attached to the exclusion from offices, in the public service, of persons who have not proved themselves to possess a certain positive amount of capacity, and even a superiority to others in comparative excellence. But in conferring the awful power of legislation, "which any man may well tremble to give or to receive," there is less of actual precaution and scrutiny, and absolutely none of the tests of competitive excellence, which are required in the appointment of an exciseman.

To delineate the election, for which the machinery has been prepared by the election agents in the manner referred to, would be an attempt to trespass on the province of the satirist. It is enough to say, that by reducing, as our system necessarily does, the literate and the ignorant, the high-minded and the corrupt, to one dead level, it probably ends in the return, as a member for a wealthy and populous borough, of some man whom it is a pure fiction to describe as its representative; and if it were to be considered other than as a fiction, it would be, as to half of the inhabitants, a mockery and an insult. "We find several very considerable classes of electors, who have little or no will in the matter." "Those who recognise, in any adequate degree, the importance of honestly exercising their judgments in the selection of legislators, and who give conscientious votes, mostly form but a minority; and the election usually hangs less upon their wills, than upon the indirect and illegitimate influences which sway the rest."[1]

The fault or the misfortune of an unworthy choice is primarily due to the absence of responsibility. There is no single elector on whom the opprobrium falls, and a disgrace which is shared with an entire electoral district is no disgrace at all. The borough, or the district, is not under responsibility to one of the greatest controlling powers on earth,—the sense of fame and estimation. The share of infamy that is likely to fall to the lot of each individual in public acts is small indeed; the operation of opinion being in the inverse ratio to the number of those who abuse power. Their own approbation of their own acts has to them the appearance of a public judgment in their favour. It is the sense of individual "fame and estimation," or, in other words, of individual and personal responsibility, that it is absolutely necessary to restore; and this individual responsibility cannot be restored unless the individual electors have, each and every of them, that power which the old patron or political leader had, of looking around, and selecting as his representative that man whom he believes to be the best suited for the office; and this cannot be if his power of choice be restricted to the two, three, or four persons who may think proper to present themselves, and solicit his suffrage.

No society, whether it be domestic, civil, or military, can prosper, unless all those who compose it have, not only their appropriate duties, but means and opportunity to perform them. The business of a nation can be conducted by no other mystery. It is of so much importance that the principle of personal responsibility in the performance of electoral duties should be realised, that it may be useful to exhibit its active operation in the other affairs of life, in which men are compelled to feel a real concern. In questions of property, the most ingenious endeavours are made to protect a man

---

[1] *Westminster Review*, vol. xii. p. 461.

from being affected by the act of his neighbour without his own consent. For example,—as a town increases in size, a landed proprietor grants to a builder the lease of a field, on which he is to erect a number of houses, and keep them in repair for a term of years, and if he omits to repair, he is to be subject to ejectment. Fifty houses are built, and sold to as many different people. The owner of No. 50 permits his house to fall into decay, and the owner of No. 1 finds that he is liable to lose his house for the default of his neighbour. This happened a few years ago to the inhabitants of a large part of Somers Town. It is a state of things which people naturally regard as intolerable. Lawyers dissuade their clients from purchasing houses unless they have an independent lease directly from the landowner. It is one of those cases against which Lord St. Leonards, in his familiar epistles on the law of property, has, no doubt, guarded his readers. Yet the owner of the house No. 1 is not more clearly deprived of his property by the conduct of the owner of No. 50, than one voter may be deprived of his power of choosing a representative by a combination of a few other voters. The situation of a shareholder in a joint-stock bank has been thought one of great hardship when he finds himself ruined by the directors ; and the constant resort to the protection of a limited liability—are all so many protests in favour of the principle of individual responsibility.

It may be thought a gigantic undertaking to bring home personal responsibility to every individual of a million of electors ; but that must be done if every individual of the million is to have a will and a voice. The other multiform duties of individuals, of family and social life, notwithstanding all the infirmities of our nature, which the divine and the moralist reprove,—are performed with sufficient exactness to preserve the general tranquillity. Why should this great social duty be alone out of the pale of morals, and be thought one which anybody may trifle with, disregard, or violate ? The same

sense of duty which assists and accompanies the performance
of the other acts of life must be attached to the act of voting.
The indispensable conditions are—to render the duty of every
man as perceptible to his understanding as it can be made,
and to remove every obstacle in the way of its performance.
The opening to every elector of the power of performing his
electoral duty is the first and prime necessity, in order to re-
establish the sense of personal responsibility, or the empire of
conscience, in electoral action. No man will feel a conscientious obligation to undertake a duty which he believes to be
beyond his resources to accomplish. Conscience, as a motive
of action, is too dull rather than too sensitive. It is not the
habit of mankind to strain all their resources in order to bring
their conduct within the dominion of conscience. It is well
if they can be led to act in obedience to conscience, when the
means are ready and the dictate clear. Lamentable will be
the error of those legislators—unhappy the condition of that
people—who think, and form their constitutional laws on the
belief, that government by representative institutions can be
safe or permanent without the aid of conscience. It may be
more or less enlightened ; but be it clear or dim, it must be
the guide ; and that it may have its full force, it should be
brought home to the knowledge and conviction of every elector
that his vote is entirely within his own control ; that he has
the power of giving it in favour of the man he deems the
worthiest of his age, and that when given it cannot be without effect. The judgment of the whole electoral body of the
kingdom must be made up of the aggregate of the judgment
of every individual, and the conscience of the whole electoral
college must be the contribution of the separate consciences
of every individual. There is not a person in Lambeth, from
the archbishop to the poorest labourer, who is not answerable
for his own acts, according to the measure of the ability which
God giveth. To the prophetic declaration, that every man
shall suffer for his own sin, both faith and reason are alike

submissive. In physical evils there may be a community of suffering—but moral responsibility is only individual.[1] The parish of Lambeth or the borough of Lambeth has no moral responsibility. A soul is not a corporate thing. There is no corporate conscience.

In order, then, to give to individuality that free agency which is the mother of responsibility, every voter must have

---

[1] "En effet, plus l'individualité est développée chez quelqu'un, plus le sentiment de sa responsabilité a grandi, et à ce développement dans le sentiment de sa responsabilité, correspond un développement parallèle de sa conscience. Atténuez, effacez l'individu; absorbez-le dans la masse; il obéira de plus en plus à des instincts, à des impulsions, et se rapprochera de plus en plus de la machine. Chargez-vous de ses affaires, il deviendra de moins en moins apte à s'en occuper."—*Le Christianisme et l'Esprit Moderne*, par Arbouisse Bastide, p. 158. "A man," observes Mr. Maurice, "will not really be intelligible to you if, instead of listening to him, and sympathizing with him, you determine to classify him."

"L'intelligence de chacun peut fleurir, tandis que son individualité se dessèche et meurt. Ni la pensée dans tout son essor, ni les passions dans tout leur excès, ne la développent ni ne la manifestent. Avec tout cela, on peut n'avoir aucun caractère à soi. L'âme ne reçoit son nom propre, sa personnalité vraie, que de la conscience, confident trop négligé, autorité trop méconnue, mais qu'il faut toujours écouter quand on ne veut pas livrer son *moi* à des influences fortuites et étrangères, quand on veut vivre de sa propre vie, quand on veut être soi-même."—*L'Education, la Famille et la Société*, par A. Vinet, p. 402.

"L'état de notre époque se caractérise par deux traits en apparence contradictoires: le relâchement de l'unité sociale par la prédominance toujours plus avouée de l'égoïsme, et la pente toujours plus forte des consciences à s'abdiquer pour se livrer au torrent de ce qu'on appelle l'opinion publique ou l'esprit du siècle. Ainsi, les progrès de *l'individualisme* d'une part, de l'autre l'extinction graduelle de *l'individualité*, voilà, par l'action d'une même cause, le double abîme, ou plutôt les deux abîmes creusés l'un dans l'autre, où nous sommes précipités. Qui nous retiendra sur ce rapide penchant ? Si quelqu'un le sait, qu'il le dise."—Id., 408. See also, on this subject, the article on "Civilization," *Mill's Dissertations and Discussions*, vol. i., pp. 161—205, a paper which was first published in 1833. These are warnings and protests, from different schools of thinkers, against the increasing prevalence and operation of a general and uniform opinion and sentiment derived from a common authority or source, and gradually enveloping individual thought and action in its powerful and inextricable folds.

the most enlarged field of choice, and the most unfettered means of exercising it.

A method of effecting these objects has been partly stated, and remains to be further explained. The first condition obviously is, that every elector, when he is called upon to exercise his franchise, should be perfectly informed of the extent of the choice before him. When it becomes his duty to select a representative, he must be told who are willing to accept the trust, that, amongst them, he may choose the man whom he shall deem the fittest to be entrusted. No proposition can be more simple or undeniable than that, properly to exercise a discretion, it is necessary to know what discretion one has to exercise. The names of all persons who may offer themselves for the political service of their country may be collected under a law, of which the following is an outline :—

VII. Upon or at any time after a dissolution of Parliament, until the time appointed for polling at the ensuing election, every person offering himself as representative in Parliament at such election, shall signify the same, in writing, to one of the said Registrars, viz—if he be a candidate for the representation of any constituency or constituencies in England, to the Registrar in London; and if he be a candidate for the representation of any constituency or constituencies in Scotland, to the Registrar in Edinburgh; and if he be a candidate for the representation of any constituency or constituencies in Ireland, to the Registrar in Dublin; and every candidate shall, in such writing or declaration, state for what constituency or constituencies he offers himself as a candidate; and shall also state whether he holds any, and if any, what office, either under the Crown or in the public service; and he shall also, on the delivery of such declaration, pay to the Registrar the sum of [£50]; and the said candidate shall not, by declaring himself a candidate as aforesaid, become therefore liable to bear or pay any further expenses, either general or local, incidental to the election.

The names of all those who may offer themselves for the political service of their country having been thus collected— without, in any measure, interfering with the individual and special efforts which any man may think proper to adopt, for the purpose of communicating with the particular boroughs or constituencies to which he presents himself,—the next step is to bring the names of all the candidates in one view before the electors.   It is thus that the nation, in the greatest of all national actions, will adopt means analogous to those which have powerfully contributed to the progress of education, of art, and of science, by concentrating their productions, and submitting them all to the test of the widest comparison.

The promulgation of the names of the candidates may be regulated by the two following clauses; in which, as in pre-scribing all the other functions of the Registrars, their duties may be so clearly defined, that nothing be left to their discre-tion.   Every step would be governed by the rigid impartiality of anterior and positive law.

VIII. The Registrars for England, Scotland, and Ireland respectively, shall, on every week-day, commencing the first day after a dissolution of Parliament, on which any candidate delivers such declaration, and makes such payment as aforesaid, and continuing until the day appointed for the general election,—prepare a list of the names of all who shall have declared themselves candidates to represent any constituency or constituencies in Parliament, and shall have made the said payment, stating in such list the respective constituencies for which they are respectively candidates; and the Registrar in London shall cause such list as aforesaid of the candidates for English constituencies to be published in the *London Gazette*, or a supplement thereto; and the Registrar in Edinburgh shall cause such list of candidates for Scotch constituencies to be published in the *Edinburgh Gazette*, or a supplement thereto ; and the Registrar in Dublin shall cause such list of candidates for Irish constituencies to be published in the *Dublin Gazette*, or a supplement thereto; and the said Registrars respectively shall transmit copies of the said lists daily to the returning officers of the said constituencies respectively, who shall cause copies thereof to be printed and published, for the use of the electors of their respective constituencies, and sold at a price not exceeding one penny for every complete list.

IX. The names of all the said candidates shall be inserted in the said gazetted list in the following order: viz., as to all persons who have there-tofore had seats in Parliament, in the order of the respective length of the periods for which they have been members thereof, beginning with the candidate who shall have sat the longest, and ending with the candidate who shall have sat the shortest, period of time in Parliament; and as to new candidates, according to their age, as the same shall be stated in the declaration delivered to the Registrars as aforesaid, beginning with the oldest, and ending with the youngest, of such new candidates; and where any such length of time, or age, shall be the same as to two or more candidates, or shall be doubtful or not stated, then, according to an alphabetical arrangement of the surnames of such candidates as to whom such particulars shall be so equal or doubtful or not declared, and which alphabetical arrangement of names as to new candidates shall be placed after the other names in the said lists.

The working of these laws will be brought more distinctly into view by placing before the eye part of a supposed *London Gazette*, containing the names of the candidates for English constituencies. It might appear thus:—

GENERAL REGISTRAR'S OFFICE FOR ENGLAND.

————— day of ————— 1859.

The persons whose names are set forth in the Schedule hereto, have declared themselves respectively to be candidates for the representation of the constituencies respectively set opposite to their said names, in the next Parliament, being the ————— Parliament of the United Kingdom of Great Britain and Ireland, and have complied with the regulations required by the Act ——.

(Signed) ————— —————

Registrar.

THE SCHEDULE ABOVE REFERRED TO.

Sir Charles Merrik Burrell, Bart	*Shoreham.*
George Granville Vernon Harcourt, Esq.	*Oxfordshire.*
Right Hon. Viscount Palmerston, G.C.B., K.G. . . .	*Tiverton.*
Hon. Henry Cecil Lowther	*Westmoreland.*
Sir John Owen, Bart.	*Pembroke.*
Right Hon. Lord John Russell	*London.*
Right Hon. Edward Ellice	*Coventry.*
Right Hon. Sir James Robert George Graham, Bart. . .	*Carlisle.*
William Miles, Esq.	*East Somerset.*

[*The Schedule will then proceed in the order specified in Clause IX., with the names of all the candidates who have been previously members of the House, in their order,—and then with the names of the new candidates, also in the order pointed out in the same law.*]

H

Nothing that has been said of the utter insufficiency of our traditional system of election for the new circumstances of society in which we are placed, must be understood as being said in forgetfulness of the illustrious names which the House of Commons still enrols amongst its members. To deny that tribute to it would be not less absurd than presumptuous. No age is, perhaps, wholly without its distinguished men; and no one can doubt that this age has its share unless he obstinately closes his eyes against all evidence. Eminence is far more difficult to attain than in any former age,—but that eminence is still attainable we have brilliant examples. It is no slight testimony to the truth of the principle—that when the disturbing causes are removed the fittest representatives will be commonly chosen,—that, amidst all the existing difficulties, some men of the highest order yet find their way to Parliament, and command the attention and respect of constituencies, fitful though that regard and respect may be. It must not be forgotten, that there is scarcely a man, however distinguished, whose exclusion from Parliament has not been at some time attempted; scarcely a man whose admission, notwithstanding a life-long public service, has not, at some time or other, been doubtful. Neither must it be forgotten—especially upon observing the distinguished names which would appear at the head of a table, prepared according to the scheme that has been suggested—how much the existing representative assembly owes to the traditional system which prevailed in times anterior to the Reform Bill, and which is now either departing, or no more.

CHAPTER VI.

THE OBSTACLES WHICH DIMINISH THE NUMBER OF
CANDIDATES.

In forming an assembly, consisting of nearly seven hundred
of those persons in whom the people "may discern that predominant proportion of active virtue and wisdom, taken
together and fitted to the charge, such as in the great and
inevitable mixed mass of human imperfections and infirmities
is to be found," every element of society requires to be laid
under contribution. The State cannot afford to reject the
services of any class, especially of any highly instructed
class, amongst its sons. Observers of the progress of society
have remarked that the more general expansion of literature
and diffusion of knowledge, invaluable as they are, do not
enlarge the proportionate number of men of great eminence;
and that, in the production of such men, nature vindicates
her exclusive prerogative. Civilisation multiplies in a vast
degree those who read and deliberate, whilst it does not produce any greater number of leading minds. It should be a
fundamental principle that all possible facilities should be
given to persons of every class to offer themselves as candidates for the representation of any portion of their fellow-
subjects. This principle is the only just foundation of the
resolution of the House of Commons, which, on the 3rd of
May, 1783, expunged from the journals all the declarations,
orders, and resolutions relating to the election of Mr. Wilkes,

and declared the previous resolution of the 17th of February, 1769, that had "affirmed his incapacity to sit in that Parliament, subversive of the rights of the whole body of the electors of the kingdom." The expurgatory resolution has been supported on the technical ground of the omission, in the resolution of 1769, of the imputed criminality which was the cause of the expulsion;[1] but it does not rest on so narrow a basis. Every law which prevents the electors of the kingdom from choosing any man whom they may consider the most fit to represent them, is in effect the adoption of a principle antagonistic to and subversive of their rights. It may possibly be justified by expediency; but the cases in which that justification can be established are very rare, and would almost entirely disappear under such a system of representation as is here contemplated, in which every member would be chosen by a quotient or nearly a quotient of the electoral body, all the electors having, at the same time, a field of choice bounded only by the intellect, the activity, or the political ambition of the age in which they live.

The impediments in the way of candidates, and which, to an incalculable extent, diminish the number from amongst whom representatives must be chosen, may be classed under three principal heads: First, pecuniary, or obstacles interposed by the expenses, which are either lawful and inevitable, or otherwise generally regarded as necessary to success; secondly, those occasioned by the peculiarities and difficulties of the manner of communication between the candidate and the electors; and thirdly, the grounds of exclusion created by positive law.

In this kingdom a large number of persons qualified for political life by their studies and habits of thought, possess but small or very moderate fortunes. Of these many would be found who would not only willingly, but eagerly, devote themselves to parliamentary and legislative labours, without

---

[1] *Blackstone's Com.*, vol. i., book i., c. 2, p. 163; *Christian's* Ed., (n. 16.)

remuneration or reward. No country in the world is more rich in the classes willing to bestow their time and attention on public business. It is one of the wholesome fruits of our civil institutions, which, from parliament to the magistracy, and the jury, have called upon every order of the people to perform their several parts and duties in the business of the State. It is a remarkable proof of the extent to which we must have departed from those natural habits that adapt, with such wonderful accuracy, the means to the end, when not only is there small sign of any endeavour to call into activity all the latent energy and talent in the country, but rejecting and throwing aside, with a careless indifference, the materials which are ready to our hands, there are classes amongst us which seek to convert political labours into a trade, and seriously propose the payment of members of parliament by stipends from the State. Whether cases may not arise, of the possession or supposed possession of special qualifications by individuals who are personally in circumstances which incapacitate them from devoting their time to such public labours without some remuneration, and whether in such cases the constituency which they serve may not with propriety contribute to their support, is a different question.[1] Such a payment would be scarcely distinguishable from those cases in which the public have paid the debts, or provided for the permanent maintenance, of the families of distinguished public servants. Wholly different in principle and effect, would be any system calculated to make all parliamentary duties venal. There is great reason to apprehend that it would deteriorate the character of the representative body, as well as diminish the respect with which it is viewed by the public.[2]

[1] In an able article in the *Westminster Review*, on "Party Government," the writer does not appear to go farther than such a case as that above supposed, vol. xiii., n.s., p. 427. See also *Parl. Deb.*, vol. cxlix., p. 1034.

[2] On this point, see Mill, *Considerations on Representative Government*,

The performance of parliamentary duties is proved not to be inconsistent with the contemporaneous prosecution of the most laborious avocations. A vigorous performance of the general business of life imparts earnestness to every occupation, and it is as belonging to that business that parliamentary duties are best executed. The constant meddling of a body of men, paid for making laws, and acting under the notion that they are bound to do something for their salaries, would in this country be intolerable; not to speak of the far more serious evil, in the diminution of that respect with which the House of Commons is now regarded. That professional labours of the most unremitting kind may be prosecuted without neglecting the duties of Parliament, is shown by the example of lawyers in extensive practice, and is proved by the amount of work—legislative, judicial, and of other kinds—which men like Lord Eldon, and others, before and since his time, have been able to accomplish. Few men would be found, whose services are of any value to the State, who would not be able to afford them without abandoning their other business and occupations.

If, on the other hand, the nation be served by its representatives without pecuniary reward, it should not require from them any pecuniary sacrifices which a prudent or an honest, and, it may be added, a comparatively poor man, is not in a condition to make. The representative house is the House of the Commons. The Commons are composed of all classes, rich and poor. The doors should be opened, to the extreme width of their portals, to admit the best and worthiest; and every impediment which clogs and obstructs their entry, is a mischief which ought to be swept away.

---

c. 10, p. 217, 2nd ed. The rejection of the Bill which proposed the payment of salaries to certain peers, for the performance of their judicial duties in the House of Lords, was regarded with much (and not unreasonable) satisfaction by many, on similar grounds.

It is greatly to be feared that an opinion, or belief, exists, and is widely spread amongst the higher and influential classes, that by rendering parliamentary elections expensive, they confine the choice of the electors to persons of wealth; and that, in this restriction, there is some chance of security, which would not otherwise be obtained. The ready assent to the clause for legalising the payment of travelling expenses to county voters, was, there is no doubt, due to this feeling. It was not adopted from any regard for the voters: the kindness was intended to be shown to the wealthy candidate, for whom, in such cases, they would necessarily vote, rather than for him who should be indisposed to expend some thousands of pounds, and possibly embarrass himself and his family in the contest.[1] It is impossible to give credit to an affectation of regard to the hard case of a county voter living at a distance, and unable to pay the expense of coming to the poll, when it proceeds from the mouths of those who have not yet discovered the hardship of excluding the resident inhabitant, for whom Mr. Locke King has for several years vainly been seeking the franchise. If the aristocratical elements in the different political parties be actuated by a feeling such as this, they are under the influence of an error, than which none will be more fatal to their chief objects. Even if they succeeded in excluding all but the wealthy, the result would be only to raise up against themselves the most dangerous of all rivals. It is the wealthy demagogue, who, by availing himself of all the aids which money can give to indulge the follies or the vices of the electors, will command success. The making of political power, the monopoly or the spoil of the

---

[1] So long as the candidate himself, and the customs of the world seem to regard the function of a member of Parliament less as a duty to be discharged than as a personal favour to be selected, no effort will avail to implant in an ordinary voter the feeling that the election is also a matter of duty, and that he is not at liberty to bestow his vote on any other consideration than that of personal fitness."—Mill, *Considerations on Representative Government*, c. 10.

rich, under such a system as ours, will afford no security to the possessors either of wealth or of hereditary rank. By the infinitely various channels of acquiring wealth, the latter are exposed to an incessant irruption of fresh enemies, ready to avenge "the outrages of a rival pride, and exalt their wealth to what they consider its natural rank and estimation." Even if they were only opposed by fortunes of less recent acquisition, a political philosopher has told them, that "there are always, in that description, men whose fortunes, when their minds are once vitiated by passion or by evil principle, are by no means a security against their taking their part against the public tranquillity. We see to what low and despicable passions of all kinds many men in that class are ready to sacrifice the patrimonial estates, which might be perpetuated in their families with splendour, and with the fame of hereditary benefactors to mankind, from generation to generation. Do we not see how lightly people treat their fortunes when under the influence of the passion of gaming? The game of ambition or resentment will be played, by many of the rich and great, as desperately, and with as much blindness to the consequences, as any other game."[1] Nor can rank alone be relied upon as a protection. "Turbulent discontented men of quality, in proportion as they are puffed up with personal pride and arrogance, generally despise their own order. One of the first symptoms they discover of a foolish and mischievous ambition is a profligate disregard of a dignity which they partake with others." "Confounded by the complication of distempered passions, their reason is disturbed, their views become vast and perplexed; to others inexplicable,—to themselves uncertain. They find on all sides bounds to their unprincipled ambition in any fixed order of things. But in the fog and haze of confusion all is enlarged, and appears without any limit. When men of rank sacrifice all ideas of dignity to ambition without a distinct object, and

[1] *Appeal*, &c., p. 134.

work with low instruments and for low ends, the whole composition becomes low and base."[1] Experience teaches that
none of these factitious aids can supply the want or fill the
place of wisdom or integrity, and that these qualities are as
likely to be found under circumstances fitted to call them
forth in one rank or condition as in another. The true
interests of all classes, the highest as well as the lowest, would
be best consulted by opening the avenues to the House of
Commons, and collecting within it the best that the nation
possesses of ability and character. This may be prevented,
but will never be assisted, by adding conditions which insure
neither the one nor the other. The prudent man, indisposed
to risk his patrimony on a game of chance, too conscientious
not to respect the claims of family, and the regard which he
owes to those who are dependent upon him,—is entitled to
greater confidence than one who is reckless of his own fortune,
or is trafficking with that of others; yet by rendering political
competition a source always of indefinite, and often of ruinous,
expense, the latter is admitted, and the former excluded.

The charges, which it is absolutely necessary that a candidate should incur, ought not to exceed a sum sufficient to
prevent any trifling or idle experiment, whereby the lists of
candidates might be encumbered with the names of persons
who can have no rational expectations of being usefully placed
in nomination. For this it is proposed to provide, by requiring a preliminary payment to the Registrar,[2] which shall
exonerate the candidate from all liability in respect of any
further expenses, except such as he may voluntarily incur.
Such voluntary expenses will of course, as now, vary according
to the peculiar circumstances of every candidate. They will
probably be in the inverse ratio of his political eminence and
distinction. Men of high character and reputation, and those
whose political conduct and discretion have been tested and

---

[1] *Reflections*, &c., p. 70.
[2] Clause VII., p. 95, *ante.* The sum there suggested is £50.

proved by experience, would stand in need of no more than that announcement of their names which the Gazetted list would publish. A man of less distinction might require something more; possibly the charges of some public meetings, and of advertisements or printed addresses, declaring his general views on political questions. This, perhaps, would be less necessary, if the candidate were a person of any mark in literature or science, and had in his previous career become known to the public. Those who would probably be compelled to spend most, would be the persons who have the least to recommend them besides their money.

The following clause would relieve the candidates from all necessary expenses, except the payment which it is proposed shall be made to the Registrars:—

X. All expenses of the erection or hire of hustings, booths, or polling-places, and the wages of clerks and officers, and the travelling expenses of the clerk in conveying the voting papers, where the same shall be necessary, to the office of the Registrar, so far as respects all existing constituencies, shall be borne by the several constituencies respectively, and shall be paid out of the county, borough, or parochial rates, or other funds, upon which the registration expenses have heretofore been or shall hereafter lawfully be charged; and as to all constituencies which shall hereafter be constituted, all such expenses shall be borne and paid in such manner as shall be directed by the order of Her Majesty in Council, constituting the same; and the sect. 71 of the stat. 2 Will. 4, c. 45; sect. 40 of the stat. 2 Will. 4, c. 65; and sect. 88 of the stat. 2 Will. 4, c. 88, are repealed.

It has been well said that the remedy for bribery, under whatever form of temptation, is to be found, not in penal laws, but in taking from one side the disposition to give, and from the other the willingness to receive bribes. It must be sought for in a consideration of the motives which ordinarily govern the conduct of mankind. The causes of bribery, and especially those causes to which most of its virulence and nearly all its public evils are owing, are not difficult to discover; and once discovered, it will be found that they are not difficult to remove, so far as they stand in the way of the candidature and success of the men whose access to the House it is most desirable to promote ; and so far also as it affects the electoral power and influence of those voters who desire to act honestly. They proceed from the same vice in the electoral system which deprives it of the salutary influences of honour and conscience. They are mainly caused by the bond which the law creates, and by which every constituency is inseparably connected together. The success of the candidate is forced to depend, not upon the votes of a competent and adequate number of his fellow-countrymen, but upon the votes of the electors who are placed within a small geographical limit. What is the necessary consequence? It is, that a certain number of votes, within that limit and no other, are made absolutely indispensable. The electors of the district or borough are first nominally or really divided into two parties, by the process of crushing all the minor differences and distinctions of thought and opinion. The hopes of each candidate depend upon the triumph of the party to which he belongs. They may, probably, from their connexions or reputation, reckon upon many votes being freely given to them. We will suppose the voters to be in number 2000, and of these, the class which has had no voice in bringing either candidate to the borough, having no sympathy with either, and, therefore wholly indifferent, and taking no part in the election to be 400. One candidate may, from the result of his canvass, expect 600, and another about 500 of the votes which are given spontaneously. There remain the residuum of 500, to be worked upon by appealing to their cupidity, their hopes, or their fears. Are not the causes of bribery, of intimidation, and of every other evil influence, plainly developed? We have given to the votes of a comparatively few of the electoral body, and these the very worst and the very poorest,—the worst who are not always the poorest, and the poorest who are far from being the worst, —a highly artificial value. It is a value to which no market price can be assigned. It is not measured by the general value of a vote; it is the special and inestimable value of those particular votes,—votes for which no others can be substituted,—for the want of which the support of all the wisdom of a senate cannot compensate. It is the *pretium affectionis*. Like the uncertain and fabulous value of a matchless painting, or work of art; or like the passion of love, which fills the mind and renders the creature of its regard the sole object in the world worthy of desire,—the voices of the small number of electors, on whose support the candidates may rely for their success, become more and more priceless, as the event becomes more and more critical and capricious. If the system—which is the result of accident—had been framed for the very purpose of giving full scope and encouragement to corruption, to provide opportunities for tempting and gratifying the needy and the base, it is scarcely possible to imagine that it could more effectually have completed the design. It is in the highest degree unjust towards the poorer electors to expose them to such influences as these. It cannot be expected that a small tradesman or artificer, labouring with difficulty to procure a subsistence for himself and his family, can reject a gift which is, perhaps, equal to his honest gains for a month. He sees no example of that self-abnegation on the part of men around him, much more wealthy than himself. It is not in the nature of things that he should rise above the temptations to which his neighbours generally succumb.

If the vote of every elector throughout the kingdom had, at all times, the same weight and the same value as a free electoral system would give to it, all these overpowering temptations would necessarily cease. No arbitrary or artificial importance would attach to the vote of any particular man; and any elector who would put a price upon his vote must deliberately seek a market in which he can dispose of it. The number of the bribed would be reduced to the comparatively few in whom the disposition to be corrupt is owing if not to an innate depravity, at least to an indifference to, or a want of, conception of the public good, accompanied by a disregard of their own character in the estimation of their neighbours.

It is not to be supposed that corrupt motives and objects will be wholly extinguished in the political conduct of any class of men by any system of things. So long as a seat in the representative assembly of this country shall be one of the highest distinctions which the people can confer—and long may that continue to be so—there will be found men ready to make great pecuniary sacrifices to reach it. In every county or town, no doubt some men will be found ready to sell their votes; and no commodity is so vile that it has not factors and dealers engaged in the traffic. If a wealthy and obscure candidate has to collect two thousand votes by this means, he is not likely to pay any considerable sum for each vote; and the members who thus obtain their seats, whether they owe their wealth to success in trade or speculation, or to inheritance, will probably have had advantages of experience or of leisure which will render them not inferior in sagacity to the average of those who now fill the House, and they are not likely to act less on their independent judgment. A member elected by these means, if he be actuated by a generous ambition, may still show by his public conduct that he is not unworthy of the position he has gained, and may at a future election deserve and obtain the support of independent men. In the mean time, in representing those alone who have voted for him, he neither prevents nor interferes with the representation of any earnest or virtuous elector; and the evil of bribery has been thus reduced to its minimum.[1]

[1] If we suppose 100 members to find their way into the House, at every general election, at the aggregate cost of half a million, and the other 558 to be elected by the spontaneous support of their constituents, undisturbed

The operation of the same system which would go so far to extinguish bribery, would also go equally far to put an end to every kind of intimidation, and other unjust and improper influences. The entire disease derives the whole of its malignity from the same cause—the fact that certain particular votes, and these votes only, are made indispensable, and are, therefore to be obtained *per fas et nefas.* To the same cause all the sacrifices of truth, of justice, of honour, and of decency, are due. Nothing is so sacred that it may not be trampled upon in a struggle which waxes more intense as it draws towards its end. The candidates become like gamblers, spurred on by the recollection of what they have already lost, and ready to peril all that they still possess upon the last stake. Such struggles serve but as excitements to morbid satiety. A Duke of Norfolk is reported to have said, that to stand a contested election for Yorkshire and win it by one, was the greatest enjoyment in life; a sentiment, which, we are told, is " thoroughly English, and to be relished only by freemen !" [2] With all admiration for those manly enjoyments which are a feature of English life, it may be permitted to an Englishman to say, that there are some things too serious to be made a game. Those who have degraded the tone of political morals, treated the most solemn duty of social life as a sport, and delighted in the satire of representation exhibited by the spectacle of the political extinction of

---

by the votes which have been bought, — the public evil would be comparatively insignificant. The persons who have accepted payment for their votes will probably, in view of the national interests, have exercised their powers by voting for members as competent as they would be likely under any circumstances to have chosen. The main current of political life has at the same time been purified. In every constituency the corrupt element has been drawn off, and the better electors are no longer injured or deprived of their just influence by the conduct of the worse. In the words of a social philosopher, it is then " only the worst people who fall into the worst ways."

[2] *Quarterly Review,* vol. cii., p. 32.

twenty thousand voices, have certainly done their part in teaching the people to abuse their political powers and despise minorities. Be sure that the sins of a nation, and of a class, will find them out.

Great as would be the national gain, from the extinction of the corrupt and illegitimate influences which now preside at elections, the benefit of the proposed system would be infinitely more extensive, in bringing into action all the better and more generous motives. It would not only depose. vice, but it would set up virtue in its place. The support which is rendered to a candidate, by the admirers of his character and political principles,—instead of being as it now is, from its absolute necessity, regarded as a favour of inestimable personal value, which the candidate is scarcely ever considered sufficiently to repay,—will become a voluntary and disinterested service. The electors will know that their support is not necessarily indispensable, and that the candidate may be returned by the votes of other constituencies; and this knowledge at once reduces the artificial and conventional value of that support to its just dimensions. The candidate and the electors are, by the present system, placed in a false position. Many of the electors are made to be mercenary in their conduct, by the very fact that their individual aid is of the greatest moment, whilst, if that were not so, they would voluntarily render to the candidate the same, or more hearty, assistance, from their attachment to his sentiments and opinions. The judges who sit in our Courts of Equity, and have occasion rigidly to scrutinise the motives and conduct of men, frequently meet with examples of the difficulty of blending together two motives, one generous and the other venal. The lower impulse is invariably destructive of the higher. Respect, admiration, and attachment, are unbought homage. The zeal and industry which, if it had not been diverted from its natural course, would have been freely devoted to uphold some public principle, is, owing to the price attached to it, perverted to

private and selfish objects. If any man doubted the consequences of grafting upon a holy impulse a venal motive, he
might try in his family the experiment of repaying the offices
of affection by pecuniary reward, and learn how the tribute of
filial duty may be converted into a mercenary service. You
cannot serve God and Mammon.

The manner in which candidates are often required, especially at the first, to enter into a communication with their
constituents, a manner which is not likely to be altered for the
best under any of the changes which are popularly urged,—
forms the second of the practical class of obstacles. Enough
has been already said on the nature of the preliminary introduction, which too commonly takes place, and is becoming
general. Supposing that stage to be passed, the process of
canvassing forms an insurmountable difficulty to many men.
It is not, necessarily, from any fastidious taste that this objection is felt; though, even if that were so, it is not wise by
making such a method of introduction commonly necessary,
to exclude the services of one who might, nevertheless, prove
qualified to be a public benefactor. A man of a well-constituted mind shrinks from affecting what he does not feel,—
from concealing any particular opinion that might be unpopular,—from pretending to assign undue weight to matters
which he knows to be trivial,—from, in fact, inaugurating his
entrance into public life, by acting a part which is not his own.
He is under the necessity of resorting to underhand and dis-
ingenuous contrivances,—to humiliating solicitations and mean
compliances. It is impossible to read the narratives of the
skill and success of men accomplished in the art of canvassing, without feeling that the affectation of friendship,
cordiality, and regard,—which are set to work on the simplicity and credulity of the voter, to cajole and surprise him
of his vote,—has a family resemblance to the tricks which,
when employed by humbler performers for the purpose of
depriving a servant-maid of her earnings, or a countryman of

his purse, are considered to be fitly rewarded by a sojourn in the oakum-yard or on the treadmill.

All these petty degradations are but the interludes of the play which the candidate is required to go through. He is to utter whatever may be the shibboleth of the hour. Instead of a candid examination of public affairs, he must deal with every subject in such a manner as to suit the prepossessions of his hearers. Rare are the cases, and eminent must be the man, who dares to appear as he is, and speak as he thinks on public questions, before those whom he addresses, and hopes to enlist in his support. Perhaps scarcely any young politician, at the entrance of his career, could venture upon such candour ;—supposing, of course, a time in which nomination boroughs do not exist. He must be initiated into political life by a discipline in deception. He must often, to please some men, approve of—or, at least, countenance—bigotry ; and if he does not positively encourage, he is obliged to wink at, corruption, intemperance, and deceit ; or shut his eyes to what he knows is taking place. In addition to this, he may be driven to competition in promises which he is aware cannot be performed. The whole process is demoralising, and tends to exclude some of the best men, and the most scrupulous and trustworthy order of minds. "Happy is he who holds that, for a public man, the first condition of capacity to serve his country is an unsullied conscience, and who, when he sees national advantages seemingly contingent upon his own moral contamination, trusts that God will raise up instruments to secure for his country all necessary goods of earth, and refuses to sell wisdom though it be for rubies."[1]

The liberation of individual electors from a compulsory union with others would enable a candidate to discard all mean and dishonest compliances, and frankly to express his sentiments, whatever they may be, relying with confidence that the kingdom contains electors enough who agree and

---

[1] *Gladstone, The State, &c., vol. i, p. 127.*

I

sympathize with him, and that he may dispense with the votes of those who do not.

The choice of the electors is not only restricted by the practical difficulties which thus exclude the vast majority of those who might otherwise be candidates, but it is also further restricted by legal grounds of exclusion. Special Acts of Parliament, all of which are of a date subsequent to the Revolution, incapacitate the holders of a great number of offices from sitting in Parliament.[1] These provisions might have been useful, as temporary measures, to meet a temporary evil—a system of representation avowedly rotten, which placed the electoral power in a few hands—but they are utterly unsuited and obstructive when they are allowed to encumber the action of a numerous and free constituency.

The late debate on the propriety of excluding the members of the Indian Council from seats in Parliament afforded satisfactory evidence of the progress of public opinion on this subject.[2] Nearly every member who addressed the House on that occasion, except the minister who had the conduct of the bill, and could scarcely be expected to abandon the clause, either opposed, or doubted the propriety of, the exclusion; and Lord Stanley expressed himself in the most guarded manner, referring to the exclusion of classes as a *fact*, and to the policy as a supposition; and he relied chiefly on the special and novel circumstances of the Indian Council. Lord John Russell affirmed the general and true principle, that "without a strong necessity, they would not say to the

---

[1] See 1 *Black. Com.*, p. 175. The following list comprises the principal disabling statutes before the Reform Bill:—5 W. & M. c. 7, s. 57; 11 & 12 W. 3, c. 2, ss. 150, 151; 6 Ann. c. 7, s. 25; 41 Geo. 3, c. 52; 3 Geo. 4, c. 55, s. 14; 10 Geo. 4, c. 50, s. 21; 10 Geo. 4, c. 62. Several others have been passed since. It has been common to introduce such clauses in Acts for administrative purposes. It displays a cheap disinterestedness,—at no cost but that of the rights of the electors, and possibly of the efficiency of Parliament,—a cost which is not felt.

[2] *Parl. Deb.*, vol. cli., p. 785.

electors, 'Here is a man you desire to elect, but there is a law which restrains you from so doing.'" Lord Grey has also pointed out the advantage of having in Parliament the aid of men engaged in official life.[1]

It can scarcely admit of doubt, that, on principle, no person should be excluded from the House of Commons on the ground of any official employment, unless there be an absolute incompatibility between the respective duties— as, for example, it would be impossible that a clerk of the House should be at the same time a member, from the impossibility of one man being at the same time both master and servant. The judges of the common law are said to be excluded because they sit in the Lords' house; which does not apply to the judges in Chancery. It is a mistake to reason upon the fact of a judicial officer having in his personal capacity a seat in the legislature, in which he only takes a part with many others, as if it were open to the objection of combining and confusing the legislative and judicial power. The person may officiate in both capacities without any blending of the power. Lord Eldon would at all times have felt as clearly his duties in the House of Lords as in the Court of Chancery, and never could have confounded one with the other. The administration of the laws affecting public liberty may distinguish the position of the judges of the superior courts from all other persons, but the distinction is by no means clear.

A general and uniform principle should be adopted as to every public officer not excluded by evident and strong necessity. If, after the possession of office had been declared and known, a numerous and free constituency choose him as their representative, there ceases to be any foundation on public grounds for the policy which would exclude him. Nothing but the absolute inconsistency of the several duties should be

[1] *Parliamentary Government*, p. 172, 1st ed.: p. 301, 2nd ed.
[2] *Westminster Review*, vol. 13, N.S., p. 418.

admitted as sufficient. The House has [ample power to compel the attendance of its members for the performance of their parliamentary duties; and if that attendance should interfere with their official labours, it will be for those who superintend the latter duties to complain. The public would approve and applaud the act of any minister, who for such just cause, and fearless of any slander of his motives, should dismiss a public officer, notwithstanding his position in the House. Considerations of this nature are too minute to be made the basis of general legislation. They must, like the current of events, be left to the solution of time and circumstance. Parliamentary annals furnish an example of a Cornet of the Guards, who, deprived of his commission for his opposition to the minister, became, therefore, not less useful to the people, and found no scanty indemnity both in honour and in fame.

XI. All enactments, whether general or special, which incapacitate any person from being elected or from sitting in Parliament, or which impose any penalty or penalties for so doing, on the ground that such person holds any office or offices which he held at the time of his election, and stated in his declaration to the Registrar,[1] are repealed.

Another excluded class are persons in holy orders. The circumstances under which the statute[2] establishing this restriction was, little more than fifty years ago, carried through Parliament by a minister whom history has not placed in any very elevated position amongst statesmen, are well known. The most attentive perusal of the debates will fail to discover the shadow of a reason for the exclusion. The bishop of Rochester adverted to what he thought the only ojection; the unbecoming nature of our electioneering system, which, as has been stated, would form more or less a difficulty to all scrupulous men, " the means by which candidates were obliged to seek admittance into the lower House, such as opening houses of entertainment, and truckling to

[1] Clause viii., p. 96.   [2] 41 Geo. 3, c. 63.

every voter."[1] These obstacles are wholly taken away, when every vote is converted into a spontaneous tribute to the qualities and attainments of the person for whom it is given. The prelate, in his speech, repudiated the notion of any incompatibility between the studies or duties of a divine, and those of a representative of the people. He pointed to the names of Usher, Pearson, and Barrow, as examples to the contrary, and urged, that divinity, as a science, was intimately blended with the principles of political justice, of morality, and the laws of nature and nations. The bill was characterised by Lord Thurlow as a bill of disfranchisement. It was, in truth, an attack on the rights of every elector in the kingdom. Lord Eldon, who supported it, like a skilful advocate, ingeniously endeavoured to divert the argument and rest the question upon another issue, by introducing a discourse of great learning to prove the indelibility of orders, a point which had nothing whatever to do with the matter in discussion. The only true explanation of this remarkable and unjustifiable law is that which was given by the immediate object of it. Horne Tooke said, " deacons and priests had sat in Parliament for more than a century, but at last one got in who opposed the minister of the day, and then Parliament determined that there should no more be any deacons and priests admitted amongst them."[2]

Nothing abstractedly could appear more unreasonable than the exclusion of a set of men whose education and functions necessarily point their attention to the greatest subjects that can occupy the thoughts of men, and whose habits and duties moreover bring them into communication with every phase of society, and especially with the poor, whose interests require the closest, the most attentive, and the most practical consideration. That the effect of local isolation, of too

[1] *Parl. Hist.*, vol. xxxv., p. 1547.
[2] *Lord Holland's Memoirs of the Whig Party*, vol. i., p. 180. See 1 *Black. Com.*, p. 175, n. (37) ; *Christian's* Ed., Lond., 1809.

exclusive an application to the same train of thought, and a want of acquaintance with secular affairs produce, in many cases, narrow views of men and things, may be admitted, although it is, perhaps, too strongly expressed in the well-known apophthegm of Lord Clarendon; but this forms no ground for the exclusion of the class, and has never been put forward as being so. It must be always recollected that the present proposal is to require about 2000 electors for every member, and if 2000 electors concurred in the choice of a minister of religion, he is not likely to be amongst the least gifted of his order.

In the great questions which arise in Parliament affecting religion and the Church, it would be in the highest degree desirable that one or two ministers of every persuasion should be present, and enabled to take part in their discussion, rather than that all such matters should be left to laymen ambitious of a dilettante degree in divinity. The more exaggerated types of every theological doctrine will be found, not amongst its ordinary teachers, but amongst its heated neophytes. These are the men who embitter discussion, exasperate differences, and regard all moderation as treachery to their cause. The true principle of representation, consistently applied, would enable every religious body, clerical or lay, to put forward as their organ whomsoever they may deem to be the best fitted for the office. Interest and feeling will alike prompt them to select the most able and accomplished exponent of their opinions to fill the important trust. The tone and temper of 'the lower House, in dealing with subjects in which the relations between public law and national worship are in controversy, would be in no slight measure improved, if, without lessening all becoming zeal, the presence and example of the Christian minister should, to that zeal, add some portion of charity.

XII. The statute 41 Geo. 3, c. 63, and sect. 9 of the stat. 10 Geo. 4, c. 7, are repealed.

In order to remove every impediment, technical or otherwise, to the possible election of any man whom the quotient of the electors may choose, the case of returning officers should be provided for. These would together form a body of five or six hundred persons, or perhaps more, all of them of some eminence in their localities. The materials of which the representative assembly is composed, are "of ten thousand times greater consequence than all 'the formalities in the world."[1]

XIII. If any person who, by virtue of his office, may be the returning officer in any election, should be a candidate at such election, it shall be lawful for such returning officer to appoint an assessor to act in his stead, and the said appointment, when confirmed by the Lord Lieutenant of the county in which such constituency shall be situated, or by the sheriff of the said county or city, or by any three magistrates for the same county, city, or borough, shall be effectual, and the certificate or return of such assessor shall be valid, as if the same were made by such returning officer.

The accumulation of exclusions which has been so inconsiderately created or allowed, is not excused or palliated by saying we have nevertheless done very well. The repeated amendments which almost every legislative Act requires, and a vast amount of costly experience, prove that many things are done very ill. In administrative subjects much of our legislation egregiously fails. New machinery is constantly erected to effect the same or some of the same objects, for which old machinery is already applicable, and then the double powers are left to conflict with and impede each other; and the expenses of the establishment go on increasing far beyond what is needful, and out of all proportion to the work which is accomplished. It is impossible to calculate the mischief occasioned by the loss of any useful legislative element which is shut out.

All such prospective and exceptional legislation, dictated, as it is vainly imagined, by a far-sighted wisdom, and in-

[1] *Reflections,* &c., p. 58.

tended to produce, by some recondite operation, a contingent good, is an attempt to accomplish objects which exceed the powers, and are beyond the province of legislators. If they have any immediate effect whatever, it must be that they produce inconvenience, and therefore peril, with scarcely the remotest probability of effecting any good. It partakes of that meddling legislation, of which our statute-book is a remarkable monument, that presumed to teach men the manner in which almost every action of life should be performed. The Parliament thought it knew better than the people themselves where they should live, and what rents they should pay— what labourers they should hire, and what wages they should pay—how they should make, and measure, and wear their clothes—how they were to pack their fish,[1] how their beer was to be brewed, and the barrels made to put it in[2]—what they should pay for their candles,[3] and how their beds and bolsters should be stuffed[4]—a legislation which permitted its subject to be neither the regulator of his own actions nor the keeper of his own conscience.

[1] 22 Edw. 4, c. 2.   [2] 35 Hen. 8, c. 8.   [3] 11 Hen. 6, c. 12.
[4] 11 Hen. 7, c. 19 : 5 & 6 Edw. 6, c. 23.

CHAPTER VII.

THE ACT OF VOTING.

IN nearly every scheme of electoral amendment that has been suggested, one part of the proposal has been to substitute a documentary form of tendering and receiving the vote, in the place of the oral form.[1] In the present plan it is proposed that the vote shall be given in the shape of a document, to be deliberately prepared and signed, and (except in some special cases, which will be the subject of a distinct chapter) personally delivered by every voter at his proper polling-place.

It will be remembered, that the system now suggested contemplates the necessity of a certain quota or number of votes for every candidate, and renders more than that number unnecessary. If, therefore, a popular candidate should receive, as is most likely to be the case, the suffrages of a very much larger number of electors than the number of the quota, it would follow that the excess of votes would be lost, if means were not provided for enabling the electors to transfer their votes, on that contingency, to some other candidate. The plan, therefore, would be incomplete, if it did not enable every elector to provide for such a contingency, and enable the vote to be transferred, as the elector shall direct,—if he shall think proper to give any such direction,—from one candidate to another, until it reaches a candidate whom the

---

[1] This has been adopted for the Universities by the stat. 24 & 25 Vict., c. 53. (Note to the 3rd ed.)

elector has named, who shall require the vote to make up his quota, and with whom the vote therefore rests. In order to give to the elector the option and the means of thus transferring his vote, the form of the document must enable him to vote, as he now can, for the single candidate, whom he may select, or to go on further, and provide for as many contingencies as he may think proper, within the scope which the gazetted lists allow him. It will be found that such a power is not only convenient and necessary for its immediate object, but that it is calculated to be of vast benefit in other respects, especially that of bringing to the duty of voting reflection, judgment, and moderation.[1]

In setting out the form of the voting-paper, it is scarcely necessary to state that no vote can be ultimately effectual for more than one candidate. The inconsistencies and absurdities of our system of election, both for parliamentary and local councillors, have been lately pointed out.[2] They have been the growth of chance and accident, and caused by the inevitable absence of any presiding design. The number of members for whom one vote may be given, on a parliamentary election, varies, in different places, from one to four. Whatever the franchise may be, whatever may be the direction in which it is extended, it should be a canon of the reform, that when the franchise is conferred,—the right of assisting in the appointment of a representative once given to any individual,—the value of his single vote, wherever be his dwelling, or his property, shall be the same as that of every other vote. There is nothing in the accidental circumstance that an elector resides, or has property, in a county, or city, or town represented by a plurality of members, which should

---

[1] In a paper on the University Election Act, in *Macmillan's Magazine*, Feb. 1862, p. 298, I have shown that an addition to that measure, rendering each vote available for no more than one candidate, and giving the contingent form of vote as above explained, would have made the scheme perfectly just, and (with some minor improvements) complete.

[2] *Edinburgh Review*, vol. c., p. 226.

entitle him to vote for more candidates than if he lived in a place which returned only one member. There is sufficient reason for giving a great community more weight in the Legislature than a small one; but there is no reason why a single elector, dwelling in the great community, should have more or less weight than a single elector in the small one. A delusion is, in truth, fostered in many minds, by the present mode of election, which gives to one in London votes for three candidates and in Finsbury or Birmingham for two, as if it were a larger privilege than that of those who in smaller boroughs can vote for one only, while the real electoral power at present is plainly far less in the greater constituency. It should always be borne in mind that it is the number of *voters* who can elect a representative, and not the number of votes which any one can give, that is the true test of electoral weight.[1] One of the first objections commonly uttered by those who have but superficially looked at the proposed system is that persons who are accustomed to a vote, which may contribute to elect several candidates, will not consent to be reduced to a vote that can elect but one. What they have to be persuaded of is, that the certain and unerring force which they may employ in the choice of one representative invests every single vote with incalculably more electoral power than any multiplication of the votes on individual electors will confer without it.[2] This gain to the electors of a self-governed nation was forcibly expressed by the late Prevost-Paradol:—" Proportional Representation is to our mind as evident and almost as important an improvement upon the majority system of representative government now in vogue, as the application of steam has been to indus-

---

[1] It is part of the same delusion which has given more popular prominence to the cumulative than to the single vote. See Appendix N, §§ 8, 9, 10, *infra*, p. 161.

[2] This will be found demonstrated by facts and figures, Appendices M and N, *infra*, pp. 351, 359.

trial pursuits."[1]   It may help to reconcile some to the rule
which gives them an effectual voice in the election of no
more than one member, if they know that in the United
States no vote can be given for more than one member of the
House of Representatives.

The law regulating the form of voting may be thus expressed :—

XIV. Every vote shall be given on a document setting forth the name
of the candidate for whom it is given; and if the vote be intended, in the
events provided for by this Act, to be transferred to any other candidate
or candidates, then the names of such other candidate or candidates must
be added in numerical order, viz. :—

County, Division of the County, City, or Borough of

The bearer of this voting paper records his vote for the candidate
named first in the subjoined list, or in the events provided for by Statute
            for the other candidates successively, in their numerical
order, viz. :—

1		6	
2		7	
3		8	
4		9	
5		10	

In the first, or if the elector approves of more than one
candidate, then in the succeeding blank spaces opposite the
several numbers on a form similar to the above the elector

[1] Article in the *Journal des Débats*, Feb. 18th, 1870.

will insert the name or names which he adopts. The candidates for his particular constituency will be made known to him, as now, by such written or personal addresses as those candidates may think proper to make; and, in addition to that which he has now, he will have a schedule before him,[1] containing the names, not only of the candidates for his own particular constituency, but of the candidates for all the other constituencies in the kingdom. This list it is entirely at the option of the elector to make use of or not; in his determination as to that, he may be guided by his education, by his knowledge, by his opportunities—by the interest which he takes in public matters, in the well-being of his town, or in the welfare of his country. In every step the object of conforming in all respects to the Ballot Act has been kept in view; but in the form of the voting paper some variation from that prescribed in the Act is necessary. It need not, however, impair in any degree that secrecy which is its cardinal purpose. The method here suggested certainly gives scope for the exercise of infinitely more thought and intelligence than there has hitherto been room for in parliamentary or municipal elections, but it leaves the illiterate voter all the facilities he now has; and it is hard upon a self-governing nation to circumscribe the use of the knowledge and discretion of the entire community until all electoral action is reduced to his level. Entering as we have now done on

---

[1] P. 97, *ante.* In order to show the variety and elasticity of application of which this principle is capable, an alternative may be introduced for the use of voters who, having perfect confidence in one candidate, wish to place their votes at his disposal, if not needed for his own election, or for the election of the other candidate or candidates they have named. A form may be used with this addition—"If this voting paper shall not be appropriated when the names of all the candidates obtaining the quota of votes shall be declared, this vote shall then be recorded in favour of such candidate as the said ——— ——— above named shall signify to the Registrar, as by this Act provided." Seo p. 189, *infra*, n. Some may think this open to the danger of consolidating power in single hands; others that it is a wise "revival of authority."

the noble task of universal education, the state may surely offer more encouragement to its children than is involved in this mean estimate of the confidence which should be reposed in them. The names of the candidates might be inserted in numerical order, or the numbers placed opposite to the names if already inserted, instead of the mark prescribed by the Ballot Act, in their order of preference. It has not been thought absolutely necessary to limit the number of candidates which shall be named on each paper. It is a question which at present may be left open, observing only, that if the use of too long a list were found to lead to the insertion of many names carelessly, after the few more distinguished candidates at the head of the voting paper, the voter might be permitted to include all or any of the candidates for places within his county, and a certain number only of those outside. Such a restriction should not, however, be adopted unless experience proved its necessity. The illiterate voters may be assisted in having the mark added for single, or the numbers if for several, candidates, as the Act prescribes.

In striving to render the act of voting a solemn and deliberate act, we pursue an object which the greatest, the best, and the most scrutinising minds, who have directed their thoughts to political subjects, have always regarded as of paramount importance. It has been the prevailing idea, that political security and happiness depend on the degree in which the votes of a free community:—the delivery of the popular judgment could be "surrounded with the best securities for rectitude, and the best preservatives against haste, passion, or private corruption."[1] Mr. Burke proclaims the foundation of the same great principle—"All persons possessing *any portion* of power ought to be strongly and awfully impressed with an idea that they act in trust, and that they are to account for their conduct in that trust to one great master, author, and founder of society. This principle

---

[1] *History of Greece*, vol. iv., p. 209.

ought to be more strongly impressed upon the minds of those who compose the collective sovereignty, than upon those of single princes." [1]

The power given to the electors, first by the information which the gazetted lists afford to them of the persons who are candidates for the representation throughout the kingdom, and, secondly, by the opportunity the voting papers afford of separating, distinguishing, and bringing out every form and shadow of political opinion, will give an immeasurable increase of force and strength to the true representative principle; and it will, at the same time, wholly extinguish the operation of the pseudo-principle of representation under which nations have suffered, and by which they are obstructed in their progress towards settled constitutional government. "In the present state of our knowledge," a late writer has observed, "politics, so far from being a science, is one of the most backward of all the arts;" [2] and certainly nothing can well be imagined more resembling a condition of barbarism than a parliamentary election. Five, ten, or twenty thousand men, comprising every diversity of education, of thought, of moral quality, and of mental endowment, are called together to elect one or two persons to represent them. If they were only, as in old times, delegates, to grant "a tenth or a fifteenth" for a foreign war, the representation might be sufficient; but a representation so created at this day, with all the varied questions which are opening and agitating mankind, is a simple impossibility, and the name is a delusion. We are rejecting the aid of letters and the facilities of locomotion, ignoring the popular intelligence, and obstinately resolving to subject ourselves to the same difficulties as our ancestors struggled with when they had no roads to travel on, when not one in a hundred had learnt to read, and not one in a

[1] *Reflections*, &c., p. 138. See *Mill, Considerations on Representative Government*. Ch. II., iii.

[2] *Buckle's History of Civilisation*, vol. i., p. 458.

thousand nad any book or manuscript to read, if he had learnt. It is plain that as the intelligence of the country has advanced, we have been receding from anything like a real representation, because it has become every year less possible for the rude forms of an earlier age to convey the varieties of expression that have in modern times been called into existence. It is no answer to say, that if we have not had representation, we have had something that has done as well,—if it has not been actual it has been " virtual." The question is, whether we are to proceed towards a system of representation, or towards something else—not representation, but a substitute for it. It is a question which every one should present to himself before he begins to reason on the subject of parliamentary reform, as the whole tenor of his argument will be necessarily governed by the answer.

The fundamental law of election, M. Guizot states to be " que les électeurs fassent ce qu'ils veulent, et sachent ce qu'ils font."[1] In the intelligent performance of the act of voting, the elector will necessarily have some preparatory knowledge, some inclination of mind, some train of thought, or some calculation of interest, disposing him to prefer one or more persons to others. The causes of the disposition are of course almost infinite. It would be useful, if it were possible, to consider them, and their operation upon every class [of mind.

The conclusions which are founded upon personal knowledge—that is, by knowledge acquired by intimate personal acquaintance and contact, must be very rare—so rare, that with reference to the great body of the electors of the kingdom, they are scarcely deserving of consideration. Knowledge of this kind of course exists somewhere as to every man, but can extend only to a small circle. In that extent this knowledge as to new candidates will of course be of great value. In a former page, the effect of giving a separate

[1] *Guizot, Gouv. Rep.*, vol. ii., p. 247.

electoral existence to every university, college, inn of court, scientific association, or other body possessing especial advantages in point of instruction or knowledge, has been adverted to as an encouragement to such bodies to put forward and recommend their most highly qualified members.[1] " Pour trouver et obtenir les hommes les plus capables, il faut obliger ceux qui croient ou qui prétendent l'être, à prouver leur capacité, à la faire reconnaître et proclamer par les hommes qui, à leur tour, sont capables de porter un jugement sur ce fait-là, c'est-à-dire, sur la capacité individuelle de quiconque aspire à être député. Ainsi se constate le pouvoir légitime, et c'est ainsi que, dans le fait de l'élection philosophiquement considérée, ce pouvoir est pris par ceux qui le possèdent, et accepté par ceux qui le reconnaissent." [2]

It is probable that to introductions by the smaller constituencies, especially where they are composed chiefly of highly instructed persons, many candidates would be indebted for their entrance into public life. There are great numbers in the country who would receive such testimony with respect. Many would act upon recommendations coming from bodies or single persons with whom they sympathize, and whom they could trust. This kind of information, although it originates in personal knowledge, is not, as to the electors to whom it is addressed, more than "hearsay," but as such they will, as all persons dealing with such evidence must do, attribute to it the degree of weight which they believe to be due to the quarter from whence it comes. Reliance on the advice or the testimony of others in whom the electors may confide is no improper guidance. Everything that contributes to establish a basis of political faith or trust, introduces a valuable element, and one which deserves to be cultivated rather than discouraged.

It is also material to observe on this point, that, whilst the present system induces a candidate—except in the case of a

[1] Supra, p. 56.   [2] *Guizot, Gour. Rep.*, vol. ii., p. 254.

majority so compact as to be enabled wholly to despise and contemn the minority—to suppress and conceal some of his opinions, lest he might lose votes by his candour, in the proposed method of introduction every candidate will be encouraged to express himself fully and distinctly, in order that he may be perfectly comprehended by minds in sympathy with his own. Such candid explanations will have both an affirmative and a negative effect. Every elector will learn with more exactness who are those with whom he can more entirely agree, and with whom he totally disagrees. The encouragement afforded on all sides to truth will immensely increase the value of the evidence as to the real character and opinions of all who present themselves.

When population was scanty, and most of the burgesses chose their townsmen or neighbours, their knowledge of them might have been personal; though even then it is propable that familiar knowledge of the chosen member had little place. At present, the knowledge which the elector has of the member must for all practical purposes be gathered by other means. He may see his face occasionally—there may be a shake of the hand at the canvass—he may have spoken a dozen words to him in the market-place—there may be an annual dinner and harangue—perhaps an address at opening a mechanics' institute or a ragged school. He may read in the newspaper an occasional interlocutory observation in the House—perhaps a set speech. He finds his name in the list of those who voted for or against this or that measure, but of any knowledge of his habits of thought, disposition, or mental qualities, the elector has none which he may not, with the same attention, gather in the daily or weekly press, concerning the members for any other constituency. What the electors in general know of any public man, at this day, is derived not from any observation of his words and conduct, which they have been able personally to make or to witness, but of what they read and gather from that ubiquitous literature which penetrates and throws light on all the important transactions of life. We find in every town, in all political conversation, except at the approach of an election, that far more is thought and known, or discussed, of the conduct of those who have been from time to time ministers, than is thought or discussed respecting the conduct of their particular member. The attention is impressed by the more prominent objects in the political world, and dwells but little on the minor ones. In perusing the gazetted lists, with a view of framing their voting papers, every elector would be able to form his judgment as well of the merits of one as of another candidate, according as he had earned distinction in Parliament or elsewhere; or if, unknown to the world, according to his appreciation by other persons who are known and trusted.

Some electors may have neither time nor means to do more than they now do—give their vote for one or other of the candidates for their own borough; and in giving that vote they may resolve to rely, not upon any view of the parliamentary conduct of the candidate, but upon personal character, as the same has come under their own observation. Suppose the case of two candidates for a country constituency, and the elector to reason thus:—"I have been over the estates of these two gentlemen. I find, on one of them, that the farms are not high-rented; but I find, also, that they are very badly farmed. No draining has been done. All the buildings are in an ill condition, and have only been patched up for many years past. Most of the labourers' cottages were pulled down thirty or forty years ago, to lessen the poor rates, and the men and boys, and women when they are employed, have to walk three miles or more every night and morning, to the next parish, where they live, huddled together in the back lane. On the other property they say the rents have been raised, and some of the tenants complain they are a little too high; but then there has been a vast deal of money spent upon the farms, and they get twice or three times as much from them as they used to do. The labourers have constant employment, and, wherever cottages have been wanted, good roomy ones have been built. They have all good gardens, and there are schools for the labourers' children. I know little of what is meant by Tory, or Whig, or Radical,—but the man who seems to manage his own business best, and attends to the good of his fellow-creatures, is the man I should rather trust, and for whom I shall vote."

It is easy to suppose the same kind of reasoning to take place in a manufacturing or a maritime town, and to be caused by like contrasts, of the conduct of different employers of labour. When no triumph can be gained, by forcing the electors to sacrifice all individual opinions to make up great majorities, and when all pressure of that nature is taken away, men will begin to think independently, and not be led by clamour. They will be governed much more by practical tests, and less by abstract and barren generalities. Those who witness and appreciate every noble effort which a man may make for the good of his neighbours or his country will be found active in his favour, and will make for him a sufficient, an independent, and probably an enthusiastic constituency.

The gazetted lists will present to the electors of the kingdom a roll of names, containing a large proportion of the most eminent men in it; for, when the obstacles which now impede the entry into Parliament are removed, there are few who will feel within themselves any competency for its labours, and have opportunities of engaging in them, who will not make the tender of their services. In the number will doubtless be found much of the dross of conceit, of self-sufficiency, and of folly; but the lists will also contain the pure ore of wisdom and virtue, if it exist,—and it is hard to believe that any generation is left destitute of those qualities. There will be the most that the nation possesses,—of high endowment,—

of the knowledge of men, gleaned by laborious study,—of science, rendering the material world subservient to the uses of man,—of literature, opening the understanding and enriching thought,—of art, conferring dignity and grace ; many of these, combined with historic fame and ancient lineage, and together comprehending all the moral and intellectual worth, which the love of country and of mankind, and the desire for honourable distinction, can call to light.

The whole of this magnificent field of choice would be open to the electors of the kingdom. The capacity of selection, and the disposition to select from such materials, would be infinitely various ; but the field, like the bounteous lap of nature, is free to all who have the intelligence and the industry to extract its treasures. Like nature, it would be barren and sterile only to the ignorant and the indolent—those who know not the wealth that it contains, or are without the industry and energy to profit by it. The pious, the learned, the scientific, the enterprising, and the philanthropic of every variety and degree, will all find a sympathetic expression amongst the candidates before them. There is a tendency in every sort of superiority to become a nucleus gathering about them kindred minds and characters. " Il y a un certain rapport, un certain lien entre la capacité d'être (un bon député ou autre chose) et la capacité de reconnaître celui qui possède la capacité d'être. Ceci est un fait dont dépose à chaque instant le spectacle du monde. Le brave se fait suivre de ceux qui sont capables de s'associer à sa bravoure. L'habile se fait obéir de ceux qui sont capables de comprendre son habileté. Le savant se fait croire de ceux qui sont capables d'apprécier sa science. Toute supériorité a une certaine sphère d'attraction, dans laquelle elle agit et groupe autour d'elle des infériorités réelles, mais en état de sentir et d'accepter son action."[1]

A representative assembly, chosen under a system thus free

[1] *Guizot. Gouv. Rep.*, vol. ii., p. 254.

and expansive, would be a reflex of the feeling and intelligence
of the people. Gradually elevated in character by the constant operation of the process of comparison which is so
powerful in every department of science, by the introduction
of the most distinguished men, and by the elimination of the
inferior, it would become a national Walhalla, worthy to form
a branch of that parliament which, having its origin in the
depth of past ages where all records are shadowy and doubtful, has gathered strength and dignity in its course, down to
our own days, and become the great model of constitutional
government, and the envy or admiration of all civilised
nations.

In reviving and calling forth periodically, at short intervals,
all proud and generous feelings connected with our country
and race,—turning the attention of every thoughtful man on
such occasions to the consideration of all that is excellent in
the age in which he lives, we nourish that love of country in
which a nation's unity and strength are found. Such love is
of no sudden growth. It must proceed from the sense that
our country contains something deserving of our affection, and
gather its force from circumstances round which the feelings
cling. " If our love for our country is to be sincere, without
ostentation and affectation, it cannot be produced immediately
by instruction and directions, like a branch of scientific knowledge. It must rest, like every other kind of love, on something unutterable and incomprehensible. Love may be
fostered ; it may be influenced by a gentle guidance from
afar : but if the youthful mind becomes conscious of this, all
the simplicity of the feeling is destroyed ; its native gloss is
brushed off. Such, too, is the case with the love of our country.
Like the love for our parents, it exists in a child from the
beginning ; but it has no permanency, and cannot expand, if
the child is kept, like a stranger, at a distance from his
country. No stories about it, no exhortations, will avail as a
substitute : we see our country, feel it, breathe it in, as we do

nature. Then history may be of use, and after a time, reflection, consciousness. But our first care ought to be for
institutions, in which the spirit of our country lives, without
being uttered in words, and takes possession of men's minds
involuntarily. For a love derived from precepts is none."[1]

The representation in its theory, or in any worthy view
of it, should be of all that is best and most instructed, omitting, as far as the separation is possible, all that is ignorant
and vicious. The representative embodiment is to be of man,
approaching, as near as his infirmity of thought and will permits him to approach, that which a lofty imagination has
pictured of his pristine dignity, when,—

> In their looks divine
> The image of their glorious Maker shone,
> Truth, wisdom, sanctitude, severe and pure
> (Severe, but in true filial freedom placed),
> Whence true authority.

The design is to represent the qualities with which man is
divinely gifted,—the noble heritage of his nature,—not their
absence and negation. Such an assembly should present "the
awful image of the virtue and wisdom of a whole people collected into a focus." The first introduction of representatives
to constituents may be viewed as the contact of two intelligences,—a higher and a lower. How is this contact to be
obtained? It must be by the higher descending to and looking
down to the lower, or the lower searching for and raising its
views to the higher. It is easier for the superior intelligence to
make itself intelligible to the lower, than for the lower to ascend
to and appreciate the excellence of the higher order of mind.
But as the latter is more difficult, so also is it an infinitely more
wholesome and beneficial exercise in human and social progress. Consider the opposite tendencies of two conditions of
things:—one in which the great mass of society remains the
passive subject of any attacks which misdirected talent may

---

[1] *Passow*, in note to *Guesses at Truth*, 2nd Ser., p. 365.

level against it, helpless itself to move until some hand be held out, and at the mercy of accident, whether it be that of a true friend or a concealed and insidious foe; prepared to be the unconscious victim of that perverted ability which is always hovering over it, ready to seize upon and turn its follies into a wicked profit;—the other, in which the same society is awakened to the value of what is truly good, by being insensibly forced to a comparison between the great and the mean.   In the table which exhibits the chief names that enlighten and adorn their times, they will see—

"Life rising still on life, in higher tone."

Can there be a doubt in which condition there will be found that upward look, and that endeavour to appreciate excellence, which is a step towards excellence itself?   It is the people who must search for and learn where knowledge and virtue are to be found.   They do not come to them unsought:—the counterfeit only will be thrust into their hands, and in taking it they embrace "the false Duessa," and must, in the end, endure the odious sight of her deformity.   "Philosophy cannot raise the bulk of mankind to her level, therefore if she is to become popular she must descend to theirs.   This she cannot do without a twofold grave injury.   She will debase herself and will puff up her disciples."

The habit of scrutinizing with attention the conduct of public men, and of forming an estimate of their relative merits, on an examination of the lists which the gazettes furnish, will naturally dispose the minds of men towards political moderation, and render them tolerant of differences, which they now regard as impassable objections.   As our views widen, our sympathies increase and multiply; all things become more precious, and in all we find good. Merits will appear, where people had before seen only adversaries.   It is party which begets party.   When an elector addresses himself to the task of forming on his voting-paper a

list sufficient to compose an entire representative assembly,
he becomes a mediator, rather than a partisan. He becomes
less narrow, and more catholic in his opinions and prepossessions. One whom he before looked upon as an opponent,
though possibly a distinguished one, he now comes to regard
as a valuable auxiliary. In a late contest for the City there
were few, if any, that voted against one of the former members, when asked whether in the present dearth of statesmen they really wished to exclude from the House one of the
small number deserving of the name, who did not answer
that their wish was only to exclude him from the representation of London, and not from Parliament. Under the proposed system his name would have appeared on most of the
voting-papers; and the preference of others, if expressed,
would have been shown only by the place which it occupied
on the voting-papers.

As the extensive capacity of expression, and the interesting
nature of the act of voting, comes to be felt, increased attention will be directed to it. Instead of that indifference to
political action which prevails so extensively that in large
constituencies only about half of the electors now take any
part in elections, there is every reason to expect that much
time would be given to the details necessary for the preparation of the voting-paper. This result can scarcely be doubted,
when we consider the degree in which political subjects form,
in this country, topics of thought and conversation. The
system attains the object to which M. Guizot points as so
desirable, that of placing " l'électeur dans une position telle
que son jugement personnel, sa propre volonté, soient non
seulement libres, mais provoqués à se produire tels qu'ils sont
en effet."[1] The attraction presented to each elector by the
power of giving effect in his vote to his especial and cherished
opinions and feelings, will, when he comes to appreciate it,
animate him with a new spirit of incalculable power. Con-

_____
[1] *Gouv. Rep.*, vol. ii., p. 247.

siderations of duty will intervene with all their force. Every
man will feel that he is personally responsible for his own
error, or his own neglect. His understanding must teach
him how to act, and his conscience guide him to the performance. It is' the sense of individual duty that preserves
every household in order and harmony. Each member of the
household has his especial function, and knows that he is
responsible for the manner in which he performs, and for his
neglect if he omits it. If this were not so, all united action
would cease; there would be no diligence, and no subordination. We may imagine the case of a family, in which no
servant has power to act without the concurrence of a
majority of his fellow-servants, and where but a few of them
can agree together as to what they ought to do. In such an
establishment there could be no certainty of the performance
of any duty; for every one might cast the blame upon the
others, and the household would be involved in inextricable
confusion. The reasoning is the same of the multitude of
families and persons who form the nation. As the individual
restraints and sanctions become more feeble, certain breaches
of duty and of justice are made the subject of municipal law.
But all blame, and all punishment for error or misconduct in
the family or in the State, assume the existence of a power
to do right. If a man be prevented by others from performing a duty,—if he be precluded from doing it by a force
which he has not himself assisted to create, and which he
has no power to overcome, he must, in justice, be absolved
from the blame of leaving the duty unperformed.

A system which first destroys individual freedom of action,
and with it the higher inducements which connect action
with duty, necessarily introduces and tolerates baser motives.
Men tempt and are tempted by each other. One covets and
seeks a public function for selfish purposes, by venal means,
and another, for like ends, helps him to obtain it. The
evil spreads. There ceases to be any belief in uprightness of

purpose. The only confidence left is of that miserable kind which relies solely upon that being done which it is the interest of another to do.

> " Thus vice the standard reared; her arrier-ban
> Corruption called, and loud she gave the word,
> Mind, mind yourselves! why should the vulgar man,—
> The lacquey, be more virtuous than his lord?
> Enjoy the span of life! 'tis all the gods afford."

The restraints imposed by penal laws are but a feeble and insufficient protection. The degradation spreads widely and becomes inveterate when the moral restraint is gone, and rich and poor, great and small, lend themselves to the same iniquity. There is no Ithuriel upon whose touch the insidious temptation starts up discovered and surprised. There is no spear of celestial temper to lay bare these foul cabals. We have no hope but in removing the causes which have tainted political life, and thereby striving to re-establish on its seat that faith in one another which we have overthrown and lost; to search through our land for men either worthy to lead, or to embody and represent all that is best and noblest amongst us, and having found such—for we need not doubt that such can be found; to give them our just reverence and implicit trust,—a reverence and trust which no man gives but by his own free consent,—which none can be forced to confer.

A system which asserts for itself the power of preventing every influence by which one man, or set of men, can control the acts of others, is necessarily brought into comparison with the ballot, which is put forward as a remedy for such evils. The advocates of the ballot cannot be supposed to have an attachment to the ballot for its own sake, and they will only contend for its introduction so long as it shall appear to them the most perfect scheme of electoral liberation. Many persons are misled by the use, in countries in which that system has been adopted, of the term "appeal to the ballot-box," and similar expressions, as if it implied that it was a palladium of liberty; the fact being that the term only refers to the popular election as the ultimate authority, by describing one of its prominent features, as we, on such occasions, say "appeal to the hustings." No greater idea of specific virtue is attached to the machine called the "ballot-box" than we do to the wooden platform called "the hustings." The secrecy which the advocates of the former amongst us chiefly desire, is for the most part, and in all countries really free, regarded as of the smallest importance.

The difference and contrasts between the system here proposed, which may be called the system of individual independence,—and that of the ballot, are these:

The ballot proposes to give to every voter a perfect freedom to vote for any of the two or three candidates who may think proper to present themselves. The system of individual independence offers him a freedom of choice, not only of the two or three, but probably of two or three thousand candidates.

It may possibly be said, that one is *freedom* of choice, the other the *extent* of choice, which the ballot does not pretend to enlarge, and that therefore it is no defect in that system that it fails to do so. This may logically be an answer. It is, nevertheless, a proper subject of comparison between the two systems.

The ballot proposes to extinguish bribery and put an end to intimidation, by depriving every person disposed to bribe or intimidate of the means of knowing how the elector has voted. The system of individual responsibility proposes to put an end to bribery and intimidation by taking away all the artificial and pecuniary value of the vote.

The ballot cannot extinguish bribery. It is almost inevitable that in a country like England, so rich in rewards for political services, a system which places bribery out of the reach of detection, and gives it impunity, will extend the practice to an incalculable degree. Why should it not do so ? The organisation for controlling elections we see is at hand. What is to prevent a candidate from stipulating that his payment shall depend 'on his success. He need not inquire who votes for him or who does not. It is sufficient that all the leaders know that their reward depends upon their skilful and resolute conduct in placing a certain candidate at the head of the poll. It is not possible to conceive anything more desperate, or more unprincipled, than such a contest may become. The system of individual independence preserves a record of every vote, with the name of the elector by whom it is given, and it prevents any struggle, by depriving every elector both of the motive and power of conquering or overruling the will of another by the force of a majority.

The ballot proposes to protect the conscience of the elector, when that conscience is called into action by a predominant sense of the superior merit of any candidate. In the larger constituencies only fifty-five per cent. of the voters, at the utmost, interfere at all, and have, therefore, any conscientious motive one way or the other.[1] The system of individual independence calls the conscience into action in the case of every elector, by making him feel that he has a personal interest and power, which he cannot misuse or neglect, without knowing that he has failed in his duty.

The ballot proposes to secure the uncontrolled exercise of

[1] Mr. Kinglake lately, at Bridgewater, mentioned the benefit that accrued to a voter who had lost his employment by his vote, and had procured, through his aid, a better situation at Woolwich. It suggests the value of investigating all such cases, and of procuring, by agency easily found, ample indemnity to every one who may be in danger of suffering from such a cause. Not only would the voter have the sympathy of all persons of his own opinion, but all would be anxious to receive him for their own sakes,— every landlord and every master knowing the inestimable value of a conscientious tenant or workman. It would at once be individual profit, economical advantage, and political amelioration, without the degradation of the ballot.

the volition of the elector, by protecting him from the influence of his fears. The system of individual independence encourages him to act by giving his sympathies and opinions, and through them his volition, scope and operation as extensive as the moral and intellectual condition of his age shall afford, and thus calls every high and generous motive into exercise.

The ballot proposes, by enabling the voter to conceal his vote, to exclude the operation of that extraneous and improper control over him, which is the symptom of a vicious state of political morality. The system of individual independence addresses itself to the disease itself, as the most certain and effectual method of removing the symptom; it puts an end to the temptation of exercising an improper control over the conscience of any, by appealing to and giving freedom of action to the consciences of all.

The ballot, moreover, proposes to prevent not only direct and open intimidation, but that tacit discouragement of the free action of electors, which is the result of partiality in dealing,—of the giving, or withdrawal, of custom,—or of the extension, or privation of other advantages, according as the opinions of the electors are, or are not, in accordance with those of the persons who have such advantages to bestow or to withhold. Upon this point the pretensions of the ballot must be more closely examined.

The argument in favour of the concealment of the political action of every individual—whatever that action may be—in order that his temporal interests may not be affected, should be stated in all its force, that it may be fairly considered. It is undeniable that, throughout our political system, the manifestation of public opinion, in county, city, and borough meetings, and in open gatherings of people on all occasions, is looked upon as one of the features of the free political life existing amongst us. A mistaken importance may be attributed to these manifestations, but they have, no doubt, for more than a century, constituted a method of mutual and national consultation and encouragement in the pursuit of public ends. The advocates of the ballot would, probably, say that they do not object to public meetings, for a man who wished to conceal his political opinions would not be obliged to attend them; and if he did attend them, he would be perfectly at liberty to applaud any opinion, however he may dislike it, and afterwards to compensate himself by voting the contrary way. The ballot, therefore, they would say, has nothing in it antagonistic to public meetings. We demand, say they, that the temporal interests of every man shall be protected from injury resulting from his opinions. No man has anything to do with the religion, the politics, or the morality of another. No man has a right, authoritatively, to determine what the religion, the politics, or the morals of another shall be; and what he cannot authoritatively determine, we demand that he shall be prevented, as far as possible, from influencing. All these things every man has a right to choose for himself. We demand for every man that none of his temporal advantages, of any kind, shall be restricted, or diminished, owing to prejudices which others may have against his religion, his politics, or his morals. A man may have prejudices in favour of Christianity, or of some special confession,—in favour of peace, of a general system of national education, or of free trade,—or in favour of a strict code of morals, and he may inculcate such doctrines, by his mouth or his pen; but he has no right to consider any of such things in the choice of his friends, his tradesmen, his tenants, or his servants. For none of these opinions is one man answerable to another,—and he usurps a right which does not belong to him who, beyond argument, attempts to exercise any influence or control on such points.

The reply to this may be,—that although it is true every man is accountable only to a higher judge for his religion, his

politics, and (except in so far as municipal law interferes) his
morals,—although all these things are matters for his private
judgment, and that judgment is free,—yet it does not follow
that all religions, politics, and morals are equally right. Every
man is entitled to be his own physician, but he has no
intuition of the medicines which he should use or avoid. He
is entitled to exercise his judgment, but there is certainly a
right and a wrong judgment. One drug may be healing and
another hurtful. So in religion; he is not responsible to man
for his choice, but the choice is not therefore indifferent.
There is a true, and there are false religions, and the consequences of error may be tremendous. In politics, one way
may lead to general tranquillity and the public good; another
way may lead to public misery or suffering, to anarchy or to
tyranny. In morals, there is a good and an evil code. It
may be true that no man is gifted with the power of pronouncing which is right and which is wrong; but it is of
paramount importance that every man should make up his
mind on all these subjects to the best of his understanding,
and, having done so, that he should act upon his conclusion
in all earnestness and sincerity. If this be so, we do not
know how to act on your principle of avoiding or excluding
the exercise of all influence. We believe this Christian
confession to be a divine truth, which offers temporal and
eternal happiness to man, and we propagate it with all our
power; we believe that these rules of national conduct will
promote the well-being of the people and of mankind, and we
promote their ascendancy to the utmost of our means; we
believe that a rigid self-denial, and the restraint of passions
and desires, are the basis of morals, and we encourage them
as far as we are able. If we did not thus labour for what we
conceive to be the good of our fellow-creatures, we should, as
it appears to us, fail in our duty, and convert life into a cold
converse of intellect, without affection or sympathy. We
should become mere dialecticians, and not men. We are, by

the operation of these motives, led to form our friendships and
our society for the most part amongst those with whom we
have opinions, and feelings, and sympathies, in common. It
is against this tendency, say the advocates of the ballot, that
we are resolved to struggle. We will deprive you of the
means of displaying such partialities, by concealing from you,
as far as we can, the opinions of your neighbours. We
cannot, indeed, conceal their religion, if they profess any, for
they cannot go to their churches or chapels in a mask. We
cannot, perhaps, altogether conceal every departure from
what you deem morality, for few of the actions of life can be
done under a mask,—but as to politics, at least we can defy
your penetration; the ballot will prevent you from knowing
how any man may vote. He shall be allowed to vote under
a mask. Be it so, is the answer. We shall still be able to
discover the political opinions of those around us, and from
those opinions we shall infer their votes. This will be
impossible, is the reply, for we enable every man to wear the
guise of agreeing with you, notwithstanding his vote may be
given in support of opposite principles. You will not know
by whom the votes were given which belie the previous
assurances that you received. You may suspect your friends
of abusing your confidence, and falsifying their professions.
The man who dines at your table, and most eagerly expresses
his concurrence in your sentiments, may be one whose act
contradicts his language. When we have established the
ballot, you will cease to believe the political declarations of any
of your neighbours, and, in the general distrust of everybody,
political friendship will be at an end. No man will value or
regard a political promise. It will cease to be asked for.
All attention, all efforts, and all reward will be directed to the
result of the ballot.[1]

[1] In the Chapter (X.) on *The Mode of Voting*, in Mr. Mill's *Considerations
on Representative Government* (p. 197, et seq., 2nd ed.), the question of the
ballot, together with the spirit it would foster, is considered in its latest
aspects, in regard to our present political condition. (Note to 3rd ed.)

In the representative system, M. Guizot observes :—" Il est vrai, et par le fait nécessaire, que la liberté, la vérité et l'erreur, les volontés perverses et les volontés légitimes, en un mot, le bien et le mal qui co-existent et se combattent dans la société comme dans l'individu, pourront également se pro-duire ; c'est la condition de ce monde ; c'est le fait même de la liberté. Mais à cela deux garanties ; l'une se trouve dans la publicité de la lutte ; c'est pour le bien la meilleure chance de succès ; car ce ne sont pas les hommes qui ont inventé l'analogie du bien avec la lumière, du mal avec les ténèbres ; cette idée commune à toutes les religions du monde, est le symbole de la première des vérités." [1]

The peace and security and strength of social and of in-dividual life depend upon our trust and our trustworthiness. Everything that tends to sap the confidence of man in his fellows, is like an insidious poison in the system,—a worm at the root of every good thought and action. Faith is not a mere theological virtue. It is not a mere metaphysical term. It is enforced as emphatically, though not with the same authority, by the economist[2] as by the divine. Without it there can be none but selfish desires,—nothing but low expectations. It is the golden cord that binds will to duty. Shakespeare has painted in living colours the growth of dark suspicions, which first torture and then madden the wretched husband who distrusts his wife's fidelity. Fenelon has shown us the dismal picture of a tyrannical and avaricious prince, isolated in his palace, his only hope of safety in the bolts and bars that secure his chamber, fearing everything, and having everything to fear, the curse of his subjects and of himself who had lost all trust in his servants and his ministers. A novelist of our day has delineated in a tale the miserable con-dition of a man without belief in goodness or truth or natural

---

[1] *Guizot, Gouv. Rep.*, vol. ii.. p. 151.

[2] *Mill, Principles of Political Economy*, vol. i., pp. 134, 135, 136 ; vol. ii., p. 449.

affection, having a heart which covetousness had hardened, rejecting alike the offices of kindness and the claims of charity,—a voluntary outcast from his species. These exhibit to us life as in a mirror, and show that to faith is assigned, in the moral world, something like that mighty office and power which are, in the physical world, fulfilled by the law of gravitation. It is faith alone that can hold the thoughts, the passions, and the actions of man in their due relation and concord with himself, his fellows, and the objects of his existence. "The foundation of domestic happiness is faith in the virtue of woman. The foundation of political happiness is faith in the integrity of man. The foundation of all happiness, temporal and eternal, is faith in the goodness, the righteousness, the mercy, and the love of God."[1]

In the action of voting, instead of destroying the remnant of belief in the fidelity of man to man, the true reformation would be to restore our faith in political honesty, by extinguishing, as far as human means can effect it, the temptations to selfishness, hypocrisy, and untruth. In that action, the only rule is that prescribed by the apostle for the government of the conscience, "let every man be fully persuaded in his own mind." The full persuasion the elector must entertain that his country has not, like a cruel and careless stepmother, left him surrounded with difficulties and obstacles in the performance of his duty; but has, with the maternal solicitude of a loving parent, carefully provided for him every means which she could devise for assisting him to perform that duty: and he must have this further persuasion that, recognising the maternal care and solicitude of his country, he has, on his part, in the same loving spirit, returned her kindness and her attention by performing the duty to the best of his power,—in selecting those whom he believes will best and most honestly serve her.

In insisting upon the absolute necessity of disentangling

[1] *Guesses at Truth*, 2nd Ser., p. 318.

individuals from the artificial bands which our political system has cast about them, the question of what has been called the "independence of individuality" should be viewed on every side. Many thoughtful minds regarded with great dread the destruction of a system sanctioned by long tradition, whereby the choice of representatives was left to the dictation of a few, and the establishment of a method of election which allowed ·every man to be his own master and guide. They foresaw the evils which have since been felt. One of the most profound thinkers of late times, reasoning on such a change, thus puts the argument :—"It is in no way necessary, for the sake of becoming free, to pull down the whole edifice of society, with all its time-hallowed majestic sanctities, and to scatter its stones about in singleness and independence on the ground. Yet assuredly it would not be more absurd to call such a multitude of scattered independent stones a house, than to suppose that a million, or twenty millions, of independent human beings, each stickling for his independence, and carrying out this principle through the ramifications of civil and domestic life, can coalesce into a nation or a state. There is need of mortar—there is need of a builder—yes, of a master builder : there is need of dependence, coherence, subordination of the parts to the whole, and to each other."[1]

Doubtless there must be the working plan,—there must be cohesion of material,—but what is the true cement, and where is the master builder? It had been proved too sadly to mankind that their rulers had no divine inspiration to guide them in their office, and that they worked with the untempered mortar of the follies, the passions, and the vices of the people. Three thousand probationary years passed over the world,—the times of history or historic fable,—

> Thebes and Pelops' line,
> And the tale of Troy divine.

The long ages of trial for the heroes and mighty princes who

[1] *Guesses at Truth*, 2nd Ser., p. 267.

led and governed men,—all were found wanting. The pagan
world bowed to the truth as spoken by Olympian Jove, that
the highest court of justice,—the court of the last appeal,—
was not an external authority, but resided in the conscience.
The evangelical prophet opened his mission, when he announced the fulness of time, by the precept, "Cease ye from
man." All record, sacred and profane,—all revelation, lead
to the recognition that there is but one power able to arrest
evil, and bind mankind together. By that divine energy and
word, a people of strangers, scattered over untravelled regions
of the east, became entitled to the apostolic epithet and name
of living stones of a spiritual house, acceptable to Him, the
only Builder and Maker. No mortar for such a work,—no
imperishable cement for the edifice of the state, or any other
institution of man, is to be found that does not dwell in the
individual conscience. All goodness, all religion is personal,
or it is nothing. "The aim of Christianity is not to stifle
the germs of individual character, and to bring down all mankind to a dead level. It, on the contrary, fosters and de-
velops the central principle of individuality in every man,
and frees it from the crushing burthen with which the lusts
of the flesh and the vanities of life overlay it." [1]

A discourse which insists on the sacred nature of the act of
voting may be fitly concluded by a suggestion on the manner
of celebrating its performance. The ancient customs of the
kingdom connect religion with its most important events and
transitions. The coronation is accompanied by a humble
recognition of the sovereignty of God over all, and a prayer
that he would grant unto the earthly sovereign the spirit of
wisdom and government,—to restore the things gone to decay, maintain the things that are restored, reform what is
amiss, and confirm what is in good order,—to be merciful and
not too remiss,—to execute justice and forget not mercy,—
judge with righteousness, reprove with equity, and accept no

[1] *Guesses at Truth,* 2nd Ser., p. 24.

man's person,—abase the proud and lift up the lowly,—
punish the wicked and protect and nourish the just;—and it
ends with a benediction that supplicates for the sovereign a
faithful senate, wise and upright counsellors and magistrates,
a loyal nobility, and a dutiful gentry; a pious, learned, and
useful clergy; an honest commonalty,—and the universal
love and reverence. These supplications are echoed, it may
be at other times and in other forms of expression, by every
Christian minister and congregation. The service should
have a suitable parallel on the day of the election of the
representative assembly, which should be set apart throughout the kingdom for the business of the election alone. A
special service might be appointed by the Church,—and all
other persuasions invited, according to their several manners,
to solemnise the public act, and seek for it the divine blessing.
In so doing, we "act on the only received and uniformly
continued sense of mankind. That sense not only, like a
wise architect, hath built up the august fabric of states, but
like a provident proprietor, to preserve the structure from
profanation and ruin, as a sacred temple, purged from all the
impurities of fraud, and violence, and injustice, and tyranny,
hath solemnly and for ever consecrated the commonwealth,
and all that officiate in it. This consecration is made, that all
who administer in the government of men, in which they
stand in the person of God himself, should have high and
worthy notions of their function and destination; that their
hope should be full of immortality; that they should not look
to the paltry pelf of the moment, nor to the temporary and
transient praise of the vulgar, but to a solid permanent existence, in the permanent part of their nature, and to a
permanent fame and glory, in the example they leave as a rich
inheritance to the world." . . . . . "Every sort of moral,
every sort of civil, every sort of politic institution, aiding the
rational and natural ties that connect the human understanding and affections to the divine, are not more than

necessary in order to build up that wonderful structure, man, whose prerogative it is to be, in a great degree, a creature of his own making, and who, when made as he ought to be made, is destined to hold no trivial place in the creation. But whenever man is put over men, as the better nature ought ever to preside, in that case more particularly he should, as nearly as possible, be approximated to his perfection." [1]

The proposal for such a consecration of the national work cannot be strange in the ears of the people, for it is in accordance with the spirit of their common prayer for the High Court of which the representatives are a part,—that all things may be so ordered and settled by their endeavours upon the best and surest foundations, that peace and happiness, truth and justice, religion and piety, may be established among us for all generations.

[1] *Reflections*, &c., p. 137.

CHAPTER VIII.

DUTIES AND POWERS OF RETURNING OFFICERS.

THE duties on the returning officer, so far as they are affected by the proposed law, will be,—upon a dissolution of Parliament,—to receive daily from the registrar of electors the " Gazette," containing the names of candidates,[1] and to direct the publication and distribution of copies at such places as shall be most accessible to the electors. On the day of the election to receive, through the agency of the polling-clerks whom he will appoint, the voting papers; and, at its close, to report to the registrar the number of votes which have been polled,[2] and after receiving the declaration of the quota[3] to make the return to the writ of the due election of the candidate or candidates for the constituency for which he officiates. In some cases, as in large constituencies, he may be able to make that return without the assistance of the registrars;[4] in other cases, as in small or very divided constituencies, he will not be able to make it until the voting papers have been sorted by the registrars. Other and subordinate duties, such as that of finally collecting, arranging, and binding up all the voting papers of his constituency, for future reference and verification if required, are mentioned elsewhere. The day of election throughout

---

[1] See Clauses VIII. and IX., pp. 96, 97, and see Form of the Gazetted List, p. 97.

[2] Clause I.   [3] Clause III.   [4] Clauses XXIII., XXV.

the kingdom should be the same. The convenience of persons having votes as well in counties as in a borough, or corporate constituency, may be provided for in a manner hereafter suggested.

XV. The same day shall, at every general election, be appointed for the poll, throughout the kingdom, and shall be specified in the writ; but such day shall not be less than   days, nor more than   days after the date of the said writ (which writ shall be framed and expressed in such manner and form as is necessary for carrying this Act into effect), and the respective sheriffs and returning officers shall, on receipt of the writ and the precept, respectively, forthwith make proclamation, and give notice of the day of such poll, and of the respective polling-places at which the same will be taken, within the limits of their respective counties, boroughs, or districts, and for their respective constituencies.

The votes should be taken at polling places opened in every parish, and if the parish be very large and populous, at several places in the same parish. If it be populous, but not of any wide extent, a larger staff of clerks at one place might be sufficient.

It is plain that a system of registration, having any pretensions to be adapted to its true purposes, facilitating the business of the election, distinguishing between those whose qualifications have ceased and those which continue,—between the living and the dead,—must be a registration effected by different means, having for its basis the *residence* of the voter, and not the place of qualification only.[1] It is in no way necessary that expense should be incurred in the erection of polling-booths. There are few parishes in the kingdom which do not contain some building applicable to a public use, as, for example, a school-room, which, without inconvenience, could be used for one day. If, in a few remote places, such a room or building could not be found, there would be no difficulty in hiring some room in a public or

---

[1] See "*Defects on the Existing Law of Registration*," &c., by W. Albert James, 1859, pp. 42, 43, 44.

even a private house for the short period during which it would be required.

In the cases of parish school-rooms, or National or British schools, a small payment of a guinea or two for the hire of the room for a day would often be thankfully added to the subscriptions by which the institution is sustained. In order to obviate all doubts which trustees and others may entertain as to their powers for so harmless an enlargement of the purposes of the edifice, a compulsory power might very properly be given to the returning officer to use the building for a single day. It may be thus expressed :—

XVI. The returning officer for every electoral district is empowered, at a general election, to take and use as a polling-place to be occupied for that purpose during the day of election, but no longer, upon giving seven days' notice of his intention to that effect, any room or rooms of competent space in any school-house or other building supported wholly or in part by any public or parochial funds, or by any perpetual endowment, or which has been built or is supported wholly or in part by any grant under the control of the Committee of Council for Education ; and he shall pay a reasonable sum for the hire of such room or place, together with the full cost of repairing any injury or damage which may be occasioned to the premises or the furniture thereof by the said use, such hire and damages, in the event of the returning officer and the managers or trustees or owners of the said premises differing about the same, to be settled by two justices of the peace, one to be chosen by the returning officer, and the other by the said trustees, managers, or owners.

The schoolmasters of the National and British Schools who would be liberated for the day from their duties, would form a class in which very intelligent clerks would be found to assist in the reception of the votes : they are not often so well paid as to make the remuneration for their extra services on that day unacceptable. The pupil teachers would in many cases also be competent and useful assistants ; nor would attention to duties of this nature be in any case undeserving of regard as an element of education. Every vote, it will be remembered, is expressed on a document, which remains as a record, and there is no room for error on the part of the clerk, which is not easy of correction.[1] The process of receiving the voting papers was pointed out with much detail in former editions. These are now, for the most part, superseded by the Ballot Act. ·As an additional provision, it is proposed that there shall be a tabular book kept at the poll by a clerk, having nothing to do with any other than the first name on the voting paper, and entering, as the voting paper comes to his hands, the number indorsed upon it in his book under that name. This tabular book is composed of a series of columns ruled vertically, one of which is appropriated to every candidate first named in any of the voting papers delivered to him. The form may be as follows :—

Borough of

Polling Place [A.]   _____, CLERK.

W. Pitt.	H. St. John.	W. Fortescue.	F. Campbell.	G. Methuen.	T. Osborne.
1	2	4	5	6	7
8	3	9	33	15	
12	28	10		16	
13		11		17	
14		20		18	
27		21		19	
		22		20	
		23		32	
		24			
		25			
		29			
		30			
		31			
6	3	13	2	8	1

The names at the head of the several columns in the above table represent those of supposed candidates, and the numbers underneath the several names are the numbers on the back of

---

[1] The Ballot Act has adopted the substance of the last clause as to the use of school-rooms, enabling them, however, to be taken free of charge (S. 6).

the voting papers. By adding up the number of votes given for each candidate, as is done at the foot of every column in the above table,—the state of the poll at that particular polling place would be known at any moment. If a certain number of lines were ruled horizontally across the tabular book, and each number written on one line, as soon as each column was full the number of votes shown in it would be ascertained even without the labour of counting. The computation of the entire result, when the register and voting papers are brought to the place of election, at which the returning officer or his assessor officiates, would be purely mechanical, and the work of a few minutes.

[In a modification of this system, in which it is proposed that the votes for the 298 constituencies of England and Wales should be transmitted to an Enumeration Office in London, to be under the superintendence of the Clerk of the Crown, and presided over by the chief officers of State, the following tabular form of record and publication is suggested. It is here introduced as suitable and convenient for the use of the registrars, in a later stage of the computation, under the system now proposed:—

Christian or First Names.	Surnames.	Abingdon.	Andover.	Anglesea.	Ashton-under-Lyne.	Aylesbury.	Banbury.	Barnstaple, &c.	Total of Votes to each Candidate.
Thomas Dyke	Acland.								
Hugh Edward	Adair .								
Rt. Hon. Sir C. B.	Adderley								
Edward	Ackroyd								
Ralph Shuttleworth	Allen .								
William Shepherd	Allen .								
Weston Cracroft	Amcotts								
&c. &c.	&c.								
Totals of Votes in each Constituency }									

The names of the constituencies, as well as the surnames of the candidates, to be printed in alphabetical order, and in the last column to the right the total number of votes given to each candidate to be entered, and in the lowest line the total number of votes given in each constituency.[1]

Under this modification the returning officers have only to receive and transmit the votes.   Mr. Dobbs, after adopting as a basis that each elector shall have one vote, and must vote in the constituency where he resides, but that he may vote for any candidate in the kingdom, proceeds,—"The votes of each part of the United Kingdom are now conveyed to the Enumeration Offices in London, Edinburgh, and Dublin.   Take London.   As soon as the poll closes, the deputy returning officer, in the presence of the public, covers and seals the slit in the lid of his box.   He then writes on a form the number of voting cards he has deposited in it; each clerk counts in the stamps in his register, and enters the amount on the form. The two numbers, if one clerk, or the number entered by the deputy and the total of the different clerks' number, should agree.   Under no circumstances may a deputy open the box, or allow it to be opened.   He is responsible for the conveyance of the box and written form to the chief returning officer of the constituency, who is waiting their arrival at an appointed place.   As they come in, they are opened in the presence of the chief officer, and of such deputies, magistrates, election agents, and electors as may choose to be present, and transferred into one box sufficiently large to contain them, which, when it has received the contents of all the boxes, is locked and sealed.   It is then delivered into the custody of the post officer who gives receipt, and thereupon the Post Office becomes responsible for its safe delivery at the Enumeration Office in London.   The chief returning officers throughout the kingdom add up the totals entered on the forms, and send the forms in a packet by post, telegraphing the total to the Clerk of the Crown in Chancery, who, on receiving the

---

[1] *General Representation*, &c., by Archibald E. Dobbs.   Longmans, 1872.   2nd edition.

totals from all the constituencies in England and Wales, publishes the sum as the total number of electors who have polled therein, and, dividing it by 493, the number of English and Welsh seats, declares the quotient, omitting fractions, to be the English quota.   On receiving the totals from Scotland and dividing by 60, and from Ireland dividing by 105, he declares the quotient to be the quota for Scotland and Ireland respectively."[1]

The latter provision assumes that the number of members for each of the three kingdoms is fixed. The system proposed in this treatise avoids any such prescribed limit, treating England, Scotland, and Ireland, precisely alike. The statement of the method thus suggested will, however, show that the application of the preferential and proportional system is not dependent on any adherence to one particular process, that it may be effected in various forms, and under different adaptations of electoral machinery.

It may appear that it is entering into an unnecessary degree of detail to undertake the explanation of these minor arrangements of the business of the election ; but, in truth, a closer consideration will show that there is no step which it is not important to make clear.   Upon the establishment of a rational system of representation, vast interests are depending. It is not possible to conceive any subject affecting the temporal welfare of mankind of greater importance.   The almost universal disposition is to turn aside from such considerations, with the despairing cry that it is impossible to make the representation pure and faithful.   It should therefore be shown that there is no difficulty in establishing a better state of things.   In what is proposed there is much less complexity than is daily encountered and overcome by the purest mechanical arrangements in the clearing-house of the London bankers, or in the General Post Office.   In explaining by a

---

[1] Ib., pp. 10–14, 21.   § 4. Of the Transmission of the Votes ; and § 5. Of the Enumeration of the Votes.   § 8. Of the use of the Tabular Form.

written narrative, the process of operation, every sort of machinery has an appearance of complexity. This would be immediately felt by any one who should endeavour, in words, to explain to another, who had not seen it, the operation of Jacquard's loom, or of the steam engine. An attempt is, however, made to bring the proceedings of an election of representatives,—such as it ought to be amongst an intelligent and free people in a civilized age,—as vividly as possible before the eyes of every reader.

We have reached the stage of the proceeding at which the voting papers,—some containing many and some few names, or a single name,[1] have been taken at the polling places. These, with the tabular books of the polling clerks,[2] are collected at the town or county hall, or other central place, where the returning officer presides. If there should be several polling places, they must be severally distinguished by a name or mark,—as by letters A, B, &c., so that, in sorting the voting papers, those received at the several polling places be always taken in consecutive order. In large constituencies, where the town hall or other chief point of concentration is ready of access from all the polling places, it would be desirable that the votes and tabular books should be collected several times during the day, that the process of sorting may be going on contemporaneously with the other business of the election. In such constituencies, it will soon be found that favourite candidates have votes exceeding in number their required quota, and which votes will therefore become available for the next candidate (if any) named in the voting papers.

It is probable that the voting papers will sometimes contain the name of a person on the gazetted lists, who has not offered himself as a candidate for the particular constituency to which the duties of the returning officer exclusively refer, but whom, notwithstanding the voter has, by selecting for the

---

[1] Page 124.   [2] Page 157.

first place on his paper, proposed as a fit person to represent it. Where any such names occur first on the voting paper, the business of the returning officer will be to forward them to the registrar. The returning officer is to confine his attention (except as to such transmission) to the voting papers in which the name of a candidate, or of the several candidates, for his particular constituency stand at the head,— that is, are named successively, one or two, or any successive number, according to the voters' peculiar predilection, down to the point at which he introduces the name of one on the list who is not a candidate for his special constituency. As soon as such other name intervenes, a further combination is introduced, which brings the appropriation within the department of the registrar.

Suppose the case of several thousand voters, and one or two candidates for the constituency, having each more than the quota required. The returning officer ascertains, first, who have the majorities, counting on this occasion only the voting papers in which the candidate has the first votes,—he then separates the 1840, or 2000, or whatever the quota may be, last polled for the candidate who has the majority, and causes his name, where it stands at the head of the other papers, to be cancelled. The second name on those papers then becomes the first, and the voting papers making up the quota for the second candidate are taken, and his name cancelled on the remaining papers, bringing a third name forward to the first place, and so on, until the name of one who is a candidate elsewhere occurs, or until the quota can no longer be made up; and the returning officer then forwards the remaining voting papers to the registrar.

These duties may be prescribed by the rules[1] or laws which follow:—

---

[1] These clauses would with more propriety form rules of the same law, but they have been made distinct clauses for the greater convenience of reference.

XVII. The returning officer of every constituency shall, at the close of the poll, and as soon as is practicable after the voting papers have been collected, ascertain and certify to the registrar the aggregate number of votes which has been polled by the constituency of which he is such returning officer,[1] and he shall then ascertain and declare the number of voters which has been polled in the same constituency for the several candidates respectively, counting for such purpose only the votes for the candidates whose names are placed at the head of or first on the respective voting papers; and when the returning officer shall have received from the registrars their declaration of the quota of voters at such general election as aforesaid,[2] if one or more candidate or candidates shall have so polled in such constituency the quota or quota of votes, then the said returning officer shall (after setting apart the said quota or quotas as hereinafter directed) forthwith return the candidate or candidates for whom the majorities or greater numbers of voters of the said constituency shall have polled (he or they having such quota or quotas as aforesaid) as the member or members to serve in Parliament for such constituency.

XVIII. The candidate, whose name is placed first in the voting papers of the constituency for which he is a candidate, shall be the candidate for whom the votes in such voting papers respectively shall be taken; and if the quota of such candidate shall not be made up by such votes, then the votes in the voting papers of the same constituency in which he shall be placed second, and then third, and so on successively, shall be taken for him in case all the names standing higher in any such voting paper shall have been cancelled as hereinafter directed.

The next law prescribes the order in which every voting paper is to be appropriated.

XIX. All the votes on voting papers in which any candidate is named alone shall be appropriated to him; and if such votes be less in number than the quota, then the votes on voting papers in which he is named first or first after any cancelled name or names shall be so appropriated, and if such votes shall exceed in number the quota required, the number of the said quota and no more (except as otherwise hereinafter provided) shall be appropriated to such candidate, and such quota shall be made up by taking—*first*, the voting papers that contain the uncancelled name of no other candidate; and *next*, the voting papers that contain the uncancelled names of one, two, or other number of candidates, successively, taking always the voting papers respectively containing a smaller, before those containing a larger number of such uncancelled names; and when it shall appear that two or more of such voting papers contain an equal number of

---

[1] Clause L, p. 25.   [2] Clause III., p. 25.

uncancelled names of candidates, *then* the quota shall be made up of the votes polled for the said candidate, beginning at the last so polled which are otherwise equal as aforesaid, and so on to the earlier of such votes in the order of their reception as indorsed on the said voting papers ;[1] and for the purpose of recording the said order, and of ascertaining which shall be taken to form the quota in case there shall be more than one polling place, the polling places shall be distinguished by consecutive letters or marks; and the votes appearing by such indorsement to have been last received at every polling place consecutively, according to the said distinguishing numbers or marks, shall be first taken *pari passu; but so much of the foregoing rule of appropriation as directs that the voting papers containing the smaller shall be taken before those containing the larger number of names, shall be subject always to the provisions regarding locality and association contained in Clause XXIV. of this Act;* and as soon as the quota of votes to be attributed to any candidate shall be thus ascertained, the voting papers making up the said quota shall be set apart by the returning officer (or by the registrar, as the case may be); and thereupon the name of the said candidate shall be cancelled on all the remaining voting papers, by being stamped across the same by a stamp of a form to be settled and provided by the registrars, and furnished by them to the returning officer for such use.

The duties of the returning officer in the appropriation of the voting papers are now at an end, and he has only to transmit the remainder to the registrar.

XX. The returning officers, after setting apart the number of voting papers which make up the quota, or respective quotas, of the candidate or candidates (if any) so returned as aforesaid, shall, as soon as possible after the close of the poll, transmit the remainder of the said voting papers; and if no candidate has obtained the said quota and been returned as aforesaid, then they shall transmit the whole of the said voting papers to the registrars respectively, by the hands of one of the sworn poll-clerks, or some other competent messenger, accompanied by a certificate of the names of the candidates for whom such votes are given, and the number of votes given to every candidate respectively, counting only the candidates first named, or first named after the cancelled name or names in the said voting papers, together with the total number of voting papers so transmitted, and the number of registered electors who have not polled at such election.

It is necessary to provide also for other new circumstances. The increase of constituencies by the admission of several hundred towns at present unrepresented, and perhaps of many ancient as well as modern corporations, of a public character,

[1] See p. 156.

—universities and colleges,—to the right of returning representatives, will probably create many more constituencies than there are, or can be members in the House.   All, or many of the contributory boroughs, also, instead of having one member to four or five towns, may apply for an order enabling them to act severally.   Candidates will, therefore, frequently offer themselves for more than one constituency.   The candidate for Ayr may be candidate also for Campbeltown and Irvine. If Trinity College, or Lincoln's Inn, had power to make a separate return of a representative, the candidate for Trinity College, of which he may be a distinguished member, might be also a candidate for his county, or a town adjacent to his estate; and the candidate for the Society of Lincoln's Inn might be a candidate also for the metropolis or for any parish in the metropolis, according as the metropolitan community should prefer to form aggregate or separate electoral bodies.   In all cases in which one person might happen to be a candidate for more than one constituency, it would only be the returning officer for the *first* constituency, which he specifies in his notice to the registrar,[1] and which is stated in the Gazette,[2] who could, immediately after the close of the poll, return him.   If this were otherwise, there might be a conflict in the action of two constituencies.   If his quota be made up in the first constituency, he cannot be returned in the second[3] until after his votes in that constituency shall have been forwarded to the registrar, and the result certified. If his quota be not made up on the first constituency, his votes will of course be also transmitted by that returning officer to the registrar.

XXI. Where one person is a candidate for the representation of more than one constituency, all the voting papers on which he is placed No. 1, which are polled in the constituencies other than the first for which he is

---

[1] P. 97.   [2] P. 97.
[3] He may titularly represent the second or other constituencies.   See Chap. X.

described in the gazetted list as a candidate, shall be forwarded by the returning officers to the registrars as aforesaid, notwithstanding they may exceed in number the quota.

The powers and duties of the returning officer thus differ in cases where the number of votes polled by the constituency affords the quota to one or more of the candidates, and in the cases of the smaller constituencies, or where great differences of sentiment prevail, and the total number of votes given, or given for any particular candidate, is insufficient to complete the quota. In the first case he will return the candidates having the majorities, supposing each to make up at least the quota,—as duly elected, and will transmit the surplus votes to the registrar; and in the latter cases he will transmit the whole of the voting paper to the registrar, without doing more than certifying the numbers polled for every candidate, awaiting the certificate of the registrar as to the fact of any of the candidates having or not having his quota supplied by votes from other places.

Aberdeen may be taken as an example of one of the first-class constituencies.   At the last election there were two candidates; and supposing that to be the case, and that under a system such as that which has been suggested some of the voters give a preference to, and place at the head of their voting papers the names of, some candidates for other places, the computation of numbers at the close of the poll might stand as it is represented in the following certificate and letter, in which the returning officer of the city of Aberdeen is supposed to communicate the result to the registrar at Edinburgh.

Aberdeen, ·   1859.

Sir,—I certify that, at a poll this day taken for a member to serve in Parliament for the city of Aberdeen, 1,850 of the electors of the said city have given their votes for William Henry Sykes, Esq., and that the said number of votes forms a majority of the electors of the said city, or is a greater number thereof than has polled for any other candidate.

I also certify, that the said William Henry Sykes having, as aforesaid, more than the number of 1,840 votes, which number of 1,840 is the quota of votes specified in the certificate, signed by the Registrars of voters for England, Scotland, and Ireland, and contained in the *London Gazette*,

dated the   I have made my return to her Majesty's
writ to the effect that the said William Henry Sykes has been duly elected
a member to serve in Parliament for the said city.

I also certify, that I have caused 1,840 voting papers of the said 1,850
polled for the said William Henry Sykes, taken in the order prescribed by
Sect. 19 of the Act, to be sealed under my official seal, and the same are
retained by me; and that the name of the said William Henry Sykes
having been cancelled on the remaining 10 voting papers, the same respectively have been appropriated to the candidates respectively secondly
named therein, and that, after such appropriation, it appears that the votes
not polled for the said William Henry Sykes, and beyond the quota
necessary for his return as aforesaid, are 2,588 in number, and that the same
have been respectively given to, and are now appropriated for, the other candidates hereinafter named according to the numbers stated opposite to their
names respectively, viz. :—

John Farley Leith, Esq. .	1549
Lord Elcho . . .	483
Henry James Baillie, Esq.	250
Hon. Arthur Gordon	225
Edward Ellice, Jun., Esq.	48
Colonel Robert Ferguson .	30
Robert Campbell, Esq. .	2
Alexander Dunlop, Esq. .	1

And I acquaint you that I have transmitted to you, by the hands
of   , one of the poll-clerks appointed and duly sworn to
officiate at the said election, the said 2,588 voting papers.

I also certify, that it appears that 119 registered electors of the said city
have not voted at the poll this day.

I have, &c.,

_____

Returning Officer for the City of Aberdeen.

To the Registrar for Scotland.

It will be observed that the names in the above certificate,
other than that of Mr. Leith, are the names of gentlemen
who are supposed not to have been candidates for Aberdeen,
but to have been candidates elsewhere, and for whom some
Aberdeen voters have thus indicated their preference by giving
unsolicited votes.

The certificate of the returning officer in the case of the

smaller constituencies would be in a still more simple form, thus :—

Ashburton,   1859.

Sir,—I certify that at a poll this day taken for a member to serve in Parliament for the borough of Ashburton, the votes of 220 electors for the said borough were polled for the several candidates hereinafter named, being the candidates first named in the voting papers respectively, viz. :—

George Moffat, Esq.	150
Sir James Weir Hogg, Bart.	22
Charles Seale Hayne, Esq.	14
John Hardy, Esq.	10
James Taylor, Jun., Esq.	8
George Pott, Esq.	8
Henry Thoby Prinsep, Esq.	7
John Gregory, Esq.	1

And I have transmitted to you by the hands of   , one of the poll-clerks appointed and duly sworn to officiate at the said election, the said 220 voting papers.

I also certify, that it appears that sixteen registered electors of the said borough have not voted at the poll this day.

I have, &c.,

————————

Returning Officer of the Borough of Ashburton.

To the Registrar for England.

Another provision with respect to the duties of the returning officers will be that which relates to the returns they will be required to make of members for their several constituencies,—not founded upon their own calculations of the number of votes, but upon the casting up of the votes in the offices of the registrars, in which the votes polled in other constituencies are brought in aid. In these cases the certificates of the registrars will be the evidence and the authority on which the returning officers will necessarily act.

XXII. Upon the receipt by the returning officer of the certificate of the registrar, that the quota of votes of any candidate for whom a vote or votes has or have been given in the constituency of which he is such returning officer, has been completed, or that such candidate has obtained a comparative majority, as hereinafter mentioned, and if the member, or full number of members which the same constituency is entitled to elect, shall not have been returned, then the said returning officer shall, if such candidate has polled a majority or greater number of votes of such constituency than any other candidate, *and any of such votes shall have been appropriated to him according to the rules hereinafter prescribed*, return such candidate so certified to him, or so many of such candidates as shall complete the number of members which the said constituency is entitled to elect, as duly elected to serve in Parliament; and if the candidate or candidates having a majority or greater number of votes in such constituency shall not have obtained the quota or comparative majority, as aforesaid, then the said returning officer shall so return such or so many of the said candidates, not exceeding the number the said constituency is entitled to elect, as shall be certified by the registrar to have obtained the quota or comparative majority, and who shall have polled in the said constituency such highest or higher number of votes, exclusive of the candidate or candidates who have so failed in obtaining the said quota or comparative majority; and in the ultimate computation of such majority or greater number of votes polled for any candidate in a particular constituency (who has obtained the quota or comparative majority as aforesaid), the returning officer thereof shall not regard the cancellation of the names of any such candidate on the voting papers thereof, owing to such votes being in excess of the quota of such candidate, but shall, in computing such majority or greater number of votes of the particular constituency, count such votes, whether the same be or be not cancelled as aforesaid, both for the candidate or candidates whose name or names has or have been so cancelled, and for the candidate or candidates to whom they have been appropriated; and shall also add thereto all other votes of the same constituency which shall be appropriated to him or them under Clause XXVI. of this Act.

The effect of this law may be illustrated by supposing, in the above case of Aberdeen, that the registrars had certified that Mr. Leith, Mr. Baillie, Lord Elcho, and Mr. Ellice had, and that no other of the candidates had, obtained the full complement of votes. Mr. Leith would then be returned as the second member. Assuming that Aberdeen were entitled to return a third member, that the other successful candidates were Lord Elcho, Mr. Baillie, and Mr. Ellice, and that none of the 250 votes given for Mr. Baillie had been appropriated to him, his quota being completed without their aid, by voters of the constituency to which he had offered himself, or the neighbouring constituencies who, according to Law XXIV., had a prior right to have their votes appropriated to him; and supposing that the whole, or part, of the 483 Aberdeen votes given for Lord Elcho had been appropriated to him, the residue of his quota being made up by his supporters in other places, he would be the third member entitled to be returned for Aberdeen.

Many other results may be supposed, to show the working of the system. Thus Lord Elcho, Mr. Baillie, Mr. Ellice, and the candidates mentioned as having a smaller number of Aberdeen votes, may all be elected by the constituencies for which they are candidates, and their names being thereupon cancelled on the Aberdeen voting papers, those votes will be given to the next candidate named on each paper. If such next candidate be Mr. Gordon (although it is of course improbable that all of them would be given to one person) the number of Aberdeen votes for Mr. Gordon would be raised from 225 to 1,039, and might, with his votes elsewhere, entitle him to be returned for Aberdeen. It would not follow in either of the cases last supposed, that, because the number of Aberdeen votes which are actually appropriated to Lord Elcho or Mr. Gordon may be few, the number of Aberdeen voters who have placed their names on their voting papers may not be very much more numerous. Many of the voters of that city who have voted for other candidates, successful or unsuccessful, whether they were candidates for Aberdeen or for other constituencies, may have placed the names of Lord Elcho or Mr. Gordon also on their voting papers, and these votes in the ultimate computation, as directed by the foregoing clause, and by a subsequent clause (XXVI.) will be reckoned as votes polled for the two unsuccessful candidates. Many of the votes given for Mr. Leith, Mr. Baillie, and others, might have contained also the name of Colonel Sykes, and many of the votes polled for Colonel Sykes might have contained also the names of Lord Elcho, Mr. Leith, and Mr. Gordon, and therefore, although as to the first votes the state of the poll appears as it is above set out by the returning officer, yet on the ultimate declaration of the poll it is not impossible (although improbable) that Colonel Sykes and the other successful candidates, whoever they may be, had as many as 4,388 votes each.   It would occupy a large space to describe all the possible results of the free manifestation of thought and sentiment which would be the consequence of the liberation and conscientious employment of the electoral forces which are now latent, and wasted or mischievously exercised.

It will be observed that the latter part of Clause XXII. which prescribes the ultimate method to be employed by the returning officers in computing the local majorities, is designed further to indicate and develop the especial preferences of local and special constituencies.   In giving to every constituency its proper share or material weight in the actual composition of the representative body, it has been necessary to equalize the force of every vote by appropriating it to one candidate only.   When the representive body is completed there is no longer any reason for refusing to any elector the full manifestation of the confidence he has expressed in the representatives of his choice, or for withholding from any member the moral influence which will naturally flow from the multiplied number, as well as the character of his constituents and supporters.   The operation of this final method of computation may be further illustrated thus :—Suppose Norwich to return three members, and that there are six candidates, A to F, whose votes, counting not only those at the head, but also the second, third, and all successive votes given for any of them on the Norwich voting papers (so long as the name of a non-candidate for that city does not intervene), stand as follows :—

A 3,500   D 1,500
B 3,000   E 1,200
C 2,500   F 1,000

The Norwich voters are here supposed to have voted some perhaps for one of their candidates, some for two, some for three or more. Some voters may even have inserted all the names in the order of their preference. In the business of appropriation, according to Law XIX., taking the quota at 2,000, the first votes given to A will be reduced to that number, and the surplus of the first votes distributed to the next names on the various papers. The same process will take place with B, distributing the surplus of his first votes and any others which B may have acquired from the distribution of A's surplus, in like manner. But 4,000 Norwich voters are now exhausted, and in doing this, perhaps a large portion of the papers on which the names of C, D, E, and F stood, may have been exclusively appropriated to A or B, and served to complete the number required for their return.

Now it may be that C, D, and E are candidates of much local popularity, but without any considerable fame beyond the walls of the city, whilst F might be a person of an eminent political, scientific, or literary reputation, or a Norfolk gentleman regarded by some of the citizens as one of the worthies of their county. F, from these causes might have numerous votes in Norfolk, in the metropolis, in the universities, or in other parts of the kingdom, and thus be returned, although no more than 500, or a smaller number, of the citizens of Norwich had given him their first votes, or their second or third votes after A or B. It then becomes the duty of the returning officer under the foregoing clause—on receiving the registrar's certificate that F has, and that C, D, and E have not, obtained a quota or comparative majority—to return F as well as A and B as members for the city of Norwich.

It is probable in the supposed case of Norwich, as in that of Aberdeen, that many of the voters for the non-candidates who have failed, may have placed the names of some of the three successful candidates in a lower place on their voting papers, and the ultimate declaration of the state of the Norwich poll may, therefore, show that each of the three successful candidates, A, B, and F, has a considerably larger number of Norwich supporters than appears in the first statement of the poll, given above.

The portion of the above law which makes it one condition of the return of a candidate for a particular constituency that some of the votes thereof shall not only have been tendered, but actually appropriated to him, when coupled with the provisions of Clause XXIV., which regulate the appropriation of votes, according to the neighbourhood or nature of the different constituencies, constitute a further security that the members shall have an intimate and personal relation with the special constituencies by which they are severally elected. The votes so appropriated must be those of the constituencies for which they were candidates, and those who are nearest to, and most likely to be connected with, and interested in, the same localities.

A word may here be added to remove any impression which a superficial view of the supposed result of the Norwich election may create, that some injustice has been done to C, D, and E, or their supporters, by the election of F. The cardinal principle is, that no vote can be appropriated to, or affect the return of, more than one member; and, therefore, when the votes for A and B are appropriated, the whole, or a large part, of those given for C, D, and E, being on the same papers, would by that means be exhausted. None of them could be used to aid the return of more than one person. And as to the Norwich votes on which either C, D, or E were placed first, it may be assumed to the credit of those voters that they have sufficient knowledge of their contemporaries, and sufficient interest in political affairs, not to confine their appreciation to those candidates exclusively, but to have provided other alternatives in their voting papers, according to which their votes will be ultimately appropriated to some member of like principle or character who may be chosen by the majorities or minorities of other constituencies.

The state of the Norwich poll, however, is not likely to be fully represented in the above table. Some citizens of Norwich might be natives of other parts of England, or of Scotland, or Ireland, and be influenced by sentiments in favour of candidates connected with such other places, or may have especial predilections overruling any local feeling, and desire to give such a direction to their votes as shall contribute to the return of candidates other than those who have offered themselves to the city of Norwich. Thus, in addition to the votes given for the candidates A to F, as above stated, suppose there are first, or first uncancelled, votes of citizens of Norwich for—

G 22		K 12
H 17		L 4
I 16		M 3

The registrars, having only to acquaint the returning officers of the ultimate result of the appropriation, will, under Clause XXV., inform them which of the candidates G, H, I, K, L, M, have, and which have not, obtained the necessary quota or comparative majority; but whether they have or not been thus successful, the Norwich return will not be affected, for A, B, and F are the successful candidates to whom the greatest number of the Norwich voters have given their primary and effectual support.

The discretion which some of the Norwich voters are thus supposed to have exercised, in setting a higher regard on general, national, intellectual, or social predilections, than on those which are governed simply by locality, cannot be a just subject of complaint by any of their fellow-citizens, for the voters so acting have done nothing which abridges or invades in the smallest degree the political power of the other inhabitants of Norwich, but, on the contrary, have in fact increased that power; for, in proposing for the choice of the electors of Norwich several other candidates, and voting for them instead of the Norwich candidates, those minorities of electors have, in fact, abdicated their power of influencing the Norwich return, and left the election entirely in the hands of the other citizens. At the same time, though powerless at Norwich, these small minorities are not necessarily so elsewhere. They may have had an important influence in assisting to complete the number of votes required for their favourite candidates, as is seen by looking at the fact which has been supposed to have taken place at this election, where a few of the voters of many other and perhaps remote constituencies, including possibly some natives of Norwich, who in distant places retain their affection for the place of their birth, have given to the 1,000 electors of Norwich—it may be of wider intelligence, higher intellectual range, or more comprehensive sympathies—the means of placing F in the position of one of the chosen candidates for that city.

One other hypothesis will suffice to explain the electoral position of such of the Aberdeen and Norwich voters, in the cases supposed, as may have placed the names of unsuccessful candidates at the head of their voting papers. None of these votes can be at first appropriated to any candidate whose name is placed lower on the paper ; because, until the general election is over, it cannot be known whether the first-named candidate might not be one of those who succeed, and to whose success that vote may contribute. Under a subsequent law (Clause XXVI.) all votes in this condition will be appropriated to the highest successful candidate on each voting paper. If the highest successful candidate of the voting paper of an Aberdeen or Norwich voter be an Aberdeen or Norwich member, the returning officer will reckon him among that constituency; but however that may be, the voter becomes part of the constituency of the member whose name stands highest on his paper, and in whom he has thus expressed greater confidence than in any other with regard to whom he has been able to obtain the concurrence of a sufficient number of his constituents. It is thus next to impossible for any elector,—except his sympathies be very narrow, —to fail of being represented by some one whom he has nominated for that purpose.

CHAPTER IX.

THE DUTIES OF THE REGISTRARS.

THE establishment of registrars of electors in London, Edinburgh, and Dublin, who may promote uniformity of action by the officers appointed to frame the local registers, and attend to their constant correction, forming a constant medium of communication in this important matter, would be of vast advantage, even if their duties ended there.[1]   They

[1] The Select Committee of the House of Lords thus reported (26th June 1860), "The present system of registration is very imperfect, and fails to make effectual provision either for placing on the register all who are entitled to vote, or for removing from it names improperly placed there. Whatever *approach* to accuracy there is in the existing register seems to be mainly due to the voluntary agency of political associations." In a pamphlet on registration, by Mr. W. A. James, the author says:—" A thorough improvement of the system generally, and a new arrangement of the registers, may be made conducive to many reforms in the present mode of completing parliamentary elections.   There is no reason why the provisions for registration should not afford every protection to the rights of individual electors, and entail no trouble or annoyance, or why the register should not be accurate and perfect.   It is simply a matter of business detail, in which few difficulties are presented, and these such as may be overcome.   Much practical experience has been gained, which was wanting at the passing of the Reform Bill of 1832, and may be brought to bear in constructing and perfecting machinery which shall effect all the results desired.   Any reform to be satisfactory must not be a mere patching up of the present system by amending it in isolated defective parts, but deal comprehensively with the whole, and in a manner in keeping with the change of circumstances time has introduced."   "The facilities derived from a vast network of railways and steam-navigation, the rapid interchange of intelligence by the electric telegraph, numerous post-office

may yet perform other very important functions in facilitating the action of voters, saving the expense and labour of travelling, and affording the means of receiving the votes of electors unable to attend personally. On these points, and others which are not necessarily connected with the scheme of representation which it is the chief purpose of the present treatise to submit, something will be said in a subsequent page.

Some portion of the duties of the registrars, in respect of this system of forming the representative assembly, has been necessarily mentioned elsewhere. They are to superintend all the local and other registers of electors, ascertain and certify the quota of voters at general elections,[1] and conduct the occasional elections.[2] They are to receive the names of the candidates, and the payments suggested, which will form a fund to be called the "Registrars' Fund," applicable to the support of the establishment, and the expense of performing its various duties;[3] and they are to publish the lists of the candidates in the respective Gazettes, and transmit copies to the various constituencies.[4]

The registrars, in their duties of sorting and appropriating the votes which are forwarded to them from the various constituencies, will be strictly governed by prescribed rules, calculated most perfectly to give effect to the will of every individual elector, as expressed on his voting paper.

The returning officers at the general election which is now supposed to be in progress will in many of the larger consti-

reforms, the advantages of book-postage and registered letters, the perfected system for the registration of deaths, and a hundred other like improvements, were unknown when the 'Registration Clauses' were under discussion. All these may be brought to bear practically upon the business of registration, and tend to its perfection." (P. 61.) That the registration of electors should be allowed to remain in its present state is a lamentable proof of the utter insincerity of public men on Parliamentary Reform.

[1] Clauses I. and III.   [2] Clauses XXIX., XXX., and XXXI.
[3] Clause VII.   [4] Clauses VIII. and IX.

tuencies, have been enabled to make their returns of members; and in those places it will be only the excess of, or unappropriated, voting papers that will be transmitted to the registrars. The completed returns will have greatly reduced the aggregate number of voting papers of which the results are undetermined,—the number unappropriated, however, would be still large. In addition to these there would be the whole of the votes given in the smaller constituencies, which have not singly sufficient electors to make up a quota, and in others, where a sufficient number had not concurred in doing so.

A large amount of clerical or mechanical labour will, of course, be necessary in dealing with the mass of documents thus brought to the offices of the registrars, and an extensive space must necessarily be occupied as office room for the few days during which the sorting and appropriation of the voting papers are in progress; but neither will probably be greater than is employed daily at the General Post-office.

The registrars will have a small permanent establishment of experienced clerks attached to their several offices. They will, on the occasion of a general election, have the assistance of the poll-clerks from the local constituencies, by whom the lists are brought from the returning officers, and of whom all the more efficient may be retained during the business of the appropriation of votes. Of these clerks there will be 400 or 500, or more. They may be further assisted by a sufficient number of clerks of character and experience, permitted to attend, at extra remuneration, for two or three days, from other public offices. The services of the several classes of clerks thus employed will be paid from the "Registrars' Fund."

At the point to which the election is now supposed to have reached, the registrars have before them the certificates of the various returning officers, and the voting papers which have accompanied them. Their duties, and the

N

laws by which those duties are to be regulated, have now to be stated.

Some of the registrar's clerks being provided with tables of the names of the candidates arranged alphabetically, at the head of distinct columns, like the tabular book before described,[1] the number of votes expressed on the returning officers' certificates to have been given for every candidate may be called over, and speedily entered under the names of the respective candidates, thereby showing how many votes every candidate has received, according to those certificates. This process, when completed—which it would probably be in an hour or two,—will show that many candidates who have been returned as elected by the constituencies which they named first in the gazetted list,[2] have received votes in other constituencies. This will doubtless be the case to a great extent with all men of high character and eminence. In all such cases, the names of the members so previously returned will be cancelled upon the voting papers in which their names are repeated, in the manner directed by Section XIX.

The registrars have then to address themselves to the cases in which no returns of members have been made. The numbers of votes expressed in the certificates of the returning officers have now ceased to be guides, as to many candidates; for by displacing the names of the members who have been already returned, the names of other candidates are brought forward to the first place on many of the voting papers, which will make so many additions to the votes now to be counted for such other candidates. The extent of this alteration will be readily ascertained by the use of the tabular books which have been mentioned. Every clerk having the charge of the voting papers of a constituency will in a few minutes ascertain the numerical variation effected in those

[1] Page 157.   [2] See Clause XXI.

papers by the cancellation of the first names upon a certain portion of them, and can report the result of such alteration, —that is to say, what additions are thereby made to the votes given for other candidates. Additions will continue to be made in like manner as the other quotas are completed, and thus the name of every candidate having the quota will soon be ascertained. The completion of such quotas must then be certified by the registrars to the returning officers of the several constituencies, where votes for such candidates have been polled.

XXIII. The registrars respectively, as soon as it appears by the voting papers appropriated to the respective candidates (according to the rules herein contained), that the quota of votes has been polled for any candidate, shall forthwith transmit a certificate of that fact to the returning officers for the respective constituencies in which votes have been polled for such candidate or candidates, stating therein the number of votes of every constituency respectively which have been appropriated to make up such quota.

The duty of the registrars, as well as of the returning officers, with regard to setting apart the voting papers appropriated to every candidate, as soon as the appropriation has been finally made, and also with regard to the cancellation of the names of the same candidates, wherever they occur, on the remaining voting papers, has already been prescribed.[1] The same clause also points out the order in which the voting papers shall be taken, up to the point at which they cease to be under the jurisdiction of the returning officers. It is now necessary to prescribe other rules as to the order in which the votes shall be appropriated to the candidates, in cases which cannot be dealt with by any particular returning officer, because the representation of two or more constituencies is involved. In these arrangements,— after disposing of the votes of the particular constituency or constituencies for which a candidate has offered himself,—it is important that there should, in the subsequent appropriation, be a prescribed order to be followed without possibility

[1] Clause XIX., p. 161.

of deviation, that the result may of necessity be accepted without the possibility of complaint.

It should be observed that the proposed law is now framed in contemplation of the cases of candidates who are found to have, amongst the unappropriated voting papers of different constituencies, more than the quota of votes ; and the simple point to be determined is, which of such votes shall 'be actually and finally appropriated to the several candidates having such excess of votes, and which of such votes shall go over to another candidate standing lower on the voting paper.

XXIV. The registrars shall, in the appropriation of the votes, proceed according to the following rules :—

A. If the candidate be a candidate for the representation of several constituencies, and shall not have been returned as a member for the constituency that appears by the gazetted list to be the first constituency for which he has declared himself a candidate, there shall be taken for him,

1, the votes polled for him in such first-named constituency ;

2, then the votes polled for him in the second and third-named and other following constituencies, for which he has so offered himself consecutively ;

3, then the votes polled for him in the remainder of the constituencies of the United Kingdom in the order hereafter mentioned.

B. If the quota of any candidate be not made up of votes polled for him in the constituency or constituencies for which he has, as appears by the gazetted list, offered himself as a candidate, then,

(a) If he be a candidate for a county or a division of a county, or other district, comprising within its geographical limits any borough or other local constituency, there shall be taken for him,

1, the votes polled for him in the constituencies comprised within such geographical limits in the alphabetical order of the names of such borough or local constituencies ; and

2, then the votes polled for him in the boroughs or local constituencies nearest to any part of the external boundary of the said geographical limit successively, in the order of their proximity, so far as they shall be included within an area of [twenty] miles from such boundary ;

3, then the votes polled for him in other local constituencies, in their alphabetical order;

4, then the votes polled for him in the constituencies of the universities, colleges, and other bodies, not restricted to geographical limits, in their alphabetical order :

(b) If he be a candidate for a local constituency, but not for any county or division of a county, or other district, having within its geographical limits any borough or local constituency, there shall be taken for him,

1, the votes polled for him in the county or division of a county, in which the local constituency for which he is a candidate shall be situated, in the order of the proximity of the locality in which such votes are registered ;

2, then the votes polled for him in the remainder of the local constituencies in their alphabetical order ;

3, then the votes polled for him in the constituencies of the universities, colleges, and other bodies not restricted to geographical limits, in their alphabetical order.

(c) If he be a candidate for any university, college, or other body, not restricted to geographical limits, there shall be taken for him,

1, the votes polled for him in all other like constituencies not restricted to geographical limits, in their alphabetical order ;

2, then the votes polled for him in the local constituencies, in their alphabetical order.

Provided always, that the votes polled by electors of constituencies of England, Scotland, or Ireland, respectively, shall be first taken for the respective candidates for whom the same are polled, who are candidates for constituencies in the kingdom in which such votes are polled, and then the votes polled in any of the same kingdoms, for candidates for constituencies in the other kingdoms respectively, in the order in which the same are above expressed, and subject to the rules of appropriation herein contained. And in order to carry out regularly and invariably the said rules, the registrars shall before every general election prepare, revise, and jointly sign, tables showing the relation of every local constituency, in respect of proximity to the other constituencies, within the respective limits aforesaid, and also showing the alphabetical order of each class of the said several constituencies in England, Scotland, and Ireland respectively, and the votes shall then be taken in the order expressed in such tables.

The Rule B., which may perhaps be modified and rendered more complete, is designed to give due effect to all local attachments and legitimate influences arising from family, traditional, territorial, or other causes. It will give to every landed proprietor the opportunity of connecting himself, or preserving his relation politically with the district in which his estates are chiefly situated, by enabling him to select a constituency embracing that portion of the country. There is no sound reason for any jealousy of such natural connections,—on the contrary, they are capable of being made the sources of some of the most inestimable of social benefits,— and which more than compensate for their occasional abuse,— an abuse which, there is reason to hope, will be constantly less and less frequent, and will cease altogether as interest and duty become obviously in harmony, and every proprietor feels that his influence depends upon the existence of an attached, a populous, and an instructed neighbourhood.

The voting papers liberated from the claim of one candidate, as his quota is completed, become votes for the next candidate who is mentioned upon them, and, being appropriated to him, will go to make up his quota. The same process of completion and cancellation will go on, according to the rules which have been stated,—hour by hour, with great rapidity, until the time comes when the remaining voting papers,—still taking only the names of the candidates which from time to time are thus made to stand first in every paper,—do not furnish enough to make up the quota for any remaining candidate. The process has been simply that of sorting the voting papers and arranging them under the several names which appear uncancelled at the head of every paper ; and as each new quota has been completed and set apart, and a member thereupon returned, the name of such member has been cancelled on all other voting papers except those which are thus set apart.

At this stage of the election,—as a quota is no longer found for any candidate, and as no voting paper can be appropriated to any name standing below the first, so long as the first is still unchosen and there is a possibility of his being elected, it becomes necessary to introduce another rule for ascertaining on which of the remaining candidates the choice of the remaining electors has fallen. Let it be supposed that 1,227,274 voters (the whole number on the register in 1857, as before stated) had polled at a general election,—that number being divided by 654. the quota would be 1,876 ; and let it also be supposed that by the process of appropriation of votes, up to this stage of the election, 300 candidates have received the quota and been returned. In this state of things 354 members are still wanting to complete the House ; and as the election of 300 members has necessarily disposed of 562,800 votes, every elector of that number being represented by the man whom he has chosen, —there remain 664,474 votes unappropriated, and which are applicable to the election of the 354 members yet to be elected. Let it also be supposed that there were originally 1,800 candidates,—somewhat less than three for every seat, and therefore that of these candidates 1,500 still remain whose success or failure is undetermined.

To obtain as nearly as possible an equal quota for all, it is necessary to adopt a process for eliminating the names of the candidates having the smaller number of votes. This was first done by cancelling their names, one by one, and thus raising on every voting paper the next name in succession to the place of the cancelled candidate, and thereby at each step bringing some other and uncancelled candidate nearer to the attainment of the quota. Following out this idea, it was, in the first edition of this work, proposed, at this stage of the election, to cancel on the voting papers, first the name of every candidate who had not, on the unappropriated voting papers, a number of votes, including both actual or contingent votes, amounting to the quota ; and if (as was most probable) the appropriation made after that process should still fail to complete the House, then to compute the number of all actual and contingent votes for each of the remaining candidates on the unappropriated voting papers, and take out, one by one, those who had the smallest number, until none but the required number of favourite, and therefore selected, candidates should remain.

The term " elimination " may be used to describe the method by which the excluded candidates are withdrawn. If no more than a hundred are to be chosen out of a thousand, however the process be conducted, nine hundred must be eliminated. Whether we begin at the least popular names and proceed upwards, cancelling the names until the hundred only are left, or begin by electing the highest on the poll, and descend until the hundred shall be chosen, and the remaining nine hundred excluded, the result, if the name at the head of every voting paper be alone regarded, will be the same ; but if the principle of contingent voting, the only method yet suggested for preventing uncertainty of action and an incalculable waste of the electoral power, be adopted, and the cancellation of each name be followed by giving the vote immediately to the next name on the voting paper, the result may be very different. It is convenient, therefore, to distinguish these methods by describing the upward process as one of *elimination*, and the downward process as one of *selection*. The result of discussion as well as of the experience gained in the tentative application of this system of voting, in the United States,[1] and gathered also from the operation of the cumulative vote in this country, has led the author to return, with little variation, to the method of eliminating the candidates having the smallest number of votes, suggested in his earlier publications on this subject,[2] notwithstanding the greater apparent complexity which had induced him to omit it in the later editions of the treatise. It is, however, desirable that each process should be stated and considered, the better

[1] Appendix M, *infra.*
[2] *Treatise on the Election of Representatives*, &c., 1st ed. (1859), pp. 214–218. *Journal of the Statistical Society*, September, 1860, pp. 351-2.

to test the comparative merits of the method of appropriation which has been ultimately adopted, and which is now proposed, as a rule not only superior to any other method which has yet been suggested, but possessing every quality that is practically needful.

1. The elimination of the candidates having less of public support, may commence with the candidate having the smallest number of votes actual or contingent,—or, in other words, the candidate whose name is mentioned on the smallest number of voting papers, whether at their head or in any other position upon them; and this being ascertained, by cancelling the name of such candidate throughout the voting papers; then that of the next candidate in like circumstances, and so on until only so many are left as shall complete the House.

This process gives an undue weight to mere aggregate numbers,—or to the multitude as compared with the few,—a preponderance which is the great danger of popular government. This effect is immediately seen when it is considered, that, by counting every name on every voting paper for the purpose of determining which candidate is the least popular that the elimination may begin by excluding him,—the effect of each paper is multiplied in the ratio of the number of names which it contains, and thereby a multiplied force is given to the combinations of large bodies of voters, or of parties, which would enable them, by the use of prepared or printed lists of candidates, to overpower the deliberate voices of the less numerous classes, and the more thoughtful electors. Although the party nominees could not be elected until their votes severally reached the quota, or placed them at the head of the poll, their success would indirectly, and scarcely less effectually, be promoted by the cancellation of the names of other candidates who were put forward by smaller numbers of voters, and who were, therefore, the first to be excluded.

2. Instead of computing the number of repetitions of each

name on *all* the voting papers, which perhaps for the most part remain with the local returning officers, it was in the first edition of this work proposed to diminish the labour of computation, by including in it none but the unappropriated voting papers after the first part of the election had been completed—namely, only the 664,474 remaining votes in the stage of the particular election now supposed. This, however, would be inequitable to the extent in which it gave an undue weight to the unappropriated over the appropriated voting papers. If, for example, one of the unappropriated voting papers should have upon it thirty uncancelled names, and it be referred to and counted thirty times on the computation which is to determine what candidates are to be excluded, it has obviously a far greater force than any appropriated paper, which, on the return of the candidate nominated upon it,—although there might have been fifty names below,—had been immediately allotted as one of the quota of the elected member, and thereafter referred to no more.

3. Every computation of actual and contingent votes which gives them an equal value, or which, in other words, permits a vote that may be in the middle or at the bottom of a list of thirty, forty, or fifty names, to have the same numerical weight in the election or rejection of a candidate that is given to the vote which the same elector has placed at the head of his voting paper, is radically inconsistent with the principle which it is the design of this system to embody,—that of giving to no vote more than a single voice, and that this voice should be the expression of the highest and most deliberate preference of the elector. The name which is placed first on every paper is that of the candidate for whom the elector votes. The subsequent names, however they may, for a contingent purpose, express relative preferences, are not to be regarded so long as a prior name remains uncancelled, and is capable of being chosen. If, therefore, the same weight be given to the name which is, say, the tenth, on the

voting paper of A, as is given to the name which is first on the voting paper of B, positive injustice is done by disregarding the will of B, to a far greater degree than the will of A can be said to be obeyed. The very moderate or faint appreciation of one is balanced against the highest expression of the preference of the other. To moderate this consequence it was first suggested that the value of every vote, for the purpose of determining the order of elimination, should be computed by its position on the voting paper. The computation would be very laborious, but that being a merely mechanical difficulty, would be overcome. A more serious objection is, that it is open to the vicious operation already referred to, of enabling numbers to obtain, by organization, an undue preponderance.

4. The method proposed in the last edition of this work was that of selection. It has been supposed that there are at this stage of the election, 664,474 unappropriated votes, and 1,500 unchosen candidates, which, if the votes were equally divided, would afford 442 for every candidate. They would be very unequally divided. Some names would probably not appear at the *head* of any of the voting papers, and some at the head of very few, and it will follow that some candidates will have many more than 442 votes. By merely sorting the voting papers, and placing together all those which have at their head the name of the same candidate, the number of actual votes for every candidate might be readily counted. The same process would be followed as to the candidate having the next greatest number, and so on, until the remaining 354 members had been thus selected. This method was recommended by its greater simplicity, and its tendency, therefore, to remove the objection that the proposed system of election was too complicated for its purpose. It is, however, in one important respect eminently defective. The result is that all the voting papers which have been appropriated to so many of the supposed 1,500 candidates as come after the 354, that by the

latest distribution have acquired the comparative majorities, are wholly thrown away and ineffectual,—however many subsequent and contingent votes there may be on such voting papers, below the unsuccessful candidate named at the head of each paper. One great purpose of the electoral system of a self-governing nation is to elicit from the voter, and encourage him to put forward, all the resources of his thought and knowledge in the choice of legislators in whom he has the most perfect confidence ; and it is of essential importance that he should not be deterred from doing this by any apprehension that owing to the obscurity or the unpopularity of the candidate whom individually he knows and would trust, his vote would be lost if he ventured to place the name of such candidate at the head of his paper. This method of selecting the remaining candidates according to their comparative majorities, regarding only the names at the head of the voting papers, notwithstanding its simplicity, has therefore been abandoned.

5. The method which it has been resolved to pursue, as combining greater advantages than any other, is to reduce the number of candidates remaining at this stage of the election, by taking out the names of all those who have the smallest number of actual votes,—that is, who are named at the *head* of the smallest number of voting papers, and appropriating each vote to the candidate standing *next* in order on each paper, until only so many candidates are left as shall be sufficient to fill the House.

The process may be embodied in the following law :—

XXV. When the votes shall have been appropriated to all the candidates who have obtained the quota of votes respectively, according to the foregoing rules, the registrars shall then cancel their names on the unappropriated voting papers, and shall sort and arrange the whole of the unappropriated voting papers, allotting them to the remaining candidates whose names are after such cancellation at the head of the same voting papers respectively, and shall compute the number of votes which have been given for the respective candidates whose names remain at the head of the respective voting papers as last aforesaid ; and shall make and publish in the London, Edinburgh, and Dublin Gazettes, a declaration of the names

of the candidates who have obtained the quota, and the number of votes
polled for every remaining candidate, computed as aforesaid;[1] and shall
then cancel the name of such one of the last-mentioned candidates as shall
stand at the head of the smallest number of voting papers, and appropriate
the same voting papers to the remaining candidate or candidates whose
name or names stand next on such voting papers respectively, and so on,
repeating such cancellation of the name remaining at the head of the
smallest number of voting papers successively, and the reappropriation of
such voting papers to the next candidate thereon respectively, until the
number of candidates is equal to the number of members remaining to be
elected; and thereupon the registrars shall declare and publish, as aforesaid, the names of such remaining candidates as have obtained the quota,
and also of such of them, if any, as have obtained comparative majorities
less than the quota, *and* so many of the said remaining candidates as
shall, together with the candidates who have previously obtained the quota
of votes as aforesaid, be sufficient to make up the whole number [654] of
members to be chosen, shall, upon the receipt of the registrar's certificate,
be returned as members to serve in Parliament, by the returning officers of
the constituencies of which they have respectively polled a majority or
majorities of votes as hereinbefore provided;[2] *and* if, upon such distribution
by the registrars, it shall appear that two or more of such candidates
having *comparative majorities* as aforesaid less than the quota, have polled
an equal number of votes, and cannot both or all be returned as members

---

[1] If the plan suggested by Mr. Dobbs (*General Representation*, &c.,
Longmans, 1872, 2nd edit.) be adopted, empowering the *candidate* to
transfer his surplus or deficient votes, where the elector shall indicate
his wish to that effect, by using a special or transferable voting paper
(see p. 124, *ante*), the following provision might be here introduced:—
[The registrars shall then collect the unappropriated voting papers
whereon the electors have directed that the same shall be transferable,
and shall compute and publish, as aforesaid, the total number thereof,
and the names of the candidates authorised to transfer the same, and the
number they are respectively empowered to transfer; and shall appropriate such votes to and among the candidates in such manner and
proportion as shall be directed in writing, signed and attested in the
presence of one of the said registrars or his deputy, by the respective
candidates empowered as aforesaid, within (24 hours) from such publication; and the registrar shall then publish as aforesaid, the names of the
candidates, if any, who have obtained the quota by such last-mentioned
appropriation; and the names of the candidates still having less than the
quota, and the number of voting papers at the head whereof they respectively stand.]

[2] Clause XXII., p. 166.

as aforesaid, then preference shall be given to the said candidates in the order of their priority in the gazetted lists of candidates prepared as hereinbefore provided,[1] and if the said candidates shall be on different gazetted lists, then in the order of their priority if they had been upon the gazetted list for the same part of the United Kingdom ; *and* to the end aforesaid the registrars shall, with all practical speed, certify to the returning officers of the constituencies in which the said votes have been polled for any of the said remaining candidates, the number of votes appropriated to them from each constituency, excluding, where two or more candidates shall have been equal, and cannot both or all be returned, the name or names of the candidates who have not the preference in the order of priority as aforesaid ; *and* if they be still equal, preference shall be given to a candidate for a constituency in Ireland before one for Scotland or England, and to a candidate for a constituency in Scotland before one in England, and to a candidate for a smaller before one for a larger constituency ; *and* the registrars shall also, as soon as possible, certify to the returning officers of the constituencies in which the said votes have been polled, the names of all the candidates who have *failed to obtain a quota of votes, or a number sufficient to form one of the said comparative majorities,* or being equal to one of such majorities have been excluded as *not having the priority* as aforesaid, signifying that in consequence thereof such candidates cannot be returned at that election as members to serve in Parliament.

In the last edition of this treatise, a clause was introduced for appropriating the votes of electors that had been ineffectual owing to having the names of unsuccessful candidates at the head of their voting papers, by assigning them as part of the constituency of any member whom they had named lower on the voting paper, in order to compensate them in some measure for the loss. It was argued that if the voter were not represented by the man whom he would above all desire, because he could not procure a sufficient concurrence of opinion or sentiment for his election, he is yet represented by the man who stands highest in his favour for whom that concurrence can be obtained : that the variation in the numbers of the constituencies which the ultimate appropriation of votes might introduce, derogated in no degree from the true principle of representation. "*A* is not the less perfectly represented by *Z* because *B* and *C* have likewise chosen *Z* to represent

---

[1] Clause IX., p. 96.

them. We do not refuse to confide our interests to a particular counsel or attorney because his eminence in character and ability has led a great number of other persons to appoint him as their counsel or attorney also. We rather expect his power to be of service to us, will be greater from that very cause." But it is clear, nevertheless, that the elector though thus represented, has not that due representative force to which he is entitled so far as it can be given to him, and which is far more perfectly secured in the manner now indicated.

If we suppose nothing more than the most ordinary degree of acquaintance with the names of a few public men, or even of one, coupled with that degree of interest in public affairs which would induce the voter to be at the pains of exercising his franchise, it is probable that under such a law every elector in the kingdom who may take the trouble to vote, will be represented by a candidate whom he has especially named and selected. An unrepresented voter will be a rare exception. By fixing on any candidate of high and general reputation, the elector will be morally certain of securing him, if no other, as his representative in the national councils; and where the elector does not rely exclusively on one name, but introduces different names, as so many alternatives, the system affords a practical application of that principle of compromise, the adaptation of the will, the pretensions, and the conduct to circumstances,—the yielding something of which we are less tenacious to secure that on which we set a still higher value,—which is of such potent influence and incalculable value in political as well as in social life. The voter expresses in effect his wish to be represented by the second person named on his paper if he cannot be by the first,—by the third if he cannot be by the second, and so on. Instead of crushing the opinions or sentiments of any elector, it leads him by a gentle and unresisted constraint to blend and harmonise them with those of others, until a voluntary unanimity is attained.

It is unnecessary to repeat the clause formerly introduced,[1] for the verification of the declared results of the poll, and for the preservation of, and means of reference to the voting papers subsequent to the election. Provisions for all these purposes are to be found in the rules appended to the Ballot Act. The secrecy of the vote now renders most of the suggestions on this point, in the preceding editions, inapplicable.

It is proper finally to provide for the possibility of a candidate being elected by a sufficient number of voters to make up the quota, and who yet may not be in a position on the poll of any particular constituency to entitle him to require that the returning officer shall return him as elected by it. Suppose, for example, that there were 700 different constituencies, and a candidate had three votes in every constituency, he might have the quota, or a comparative majority, but not a majority in any place. The supposed state of things is of course highly improbable, but there ought to be no possible defect in the operation of machinery designed to act perpetually, and under all circumstances. If any cases should arise, such as has been supposed, it may be left to be dealt with by the House, upon a form of proceeding which the candidate, or any of the electors interested, may be allowed to imitate.

XXVIII. When it shall appear by a certificate of the registrars that any candidate has polled such a number of votes as shall amount to the quota, or to a comparative majority, and he shall yet not be returned by any returning officer as a member to serve in Parliament; and such candidate, or any of the electors by whom he has been chosen, shall present a petition to the House of Commons stating such facts, and praying that he may be admitted as a representative, it shall be lawful for the House, upon hearing the said certificate of the registrar, to declare, by resolution, that the said candidate has been duly elected as a member of the said House, and that he shall be designated as an additional representative of the three constituencies in which he shall have polled a greater number of votes than in any other three constituencies, and if such numbers in so many several con-

---

[1] Sect. XXVIII., p. 197, 3rd ed.

stituencies should be equal, then that he shall be designated representative of such three constituencies as shall contain the greatest number of
registered electors; and such declaration shall have the same effect as if
he had been duly returned under the writ as aforesaid.

In the above electoral law it has not been thought necessary thus far to depart from the form originally adopted to
show in what way proportional representation might be
established, or to borrow the more succinct phraseology in
which rules of a like or analogous purport have been expressed in subsequent adaptations of the principle. With a
view, however, to the practical introduction of the system, it
is of great importance to show how much the form of an
electoral law for that object may be simplified as well as
abridged. The labours of other minds in England and in
America, bringing to the task their varied experience in the
work of legislation, have succeeded in framing in fewer words
rules which effect substantially the same object. One example is given in the four simple rules which suffice for
expressing what was to be done, on the nomination of overseers of Harvard University.[1] The Proportional Representation Bill[2] of the last session embodied every essential condition in the three following clauses :—

" 10. The following provisions shall have effect with reference to a poll :
  (i.) Each elector shall have one vote only :
  (ii.) The votes shall be given by voting-papers delivered by the electors
      in person :
  (iii.) The voting-paper of an elector shall be deemed to have been
      given for the candidate first named thereon, but the elector may,
      if he think fit, designate one or more other candidates to
      whom in succession, in the designated order of priority, he de-
      sires that his vote should be transferred, in the event of its not

---

[1] See Appendix M, p. 351, *infra.*

[2] Prepared and brought in by Mr. Morrison, Mr. Auberon Herbert, Mr.
Fawcett, and Mr. Thomas Hughes. Ordered by the House of Commons to
be printed, 28th Feb., 1872. Motion for the second reading, 10th July,
1872. Hansard, *Parl. Deb.*, vol. ccxii., pp. 890–926. The form of the
voting paper, in the third schedule of this Bill, is substantially the same as
that given in p. 124, *ante.*

being required to bé used for the return of any prior candidate. The number of candidates named on a voting-paper, including the candidate first named, must not be greater than the number of vacancies :

(iv.) A candidate, in order that he may be returned at an election, must (subject as herein-after in this Act expressly provided) have given for him a number of voting-papers (herein-after in this Act referred to as the "quota") to be found by dividing the total number of voting-papers given at the election by the number of vacancies to be filled at the election (the fraction, if any, remaining from the division being disregarded) :

(v.) A voting-paper shall be filled up in writing by the elector at the polling booth, provided that the returning officer shall, at the request of an elector who states that he is unable to write, fill up the voting-paper of such elector as he directs :

(vi.) Every voting-paper shall be void which either—

(a.) Contains the names of more candidates than there are vacancies, or

(b.) Contains any mark by which the elector can be identified ; and a void voting-paper shall not be counted or deemed to have been given.

11. After the close of a poll the voting-papers shall be dealt with by the returning officer as follows :

(i.) He shall cause the voting-papers to be collected, and shall ascertain the total number of voting-papers, exclusive of void voting-papers and of voting-papers on which no candidate is legibly named. His decision as to whether a voting-paper is void or a name is illegible shall be final, subject to reversal on a petition :

(ii.) He shall ascertain and declare the quota necessary for the return of a member :

(iii.) He shall arrange the voting-papers given for the several candidates in separate parcels, and shall in the parcel of each candidate sort his voting-papers according to the numbers of names upon them, placing at the top those voting-papers in which no other candidate is designated, and then those in succession in which the fewest other candidates are designated, and placing last those in which the greatest number of other candidates are designated :

(iv.) He shall proceed to make one or more scrutinies (as the case may require) according to the provisions herein-after in this Act contained :

(v.) He shall give to each candidate, on application by him or his agent, two orders of admission to the place where a scrutiny is to be made, and each such order shall entitle the bearer to be present at the ascertaining of the number of voting-papers, and of the quota, and at any scrutiny.

12. The first scrutiny shall be made in the following manner :

(i.) The total number of voting-papers given for each candidate shall be counted in the order in which they are arranged, and shall be recorded; and every candidate whose voting-papers equal or exceed the quota shall be declared elected :

(ii.) When a candidate is declared elected, his voting-papers shall be dealt with as follows :

(a.) His voting-papers used in making up his quota shall be set aside as exhausted :

(b.) His voting-papers counted after his quota was reached shall be deemed to be unused :

(iii.) An unused voting-paper of an elected candidate shall be transferred to and be deemed to have been given for the unelected candidate (if any) first designated thereon, and shall be counted to him after and in addition to the voting-papers (if any) originally given for him ; and any candidate whose voting-papers are by this means raised to the quota shall be declared elected, and his voting-papers shall be dealt with as voting-papers of an elected candidate.

The unused voting-papers transferred to a candidate may be counted to him in any order in which they happen to be taken. ·

13. A second or other scrutiny shall (if necessary) be made in the following manner :

(i.) The lowest candidate on the preceding scrutiny shall be excluded and declared not elected; and, if there still remain more candidates than vacancies, all the voting-papers of the excluded candidate shall be deemed to be unused, and shall, with the unused voting-papers (if any) remaining from the preceding scrutiny, be respectively transferred to and counted for the first of the remaining candidates (if any) designated thereon, and any candidate so obtaining the quota shall be declared elected, and his voting-papers shall be dealt with as voting-papers of an elected candidate :

(ii.) The same process of excluding the lowest candidate on the preceding scrutiny, and of transferring unused voting-papers, shall be repeated so often as may be necessary until all the vacancies are filled by the election of candidates obtaining the quota of voting-papers, or there remain no more candidates than vacancies :

(iii.) When there remain no more candidates than vacancies, all the remaining candidates shall be declared elected, whether they have obtained the quota or not :

(iv.) In case two or more candidates have equal numbers of voting-papers in a scrutiny, that one of them shall be deemed to be the lowest who had the fewest votes on the first scrutiny, and if they are still equal the returning officer shall have a casting vote or votes."

It is true that the division of England and Wales into sixty-nine constituencies,[1] acting independently of one another, rendered unnecessary several of the provisions required where, as in the method herein contemplated, the existing constituencies would not only be much increased in number, but are so far connected that the electoral weight of the votes is measured by the same numerical standard, and individual voters may transfer themselves from one local constituency to another.

In the Proportional Representation Bill, from which the foregoing clauses are extracted, the number of members to be returned at the next general election by the several con-

[1] They are specified in the first Schedule. The principle of division was to give distinct representation to the larger towns, and include the smaller in the counties. It allots to the Universities of Oxford, Cambridge, and London, 5 members, and to cities and boroughs as follows:—Plymouth and Devonport, 3; Bristol, 4; Portsmouth and Southampton, 4; Greenwich, 4; Newcastle-on-Tyne, Tynemouth, and North Shields, 6; Wolverhampton, Wednesbury, and Walsall, 7; Lambeth, 8; Southwark, 4; Birmingham, 7; Kingston-upon-Hull, 3; Leeds, 6; Sheffield, 5; Bradford, 3; Halifax, Huddersfield, and Dewsbury, 4; Liverpool, 11; Manchester and Salford, 11; City of London, 4; Finsbury, 9; Mary-le-bone, 10; Tower Hamlets, 8; Hackney, 8; Westminster and Chelsea, 11. The Schedule then distributes the county seats, exclusive of the foregoing boroughs, thus:—Bedfordshire, 3; Berkshire, 4; Buckinghamshire, 4; Cambridgeshire and Huntingdonshire, 5; Cheshire, 12; Cornwall, 8; Cumberland and Westmoreland, 6; Derbyshire, 8; Devonshire, 10; Dorsetshire, 4; Durham, 13; Essex, 10; Gloucestershire, 8; Hampshire and the Isle of Wight, 8; Herefordshire, 3; Hertfordshire, 4; Kent, 15; Lancashire, Northern Division, 6; Lancashire, North-Eastern Division, 7; Lancashire, South-Eastern Division, 16; Lancashire, South-Western Division, 9; Leicestershire, 6; Lincolnshire, 9; Middlesex, 6; Monmouthshire, 4; Norfolk, 9; Northamptonshire and Rutlandshire, 6; Northumberland, 5; Nottinghamshire, 7; Oxfordshire, 4; Shropshire, 5; Somersetshire, 10; Staffordshire, 11; Suffolk, 7; Surrey, 11; Sussex, 9; Warwickshire, 6; Wiltshire, 6; Worcestershire, 7; Yorkshire, North Riding, 6; Yorkshire, East Riding, and York, 4; Northern Division of West Riding of Yorkshire, 6; Eastern Division of West Riding of Yorkshire, 6; Southern Division of West Riding of Yorkshire, 9; North Wales, consisting of the counties of Anglesea, Carnarvon, Denbigh, Flint, and Montgomery, 10; South Wales, consisting of the counties of Brecon, Cardigan, Carmarthen, Glamorgan, Pembroke, and Radnor, 16.

stituencies in England and Wales, to which part of the
United Kingdom it exclusively applied, are set forth in the
schedule; but the numbers are to be subject to alteration
according to the population at every decennial census. Such
a distribution of seats was objected to in the debate, on the
ground that the number of registered *voters*, and not population, should form the standard. The argument at once
suggests the question whether the principle which is at the
basis of the system advocated in this treatise might not be
well introduced into any measure for a just apportionment of
political power, however rigidly local the electoral districts
may be framed. The election of members for Birmingham
may be confined to the voters for Birmingham, and that for
Warwickshire to the county voters, by whatever measure the
number of members they are respectively entitled to elect
shall be ascertained. The subject of exclusive local action in
its general character and results is treated in an earlier
chapter,[1] but the possibility and advantage of measuring
the political power of localities by a rational method—a
method dependent on the part their inhabitants are willing
or disposed to take in public affairs—should not be passed
over while we are adverting to this recent and practical attempt
to establish proportional representation, and the objections
which it elicited.

It cannot be too often repeated that the constant statement
that the author has neglected or ignored the local character
of representation is entirely a mistake. He has sought, on
the contrary, to develop the activity of our local system
more completely than ever,[2] making local divisions, as elsewhere said, "facilities and not fetters" of political action.
He proposes for this purpose first, to determine the number

[1] Chap. III.
[2] See p. 52, n. M. Morin understood this care of localities, and concludes his examination of the system by saying, "L'intérêt général et
l'intérêt local paraissent heureusement associés."

of members every county, city, or borough may return, not by the number of its electors on the register, but by the number of those electors who take the trouble to vote at the election.[1] It is the same in effect as if the whole nation, all the adult and trusted of the people to whom the suffrage is given, had been summoned to meet on some great central plain, and the business of the assembly is then and there determined by those who obey the summons and attend, and not by those who are absent; in fact, every elector who does not go to the poll is absent from the great national conclave, and it is but just that he should be so regarded. This principle of the system might have formed part of the proposed measure of the last session, or might be adopted in any future Reform Bill. It cannot be doubted that it would operate as a powerful appeal to the public spirit and patriotism of every voter, to be careful not by his abstention to diminish the fair political influence of his town or county. It would in fact put all the people of Britain as it were on their mettle that they may not fall behind others in the performance of their electoral duties, and lose that influence in the state which is its consequence.

In working out the details of that phase of this system which equalizes and adjusts the comparative power of every voter, to whatever constituency he belongs, and liberates him at the same time from every restriction which at present abridges his opportunities of association with others of like sympathies, two things have been contemplated; first, this equality of numbers making up the quota sufficient to return a member, and which the foregoing explanation will show to be applicable to constituencies however rigidly localized; and secondly, the enlarged and vast extension of the field open to the individual elector by enabling him to carry his vote to the aid of those with whom he agrees, and whose candidate he would desire to see elected, whether within or without

---

[1] See pp. 25-31; and Sect. XXXIII., p. 219.

the local boundary of his own constituency, and thus open to every voter full scope and exercise for his predilections, whether of birth or neighbourhood—from community of interest, thought, or opinion, or from any other governing sentiment —an opportunity which under the proportional system it must be remembered may be used as a means of help, but not of conflict or defeat. If a voter whose residence and qualification is in London, but whose early associations are with Cornwall or Devonshire, should prefer to preserve his connection with and vote in the county rather than in the city, he would in no degree interfere with the electoral power of the county voters. He might come to the aid of a minority or add one to the majority who vote for a county candidate; but when it is no longer a struggle on one side to exclude the other, the addition would be felt as purely beneficial in its tendency, as increasing the aggregate county influence without diminishing that of any party or section in it. The election with the proportional system is no longer a strife for mastery, but an exercise in which all are stimulated to do their best, allowing their neighbours to do the same. This character of the system, however, is not generally realised in the popular mind, and therefore it is desirable to show that the provisions introduced to effect the second of these objects are entirely distinct from those which relate to the first, and that the second may be omitted while the first is adopted.

Instead, therefore, of prescribing, as in the Proportional Representation Bill, that the number of members to be returned by the several constituencies in the schedule should be found by dividing the population, as ascertained at the census from time to time, by the number of members to be returned for England and Wales, and assigning to each so many members as the constituency contains entire multiples of the quotient,[1] or even of making the number of registered

---

[1] Sect. VII. Other boroughs were to be withdrawn from the counties and added to those enumerated in the note (p. 196) as soon as they should contain a population equal to three multiples of the quotient.

electors the dividend, as was contended for in the debate, the Clause XXXIII. of the Act, the draft of which is herein given,[1] might be conveniently substituted, and by its self-acting force may reasonably be expected to have a far better effect than the penal denunciations of the Solonic table,[2] awakening voluntary effort, and rendering compulsion needless.

The method formerly proposed for supplying occasional vacancies of seats, owing to the acceptance of office, resignation, or death of members, or other causes, is since the Ballot Act no longer possible. The clauses for this purpose are therefore omitted. The occurrence of these accidents has been mentioned by some writers as an objection to proportional representation. It is quite possible to regard them as increasing its advantages. Various adaptations of the system for the purpose of supplying such vacancies have been proposed.[3] Perhaps, a better method than any other would be to allow them to continue until the number reaches four or five, and then to vest the election in the House itself, under the same proportional system, which would enable any considerable party to introduce any known or rising politician, in whom it has confidence or hope. Such an opportunity of bringing into the national assembly, and thereby to prominent and public notice, minds of especial eminence or promise, who had not sought, or not obtained, the popular suffrage, would sometimes be of no small value.

---

[1] P. 219.   [2] See pp. 251, 252, *infra*.   [3] Appendix M, p. 353.

CHAPTER X.

A SYSTEM which anticipates the progress of the nation, and admits of the formation of new constituencies, as the occasion and desire shall arise, must also contemplate, as has been already observed, the existence of many more constituencies than there can be members,—and, therefore, that one member may represent several constituencies.[1] This is substantially the case at present in the contributory boroughs. The member for Ayr, for example, may be called with indifferent accuracy the member for Campbeltown or Irvine. So, in the proposed system, it would be unimportant, in point of nomenclature, whether a member who had been returned for several constituencies should, in the ordinary appellation by which he is addressed in the House, be styled as the member for one rather than the other, although it would be reasonable that he should be usually referred to as the representative of that constituency for which he had also been especially a candidate.

Throughout the frame of this scheme it has been an object to create and maintain a connection between the member and the constituents, which shall be due to no selfish or sordid cause, but be solely owing to the estimation by the one of the virtues of the other. Under the existing system of majorities, every elector may throw upon others the blame of a contemptible choice. "Thou canst not say I did it," may

[1] See pp. 50—54, 56.

be the answer to every remonstrance. But the case will be
very different when every elector may personally acquire
respect, or incur disgrace, by the selection which he makes.
In addition to what is merely personal, another powerful
feeling of an elevating character, which has already been
spoken of,[1] will be called forth. A collective or corporate
feeling of pride is brought into existence,—for, although men
readily discover reasons for not ascribing to themselves any
part of the ignominy that attaches to an act which is dis-
graceful to the body they belong to, yet they are always
prompt to claim a share of the credit their community may
have gained, and which they commonly appreciate at the
utmost of its worth. Dispositions such as these are moral
levers. In them we have presented to us a field, both for
merit and praise, boundless as the imagination; the civic
honours which the people may confer on their more worthy
countrymen, by placing them in the front ranks of the Commons of the kingdom, have no limits but the public appreciation of high desert and of the value of such a reward. In the
proposed system of election the return of the same member
may be double or multiple. The majority in every constituency will confer upon their chosen candidate the title of
representative for their particular body; but as the purely
political object ceases when the quota is made up, the majority,
in placing one member rather than another in the first place,
will commonly have no motive but the laudable one of showing the nation that they delight to honour one of its worthiest
sons. The prevailing sentiment will be that which we observe to govern the members of ancient institutions and
learned and scientific bodies, in nominating as their chan-
cellors, their rectors, or their presidents, the eminent persons
of their time. There is no borough, or electoral community,
which may not be titularly represented by the most distinguished men, without, in any degree, interfering with their

[1] P. 56.

further representation by the members to whom their votes have been specifically appropriated. The spontaneous testimony of public admiration thus offered will not,—because it is an unsolicited tribute to high qualities, adding only to the moral influence of him to whom it is given,—be therefore less honourable to the givers than to the receiver. In a time when every effort is devoted to the acquisition of material riches, nothing is without its worth that confers extrinsic dignity or power. We are too prosaic to clothe

> " The olive wreath, the ivied wand,
> The sword in myrtles drest,"

with the symbolic value given to them by a more imaginative people in an earlier age; but we have not yet lost the estimation of what is great, and no means should be neglected which our institutions can offer of giving prominence to true worth, and impressing upon it the seal of the general approbation. That " virtue is its own reward " is for the individual a sublime truth, but for society it would be a niggard maxim. We cannot afford to part even with the faint and reflected gleams of human glory. Divinely taught wherein true heroism consists, we may restore again our long-forgotten shrines of hero-worship, and find something better and nobler than an universal idolatry of money. When we have undone the fetters of our electoral bodies,—shaken off, so far as any human arrangements can do so, all that is mercenary and degrading, and given them health and elasticity,—the free spirit, no longer enslaved by the lower desires and appetites, will ever rise and soar towards that which shall be more and more excellent; and the law should encourage a disposition in every constituency to nominate as their representative him whom they regard as the highest living model of worth.

XXXII. A candidate shall be entitled to be, and shall be returned as a member for any constituency in which a majority of votes has been polled for him, notwithstanding that under section XVIII. or section XXIV. all the votes actually appropriated to him shall have been polled in another constituency or other constituencies; and in such case the constituency for which he is by this law declared to be entitled to be returned, and the votes whereof are appropriated to other candidates, shall be entitled to return one other member for every candidate so elected, in addition to the number which is to be returned for it under section XXXIII. next hereinafter contained.

The effect of the law may be illustrated by supposing that James Watt had been a candidate for Birmingham, and that Glasgow, remembering the "frown severe" with which she had beheld his earlier exertions, desired to testify her sense of the debt the marvellous city of the Clyde owed to one who was, almost by inheritance, the tutelary genius of that river, by placing him in the front rank as her representative. James Watt might have been at the head of the poll, and returned for Glasgow as well as for Birmingham, whilst Glasgow would have, in addition, her complement of representatives under the general rule expressed in the succeeding law.

It is important in so great a national work as the election of a representative assembly, to secure the aid of all the better feelings and higher motives,—to bind the representative and the constituent by the ties of mutual respect and attachment, and thus render names subservient to things. With this view the designation of members is a subject of no slight moment. It is the sign, as well as the result of the intimate connection of the members with the various constituencies dispersed throughout the length and breadth of the land. The names by which the members are severally designated constitute the marks or imprint in the Parliament of the distinct vitality and force of every part of Britain. Still, all these distinct sources from which the members receive their appellation and derive their function and authority, are to be regarded, to use the words of Bacon, as lines and veins rather than as sections and separations. Or, to borrow an illustration from physiology, they may be likened to the nervous centres whence the human frame is supposed to receive its impulse and power of harmonious action. It is the people, and not the surface of the earth, or the constructions which man has heaped upon it, which must be represented. The principle of personal representation is the great political doctrine of modern times.[1]

Every project for the distribution of seats, and indeed every actual distribution, has professed to have regard to the number of voters in the constituency. All schemes, except that of the Duke of Richmond, have proposed a distribution more or less grossly disproportionate, or if not, of divisions more or less arbitrary. It is obvious that a just and natural distribution throughout the kingdom of the sources of political power requires, as its basis, that the same rights of suffrage should exist in every part of the kingdom. A consideration of the great question of the suffrage is reserved for a subsequent chapter. It is sufficient here to remark, that a right of suffrage, extensive and impartial, is, as Mr. Calhoun says, "the indispensable and primary principle,"[2] and that in conferring it, in the language of M. Guizot :—" Le gouvernement représentatif considère quel est l'acte auquel vont être appelés les individus ; il examine quelle est la capacité nécessaire pour cet acte ; il appelle ensuite les individus qui sont présumés posséder cette capacité, *tous* ceux-là, et ceux-là *seuls*. Il cherche ensuite la majorité parmi les capables. C'est ainsi, en fait, qu'on a presque toujours procédé partout, même quand on a cru agir en vertu de la souveraineté du peuple. Jamais on ne lui a été vraiment fidèle ; on a toujours exigé, pour les actes politiques, certaines conditions, c'est-à-dire, les signes d'une certaine capacité. On s'est trompé en plus ou en moins, et l'erreur est grave, soit à exclure des capables, soit à appeler des incapables. Mais on a obéi au principe du droit mesuré selon la capacité, même quand on professait le principe du

---

[1] *Buckle's History of Civilisation.*   [2] *Disquisition,* &c., p. 13.

droit dérivé de la simple qualité d'homme."[1] It may be assumed that in any law regulating the suffrage, to the extent in which it is given, it will be founded on the supposition of capacity; and to the extent to which it is restricted, it will be restricted on the supposition of incapacity. Any statesman who shall attempt to carry an electoral law on a narrower basis than this—even if any party combinations should give him a temporary success,—will most assuredly prepare the way for future political difficulties. If a standard of capacity be once adopted—whatever be its elements—the next question for the consideration of statesmen in this country is,—whether any ground exists for disturbing this general standard of capacity by exceptional privileges or restrictions dependent on the place in which the individual elector resides? It is only in a social condition which is become highly artificial that such a question could be seriously proposed. No one will gravely argue that the residents of one district of the United Kingdom, when subjected to the same tests, are so inferior in capacity or character to those who reside in another district, that a different and exceptional standard of electoral capacity should be adopted. No reasons for such a difference, founded on intellect, opinion, disposition, or any other conceivable quality, are applicable to the people of these islands within any specific geographical or other line. The same general standard applies to the Englishman in Cornwall and in Cornhill. None will probably deny that in scientific acumen and courageous enterprise the county may fearlessly sustain a comparison with the city.

Those who would refuse to the inhabitants of the country districts their equal title to electoral power, will, when subjected to close scrutiny, be found to be a class of small weight or influence. The remarks of a leader of the reformers on this subject are significant. He observed:—"I know no good reason why the franchise in counties should

---

[1] *Gouv. Rep.*, vol. i., p. 110.

not be as extensive as in boroughs; but there appears to have
been an understanding of late years, that the next step
with regard to the county suffrage shall be short of that, and
I shall not quarrel with any measure on that ground."[1] It
is true, that the inhabitants of the towns who have agitated
the subject of parliamentary reform, not only have not
thought it desirable to advocate the interests of those who
reside in the counties, but have given little support to the
principle of residential equality. The people residing beyond
the limits of towns and boroughs have comparatively small
means of combining to forward their own claims. " The
very nature of a country life, the very nature of landed property, in all the occupations and all the pleasures they afford,
render combination and arrangement (the sole way of procuring and exerting influence) in a manner impossible
amongst country people. Combine them by all the art you
can, and all the industry, they are always dissolving into
individuality. Anything in the nature of incorporation is
almost impracticable amongst them. Hope, fear, alarm,
jealousy, the ephemerous tale that does its business and dies
in a day,—all these things, which are the reins and spurs by
which leaders check or urge the minds of followers, are not
easily employed, or hardly at all, amongst scattered people.
They assemble, they arm, they act with the utmost difficulty
and at the greatest charge. Their efforts, if ever they can
be commenced, cannot be sustained. They cannot proceed
systematically."[2] It might have been expected, by a
foreigner unacquainted with the working of our representative institutions, that the landed proprietors, who are in a
condition to make themselves heard in Parliament, would
have been the efficient protectors of their neighbours, the
inhabitants of the country,—that they would have indignantly repelled any insinuation of mental or physical inferi-

[1] Mr. Bright. *Speech at Birmingham*, Oct. 27, 1858.
[2] *Reflections*, &c., p. 286.

ority, and demanded for them, at least, an equality of political rights. He would be surprised to learn, that, so far from finding advocates in their territorial and natural chieftains, it is from some of them that the attempt to confer upon the inhabitants of counties a franchise, nominally of an equal, but really of a greater, amount than that existing in the towns, has met with the greatest opposition. Mr. Bright gave utterance to what a correct sense of truth prompted, when he characterised the indifference to the rights of the county inhabitants, as an "understanding," and with an equal sense of justice he informs them beforehand, that it is not his province to become their champion. An "understanding" every lawyer knows is a covert expression, generally introduced when one person wishes to impose upon another terms which have not been agreed upon between them. One party is sufficient for an understanding, but two are required to an agreement. The understanding has not yet been ratified by the persons whose political equality it menaces.

It will be said, that the distinction between the electoral standard in the boroughs and in the counties is founded not on any inferiority in capacity or in any consideration of danger in the opinions or dispositions of the people in the country districts, but on the constitutional necessity of guarding in this manner the interests of the proprietors of the land. The argument, of course, assumes—first, that there exists in the country an antagonism between the proprietors and those who are occupiers, and not proprietors, of houses or lands; and secondly, that the constitution affords no adequate protection to the proprietary class, except by the exclusion as far as possible of county voters who are not proprietors. In the long discussions on representation which took place before the Reform Bill, the antagonistic bodies were supposed to be the landed and the mercantile classes;[1] and it is a doctrine of

[1] "There is one great and eternal distinction arising from the nature of things, which no wisdom can annihilate and no artifice disguise; and that

a very recent date, which places the landed proprietors and rural population in supposed hostility to each other. In truth, the antagonism is perfectly imaginary. By giving health and activity to all the fibres which grow out of interests in land, and which stretch their roots deeply and widely, and take more or less hold on every class in society, the proprietors of land will always find that their true interests and just rights are too firm to be shaken. It may, indeed, be possible for the great proprietors of land to insist upon upholding a system which will sever all these multitudinous ties, and leave them isolated and exposed.

It may well be hoped that when our representative institutions shall come under revision, there will be found in their places in both houses of Parliament some at least of the hereditary leaders of the yeomanry of the kingdom, demanding for them, as county inhabitants, individually and collectively, the same measure of political justice as shall be given to the inhabitants of the towns.

The fidelity and adequacy of the county representation is one of the chief points on which every one who may take a part in the business of parliamentary reform, with a single-minded view to the establishment of a system universally just and true, ought resolutely to insist. The title of the county inhabitants to an equal representation to those of the towns, according to their numbers, measured by the same rule, is alike indefeasible and undeniable. Cheshire, with its 16,000 electors, increased by the extension of the suffrage perhaps to 20,000, would unquestionably be 'entitled to return ten members, if every constituency of 2000, on the average, returned one member. Yorkshire, with its 56,000 electors, increased to 70,000 by the extension of the franchise, would, on the same rule, be entitled to thirty-five members; and so

is the distinction between the landed and mercantile interests !"—*Oldfield's Representative History,* vol. i., p. 163. London, 1816.

P

with the rest of the counties. What is the objection to this demand? There should be no shrinking on any side from principles of indisputable justice. It is the duty—and duty is always true policy—of the ministry who may conduct the affairs of the State,—of the peers, who are, by tradition and constitution, hereditary guardians of justice and liberty,—of every member of the lower House who can rise above mere party attachment, to insist upon this measure of justice for those whose position do not enable them to combine for the purpose of demanding it. If, in the discussions to arise, they shall be led by rectitude of principle to the conception of political wisdom, they will insist upon perfect and equal rights for the dwellers in the counties, regulated by the same measure, to the uttermost fraction,—abating not one jot or tittle from what is conceded to those who live in towns,— and demanding nothing more. If their demands be tainted with a desire to secure a monopoly, or an unjust partition of influence or power, they deserve to fail ; but, in requiring equality, their position is impregnable. The English people, from the impromptu-crowd which gathers in the street, to the most august court in the land, are lovers of fairness and justice, and they will scorn the sophistry which shall attempt distinctions between their countrymen, founded upon the difference of the spot on which they may happen to live.

An equal measure of justice must be extended to the towns. On this point, the metropolis seems to appal even some of the most extreme reformers. On calculating its vast population, and the corresponding share which it may claim in the representative assembly, the agitation for reform, like fear, " recoils at the sound itself has made." An extensive metropolitan representation, framed as it has hitherto been, may well be dreaded ; but, constructed on a system which is freed from the ties of parish or boundary, it might be the strength and anchor of the constitution, if such a character or office could be attributed to any part of the kingdom rather than to another. A true representative reflex of all the better elements which are found in the metropolis, should present a body of men as illustrious as any in the world.

Of what does the metropolis consist? It contains the abode of the sovereign, and of the regal house and household, and of all who compose the court and council of the Queen. It contains the mansions of an ancient and powerful nobility, and their numerous connexions and dependents. In it are all the chief military and civil departments of the army, the navy, the ordnance, and the control of their vast equipments; the public treasury, the mint, and the multitude of offices which are concerned with the receipt of the revenues of the kingdom from foreign and inland trade, and all the subjects of taxation, and for the appropriation and liquidation of the principal and interest of a public debt equal in amount to the value of the fee-simple of the dominions of some not insignificant monarchs,—and with the collection and audit of the public accounts of the empire. In the metropolis are the chief stewardships of the great estates of the crown and its palatinates. In it reside all the functionaries connected with the imperial Parliament,—the secretaries, councils, and officers engaged in communications between the government and its dependencies, — the Canadas, Australasia, Africa, and the Indies,—and with foreign nations. In it are the immense establishments of the Post-office, the great triumph of civilisation,—sowing, daily and hourly, with its myriad hands, the seeds of public and private intelligence gathered from every part of the habitable globe. In the metropolis are the seats of the Courts of Equity and Law, and to it are brought all appeals, in the last resort, from every territory and colony. Here reside the bar, and the other professors of legal science concerned in the supreme administration of justice, and in the settlement and transfer of most of the great properties in the kingdom. In this detail is comprehended but a few of the multitude of conditions and occupations engaged on the affairs of the empire. There is the Bank of England, and the other companies and firms of bankers, whose money transactions represent no small portion of the dealings and commerce of every quarter of the earth. Here are the managers, directors, and staff of the principal associations which, by ships and railways, conduct the intercourse of the people of all nations. There are classes almost beyond the possibility of recapitulation,—merchants, shipowners, brokers, manufacturers of an infinite variety of fabrics,—traders, capitalists, composed of companies and individuals, having ramifications of business with every port, inland town, market, and village. Here are associations, academies, and museums, for the promotion of learning, and science, in all their developments. Ireland sends its brilliant imagination and its romantic bravery; Scotland, its keen intellect and its untiring perseverance. The metropolis attracts to itself much that the kingdom produces of high talent or superior energy ; it gathers together the diversities of gifts with which nature endows her most favoured sons. Here the learning of Johnson, the erudition and wisdom of Burke, the genius of Reynolds, of Lawrence, of Flaxman, and Chantrey, found their home. Here the eloquence of Erskine, of Copley, and of Brougham, had their appropriate theatre. It is here that Wren achieved his triumphs ; and here it may be given to Scott to realise his conception of what Gothic architecture is capable. Davy brings hither from Cornwall his researches in chemistry ; Stephenson, from Northumberland, his applications of mechanics ; Herschel, from Somersetshire, his astronomical observations. Here, Abernethy, and Cooper, and Brodie, held their daily levees. From the rapidity of communication and of travel, the metropolis has now robbed the old provincial capitals of much of their lustre. It is the dwelling of the gentry of the kingdom. Hither thousands, whose skill and industry have been crowned with success, retire, and bring their acquired wealth, and find repose in contemplating that progress in the labour of which they have ceased actively to participate, and in the society of kindred minds. From the metropolis flows that comprehensive literature, the seemingly ever-increasing and inexhaustible stores of which are daily poured forth in article and volume, to feed and guide the realm of thought.

Foreigners should behold in the representation of this mighty community a condensed picture of the greatness of our country, and be compelled to recognise in it a triumphant display of the dignity and virtue of its institutions. Instead of this, the product which our political chemistry extracts from this abundant wealth of material is so immeasurably small that it may well create the deepest alarm in the mind of any statesman, looking to the future, and beholding the shoals into which the representative institutions, even in a highly-intelligent age, may be permitted to drift. With an accidental exception or two, we are unable to refer to the metropolitan constituencies as having given to the senate any members to whom the nation can point, not to say with pride, —but with even the shadow of satisfaction, as illustrating a single ennobling feature of the national character. Under a system which forces every man either to submit to political extinction or to make one of a majority, in which he utterly sacrifices all that in which he differs from the rest in judgment or opinion, it cannot be otherwise. An electoral community formed of thousands of persons, including every diversity of thought, intelligence, education, and feeling, is driven together, and told,—what is, in effect, a cruel irony,— to elect a *representative*. If it be only that the person chosen is to support this or that minister,—or this or that dogma which the majority in its caprice or its ignorance has set up, the representation may be enough,—but if it be to exercise a judgment on all the subjects which at this day become matters of legislation, then it may be confidently said, that no fable, legend, or allegory, has personified a creature capable of adequately representing such a heterogeneous combination of men. The result is inevitable. The crowd of electors is persuaded by the more cunning to apply some test, which affords no more proof of the fitness of the candidate for a legislator than if they had taken him by weight or measure, —something which the most ignorant man may answer. The small degree in which he differs from the lowest and commonest order of mind amongst them may be his recommendation. The chance of any candidate of a higher order of intelligence is so small, that no man will waste his fortune upon it; and the very considerable number of components of the electoral body, who, with delight, would have chosen a superior man, have no opportunity of judging by comparison, or of making a better selection.

It can hardly admit of doubt that, if our statesmen would offer to the metropolitan electors the opportunity of adopting, in the metropolitan constituencies alone, the system proposed in this treatise, it would be regarded as an incalculable boon by a very large number of the intelligent inhabitants; probably by almost all, excepting those who are able by the present arrangements to acquire some profit, or some undue advantage over their fellow-voters. Let us suppose that all the eighteen members are to be elected at one poll, and that the candidates are not liable to be charged with any election expenses beyond a deposit of £50 apiece. There would be probably not less than forty or fifty candidates, including men of eminence in science and literature, in political life, in the army or navy, and at the head of various departments of manufacture and trade. Every elector would have this vastly increased extent of choice, and selection, and in the method of contingent voting may place on his voting paper the names of all, or any, that he may approve of, rejecting as many as he pleases. The whole number of votes being divided by eighteen will give the quota, and the excess being struck off from the more popular candidates would be carried to the next names. The deficient votes would be dealt with in like manner, and thus the sympathies of all would be awakened and called into exercise.[1] The electors in the metropolis, emancipated from the trammels by which they are now restricted, and having before them a field of choice, including many men amongst their contemporaries whose names they have been accustomed to admire or venerate, would gather together members certainly not less eminent than those of any other constituency in the kingdom. In an equal system of suffrage in counties and boroughs—and of individual independence—it is probable that the county electors between the Humber, the Mersey, and the Tees—or the county electors south of the Severn, would be entitled to nearly the same number of members as the electors of the metropolis; and a competition between the metropolis, the north, and the south, to be represented in the state by the most distinguished of contemporaneous statesmen, would impart a new and incalcu-

---

[1] The author pointed out this method in his evidence given before the Select Committee of the House of Lords on the Franchise (Report, June 26, 1860). See also the 'Journal of the Social Science Association,' April 10, 1865. The practical objection to an application of this system to the metropolis alone, of course, is the immediate effect it would have in transferring power from one party to another. It must in justice be accompanied by a redistribution of seats, giving to the metropolis its due number of members, and thus full representation both to Liberals and Conservatives.

The division of the capital into new boroughs, as Finsbury, Marylebone, &c., has not the justification that it preserves the bonds of neighbourhood, local sympathy and intercourse which exist in provincial towns. These ties are scarcely known in the metropolitan localities. It was desired that the School Board should contain ladies practically acquainted with the education of girls, yet of 38,000 surplus votes for Miss Garrett in Marylebone, none could go to make up the 100 wanting for Mrs. Grey in Chelsea. It is absurd enough that the seat of Mr. Gladstone in Parliament, for whom 100,000 electors would have voted if they could, is made to depend upon a majority of the voters of Oxford University, of South Lancashire, or of Gravesend. But it is, if possible, still more absurd that the 6,000 electors south of Oxford Street, who vainly struggled to be represented by Mr. Mill, could not be reinforced by any of the vast number of voters at the north of the same street who would have rejoiced to lend their aid. Note to 4th edition.

lably higher tone of life to our national politics. A few thousand electors might still make choice of men who could do them no honour, but the system thus affords a kind of safety-valve, by which deficiency of judgment or public spirit is drawn off,—for every quota that makes a mean selection is thus prevented from lowering the tone and character of any other constituency, which such a number of voters is now able to do; and the objects of their choice will find their proper level.

Another condition of the population of London, and one which may be expected to operate to an immense extent in a system of individual independence, must also be taken into account. At the census of 1851, of 1,395,000 persons above twenty years of age, then in London, 588,000 were born in other parts of England, including every English county, 14,000 in Wales, 26,000 in Scotland, and 89,000 in Ireland. It is a habit of mankind to cling tenaciously to early associations. A native of Scotland or Ireland, or of a distant county, whom a profession or a trade has drawn to London, retains still his attachment to his birthplace. His sympathies are with it, as his mind dwells on the memories of home, and of youth or early manhood. Not in London alone would the attachment to country and early associations operate. It would be found throughout the kingdom, especially in all the great centres of industry. Lancashire contained, at the same census, 378,000 persons not born within that county. Of these, 26,000 had their birthplaces in Scotland, and 190,000 in Ireland. Of the inhabitants of Yorkshire, about 8,000 were born in Scotland, and 43,000 in Ireland. In Wales, there were 2,200 from Scotland, and upwards of 20,000 from Ireland. Scotland contained 75,000 born in Ireland, and 45,000 in England. The extent to which the means of travelling have been facilitated within the last few years will operate, in a degree which has never before been felt, to preserve the connection between individuals and the places of their more cherished associations.

and from which, notwithstanding their business may employ them at a distance, they can scarcely be said now to be permanently removed.   Under a system of individual independence, full scope would be given to every local attachment,—a regard which, if it exists at all, must be of free and spontaneous growth.   Scotland would not complain of neglected interests, for every Scotchman, wherever his lot in life had cast him, would, in the choice of his representative, turn with filial love to the land of his sires.   Ireland would complain of no cold disregard, for it would find friends in every spot in which, the warm-hearted and unchanging faith of her sons, and the exquisite loveliness of her daughters, had won affection.

It is obvious that causes arising out of country, of property, and of every species of actual or possible association, would all operate materially on the votes which would be given in the metropolis and in other populous cities.   To a large number of persons, the success of the local candidate would be a matter of less importance than that of some candidates for distant places, in which they may feel a greater interest. The desire and temptation to achieve a party triumph would be encountered by feelings and motives more wholesome and genuine.   Instead of local interests being neglected, they will receive, by the accession of voluntary strength from without, greatly increased impulse and power; the impediments which merely local jealousies create being at the same time softened or removed.

It will be seen that the system of individual independence is consistent with the most perfect devotion to local objects, whilst, on the other hand, a geographical or territorial system is perfectly inconsistent with individual independence. The geographical system constrains every man's will, and destroys all personal independence.   On the other hand, the power of voting for whom he thinks proper, permits every man to make the place in which he lives, or in which his property is situated, the first object of consideration. Local obligations can go no further than this full liberty extends, —unless it be really meant that the duty of protection is attached, not to men but to inorganic nature, as to the soil or the houses; or to unsentient life, the woods and forests, and other productions of the vegetable kingdom. It is only on the supposition that these existences are to control the human will, that there can be any necessity for adhering to an electoral system forcibly bound by territorial limits.

A system of individual independence is not only consistent with every territorial view which the elector may entertain, but the method of election which is here proposed does not permit an elector of one constituency to interfere with the electors of another. The distinct and independent action of every constituency is perfectly preserved. No elector for Marylebone can interfere with the electors for Warwickshire, nor the elector of Warwickshire with those of Marylebone. An elector of Marylebone may vote for a candidate who may be a candidate for the county of Warwick, and the votes of electors of Marylebone may furnish a quota who may return him,—but not for Warwickshire. Nothing but a majority in that county could return him as a member for it, as the fact of a return of the candidate by votes from Marylebone, in the case supposed, when he had no sufficient majority in Warwickshire, would be the same thing in effect as if he had been at the first a candidate for Marylebone. It would be that borough he would be returned to represent, and not Warwickshire.

The adoption of a rule giving to every unanimous quota of votes the power of electing a representative, would operate in fact as a perfect and self-adjusting system of electoral division, at all times corresponding with the fluctuations of population and wealth. One of the suggested provisions[1] is directed to the object of admitting the separation of the larger

[1] Clause V., p. 50.

THE DESIGNATION OF MEMBERS AND CONSTITUENCIES. 219

into smaller constituencies; but after this has been done so far as this is likely to be sought, there will no doubt still remain counties, cities, and towns, the inhabitants of which will not desire or consent to any division. Liverpool, for example, would probably insist upon remaining—and there is no reason why it should not remain—an entire and undivided constituency. It now contains 17,333 voters, and is increasing in magnitude. The electors of Liverpool, even if the quota were largely increased, might still be sufficient in number to return seven or eight members. It is impossible to foresee the extent of the changes, or the development which any of the great centres of population may undergo. Under a system in which political weight is perpetually regulated by the magnitude and importance of the community, there is no reason for preserving an arbitrary limit prescribed under an obsolete condition of things, and the nominal representation may be determined by, and correspond with, the real position of the electors.

XXXIII. Every constituency which is, or shall hereafter be entitled to return a member or members to serve in Parliament, shall be summoned by writ to return so many members as shall be equal to the quotient of the number of the electors of the same constituency, who shall vote at the election thereby directed to be made, divided by the number of the quota for the time being declared and certified according to sections I. and III., hereinbefore contained, and one member for every fractional part of such dividend; and in cases where the number of such electors shall be less than such quota, one member, and no more,—except in cases falling within section XXXII., hereinbefore contained; and it shall not be necessary to specify in the writ otherwise than as aforesaid, the number of members to be returned by any constituency.

The operation of this law will be explained by supposing that in North Cheshire, after an extended franchise, there should be 11,000 voters, and that the quota be 2,000. The number of electors, divided by the quota, gives a quotient of five, and a fractional number, which will make it the duty of the sheriff to return five, and one for the fractional number, making together six members for North Cheshire. The arrangement of the number of members to be returned for every constituency, under a system regulated by its magnitude, whilst it gives to every locality an effectual and substantial representation, becomes, so far as relates to form, no more than a question of nomenclature.

The contest in which the nation will, so long as the present system continues, be periodically and more or less fiercely engaged, with reference to the relative importance and right of counties, cities, and towns, and other constituencies, to return severally one or more members, and to the propriety of disfranchising boroughs, the only fault of whose inhabitants is, that nature has not placed them on a seaboard, or on some great stream of communication, or enriched them with mineral treasure,—is worthy of the times when laws were made to enable one city or class to exercise privileges hostile to another, and when the statute of Kilkenny was in force. It will not continue for an hour after our leading statesmen and public men shall be able to perceive that there is no more wisdom in incumbering our political institutions with the difficulties, and deteriorating them by the rude and barbarous practices of bygone ages, than there would be in rejecting the aid of modern science in the performance of any other operation.

CHAPTER XI.

THE HOUSE OF COMMONS AND THE IMPERIAL GOVERNMENT.

THE American statesman, whose "Disquisition on Government" has been referred to, observes that all history and experience testify that the same predominance of the individual over the social feelings which makes government indispensable to preserve society, produces also on those who administer the government a strong tendency to abuse its powers. "Liberty," he says, "is little more than a name under all governments of the absolute form, including that of the numerical majority, and can have only a secure and durable existence under those of the concurrent or constitutional form."[1] It is only a constitution, by whatever name it may be called, which can prevent an abuse of power. "Having its origin in the same principle of our nature, *constitution* stands to *government* as *government* stands to *society*, and as the end for which society is ordained would be defeated without government, so that for which government is ordained would, in a great measure, be defeated without constitution. But they differ in this striking particular. There is no difficulty in forming government. It is not even a matter of choice whether there shall be one or not.

---

[1] *Calhoun, Disquisition,* &c., p. 60. See *Niebuhr, Hist. Rome,* (*Hare and Thirlwall's Trans.*), vol. ii., p. 298, Camb., 1832, where there are several illustrations from ancient and modern history; *Buckle, Hist. Civilization,* vol. i., p. 71.

Like breathing, it is not permitted to depend on our volition.
Necessity will force it on all communities in some one form
or another. Very different is the case as to constitution.
Instead of a matter of necessity, it is one of the most difficult
tasks imposed on man to form a constitution worthy of the
name; while, to form a perfect one,—one that would completely counteract the tendency of government to oppression
and abuse, and hold it strictly to the great ends for which it
is ordained,—has thus far exceeded human wisdom, and
possibly ever will."[1] "The question involves difficulties,
which, from the earliest ages, wise and good men have
attempted to overcome. For this purpose many devices
have been resorted to, suited to the various stages of intelligence and civilisation, through which our race has passed. The
only materials which the early ages afforded for the construction of constitutions, were applied with consummate wisdom
and skill. To their successful application may be fairly
traced the subsequent advance of our race in civilisation and
intelligence, of which we now enjoy the benefits. For, without a constitution,—something to counteract the strong
tendency of government to disorder and abuse, and to give
stability to political institutions,—there can be little progress
or permanent improvement."

The writer who, in our own times, has combined the characters of the laborious historian, the practical statesman, and
the calm philosopher, divides power into that which exists *de
facto*, and that which is *de jure* : not the *jus* of the lawyers,
founded on the accidents of history,—but that which rests on
immutable principles of truth and justice. He cites the
words of Pascal, "*La multitude qui ne se réduit pas à
l'unité est confusion. L'unité qui n'est pas multitude est
tyrannie.*"[2] This, says M. Guizot, "est l'expression la plus

---

[1] *Disquisition*, &c., p. 8.

[2] The causes of the practical failures of M. Guizot are perhaps nowhere
more candidly weighed than by M. Lanfrey (*Etudes et Portraits Politiques*,

belle et la définition la plus précise du gouvernement représentatif. La multitude, c'est la société : l'unité, c'est la vérité—c'est l'ensemble des lois de justice et de raison qui doivent gouverner la société. Si la société reste à l'état de multitude, si les volontés isolées ne se réunissent pas sous l'empire de règles communes, si elles ne reconnaissent pas également la justice et la raison, si elles ne se réduisent pas elles-mêmes à l'unité, il n'y a pas société, il y a confusion. L'unité qui n'est pas sortie du sein de la multitude, qui lui a été violemment imposée par un ou plusieurs, n'importe le nombre, en vertu d'un droit à eux personnel, est une unité fausse et arbitraire ; c'est la tyrannie. Le but du gouvernement représentatif est d'empêcher à la fois la tyrannie et la confusion, de ramener la multitude à l'unité en la provoquant à la reconnaître et à l'accepter elle-même." [1]

Mr. Burke adverts to the error of the theorists who sophistically confound the right of the people with their *power*. " The body of the community, whenever it can come to act, can meet with no effectual resistance ; but, till power and right are the same, the whole body of them has no right inconsistent with virtue, and the first of all virtues, prudence. Men have no right to what is not reasonable, and to what is not for their benefit." [2] " One of the first motives to civil society, and which becomes one of its fundamental rules, is, *that no man should be judge in his own cause.* By this, each person has at once divested himself of the first fundamental right of uncovenanted man, that is, to judge for himself, and to assert his own cause. He abdicates all right to be his own governor. He inclusively, in a great measure, aban-

---

Paris, 1864). It was "l'esprit de conservation à outrance, qui exigeait l'inertie en système."—"Nous sommes dans la charte, la charte est notre forteresse."—" C'est bien l'image exacte de ce système fermé, sans expansion, sans avenir, et sans issue. On ne songeait pas que tout forteresse appelle un siége." Pp. 352, 353. *Du Régime Parlementaire.*

[1] *Guizot, Gouv. Rep.*, vol. i., p. 94.   [2] *Reflections*, &c., p. 92.

dons the right of self-defence, the first law of nature. Man cannot enjoy the rights of an uncivil and of a civil state together. That he may obtain justice, he gives up his right of determining what it is in points the most essential to him. That he may secure some liberty, he makes a surrender in trust of the whole of it."[1]

The question of the ultimate deposit of political power is presented by the European statesman in its philosophical, and by the Transatlantic statesman in its practical shape,— " Comment garantir à la société que le pouvoir absolu en fait, auquel toutes les relations sociales viennent nécessairement aboutir, ne sera que l'image, l'expression, l'organe du pouvoir absolu en droit, seul légitime, et] qui n'est déposé nulle part sur la terre ? C'est là le problème du gouvernement."[2] How, asks Mr. Calhoun, is the tendency of government to oppression and abuse " to be counteracted,—how can those who are invested with the powers of government be prevented from employing them as the means of aggrandising themselves, instead of using them to protect and preserve society ?"[3]

The answer to these questions, as they are the conclusions from facts, first assumes a negative form, by showing that as no selection of one, or of a class, be it few or many, constitutes any security from oppression, so the vesting of power in the greater number—in the numerical majority—is at least equally a despotism in principle ; and a despotism which is more hopeless from the numbers of which it is composed, and the assistance and countenance of a multitude which creates its own standard of morals, and is blind to what is base, when it serves the popular object.[4] When the contest is reduced to one of numbers—to a question of numerical majority—the conflict between the two parties " tends neces-

---

[1] *Reflections*, &c., p. 88.   [2] *Gouv. Rep.*, vol. i., p. 120.
[3] *Calhoun, Disquisition*, &c., p. 8. See *Mill, Considerations on Rep. Gov.*, chap. vi.
[4] *Niebuhr. History of Rome (Hare and Thirlwall*, Tr.), vol. ii., p. 407.

sarily to settle down into a struggle for the honours and emoluments of the government, and each, in order to obtain an
object so ardently desired, will in the process of the struggle
resort to whatever measure may seem best calculated to effect
this purpose. The adoption, by the one, of any measure,
however objectionable, which might give it an advantage,
would compel the other to follow its example. In such case,
it would be indispensable to success to avoid division and
keep united; and hence, from a necessity inherent in the
nature of such governments, each party must be alternately
forced, in order to insure victory, to resort to measures
to concentrate the control over its movements in fewer and
fewer hands, as the struggle became more and more violent.
This, in process of time, must lead to party organization,
and party caucuses and discipline, and these, to the conver-
sion of the honours and emoluments of the government into
means of rewarding partisan services, in order to secure the
fidelity and increase the zeal of the members of the party.
The effect of the whole combined, even in the earlier stages
of the process, when they exert the least pernicious influence, would be to place the control of the two parties in the
hands of their respective majorities; and the government
itself virtually under the control of the majority of the dominant party for the time, instead of the majority of the whole
community, where the theory of this form of government
vests it. Thus, in the very first stage of the process, the
government becomes the government of a minority, instead
of a majority,—a minority, usually, and, under the most
favourable circumstances, of not much more than one-fourth
of the whole community.[1]

[1] "It has come to this, that one man, Caleb Claptrap, for example, who has
a certain influence with three other men, selects the man who, for the space
of four years, if elected, is to divide 120 millions of dollars amongst his
friends and their friends."—*American-Whig Review*, vol. xvi., p. 175. New
York, 1852.

"But the process, as regards the concentration of power, would not stop at this stage. The government would gradually pass from the hands of the majority of the party into those of its leaders, as the struggle became more intense, and the honours and emoluments of the government the all-absorbing objects. At this stage, principles and policy would lose all influence in the elections; and cunning, falsehood, deception, slander, fraud, and gross appeals to the appetites of the lowest and most worthless portions of the community, would take the place of sound reason and wise debate. After these have thoroughly debased and corrupted the community, and all the arts and devices of party have been exhausted, the government would vibrate between the two factions (for such will parties have become) at each successive election. Neither would be able to retain power beyond some fixed term; for those seeking office and patronage would become too numerous to be rewarded by the offices and patronage at the disposal of the government; and these being the sole objects of pursuit, the disappointed would, at the next succeeding election, throw their weight into the opposite scale, in the hope of better success at the next turn of the wheel. These vibrations would continue until confusion, corruption, disorder, and anarchy, would lead to an appeal to force,—to be followed by a revolution in the form of the government. Such must be the end of the government of the numerical majority; and such, in brief, the process through which it must pass, in the regular course of events, before it can reach it.

"This transition would be more or less rapid, according to circumstances. The more numerous the population, the more extensive the country,—the more diversified the climate, productions, pursuits, and character of the people, the more wealthy, refined, and artificial their condition; and the greater the amount of revenues and disbursements, the more unsuited would the community be to such a government, and the more rapid would be the passage."[1]

It is not by instituting a higher power to control the government, and those who administer it, that the tendency to abuse can be counteracted. " This would be but to change the seat of authority, 'and to make this higher power, in reality, the government, with the same tendency to pervert its powers into instruments of aggrandizement. Nor can it be done by limiting the powers of government, so as to make it too feeble to be made an instrument of abuse ; for passing by the difficulty of so limiting its powers, without creating a power higher than the government itself to enforce the observance of the limitations, it is a sufficient objection that it would, if practicable, defeat the end for which government is ordained, by making it too feeble to protect and preserve society."[2]

Absolute and rightful power,—the power *de jure*,—is divinely given, and attributable to none,—" la souveraineté de droit," says M. Guizot, " n'appartient à personne, parce que la connaissance pleine et continue, l'application fixe et imperturbable de la justice et de la raison n'appartiennent pas à notre nature imparfaite."[3]

The lessons of experience having shown that absolute power can be safely reposed in no single authority, the question recurs, how the government must be constructed to counteract its tendency to abuse? " There is but one certain mode in which this result can be secured, and that is by the adoption of some restriction or limitation, which has so effectually prevented any one interest, or combination of interests, from obtaining the exclusive control of the government, as to render hopeless all attempts directed to that end. There is, again, but one mode in which this can be effected, and that is, by taking the sense of each interest or portion of the

---

[1] *Calhoun, Disquisition,* &c., p. 42.   [2] Id., p. 9.
[3] *Guizot, Gouv. Rep.,* vol. i., p. 93.

community, which may be unequally and injuriously affected
by the action of the government, separately, through its own
majority, or in some other way, by which its voice may be
fairly expressed ; and to require the consent of each interest,
either to put or to keep the government in action. This,
too, can be accomplished only in one way, and that is, by
such an organism of the government, and, if necessary for
the purpose, of the community also, as will, by dividing and
distributing the power of government, give to each division
or interest, through its appropriate organ, either a concurrent
voice in making and executing the laws, or a veto in their
execution.   It is only by such an organism that the assent of
each can be made necessary to put the government in motion ;
or the power made effectual to arrest its action when put in
motion ; and it is only by the one or the other that the different interests, orders, classes, or portions, into which the
community may be divided, can be protected, and all conflict
and struggle between them prevented, by rendering it impossible to put or to keep it in action, without the concurrent
consent of all." [1]

It is upon an application of these truths that the constitution of this kingdom rests,—a constitution we may yet be
permitted to describe, as "in theory the most beautiful of
any—in practice the most approved,"—and, may it still be
our trust,—"in duration the most permanent." [2]   It does
not, indeed, owe its foundation to any original and scientific
conception of the necessity of such a balance and distribution
of power.   "Les gouvernements ne se font pas plus à priori
et en vertu des préceptes que les grands poëmes."   The
labours, — now conflicting and now combined, — of divers
ranks, classes, and interests, have erected the British Parliament, and composed it of three constituent parts—"the
King, the Lords spiritual and temporal, and the Commons ;

---

[1] *Calhoun, Disquisition,* &c., p. 25.   [2] 1 *Black. Com.,* p. 217.

parts, of which each is so necessary, that the consent of all three is required to make any new law that shall bind the subject."[1]

It is by the action of these co-ordinate authorities that unity, the combination of the power and the right, is sought. Nothing human is infallible; but, from their joint and harmonious concurrence in any public act, the people have the greatest security which the institutions of man can afford, that the measure will be conformable to the laws of truth and justice. If they differ, the difference involves the necessity of an appeal to reason, guided by the individual conscience. The sovereignty of right resides in no man or collection of men, but dwells, says M. Guizot, " Dans sa vie intérieure, dans ses rapports avec lui-même, si je puis ainsi parler, comme dans sa vie extérieure, dans ses rapports avec ses semblables, l'homme qui se sent libre et capable d'action, entrevoit toujours une loi naturelle de son action. Il reconnait quelque · chose qui n'est pas sa volonté, et qui doit régler sa volonté. Il se sent raisonnablement ou moralement obligé à quelque chose ; il voit ou il sent qu'il y a quelque chose qu'il doit faire ou ne pas faire. Ce quelque chose, c'est la loi supérieure à l'homme et faite pour lui, la loi divine. La vraie loi de l'homme ne vient pas de l'homme ; il la reçoit, il ne la fait pas. Alors même qu'il s'y soumet, elle n'est pas sienne, elle est extérieure et supérieure à lui.

" L'homme ne se soumet pas toujours ; en sa qualité de force libre et de nature imparfaite, il n'obéit pas toujours à sa loi. Il porte en lui d'autres mobiles d'action que cette loi suprême, et quoiqu' il sente le vice de ces mobiles, souvent il y cède. Mais, obéie ou non, la loi suprême de l'homme est toujours là ; il n'y peut songer sans reconnaître qu'elle est placée au dessus de lui.

" Voilà donc l'individu toujours en présence d'une règle, d'une règle qu'il n'a pas faite, et qui l'oblige, et qui ne l'aban-

[1] 1 *Black. Com.*, p. 160.

donne jamais. S'il entre ou se trouve en société avec ses semblables, quelle autre règle aura-t-il que celle là? La société humaine serait-elle une abdication de la nature humaine? non: l'homme, dans la société, doit rester et reste effectivement ce qu'il est; et comme la société n'est qu'une collection d'individus, la loi suprême de la société doit être celle qui a droit de régir les individus eux-mêmes.

" Voilà donc la vraie loi du gouvernement trouvée. C'est la même loi qui oblige les individus. Et comme pour l'individu, la vraie loi est souvent obscure, et que l'individu même quand il la connaît bien, ne la sait pas toujours, de même pour le gouvernement, quel qu'il soit, la vraie loi, qui a toujours à passer par l'esprit de l'homme, toujours borné et passionné, n'est ni toujours connue ni toujours obéie. Il est donc impossible d'attribuer à un homme ou à plusieurs, la souveraineté de droit, car ce serait supposer qu'ils savent et veulent dans tous les cas, ce que veulent la justice et la raison. Supposition inadmissible, à raison de l'imperfection radicale de notre nature."[1]

The possibility that the union of constitutional power with the law of reason and justice may not be attained, after the discussion to which differences between the co-ordinate powers would necessarily give rise, is a possibility which positive law cannot contemplate, for it is unable to create any power above the constitution. The concessions which may be necessary to be made by any of the three co-ordinate powers to the other, are left to the direction of the individual conscience, and the imperious demands of necessity. Human law cannot abrogate the divine, and, therefore, no member of any of the three powers, from the sovereign downwards, can be required to disregard the dictates of conscience; but, on the other hand, necessity compels all to submit to the consequences, be they what they may, which may follow either

---

[1] *Guizot, Gouv. Rep.*, vol. i., p. 92.

obedience or neglect of conscience.[1] Publicity of debate, free discussion, the extraneous and powerful help of the press, all tend to the concurrent determination of disputed questions; and thus to realise the idea of Pascal,—"il provoque la multitude à se réduire à l'unité et il fait sortir l'unité du sein de la multitude." "When something *must* be done, and when it can be done only by the united consent of all,—the necessity of the case will force to a compromise." "On all questions of acting, necessity, where it exists, is the over-ruling motive; and where, in such cases, compromise among the parties is an indispensable condition to acting, it exerts an overruling influence in predisposing them to acquiesce in some one opinion or course of action. Experience furnishes many examples in confirmation of this important truth: among these, the trial by jury is the most familiar."[2]

It cannot, however, be for a moment forgotten, that the equality of power in the three co-ordinate branches of the Parliament—sacred as the constitutional principle may be—is still but a principle. The rights of the sovereign, which stand alone, are the symbol and safeguard of every lesser right; but they rest upon law, and not upon force. The dignity of the peerage forms a graduated hierarchy round the throne, rendering it more difficult to approach without reverence the earthly embodiment of justice, of freedom, and of honour; and their hereditary privileges,[3] by a parity of right,

[1] These consequences, as they respect the sovereign, are discussed by Blackstone (*Com.*, vol. i., p. 211). As they regard the House of Lords, perhaps the events which followed its resistance to the Reform Bill, and the ground on which the resistance was overcome,—"that," as Earl Grey said, "otherwise the government would be in fact an oligarchy," will afford an illustration. See also pp. 18—20.

[2] *Calhoun, Disquisition,* &c., p. 65.

[3] There are not wanting those who speak of hereditary legislators as an institution which the progress of society is destined to abrogate. The friends of the constitution may be allowed to hope that such opinions may not hereafter derive strength from the course taken by the House in ex-cluding a peer created for life,—a course justly described in one of their Lordship's protests as "an unauthorised extension of the privileges of the

preserve its peaceful succession and descent. The whole combination of degrees, whilst it wisely gratifies, also sets bounds to the restless and insatiate cravings of human ambition, and forms a protection to man against his passions. These rights and privileges, again, rest upon law, and not upon force. The third estate—the representative body—stands in the place of those who are, in number and physical power, beyond comparison greater than the two other estates, and without whom the two other estates could have no existence. The will of the great constituent body, when definitively expressed,—and after every opportunity shall have been given to the people of considering and revising the determination,—must be obeyed.

It follows, then, from the vast powers with which the representative body is necessarily invested, that in its construction every avenue should be opened by which the sense of right, of justice, of prudence,—the dictates of the inward law,—can find expression within it. If it should err in its course,—if it should fail in arriving at that unity which embodies at once power, reason, and justice, the people cannot rely on the internal strength of the other two estates, for any permanent resistance to what it may demand,—nor does even the theory of the constitution justify any such reliance. The representative body should, therefore, be regarded, for the purpose of determining on its construction, as if it were the

---

House, not resting on any parliamentary precedent, and in derogation of the just prerogative of the Crown." Parl. Deb., vol. cxl., p. 1311. The step was supported by the expression of what certainly seem but mean ideas of that in which personal dignity consists, and of what constitutes the heritage of an illustrious name. The whole argument against the admission of Lord Wensleydale to his seat may be described with sufficient respect by saying it was not worthy of the peers from whom it came. The resistance to any expansion of the Lower House in 1828 and 1830 bears no little resemblance to that in the Upper House in 1856.—See *Mill's Considerations on Representative Government*, chap. xiii., on the Constitution of a Second Chamber. (Note to 3rd ed.)

sole power,—which from the force of circumstances, and its means of arresting the operations of government, it may at any time in a great measure practically become.   In order to complete that constitutional security which depends on a real and not on a nominal partition of power, the representative body should be composed of every distinct variety and combination of thought, of sentiment, of feeling, of opinion, and of interest which exist in the constituent multitude.   All these diversities form so many pillars to support and give unity to the constitutional edifice.   If the representative body be the creature of numerical majorities, the constitution will be ultimately drawn into the vortex to which governments by such majorities are exposed.   In such a case, Mr. Calhoun cautions the minority, not "to indulge the folly of supposing that the party in possession of the ballot box and the physical force of the country could be successfully resisted by an appeal to reason, truth, justice, or the obligations imposed by the constitution."[1]   If these could be relied on, he observes, government might be dispensed with.   The end of the contest between the majority and the minority would be "the subversion of the constitution, either by the undermining process of construction,—where its meaning would admit of possible doubt,—or by substituting in practice what is called party usage, in place of its provisions ;—or, finally, when no other contrivance would subserve the purpose, by openly and boldly setting them aside.   By the one or the other, the restrictions would ultimately be annulled, and the government be converted into one of unlimited powers."

A representative body composed, not of the nominees of the numerical majorities, but of the actual representatives of all varieties of disposition and interest which make up society —none being suppressed, would form within itself an assembly in which the majority must necessarily be concurrent, and comprehend the elements to which Mr. Calhoun attributes,

[1] *Calhoun, Disquisition, &c.,* p. 33.

not unreasonably, so much virtue.   Under such a form of composition, every division of the constituents, "in order to advance its own peculiar interests, would have to conciliate all others, by showing a disposition to advance theirs; and for this purpose, each would select those to represent it whose wisdom, patriotism, and weight of character, would command the confidence of the others.   Under its influence, and with representatives so well qualified to accomplish the object for which they were selected,—the prevailing desire would be, to promote the common interests of the whole; and, hence, the competition would be, not which should yield the least to promote the common good, but which should yield the most. It is thus that concession would cease to be considered a sacrifice,—would become a free-will offering on the altar of the country, and lose the name of compromise.   And herein is to be found the feature, which distinguishes governments of the concurrent majority so strikingly from those of the numerical.   In the latter, each faction, in the struggle to obtain the control of the government, elevates to power the designing, the artful, and unscrupulous, who in their devotion to party,—instead of aiming at the good of the whole,—aim exclusively at securing the ascendancy of party.   When traced to its source, this difference will be found to originate in the fact, that, in governments of the concurrent majority, individual feelings are, from its organism, necessarily enlisted on the side of the social, and made to unite with them in promoting the interests of the whole, as the best way of pro- moting the separate interests of each; while in those of the numerical majority, the social are necessarily enlisted on the side of the individual, and made to contribute to the interest of parties, regardless of that of the whole.   To effect the former,—to enlist the individual on the side of the social feelings to promote the good of the whole, is the greatest possible achievement of the science of government; while, to enlist the social on the side of the individual, to promote the interest of parties at the expense of the good of the whole, is the greatest blunder which ignorance can possibly commit.

"To this, also, may be referred the greater solidity of foundation on which governments of the concurrent majority repose. Both, ultimately, rest on necessity; for force, by which those of the numerical majority are upheld, is only acquiesced in from necessity; a necessity not more imperious, however, than that which compels the different portions, in governments of the concurrent majority, to acquiesce in compromise. There is, however, a great difference in the motive, the feeling, the aim which characterise the act in the two cases. In the one, it is done with that reluctance and hostility ever incident to enforced submission to what is regarded as injustice and oppression; accompanied by the desire and purpose to seize on the first favourable opportunity for resistance:—but in the other, willingly and cheerfully, under the impulse of an exalted patriotism, impelling all to acquiesce in whatever the common good requires."[1]

In this kingdom, a system, peculiarly national, sometimes called "Parliamentary," and at other times "Party Government," has grown up. Its essential feature is the predominance of a compact party, of which the ministers of the crown are a portion, and which is encountered in the House of Commons by another compact party, who expect to succeed it in power, on a detection and exposure of any error into which it may fall,—on the discovery and adoption of some tenet of greater popularity, or by the more skilful employment of parliamentary forces. So little difference has been understood to exist between the two parties, other than that which is founded on the possession or expectation of power, that an orator who adverted to the party out of office as "His Majesty's opposition," was applauded as the author of a felicitous appellation. It was a conflict of two hostile bodies, over ending, and ever to be recommenced, which, but for its

---

[1] *Calhoun, Disquisition,* &c., p. 70.

vicissitude, might, without irreverence, be compared to those occupations of a perpetually renewed warfare, with which the Scandinavian paradise tempted the heroes of Odin,—

A round of listless joy, and weary strife.

As the system advanced towards maturity it became subjected to rules of indefinite stringency,—requiring, in order to secure majorities, that abnegation of individual opinion and perfect external harmony, to which majorities of electors are now reduced, in order to insure success. In the progress of general knowledge, it was found that innumerable subjects which had not been anticipated, became matters for parliamentary discussion, and some of the restrictions on differences of opinion were relaxed. "Open questions," were admitted to be lawful. The later parliamentary theory and practice on the subject cannot be better described than it has recently been by a statesman thoroughly experienced in it. "When I first entered Parliament, the House of Commons was divided into two camps. A leader guarded both ; a leader whom no man questioned, and whom every man on his side followed. All the trouble was in his hands. His party acquiesced in everything he thought best, and, five minutes after his decision was announced to them, they were heart and soul engaged in it, clamorous that it was the only one that could be arrived at. This was a great advantage in some respects, for it saved a world of thought. But in the House of Commons of the present day we have a different state of things. The House is divided into many parties, or, rather, no party—and why? Because the country is divided into many parties, or no party. At the time the House was divided into two camps, the country was divided into two camps also. One man was blue, another yellow. Each had his own lawyers, and there was the sharpest line of demarcation between the two. The mass of people now judging for themselves, find some good on one side, some on another, and they will not yield themselves blindly to the lead of any one man or party in the State. Now, there is great complaint of this throughout the country. Men are disturbed and unsettled by it, and they are devising means whereby the country and Parliament may be again divided into two camps. But, instead of lamenting the existence of such a state of things, and devising means to restore what I believe will never be restored again, I think we had better look our difficulties in the face. I don't lament the change. Many of the old public men in the House of Commons regret it enormously ; they are bewildered by it ; and they are perhaps right in their regret as public men, because it increases the trouble and difficulty of public men. But all they have lost in comfort the country has gained in public good. The result is this, that the impulsion comes from below—that the country, instead of being partisans, are now become a calm, reasoning jury; and it is necessary, now that they are to constitute the jury, that they should be capable of deciding upon the arguments laid before them. The more great measures are passed by consent, and party bitterness is extinct, the more necessary it becomes that we in the country should understand the contemporaneous political opinions we are called upon to decide." [1]

If the representation is to be constructed with the view of perpetuating party government, two considerations arise,—first, the method of effecting the object,—secondly, what would probably be the result ?

The division of every constituency into two bodies, each distinguished by a political dogma, and ignoring or suppressing every opinion which these dogma do not comprise, is

[1] Mr. Sidney Herbert, Address on opening the Warminster Athenæum, Oct. 1858.—*Times.* I may be allowed to express my gratification at having collected, and presented in this place, these words of truth and soberness, proceeding from the lips of one of the best and greatest men of our time, who has since passed from among us, leaving to his country his wise counsels, and his pure example. (Note to 3rd ed.)

likely to create a representative body also divided into two
parties. In order thus to procure a representation of opinions
not popular with the majorities, constituencies must be
created which are not popular,—or which, being popular, can
be led by corruption. For these purposes the county representation may be made as full as it can be in point of
members,—as restricted as possible in point of suffrage.
Every effort may be made in the closer counties to keep land
out of the market, and arrest the progress of building and
building societies. The borough suffrage may be widened to
any extent, and the ballot introduced, in order to obtain, by
a wholesale corruption of the poor and ignorant, a direct influence for property. We may hope that there are few who
could look forward with any complacency to such a scheme.
It is indeed impossible to hear, without pity at their ignorance, or disgust at their hypocrisy, the warnings of prominent party men against improvements in our electoral
system, founded on appeals to the condition of the United
States, when every reader of their history knows that it is to
the overwhelming power of party, pushed onwards by a
covetous greed of the profits of party, and subduing all individual conscience and action, that the evils of political life in
that country are owing.

What would be the result of a contrivance to render party
organization omnipotent in elections in this country? An
attempt to foretel the future would be presumptuous. We
have seen the struggles made to gain electoral majorities.
We know the nature of man,—we can scarcely doubt,—that
an abject submission to the occasional will of the greatest
number in any assembled multitude, will "extinguish in those
who serve them all moral principle, all sense of dignity, all
use of judgment, and all consistency of character." "When
the leaders choose to make themselves bidders at an auction
of popularity, their talents in the construction of the state
will be of no service. They will become flatterers instead of

legislators; the instruments, not the guides of the people. If any of them should happen to propose a scheme of liberty, soberly limited and defined with proper qualifications, he will be immediately outbid by his competitors, who will produce something more splendidly popular. Suspicions will be raised of his fidelity to his cause. Moderation will be stigmatized as the virtue of cowards; and compromise as the prudence of traitors; until, in hopes of preserving the credit which may enable him to temper and moderate on some occasions, the popular leader is obliged to become active in propagating doctrines and establishing powers which will afterwards defeat any sober purpose at which he ultimately might have aimed."[1]

The office of the House of Commons, as the exponent of public opinion, is of vast importance, and deserves the utmost attention. In that assembly, public opinion should be gathered and expressed with clearness and certainty. It should be registered there with an accuracy resembling that of the thermometer; and that can only be when the House collects and receives all varieties of opinion from without. There is nothing else connected with the science of government which it is of equal importance in a free state that the minister should always be able to ascertain. Any defect in the representative constitution which leads the minister or the people to look elsewhere for the manifestation of public opinion is fraught with the gravest dangers. Public opinion is a sea over which a well-taught pilot may navigate in safety; but, to the uninformed, it is the " gulf profound "

Where armies whole have sunk.

It is strewed with the wrecks of governments. The rarest and most necessary qualification of a statesman is " the faculty of discerning what the nation really desires and thinks; of distinguishing between the intelligent and the unintelligent

<hr />

[1] *Reflections*, &c., p. 361.

public opinion,—between the orators and the organs that have weight, and those that have none,—between the voice which is influential and the voice which is only loud ;—in a word, between the popular *pronunciamento,* which it would be weakness and wickedness to listen to, and that which it would be unpardonable to disregard, and idle to dream of opposing. The task demands no little care, and no ordinary tact ; it belongs to a sagacity partaking of the character of an instinct, which some men of very moderate genius have in perfection,—of which others of far loftier intellect are entirely destitute. It requires singular accuracy of judgment and acuteness of perception ; a practical acquaintance with every rank and class of the community, or that intuitive insight which, with some men, appears to supply its place ; and a mental ear so fine, sensitive, and subtle, as to be able (so to speak) to hear the language of the silent, as well as that of the outspoken and the noisy, and to discriminate between the tones of resolute earnestness, and those of mere bustling loquacity." Without this rare discernment, he " is for ever steering between two dangers : that of opposing a stolid and insensible defiance to the real and serious demands of the popular will, and that of yielding a weak obedience to the noisy outcries of a worthless, insignificant, and powerless few, and incurring thereby the infinite disgust of the influential, but silent and contented class."[1] If the House of Commons be not the actual, as well as the constitutional organ of public opinion, the nation is left open to the attacks and the enterprises of irresponsible persons, who are thereby encouraged to usurp its office. It is impossible to estimate the mischief to which a misconception of public opinion may lead. The tendency in the mind to believe what it desires to think, is expressed in the proverb, that "the wish is father to the thought." It is not less inclined to fancy that the opinions of others assimilate to its own.

[1] *Edinburgh Review,* vol. xcv., p. 234.

There is, again, a disposition in most minds to exaggerate any circumstance or action which they have themselves witnessed, or in which they have borne a part. A sort of imaginary importance or glory is acquired by being able to narrate something out of the common. We are, perhaps, told of a numerous and influential public meeting in London, attended by merchants, bankers, traders, and persons of all classes; and the concurrence of their opinions on some agitated subject is dwelt upon as a great fact. If during the hour that this meeting was held we had gone to the banks, to the merchants' and brokers' offices,—the exchanges,—the docks,—the shops of the principal tradesmen,—we should probably have found all the ordinary work of the establishments going on, and few or none of the active heads of any business absent from their usual posts. We are told of the names of many who were present, but such an array is easily made imposing; and if examined, it would very likely appear to have been,—besides those who led the movement,—only a few of the senior members of firms, in the business of which they are no longer regularly or personally engaged, and who are gratified with celebrity in the public journals,—a few others desiring, or glad of an excuse for, an hour or two of relaxation;—a number of unemployed persons in easy circumstances, to whom the opportunity of hearing speeches on a popular topic is a pastime, or a harmless kind of dissipation;—and the idle, who, when not kept at home by the rain, are always ready to make up a crowd. The men of business, upon whose industry and labour the wealth of the nation depends, are unconcerned, and take no interest in the matter. Of course, it *may* be otherwise; but the public has little or no evidence one way or the other; it may be deluded, either by those who exaggerate, or those who disparage the value of the expression. It may be misled by the statement that a great manifestation had been made, and be induced to imitate it elsewhere; and thus a comparatively few

R

persons may give to their own notions the semblance of the popular voice.

One example of a declaration of public opinion has occurred to this generation. The political convulsions on the Continent ten years ago caused great excitement amongst the poorer classes in England, and an urgent demand arose for changes in the representative system. The claim was asserted in the calm and constitutional form of addressing Parliament by petition; and in order to give it further weight, a public meeting on Kennington Common was resolved upon. The belief of the intensity of feeling on the points in question, caused great apprehension to be felt by the more wealthy classes; who remembered that a few years earlier even the Duke of Wellington had been led by apprehensions of disturbance to advise the King not to attend an entertainment in the city of London. On the appointed day business was suspended. The petitioners assembled in great numbers,[1] and the opponents of the movement occupied the public buildings and halls north of the Thames. Nothing occurred to provoke any collision,—nor was there evidence that any outrage was intended. The exaggerations of the statements with regard to the popular expression which had been dispersed, and excited so much terror, were very remarkable. The petition, which was for annual parliaments, universal suffrage, equal electoral districts, and the payment of members, was presented by Mr. Feargus O'Connor, a gentleman of great earnestness and undoubted personal integrity. He stated,—and justified the statement by letters he had received,—that the petition was signed by 5,706,000 persons. The Committee on Public Petitions ascertained and reported that the signatures were 1,975,496, that many consecutive sheets were in the same handwriting, and many signatures fictitious. The meeting on Kennington

---

[1] April 10, 1848.

Common, where half a million were said to have assembled, was shown never to have exceeded at any time 23,000 in number.

In a case which could thus be subjected to accurate measure·ment, we find an example of the error to which the Government and the public are exposed in the reception of statements relating to the general feeling or opinion when it is gathered from mere assertion and rumour. . If the nominal representative body do not truly represent the people, or if it represent only a majority of numbers out of which all distinctive individuality, which is the essence of character and opinion, has been extracted in the process of its formation, public opinion will be necessarily sought for by other means, however imperfect or deceptive.

Amongst the causes enumerated by Mr. Calhoun as contributing to make monarchies the most prevalent and usually the most durable governments, he mentions, as the leading one, their greater capacity of improvement. When,—he observes,—the hereditary form is well defined, it identifies the interests of the Sovereign and the subject, excludes the suspicion and hostility incident to insecurity, and creates the strong feelings of paternity on one side, and loyalty on the other. When,—he adds,—the hereditary principle is extended to other families, and a powerful body of nobles surround the Sovereign, they oppose a strong resistance to . his authority, and he to theirs, tending to the advantage and security of the people. Such governments settle down on some fixed rules of action, by which increased protection and security are acquired by all;[1] and thus, under the enlightened monarchies of Europe, the people have made such

---

[1] " The ruin of the ancient democracies was, that they ruled as you [the French National Assembly] do, by occasional decrees, *psephismata*. This practice soon broke in upon the tenor and consistency of the laws; they abated the respect of the people towards them, and totally destroyed them in the end."—*Burke, Reflections*, &c., p. 305. See the Psephisms contrasted with the respect for law, in *Lucas's Secularia*, pp. 16, 17.

great advances in power, intelligence, and civilization.[1] " It remains to be seen, whether they will continue to retain their advantages, under the great and growing influence of public opinion, and the new and imposing form which popular government has assumed." " To comprehend more fully the force and bearing of public opinion—and to form a just estimate of the changes to which, aided by the press, it will probably lead, politically and socially, it must be considered in connexion with the causes that have given it an influence so great, as to entitle it to be regarded as a new political element."[2] The more prominent of the causes referred to, are the discoveries and inventions of the last few centuries; printing, the compass in navigation, gunpowder in war, the application of mechanical and chemical laws to the arts of production, and of steam to machinery, facilitating travel and transportation by land and water. Hence the increase and diffusion of knowledge; an impulse to progress and civilization heretofore unexampled, accompanied by unprecedented mental energy and activity, to all which causes, public opinion, and its organ the press, owe their joint and powerful influence. "Already they have attained a force in the more civilized portions of the globe, sufficient to be felt by all governments, even the most absolute and despotic. But, as great as they now are, they have as yet attained nothing like their maximum force. It is probable, that not one of the causes which have contributed to their formation and influence, has yet produced its full effect; while several of the most powerful have just begun to operate, and many others, probably of equal, or even greater force, yet remain to be brought to light." When they have produced their full effect, "they will give a force to public opinion, and cause changes, political and social, impossible to be anticipated. Their final bearing, time only can decide; but, that they would improve the condition of man, it would be impious to doubt." " The first effect

---

[1] *Calhoun, Disquisition,* &c., p. 85.   [2] Id., p. 87.

of such changes on long-established governments will be, to unsettle the opinions and principles in which they originated, and which have guided their policy, before those which the changes are calculated to form and establish are fairly developed and understood. The governments of the more advanced and civilized portions of the world are now in the midst of this period of transition. It has proved, and will continue to prove, a severe trial to existing political institutions of every form. Those governments which have not the sagacity to perceive what is truly public opinion,—to distinguish between it and the mere clamour of faction, or shouts of fanaticism,—and the good sense and firmness to yield timely and cautiously to the claims of the one,—and to resist, promptly and decidedly, the demands of the other, are doomed to fall. Few will be able successfully to pass through this period of transition, and these not without shocks and modifications, more or less considerable. It will endure until the governing and the governed shall better understand the ends for which government is ordained, and the form best adapted to accomplish them, under all the circumstances in which communities may be respectively placed."

The press must at this day be regarded as an important political element, and has not, without great truth and significance, claimed for itself the title of the "fourth estate." It exercises *two* functions, one of which it performs much more perfectly than the other. It creates the public opinion of which it is the exponent, and professes to expound that which it has created. The press, taken in its largest meaning, is the lever of the mind. It cannot eradicate the desires or the passions of mankind; but, with this limit to its power, it is hardly possible to exaggerate its importance, or its value in education,—in producing salutary changes on the condition of society,—in exploding political errors,—in promoting the social and benevolent, as opposed to the individual and selfish feeling,—and thereby bringing public opinion to a sound and

wholesome state. When we come to observe its other function, that of expressing and making known the opinion which
the public have formed,—we begin chiefly to consider the
periodical press,—a very powerful part, but not the whole,—
and we immediately perceive how insufficient for such an
office are the materials of which it can be in possession. Of
the many millions of persons composing the nation, how few
think it necessary to divert their attention from their ordinary
pursuits, even to make up their minds on most of the public
questions which arise;[1] how few, again, distinctly express
their opinions,—how few communicate them to the press.
The press has no statistical or other means of ascertaining the
opinions of the vast and silent mass. "It is strange that all
our institutions are to be at the mercy of one authoritative
voice, and that of the utterances of that voice there should not
be as much as one authorised reporter."[2] If every one of the
2,866 persons who were in the census described as "authors
and literary men," divided the kingdom amongst them, and
devoted themselves to the business of gathering the opinions
of the people on the immense number and variety of subjects
connected with the public welfare, they would fail to ascertain
any true public opinion. Their numbers would be unequal
to grapple with the multitude of people and of questions:
they would find comparatively few to respond to their inter-
rogatories; and the catechism would be upon matters as to
which the vast majority had as yet formed no creed or opinion.

In fact, however, literary men are not engaged in such a
profitless inquiry. They have a more elevated function. It

---

[1] Mr. Henry Taylor, in *The Statesman* (p. 56), London, 1836,—observes
on the fact, that most men put off making up their minds, even on matters
affecting *themselves*, until they have to act, write, or speak respecting
them.

[2] Sir James Stephen. I may refer also to the well-known and curious
inquiry of Mr. Kinglake, in his work on the *Invasion of the Crimea*,
of the manner in which public opinion has been supposed to be sounded
and urged on. Vol. ii., pp. 74—86.

has been observed,[1] that formerly the debates in the House of Commons guided, strengthened, and ruled public opinion; but that they do so no longer, because the speakers are anticipated, and public questions better and more completely treated in the articles contained in periodical literature. It is to the press, it is said, "that we must look for the formation of the great mass of public opinion on political and social questions, and it is of importance to watch with the greatest care any defects capable of remedy which diminish the good influence the press exercises; and if any one can contribute to improve the strength of the press for good, and to diminish it when it tends towards evil, he can confer no greater benefit upon the community at large."[2]

All, or nearly all important subjects, will necessarily be discussed in the press, before they are considered in the Legislature; for the Legislature is a limited body with a definite purpose, whilst the press is illimitable in diffusion, and boundless in capacity. It is in its great office, as the vehicle of public instruction, that the inestimable value of the press consists. As the universal repertory of ever-multiplying facts, and of the reasoning to which they may lead, it has become the indispensable daily food of civilisation. It is only in the event of its reporting, or assuming as *fact*, that which is *not* fact,—and of its reasoning on such false representation or assumption, that it may mislead. Such errors must be as prejudicial to the progress of political, as of every other science. They are more dangerous in political science, from the difficulty of testing them,—the infinite varieties of capacity amongst those who are more or less engaged on the subject,—and the passions which interfere to disturb inquiries so much more largely in moral than in physical science. It is

---

[1] Mr. Sidney Herbert, in the address already quoted, p. 237.

[2] The most important questions here raised have been considered in Mr. Mill's *Dissertations and Discussions*, 1859. See article on *Civilization*, vol. i. (Note to 3rd ed.)

very possible for a writer, who has a strong feeling or bias on
any particular subject, honestly to believe and represent that
which is his own opinion to be the opinion of the public. As
a supposed organ of public opinion, the press is at all times
imperfect, and may become dangerous.

The danger would result from trusting any body of men,
however high in character, to wield a machine of such vast
power as "public opinion." In *forming* public opinion we
have seen that the press is the most potent of material gifts
which has been vouchsafed to man. Diverse and antagonistic
views and interests may all invoke its aid, and be heard before
the great court of reason and conscience. But when the press
assumes to *declare* public opinion, it ceases to be the advocate
and takes the office of judge. In preparing itself for this
high function, it is assailed by all the disturbing causes of
party and private influence and interest, which bias the conduct and corrupt the judgment of mankind. It is also important not to forget, with reference to the public journals, that
they must necessarily be conducted on mercantile principles.
They must be remunerative or they cannot long continue.[1]

"If what is called public opinion were always the opinion
of the whole community, the press would, as its organ, be an
effective guardian against the abuse of power, and supersede
the necessity of the concurrent majority; just as the right of
suffrage would do, where the community, in reference to the
action of government, had but one interest. But such is not
the case. On the contrary, what is called public opinion,
instead of being the united opinion of the whole community,
is, usually, nothing more than the opinion or voice of the
strongest interest or combination of interests, and not unfre-
quently, of a small but energetic and active portion of the
whole. Public opinion, in relation to government and its
policy, is as much divided and diversified as are the interests

[1] See this point succinctly stated in a short note to Mr. Wingrove Cooke's
History of Party, vol. iii., p. 613.

of the community ; and the press, instead of being the organ
of the whole, is usually but the organ of these various and
diversified interests respectively, or rather of the parties growing out of them. It is used by them as the means of controlling public opinion, and of so moulding it as to promote
their peculiar interests, and to aid in carrying on the warfare
of party." "As the instrument of party warfare, it contributes greatly to increase party excitement, and the violence
and virulence of party struggles, and, in the same degree, the
tendency to oppression and abuse of power. Instead, then,
of superseding the necessity of the concurrent majority, it
increases it by increasing the violence and force of party feelings,—in like manner as party caucuses and party machinery ;
of the latter of which, indeed, it forms an important part." [1]

The opinion which is declared by the press to be that of
the public is very likely to become so if the declaration be
believed, however unhappy or evil may be the course to which

[1] *Calhoun, Disquisition*, &c., p. 77. " The present vitiated state of the
public taste admits of no neutrality ; no lukewarmness. The mangling of the
public and private character of political men, the debasing of the motives of
action of the loftiest and purest to a level with the meanest, the fomenting of
party rage and party hate, these are the dishes that are devoured with most
avidity. At this day no politician cares for the boldness, frankness, or
integrity of an individual editor. He buys a paper because it is an agent of
his party, to promote or to preserve its elevation. Whenever an editor
undertakes to think for himself or differently from party dictation, the party
ceases to sustain him. The editors do but imitate our leading politicians,
who themselves imitate the lawyers. They handle all political questions
like fee'd advocates, and consider themselves as standing in that attitude
before the country ; and, as such, feel justified in making the most of the
cause in which they are enlisted, good or bad. All this is most pernicious,
when we consider the immense influence they exercise over public opinion
and public morals. Though a politically debased public press is rather the
consequence than the cause of a vitiated state of public morals, yet such is
the influence of the press in augmenting such a state of morals, that
nothing is better deserving an anxious care than the preserving it pure,
independent, and respectable, and the removing from our institutions
everything that bears upon it with a contrary tendency."—*Conservative
Essays, Legal and Political*, by S. S. Nicholas, of Louisville, Kentucky,
pp. 473, 474. Philadelphia, 1863.

it leads. People yield their assent and concurrence to what seems to them inevitable. If it should happen to become the opinion of an apparent majority, and be adopted by those in power, it proceeds with a vastly accelerated rapidity, over-whelming all opponents. "The negative power is always far weaker, in proportion to its appearance, than the positive. The latter having the control of the government, with all its honours and emoluments, has the means of acting on and influencing those who exercise the negative power, and of enlisting them on its side, unless it be effectually guarded; while, on the other hand, those who exercise the negative, have nothing but the simple power, and possess no means of influencing those who exercise the positive power."[1]

It has been lately said, that "political principles are at best but the product of human reason; while political practice has to do with human nature and human passions, of which reason forms but a part; and on this account the proper business of a statesman is to contrive the means by which certain ends may be effected, leaving it to the general voice of the country to determine what those ends shall be."[2] A House in which every member would sit as the representative of an unanimous constituency will effectually prevent any successful counterfeit of the public voice, for he will have been selected as the most accurate medium for conveying the opinions of his constituents, not only on the subjects on which those opinions had been awakened, but on those on which they were latent, and might be evoked by new and unexpected circumstances. They agree with him from sympathy or from deference. The general opinion of the nation,—including that large body which now silently and passively submits to disturbing elements and causes, will thus be readily and habi-tually manifested. The operation of the system in this respect is so important that it requires especial comment.

[1] *Calhoun, Disquisition, &c.,* p. 284.
[2] *Buckle, Hist. Civilisation,* vol. i., p. 475.

It is from the regular exercise of political functions by those who are entitled to exercise them, that the steady operation of the great machine of state can be relied upon. If such duties be only taken up in times of excitement, its action will be spasmodic rather than sober and progressive. "A system of rule under which the sovereign power is dormant and inert when ordinarily comfortable, and called into action and made omnipotent only when frantic with misery;—under which it abnegates its functions in hours of calm, to resume them in its moments of passion;—under which it drops the reins when the driving is easy and the road is smooth, to snatch them at those difficult and perilous passages when the cool and dexterous hand of long experience is especially required,—surely carries its own condemnation on its face."[1] And to guard against this irregularity, it has been suggested that, on any considerable extension of the franchise, it would be desirable to make its exercise compulsory.[2] The proposal is directed in effect to the same object as that of the well-known law of Solon,—coeval with democratic institutions,—which decreed disfranchisement and dishonour to him who, on the occasion of a division and tumult in the city, should stand aloof and take part with neither side.[3] It would naturally be a part of the first conception of a democratic body, that its action should be like that of ONE man. It is only by giving it the energy and decision of a single will that a multitude can deal with its internal interests or be dealt with by strangers as a competent and self-acting body. The more fitful and irregular its action the more it becomes feeble and open to intrigue. To the extent in which every individual will is actually comprehended in any expression which purports to be that of the general will, to that extent its own members as well as strangers may depend upon the national firmness and persistency. It can hardly be doubted, that, if

[1] *Edinburgh Review*, vol. xcv., p. 277. [2] Id.
[3] *Plut. in Solon*, i., 80.

the feeling of the British people upon the late designs of
Russia against Turkey had been perfectly known, these
designs would have been abandoned, and an unhappy war
would have been averted. Mr. Grote, speaking of the law of
Solon, observes that it "seems more in the nature of an emphatic moral denunciation, or a religious curse, than a legal
sanction, capable of being formally applied in an individual
case, and after judicial trial." "We may, however," he adds,
"follow the course of ideas under which Solon was induced to
write this sentence on his tables, and we may trace the influence of similar ideas in later Attic institutions. It is obvious
that his denunciation is confined to that special case in which
a sedition has already broken out: we must suppose that
Kylon has seized the Acropolis, or that Peisistratus, Mega-
klês, and Lycurgus, are in arms at the head of their partisans. Assuming these leaders to be wealthy and powerful
men, which would in all probability be the fact, the constituted authority—such as Solon saw before him in Attica, even
after his own organic amendments—was not strong enough to
maintain the peace; it became in fact itself one of the contending parties. Under such given circumstances, the sooner every
citizen publicly declared his adherence to some one of them,
the earlier this suspension of legal authority was likely to
terminate."[1] Mr. Grote does not suggest any reason for
limiting the operation of the law to cases of such extreme
emergency. It would be of efficacy and value in every case
of tumult,—every strong manifestation of adverse opinions,
—every standing apart in the public assembly, or every case
arising out of the power which the Solonic constitution gave
to the people in that assembly. Commentators of the law
have considered its principle to be deserving of very wide extension.[2] It is agreeable to all theory and all experience,

---

[1] *Grote, Hist. of Greece,* vol. iii., p. 190.
[2] *Aulus Gellius, Noct. Attic.,* ii., 12; *Voy. du Jeune Anacharsis,* vol. i.,
p. 111. Paris, 1790.

that in every great question by which a nation can be agitated or divided, nothing could sooner tend to bring the contest to an end, than an expression of the general will.

"There is in all parties, between the principal leaders in Parliament and the lowest followers out of doors, a middle sort of men, who, by the spirit of that middle situation, are the fittest for preventing things from running to excess. But *indecision*, though a vice of a totally different character, is the natural accomplice of violence. The irresolution and timidity of those who compose this middle order, often prevent the effect of their controlling situation. The fear of differing with the authority of leaders on the one hand, and of contradicting the desires of the multitude on the other, induces them to give a careless and passive assent to measures in which they never were consulted : and thus things proceed, by a sort of activity of inertness, until whole bodies, leaders, middle men, and followers, are all hurried, with every appearance, and with many of the effects, of unanimity, into schemes of politics, in the substance of which no two of them were ever fully agreed, and the origin and authors of which in this circular mode of communication, none of them find it possible to trace." "The sober part give their sanction, at first through inattention and levity ; at last they give it through necessity. A violent spirit is raised, which the presiding minds, after a time, find it impracticable to stop at their pleasure, to control, to regulate, or even to direct."[1]

The press not only, it is observed, takes from the statesman his initiative action, but it supersedes the function of the orator. "As printing and book-reading increase, the gifts of public orators will become of little or no value."[2] There is little doubt, as Parliament shall become composed of men of a more reflective order of mind, it will be less an arena for the display of mere extempore crudities. The debates may here-

---

[1] *Appeal from the New to the Old Whigs*, p. 122.
[2] Mr. Sidney Herbert, see p. 237.

after be the brief expression of condensed thought. Instead of many of the oral addresses, the habit may be adopted of embodying and conveying reasons carefully prepared in the shape of propositions, to be entered on the proceedings of the House,—having some resemblance to the protests in the Lords. The economy of time, and the improvement in logic by such a process would be incalculable. It requires a different, and, for a deliberative body, a more valuable order of mind than mere oratory demands. It is more difficult to convince the understanding by close reasoning and irrefragable proof, than to captivate the mind by vague generalisations and plausible analogies. The positive is always restricted to some narrow and rigid limits,—to what is imaginative there are no bounds. It is, indeed, impossible to conceive any step in our progress onwards which will not require an increase of legislative talent and power,—whether it be to lead, to guide, or even to retard, where further deliberation may be necessary.

Another effect of a perfect system of representation, such as that which has been proposed, would be to strengthen the executive government. It would give to the ministry that assurance of the confidence of the people, which none of the existing machinery can afford. It would probably become the habit of every intelligent elector to place on his voting-paper, in addition to the name of his local candidate, the names of the statesmen he regarded as the most eminent, and an expression of the general opinion would be thus afforded which none could despise. The grounds of opposition to the measures of a cabinet in support of whose members some hundred thousands of electors had declared their willingness to vote, must be far other than selfish or factious, before a parliamentary majority would unite to displace them,—and thus incur the danger of a step which might be suicidal for themselves.[1]

[1] The appropriation of no more than the quota of votes to any member,

It would also further strengthen the position of every government, by the perfect security of the seats of all the principal statesmen in the House from the effect of local or individual prejudices or enmities. Under the present system, all the consideration which is due to knowledge, experience, integrity, and industry, displayed in a laborious life, may be disregarded, and their possessor. excluded from Parliament, from some accidental offence to a few influential members of a constituency, or from some petty and miserable pique. Against all such sinister influences the statesman might,

---

however numerous his supporters might be, appeared to M. Morin a defect in the system, which required amendment in its application to Geneva. "Attribuer," says M. Morin, "le même nombre de voix à tous les deputés qui ont obtenu le quantum voulu et les représenter comme n'ayant pas plus de valeur les uns que les autres aux yeux des votants c'est s'écarter de la vérité et ne pas exprimer la pensée réelle du corps électoral. Dans un pays comme l'Angleterre, où le pouvoir est stable dans la personne du souverain, cette uniformité factice serait probablement sans grand inconvénient ; mais dans une république, il est utile que les députés sachent, en vue de leur influence ultérieure, qu'ils sont les élus d'une parti plus ou moins notable du corps électoral. Cette connaissance est de nature à leur inspirer une certaine confiance en eux-mêmes, proportionnée à celle qu'on leur a témoignée, et peut, dans les circonstances très-graves, leur donner la hardiesse et le courage nécessaires pour détourner l'orage. Dans la vie des peuples il y a des crises, des occasions solennelles, pour lesquelles, le crédit personnel d'un deputé, le caractère ferme et décidé d'un citoyen estimé sont comme des forces, tenues providentiellement en réserve, qu'il y aurait imprudence à anéantir."—(De la Représentation des Minorités, p. 17.) Neither the public estimation, nor the self-confidence of the statesman or patriot, would be diminished by a law which enables a comparatively small number of his countrymen to elect him. The withdrawal of the excess of votes given to the more distinguished candidates beyond the quota necessary for their return, and the appropriation of those votes to other candidates, will in no respect lessen the weight which the first derive from the extent of support proffered to them. Not only will the recorded sympathy of a great number of voters have its moral force in commanding due attention to their opinions and measures, but the election of other members by their supporters will generally tend to augment their power in the legislative body, by strengthening the party to which they belong.

under a condition of individual independence, safely appeal to the electors at large, who will be actuated by no such narrow motives. The most important interests of a great people may be set at nought by the jealousies or caprices of the voters within a certain limited borough,—voters possessing none of the high qualifications above their fellow-men which could entitle them to pronounce such a veto. It would no longer be possible for the electors of any particular constituency to ostracise an eminent member of the House. Every one might fearlessly pursue an independent course of conduct, satisfied that if he should lose the support of one portion of his constituents, there was little doubt of his gaining that of others.

The free action of individual minds extending over a vast population, not cramped or distorted by party or selfish objects, would bring to the aid of the Government and to sound political progress, the operation of those large and general causes, the force of which has hitherto been excluded. It is found that physical laws,—which in their operation on single individuals appear so uncertain and capricious,—when examined in their bearing and effect on large numbers of persons, proceed with undeviating regularity. The uncertainty which exists of the duration of an individual life ceases when the lives of a large number of persons are taken into the account, and companies for the insurance of lives accumulate large funds by a calculation of profits which they can form with mathematical accuracy. Not only mortality but crime is found to be governed by laws which operate with wonderful uniformity, and even inadvertencies happen in a ratio which corresponds with the repetitions of the act in which they occur. It is asserted, with no unreasonable confidence, that statistical knowledge will be hereafter the basis of history,—and that it will be "as rare to find an historian who denies the undeviating regularity of the moral world, as it is now to find a philosopher who denies the regularity of the material world."[1] By connecting public events and the business of the state with the caprices of will and disposition, and the other disturbing and corrupting causes which are encouraged to interpose in detached and limited bodies of electors, the action and fate of the Government, and of its members, are disturbed by the same causes, and made capricious and uncertain, exhibiting vicissitudes, which, it has been recently remarked, sometimes bear almost a resemblance to the condition of ministers under an oriental despotism. The votes constantly given by one or two millions of persons,—subjected to no disturbing influences of any extensive operation,—may be expected to preserve such an uniformity of contemporary character and opinion, as will give general stability to good government. Instead of shrinking from the inconvenience and dreading the consequences of frequent parliamentary elections,—their frequency would be regarded by the minister as a source' of confidence and strength. It may be assumed that he will be a man of the highest talent and character,—able to ameliorate while he also preserves,—and, therefore, one on whose activity and moderation vast numbers will be content to rely. His own seat in the House would be in no danger. He would be re-elected with the tranquil certainty with which a director of the Bank is replaced. The result of every general election would be to furnish him with a faithful index of the progress and existing state of public opinion. A triennial election would be soon considered as recurring at too long rather than too short an interval,—for the minister would find his main support not in any party arrangements or complications, but in the sense and approbation of the people.

[1] See *Buckle's History of Civilisation*, vol. i., p. 30.

CHAPTER XII.

THE SUFFRAGE.

THE subject of the suffrage has been reserved, as a matter which, in one respect only, is necessarily affected by, and affects, the system of representation suggested in this work. A provision has been introduced for enabling any district, town, or parish, to obtain a charter, entitling it to return a representative,[1]—or in another, and perhaps better understood form of expression, to constitute itself one of several contributory boroughs. The right is proposed to be conferred by an order of the Queen in council, and is designed to be purely a change in division and arrangement in no respect affecting the right of suffrage. If a distinction of the right of suffrage depending on the place of residence be obstinately adhered to, it might in certain cases be an impediment to the equal operation of such a law,—for a village, which, having grown into a town, should apply for incorporation as a borough, would find itself with a different suffrage from other boroughs, as it would be framed on the county franchise. It would not be proper to vest in the executive government the power of affecting the suffrage.

It may be hoped, however, that when the subject is examined in all its bearings, every party will agree on the abolition of distinctions, which are unworthy of the age in

[1] Clause V.

which we live, and carry us back to the times of the Norman
villeins or the Saxon thralls.   The true principle on which
the bill of Mr. Locke King for a £10 franchise in counties
should be supported is, that it proposes the adoption of the
same electoral standard in the counties as obtains in the
towns: the principle is equality of the suffrage, wherever the
place of residence may be.   If any persons delude themselves
with the thought that a concession of a £10 suffrage in the
counties,—if it be reduced below that standard in the
boroughs,—will be a final measure, they cannot be too soon
undeceived.   If it be made £5 in the boroughs, and £10 in
the counties, they may be assured of this consequence,—a
consequence which may be safely predicted without any pretensions to the spirit of prophecy,—that in the session of
Parliament which follows such an Act, some county member,
who, like Mr. Locke King, is able to regard himself as representing his county, and not merely a privileged class of its
inhabitants, will ask for leave to bring in a bill reducing the
standard to £5 in the counties.   It is a logical, a necessary,
and an inevitable result.   It may fail the first time, or the
second,—but that which is undeniably just will, at no distant
day, assuredly prevail.   By withholding it as long as that can
be done, its adversaries may succeed in producing hostility
and rancour.   They may alienate those who otherwise would
be their friends,—but for any purposes of good, their efforts
will be impotent.   When other anomalies are removed, many
of the representatives of the counties will perceive the impro-
priety of preserving one which treats the rural inhabitants as
a servile class, stamped by the legislature with the seal of
inferiority.   As they ride through the country,—the retired
hamlet, and the antique market-village,—they will experience
an ingenuous shame at beholding men, many of whom, by
long converse with the external world,—

> Amid the bounties of the year, the peace
> And liberty of nature,—

have acquired "the wisdom which works through patience," whom they had yet allowed to be excluded from the highest of civil rights,—rights which are conceded to others far inferior to them morally or physically, in some neighbouring borough. So much it has been thought necessary to say on behalf,—not of any particular qualification,—but of an equality of qualification,—not an equality of every man with every other, which the common sense of mankind has in all ages repelled,—but an equality of every man of any rank and class with others of the same rank and class as himself, —an equality wholly unaffected by the plot of ground which may constitute his freehold, or be the site of his dwelling.

The proper qualification to be adopted as the test of the right of suffrage is a question independent of that of its equality. It deserves much consideration, to what extent there is any just reason for lowering the general standard of qualification adopted in the Reform Bill. It would be desirable to try the effect of good laws in enabling the great masses of the people to rise to that standard; but the misfortune is that such laws are obtained slowly, and with difficulty, if obtained at all, in the absence of sufficient members of the legislative body really interesting themselves for the poorer of the working classes. It is important to consider the true principle to be observed in conferring the suffrage.

The question of *right* may be first considered. "If civil society be made for the advantage of man, all the advantages for which it is made become his right. It is an institution of beneficence; and law itself is only beneficence acting by a rule. Men have a right to live by that rule—they have a right to justice—as between their fellows, whether their fellows are in politic function or in ordinary occupation. They have a right to the fruits of their industry, and to the means of making their industry fruitful. They have a right to the acquisitions of their parents,—to the nourishment and improvement of their offspring,—to instruction in life, and consolation in death. Whatever each man can separately do, without trespassing upon others, he has a right to do for himself; and he has a right to a fair portion of all which society, with all its combinations of skill and force, can do in his favour. In this partnership all men have equal rights, but not to equal things. He that has but five shillings in the partnership has as good a right to it as he that has five hundred has to his larger proportion. But he has not a right to an equal dividend in the product of the joint estate; and as to the share of power, authority, and direction which each individual ought to have in the management of the state, that I must deny to be among the direct original rights of man in civil society; for I have in my contemplation the civil social man, and no other. It is a thing to be settled by convention. If civil society be the offspring of convention, that convention must be its law. That convention must limit and modify all the descriptions of constitution which are formed under it. Every sort of legislative, judicial, or executory power are its creatures. They can have no being in any other state of things; and how can any man claim, under the conventions of civil society, rights which do not so much as suppose its existence?—rights which are absolutely repugnant to it?" "Government is not made in virtue of natural rights, which may and do exist in total independence of it, and exist in much greater clearness, and in a much greater degree of abstract perfection: but their abstract perfection is their practical defect. By having a right to everything, they want everything. Government is a contrivance of human wisdom to provide for human *wants*. Men have a right that these wants should be provided for by this wisdom. Among these wants is to be reckoned the want, out of civil society, of a sufficient restraint upon their passions. Society requires not only that the passions of individuals should be subjected, but that even in the mass and body, as well as in the individuals, the inclinations of men should be frequently thwarted, their will controlled, and their passions brought into subjection. This can only be done by a *power out of themselves ;* and not, in the exercise of its functions, subject to that will, and to those passions which it is its office to bridle and subdue. In this sense the restraints on men, as well as their liberties, are to be reckoned among their rights. But as the liberties and the restrictions vary with times and circumstances, and admit of infinite modifications, they cannot be settled upon any abstract rule ; and nothing is so foolish as to discuss them upon that principle. The moment you abate anything from the full rights of men, each to govern himself, and suffer any artificial positive limitation upon those rights, from that moment the whole organisation of government becomes a consideration of convenience. This it is which makes the constitution of a state, and the due distribution of its powers, a matter of the most delicate and complicated skill. It requires a deep knowledge of human nature and human necessities, and of the things which facilitate or obstruct the various ends which are to be pursued by the mechanism of civil institutions. The state is to have recruits to its strength, and remedies to its distempers. What is the use of discussing a man's abstract right to food or to medicine ? The question is upon the method of procuring and administering them." [1]

" The rights of men in governments are their advantages ; and these are often in balances between differences of good ; in compromises, sometimes between good and evil, and sometimes between evil and evil. Political reason is a computing principle ; adding, subtracting, multiplying, and dividing, morally, and not metaphysically or mathematically, true moral denominations." [2]

The question with which we are met on the threshold is,

---

[1] *Reflections*, &c., pp. 89, 90.

[2] Id., p. 92. See on this subject *Mill's Considerations on Representative Government*, chapters iii. and viii.

whether, in conferring the franchise, there should be *any* test of capacity,—and, if that be answered in the affirmative, the next is, what that test of capacity shall be. It has never been denied, by those who have condescended to enter upon details, that the first question must be answered in the affirmative,—although that which was at one time the popular formula, *universal* suffrage, apparently repudiates any test, whether of condition, of sex, or of age. The term "manhood" suffrage, implies that "manhood" is to be the test. It must be applied by the aid of the lawyer, the physiologist, or the statistician.

The law gives to one whose father has died without appointing him a guardian, and who has no mother, and no property attracting a guardianship by tenure, the power even *before* fourteen years of age, of electing a guardian for himself; and "as to a guardian *after* fourteen, it appears, from the ending of guardianship in soccage at that age, as if the common law deemed a guardian afterwards unnecessary."[1] It would probably be about that age at which the definition of the physiologist would properly attribute the term "manhood."[2] Other applications of the description are furnished in statistical classifications of the ages of life.

In the report of the Registrar-General on the census, printed in 1854, we have the description of two ages of manhood:—"The second age or vicenniad (20—40), of which *thirty* years is the central point, embraces the early period of manhood. Growth is completed; weight, stature, and strength are at their maximum. It is the athletic, poetic, inventive, beautiful age,—the prime of life. It is the soldier's age. The apprentice becomes the journeyman, who attains at the end the highest mechanical skill, and earns the highest wages. Marriage is contracted, and the man first hears the name of father from the lips of his children. In bad natures

---

[1] *Co. Lit.*, 88, b. (u) 16: ed. 1832, by *Hargrave and Butler*.
[2] See *Eng. Dict.* in voc.

and in unfavourable circumstances it is the age of crime, of
passion,—of madness, which breaks out in its wildest forms,
—as well as of wasting maladies.

"In the third vicenniad (40—60), of which the middle
point is *fifty* years, we see men in the highest professions
first attain eminence ; the capital which has been expended
in their education returns rapidly ; their established character
gives them the confidence of their fellow men ; experience
and practice enable them to deal as proficients with the great
interests and questions of the world.   They see their children
enter life.   The edifices, of which the foundations were laid
before, spring up around them.   The prudent, tried, skilful,
inventive man, now often becomes, in England, a master, and
controls establishments in which he was once the clerk, the
workman, the apprentice boy.   It may be justly called the
intellectual age, — the legislative, the judicial age.   The
statesman speaks, and his voice reverberates over an attentive
nation.   But the passions and labours of life wear deep
furrows ; the health of the workman is shaken in great
cities, and he falls before their pestilences ; the heart and the
brain are sometimes overwrought ; diseases acquire force, and
the man easily falls their victim."

Positive laws in different countries have adopted other ages
of man as the time at which different rights shall belong to
him.   The Roman could acquire no property which was not
immediately lost in the property of the father during his life.
Neither age, nor rank, nor the consular office, nor the honours
of a triumph, could exempt the most illustrious citizen from
the bonds of filial subjection.   In our own law the age of
twenty-one has been adopted as the age at which binding
contracts may be made, and at which the rights of property
may be asserted.   The constitution has also adopted that age
as one of the tests, but not a sole test, of capacity for the
franchise.

It is obvious, that if what is called "manhood" suffrage

were adopted as a qualification,—"the good of the citizens at large being,"—according to the most uncompromising asserters of right,—"the proper end of civil government, whatever its form,—whatever its history or traditional origin,"[1] the question of the age to be adopted, must be determined by considerations of prudence and convenience. If there could be any natural solution of the question of right attaching more forcibly at one time than at another, it would be that which the Roman law and the patriarchal system exhibited, and which reserves to the parent that power over the interests of all his descendants, which nature has conferred, until nature herself deposes him. "Without fear though not without danger of abuse, the Roman legislators reposed an unbounded confidence in the sentiments of paternal love; and the oppression was tempered by the assurance, that each generation must succeed in its turn to the awful dignity of parent and master."[2]

Another test or condition has also been introduced amongst us,—the possession of certain property, as a freehold, or a certain social position, as that of paying rates or taxes, or the occupation of a tenement of a certain value. In the classification of citizens,[3] Montesquieu observed, "that the great legislators of antiquity made the greatest display of their powers, and even soared above themselves."[4] These, being questions of capacity, must obviously be determined by the condition of society and the state of education. It is the business of our legislators to select, amid the examples before them, that which is the test or qualification best suited to our country, our age, and our social condition. In considering the form which it should assume, there are certain principles of which it is important not to lose sight.

[1] *Westminster Review*, vol. x., p. 195, N. S.
[2] *Gibbon, Decline and Fall*, vol. vi., p. 91. 8vo ed. 1809.
[3] *Reflections*, &c., p. 272.
[4] And see *Grote's History of Greece*, vol. iii., pp. 155-159.

The test of capacity should be one which will exclude no man of ordinary industry and skill in his calling, and ordinary prudence and self-denial in his conduct. It cannot be necessary that the suffrage should be given to every youth as soon as he is out of his apprenticeship :—it is not necessary that it should be given, without regard to property, or to position, as the head of a family, or to participation in the burdens of citizenship, at least to one in early manhood, whilst the character is in process of formation, and the pleasures and anticipations of life exercise a strong influence on his conduct, and divert him from more serious thought on subjects not directly affecting his own career. He does not at that time of life require it from any regard to liberty or security, for the possession of the franchise by his seniors of the same class, having similar interest for themselves and their children, is a sufficient guard, and every day brings him nearer to the time when he may himself attain it. The qualification, however, should be accessible to every man when he acquires a home, and settles to the fixed occupation for which the preparatory course of his earlier years has fitted him.

It should be applied equally to all classes and conditions, without regard to employment or situation. If certain boundaries are fixed, and persons beyond or without such boundaries are placed under a different law, it may operate as a perpetual exclusion as to such persons. It may be impossible for a man to change the place in which his business and connections have formed themselves, and it may therefore be a mockery to tell him, that if he would take any interest in the political condition of his country he must go elsewhere. Another condition of the test should be, that it is of easy and ready application to large numbers of persons. The practicability of universal application necessarily causes the test to be of a rude and general character; but one which assumes the possession of the fit qualifications of an elector from his possession of their fruits, is not ill adapted to supply the place of that more accurate and refined examination to which it is impossible to resort.[1]

An alternative which has been sometimes proposed, and even resorted to, where the numbers to be admitted to the suffrage are large, and there are great inequalities of position, is that of indirect election, or the formation of bodies of electors, who, when chosen, are to elect the representative. This system, whether in great or small institutions, is almost in every case ineffectual for any useful purpose. There is no object which would not be better fulfilled by a direct choice. The electoral college of the United States, chosen for the purpose of appointing the President, is a remarkable example of the entire failure of such a preliminary election to effect that which its authors propose to themselves. The object was to form a conclave of the wisest and most unbiassed of the American citizens,—separated from all the other political bodies in the state and not connected with any party, having only one cause of existence, and one object, that of electing as President the man in whose hands the vast interests and powers of the republic can be most safely deposited. Such an unbounded confidence the American people have not reposed in any college of men. The spirit of the institution is wholly disregarded in the literal execution of its office. The electors thus chosen are the mere machines of party. The effect of the interposition of intermediate electors will be either to produce such a result, or, if not, to destroy all interest in the election on the part of the primary voters.

" Or, ce qu'on cherche, c'est le bon député. La capacité supérieure en appelant à la reconnaître toutes les capacités qui, bien qu'inférieures, sont en rapport naturel avec elle.

---

[1] On the educational tests which may be applied, see Chapter VIII., on the "Extension of the Suffrage," in Mr. Mill's *Considerations on Representative Government.* The heated discussions in the Ballot debate on the necessity and method of securing the suffrage to the illiterate voter are a curious feature in this argument. (Note to 4th ed.)

Si au contraire vous commencez par faire élire les électeurs, qu'arrive-t-il?—vous avez à accomplir une opération analogue à la précédente; mais le point de départ est changé, la condition générale est abaissée. Vous prenez pour base la capacité de l'électeur, c'est-à-dire, une capacité inférieure à celle qu'en définitive vous voulez obtenir; et vous vous adressez forcément à des capacités encore inférieures, hors d'état de vous conduire, même sous cette forme, au résultat plus élevé auquel vous aspirez; car la capacité de l'électeur n'étant que celle de reconnaître le bon député, il faudrait être en état de comprendre celle-ci pour comprendre celle-là, ce qui n'arrive point.

"L'élection indirecte, considérée en elle-même, déroge donc au principe primitif comme au dernier but du gouvernement représentatif, et abaisse sa nature.

"L'élection indirecte dérive de la souveraineté du nombre et du suffrage universel; dans l'impossibilité de faire passer ces deux principes dans la pratique, on s'est efforcé d'en retenir quelque ombre. On a violé le principe du gouvernement représentatif, abaissé sa nature et énervé le droit d'élection pour demeurer, en apparence, conséquent à une erreur. Qui ne voit en effet qu'un tel système de l'élection directe lui conserve seul sa réalité et son énergie? *Toute action dont le résultat est éloigné et incertain inspire peu d'intérêt;* et les mêmes hommes qui concourent avec beaucoup de discernement et de vivacité au choix de leurs officiers municipaux donneront aveuglément et froidement leur suffrage à des électeurs futurs que leur pensée ne suit point dans un avenir où ils interviennent si peu. Ce prétendu hommage à des volontés trop peu éclairées, pour qu'on leur fasse, dans le choix des députés, une part plus efficace, n'est au fond qu'une misérable charlatanerie, une adulation mensongère; et sous une prétendue extension de droits politiques, se cachent la restriction, la mutilation, l'affaiblissement de ces mêmes droits dans la sphère où ils existent réellement, et où ils s'exerceraient dans toute leur plénitude, avec tout leur effet."[1]

[1] *Gouv. Rép.*, vol. ii., p. 262.

The independence of the representative body thus chosen, of the real constituent body, the people, is thus set forth by Mr. Burke:—" There is no way to make a connection between the original constituent and the representative, but by the circuitous means which may lead the candidate to apply in the first instance to the primary electors, in order that, by their authoritative instructions (and something more perhaps), these primary electors may force the succeeding bodies of electors to make a choice agreeable to their wishes. But this would plainly subvert the whole scheme. It would be to plunge them back into that tumult and confusion of popular election, which, by their interposed gradation-elections, they mean to avoid, and at length to risk the whole fortune of the State with those who have the least knowledge of it, and the least interest in it. This is a perpetual dilemma, into which they are thrown by the vicious, weak, and contradictory principles they have chosen. Unless the people break up and level this gradation, it is plain that they do not at all substantially elect to the assembly; indeed, they elect as little in appearance as reality.

" What is it we all seek for in an election? To answer its real purposes you must first possess the means of knowing the fitness of your man, and then you must retain some hold upon him by personal obligation or dependence. For what end are these primary electors complimented, or rather mocked, with a choice? They can never know anything of the qualities of him that is to serve them, nor has he any obligation whatsoever to them. *Of all the powers unfit to be delegated by those who have any real means of judging, that most peculiarly unfit is what relates to a personal choice.* In case of abuse, the body of primary electors never can call the representative to an account for his conduct. He is too far removed from them in the chain of representation."

" As, in the end, all the members of this elective constitution are equally fugitive, they may be no longer the same persons who had chosen him, to whom he is to be responsible when he seeks for a renewal of his trust. To call all the secondary electors to account is ridiculous, impracticable, and unjust; they may themselves have been deceived in their choice, as the third set of electors may be in theirs. In your elections responsibility cannot exist."[1]

The practical and vigorous mind of Major Cartwright rejected a system in which he saw merely an ingenious refinement, destroying all the force and value of the principle of representation. Writing of the then Spanish Cortes, he observes, that, from the successive strainings, "there can be nothing more likely than that in the end the representative chosen by the very few who have the final straining may be one whom a great majority of the collective body would not have elected. This erroneous practice was recommended by David Williams to the French at the time of their revolution. It had before been recommended by Hume."[2]

---

[1] *Reflections*, &c., pp. 277–279.

[2] *Life and Correspondence of Major Cartwright*, vol. ii., p. 227. Mr. Mill, in his *Considerations on Representative Government* (Chap. IX., "Should there be two stages of election?"), has concluded that indirect election has many disadvantages peculiar to itself, while it has no benefit which is not attainable by direct election. Lord Grey is not satisfied with the argument, and compares the case of a poor man [why not a rich man?], one of 10,000 voters for a large town, with the same man if he were one of twenty friends, empowered to appoint a deputy to vote for them in a constituency thus reduced to 500,—when he thinks that the vote would be more considered and valued by the voter. (*Parliamentary Government*, pp. 257–263, 2nd ed.) It is true that our present method of dealing with such large constituencies must be felt by every thoughtful person as a mockery of representation. I pass by what might be said of this method of diminishing the number of the rich voters; but I confess I should deprecate most strongly its adoption in the case of the poorer electors. It would, I think, be the most downward and fatal step that could be taken in the progress of representative institutions. One cannot but imagine the petty intrigues, favouritism, and jealousies of the workshop, the factory, and the club-room, which such a system would inaugurate. The more cunning workmen, or foremen, would soon find that a twenty-vote power was of some value in securing them a certain notice and attention, and would learn how

The suffrage should be regarded as a right of value, and one not thrown heedlessly to any. It should be felt that in conferring it the state adopts all the tests of quality and of worth that are consistent with placing the suffrage on a broad and comprehensive basis. The right of taking part in the social government is so sacred, that the state may be justified in adopting the precept, — "cast ye not your pearls before swine." Like other rights of value, it would be not too much to require some proof of appreciation from every man who would possess it. One of the most valuable improvements adopted by the Reform Bill was that which established the register of voters. The more the population increases, the more important will the register become. Without it, parlia-

---

it might be turned to account. They would no doubt be successful in overcoming the inertia or indifference of their fellow-labourers, sufficiently to secure their own nomination; but when a workman is canvassed by three or four of his companions for the same petty advantage, the scale is not likely to be turned by arguments the best fitted to enlighten the understanding or improve the character. Nor would the small eminence thus gained by the deputed voter be generally salutary to himself. He will often have acquired it by some of those persuasive arts which have no elevating tendency, while he will be apt to form an exaggerated estimate of the personal importance conferred by his exceptional privilege. It is the common habit of most persons to magnify any small measure of distinction which gratifies self-importance. Circumstances can hardly be conceived more calculated to create a disposition unfavourable to disinterested action than the interposition of such intermediate depositories of political power. They would cut off the primary electors from all direct and necessary contact and relation with public men of superior intelligence and character,— narrow instead of enlarging the field from which the voter must seek concurrent sympathies in opinion,—narrow also his direct interest and therefore his scope of thought on public subjects, which would be one of the main educational advantages of the franchise. I believe that indirect voting would seriously detract from the good results of representative government, and multiply some of its worst evils. If there be any portion of the people qualified to take a part in political affairs, to whom the state cannot entrust more than the twentieth of a vote, let us, for the sake of straightforwardness and honesty, hope that this fraction of suffrage may be given at once and directly to the elector, and not through the mediation of another. (Note to 3rd ed.)

mentary elections would become a scene of riot and confusion.
" When, after the social war, all the burghers of Italy were
admitted free citizens of Rome, and each had a vote in the
public assemblies, it became impossible to distinguish the
spurious from the real voter, and from that time all elections
and popular deliberations grew tumultuous and disorderly,
which paved the way for Marius and Sylla, Pompey and
Cæsar, to trample on the liberties of their country, and at
last to dissolve the commonwealth." [1] The cost of registration in England and Wales amounts annually to upwards of
£100,000, and notwithstanding the unpaid services of a great
number of overseers and other officers, the machinery is
extremely imperfect. It is not impossible to make the process of registration of the voter ancillary to that of his due
identification at the poll. The Registration Act abolished
the payment of a shilling imposed by the Reform Act. A
small payment, even of two or three pence, might be usefully restored, and collected on the annual delivery to the
elector of a ticket containing his name, address, and number
on the register. This might be done on a house to house
visitation by an officer charged with the duty of keeping the
lists constantly accurate, and of withdrawing the names of
deceased persons. A yearly struggle of parties in the registration courts, for the purpose of expunging the names of
voters, without any regard to their intelligence, their worth,
or their capacity for bringing a deliberate and instructed
judgment to the choice of legislators, is not the least contemptible feature of modern political life.

The retention, since the Reform Act, of the laws that disfranchise a large number of persons holding offices in the

---

[1] *Black. Com.*, vol. i., p. 159. At a meeting of the Ballot Society, Mr.
Pliny Miles, of New York, stated that one of the principal causes of elec-
toral corruption in that city was the want of any register of electors.—
Star, Dec. 31, 1858. See also the note on the registration, p. 175, *supra*.

public service¹ can only have happened from a remarkable inadvertence. The principle and cause of the exclusion was intelligible under the system of restricted electoral rights and close boroughs, but it is now utterly indefensible. It has probably done no little towards lowering some of the metropolitan constituencies—especially at the east, north, and south of London—by excluding an extensive body of respectable and intelligent householders. It would be an extraordinary condition of things, if, after establishing a competitive examination, and collecting a great number of the most able of its people in its service, the state should go on to deny them that franchise which it gives to classes far inferior to them in character, education, and talent. It is absurd to suppose that they would form a class of electors favourable to an extravagant expenditure of the public income. There would be few classes more interested in or anxious for general economy. It is where the resources of the household are properly husbanded, and not in the establishment of a spendthrift, that the servants chiefly look for the due remuneration of steady and honest service. No class of voters would be less inclined to act corruptly, for under the system which is here proposed, no class of voters would have stronger reasons for choosing the best men, and none would be more impotent for any purpose of mischief, even if they combined to choose the worst.²

¹ Excise, 5 W. & M., c. 20; Customs, 12 & 13 W. 3, c. 91; Post Office, 9 Anne, c. 10; Police, 3 W. 4, c. 19, &c.
² On this point I am compelled to take a view the very reverse of that adopted by Lord Grey, who recommends that, instead of removing the prohibition of persons engaged in the revenue from voting, that exclusion should be made to extend to all who are employed in the permanent *civil* service (*Parliamentary Government*, p. 235, 2nd ed.), and he alludes to the defeat of the government on the Civil Service Bill of 1857 by the skilfully-organized agitation of those interested in the measure. (Id., pp. 91, 92.) An electoral system which so balances the chances of a candidate as to place him in a condition in which he may be defeated by two or three votes being withdrawn from him and given to his adversary, is precisely suited to the exaction of petty pledges, and especially those by which he may hope

T

All persons engaged in maritime employment, and there-fore necessarily absent, should be allowed, by depositing their voting papers with the registrars, to exercise their franchise. The same facility may be afforded to all civil, military, and naval officers in the public service, absent from the country on their public duties. Nowhere could more intelligent and valuable electors be found than these classes would afford. There does not seem to be any reason why a like privilege should not be given to English subjects travelling in foreign countries, or residing there temporarily for mercantile or other causes. Such opportunities afforded to an elector of exercising his national rights would call forth at all times his interest in and affection for his country. Some modification of the suffrage might be made in order to give effect to the opportunities of voting thus afforded. They would be, of course, applicable to all freehold votes; and as to votes founded on qualifications which require residence, it might be made sufficient if any portion of the family of the elector had resided in the house giving the qualification; without ren-dering it necessary, in such cases, that he should himself have been resident within so short a preceding period as is at pre-sent necessary.

Lord Harrowby, in presenting a petition,[1] in 1852, on the subject of the representation, remarked that if it were purely internal, or even confined to national interests, we were "in danger of neglecting altogether those considerations which arise out of our colonial connections;" and the question of the propriety of establishing some connection between our

---

to gain a few friends, and create no enemies. An abolition of the system which exposes candidates to such injurious influences is the true remedy. There can be no more certain proof of the existence of a great vice in any social institution than the fact that, in order to effect its object or secure its working, it requires that any class of persons of whom the society is composed shall be either physically, morally, or politically dwarfed.

[1] *Parl. Deb.*, 27th May, 1852.

national and colonial representation has been repeatedly discussed. A freehold suffrage might afford the means of keeping up this intercommunication and representation of interests, and sympathies which are even of more importance than interests. There would be no difficulty in the system, of which an outline has been here presented, of enabling any British subject holding a freehold of a prescribed value in the United Kingdom, and residing in any of her colonies, territories, or dependencies, to transmit his voting paper, with evidence of his identity, to the registrars, and of thus exercising a right of suffrage in the mother country. The colonial legislatures would, there is little doubt, willingly create reciprocal rights, and thus the institutions of the mother country and the colonies — without interfering with the operation of each other—would be intimately blended. The inhabitant of the colony, as well as he of the mother country, would feel himself a subject and citizen of the same great empire, and the associations of the inhabitants of different hemispheres would be connected by a multitude of new ties, preserving an unity of feeling which has been hitherto rarely sustained after a few generations.[1] The rapidity of telegraphic communication would afford opportunities of action which were impossible in earlier times.

In all cases where a woman is *sui juris*, occupying a house

[1] Since the publication of this treatise, the nature and permanency of the connection between the mother country and her colonies, and their several duties and responsibilities, have been discussed ,'both by statesmen and philosophers, nor is the discussion yet exhausted. The practicability and advantage of creating such personal and abiding ties as are above suggested would not be undeserving of consideration in that argument. (Note to 3rd ed.) An objection may be made that this would tend to the creation of an absentee proprietary. It would, however, be easy to annex to the electoral privilege when claimed by absentees, a condition securing the administration of the estate, which forms the qualification, with due regard to the public interest. It might be that they should be dealt with as was proposed with regard to estates in mortmain, under the Public Lands and Commons Bills, of sessions 1871 and 1872. (Note to 4th ed.)

or tenement, or possessed of a freehold, or is otherwise in a position which, in the case of a male, would amount to a qualification, there is no sound reason for excluding her from the parliamentary franchise. Since the first publication of this work, the municipal franchise has been secured to women, and it is impossible to doubt the speedy abolition of an anomaly which is so entirely without any justifiable foundation, as their exclusion from the full rights of citizenship.

The suffrage is a matter so distinct from electoral organisation, that the legislature should deal with the two things in separate Acts. Blending them together tends to confuse and embarrass the discussion of both, and is convenient only to those who would divert the public mind from true conclusions on the question of representation.

CHAPTER XIII.

THE progress of population and wealth, the activity of commerce and intercommunication, the discovery and employment of new methods of labour, requiring large combinations of means and their scientific application, and the changes which the face of the country is undergoing from these and other causes, are now constantly requiring the creation for local purposes of new powers.[1]   Every successive year it becomes more and more difficult for Parliament to deal properly and beneficially with the innumerable local matters on which legislation is called for.   During the last five-and-twenty years many public Acts have been passed conferring, under various conditions, powers of local government which before that time could only have been obtained by special Acts. Some of our cities and towns, at this day, having regard to their wealth and population, and to the intelligence and culture of their inhabitants, are not inferior to many communities which in an earlier stage of European history stood in the rank of independent States.   The more closely the condition and wants of society are examined, the more clearly it

---

[1] Part of this chapter has been borrowed from papers read by the author before the Social Science Association. (Note to 4th ed.)

will be seen to be necessary that counties, cities, and towns
should be everywhere entrusted with far more comprehensive
powers for public improvement, and for the promotion of
every beneficent object, educational, moral, and physical,
within their boundaries. It is not necessary to dwell on the
expense of local Bills, or on the impossibility, from their
number and the character of their details, that they can have
that attention in Parliament which their importance requires ;
or the extreme difficulty of bringing before Committees the
true facts and bearings of questions on local works, or the
considerations and arguments for or against their allowance or
rejection which ought to prevail—reasons which for the most
part are perfectly well known to the inhabitants of the locality.
The failure of the evidence commonly so given to convey the
true facts in contested matters is now almost proverbial. In
railway legislation it has been remarked that a certain number
of great companies have parcelled out England and Wales
between them, and bring forward schemes in their own
interest, the public interest being wholly lost sight of ; and
powers are conceded to them upon evidence justly charac-
terized as unexampled in any other time or place. Experts
of all kinds are called to depose to one thing one day and the
very contrary the next day, their ingenuity being exercised to
distinguish the cases, whenever the contradiction is likely to
be exposed. Gas companies, water companies, and other
bodies seeking special powers, all more or less employ these
means of success. Well-constituted local governing bodies
would determine on the necessary and useful public works
required in the locality, in an inexpensive and far more satisfactory manner.

   The object to be sought is not merely means of accomplishing works for the public advantage when the desire for them
in local governing bodies is sufficiently strong to produce the
effort, but such an organization as shall give to all the latent
forces existing in each community in the shape of aspirations

for improvement of every kind, their proportionate measure of political power, and thus overcome inertness and indifference, and stimulate and encourage effort. The governing body should accurately represent the interests of the town and of all the inhabitants of the town or district, and when so constituted as to entitle it to public confidence, it may safely be empowered to frame and adopt laws of limited application for establishing public works and effecting improvements within the locality for the general benefit of its inhabitants; and for such purposes to incorporate in these powers the Lands Clauses, and Railway Clauses Consolidation Acts, and such other general Acts as may be deemed necessary, and to impose local rates. These limited statutes, in order to become law, should be subject to the confirmation of the Local Government Board, and the assent of the Crown, through one of the Secretaries of State. It would of course be competent to these authorities on any question which may arise on a proposed statute, to require the opinion of legal or other sufficient advisers.

It is with the constitution of such local governing bodies, whether in existing municipalities, or county or parochial boards, that it is the purpose of the present chapter to treat.

A generation has gone by since the passing of the Municipal Corporation Act of 1835. It was not without a manifest distrust of its successful operation that its very framers, if they did not actually propose, at least readily acquiesced in excluding from the newly-created bodies the control of the valuable charitable endowments which were under the government of the old corporations. Its provisions are certainly unsatisfactory in several important points.

First, it divides the municipalities into wards instead of enabling the burgesses to group themselves according to their own discretion. This admits of the employment of that ingenious party artifice which is known in the United States as "gerrymandering," or such an arrangement of the boundaries of each ward, that on a poll of the ward will enable a dominant part of the inhabitants to obtain a majority. All experience tends to prove that the larger the area of the electoral district, the greater is the interest that is felt, and the more extensive will be the choice offered to the electors. In the last session of Parliament an attempt was made to afford facilities for revision of the boundaries of wards. It is not to be regretted that the apprehension that this would do no more than expose the electors still more to the gerrymandering artifices, caused the rejection of the measure. The true remedy in fact is the abolition of the ward system, or at least of its restrictive provisions, especially now that a practical method is known, of liberating the electors from such restrictions, with far greater convenience for taking the poll than any divisional system can possibly afford.

Secondly, it introduced certain qualifications of property or rating as indispensable for those who are to be chosen on the municipal councils. The object of electoral laws is above all things to provide for the choice of the most fit and competent persons for the functions entrusted to them; and to obtain such persons, the first and most simple condition is, that those in whom the selection is vested have the widest and most unfettered choice. It is in the degree in which effectual means of comparison, with unrestricted powers of selection, have been gradually opened, that all things necessary for convenience, comfort, and health, have been developed and improved in the material world, and we have no better course to follow in the pursuit of moral benefits, of which good government is one of no small importance. Clearly the first thing to be done is, as far as possible, to remove out of the way every obstacle which does or may unnecessarily obstruct any elector in making the best choice he is able, according to his most deliberate judgment, of the persons by whom the public business of the community in which he lives is to be managed or administered. The greatest obstacle of course is

ignorance.   Ignorance, perhaps, of what is needful to be done;
ignorance of the persons who would be the fittest to do it, if
they were called upon for the work; of their relative capacity,
integrity, or other qualifying or disqualifying elements, or of
their willingness to undertake it.   We cannot expect that difficulties of this nature will be ever wholly removed, although
much may be done, and probably is in progress, for the
education of individuals and of society in the business of self-
government.   One step, however, can be immediately taken.
All obstacles, purely artificial, may be got rid of.   In a former
chapter I have dwelt on the expediency of abolishing all
arbitrary disqualifications for sitting in the House of Commons.   In the matter of local and municipal government, no
qualifications of property, rating, residence, or otherwise,
should be required.   The first introduction arbitrarily of a
certain rank or status as indispensable to the person who fills
an elective office, was probably due to the desire to exclude all
below a certain class; and since this feeling has ceased, or has
come to operate less forcibly, the continuance of such arbitrary
distinctions has perhaps been owing to the reasons applicable
to one kind of function, or to certain principles of selection,
having been illogically applied to other functions or methods
of choice, with which they have really nothing in common.
A physician or surgeon, a lawyer, a master of a ship, may be
reasonably required to pass a prescribed examination, for they
are entrusted with the properties or lives of multitudes who
have no sufficient means of judging whether they are qualified
to undertake the tasks upon which they enter, and who stand
in need of some certificate upon which they can rely.   There
may be physical grounds for demanding a certain standard of
size and of health for men to be received into the army or the
police.   It is right for divers reasons to require proof of some
amount of intellectual cultivation from those who desire to
enter the civil service, but an electoral test of this nature has
not been seriously proposed.   When the people, who are too

numerous to be convened to determine on the details of business affecting the common weal, are invited to elect representatives to act in such matters on their behalf,—to impose terms upon the discretion thus implied, instead of fully trusting them to make the best choice they are able, is to withdraw with one hand the power tendered in the other. Not many years ago certain property qualifications were required in members of the House of Commons, but these were found to be frequently obstructive, were commonly evaded, and were ultimately swept away as intolerable. It is matter almost of astonishment that qualifications of a like nature should be still insisted upon for aldermen, members of town councils, and should be even proposed for other elective offices. The town council of Birmingham has, however, recently applied to Parliament for their repeal. If there were anything in such qualifications which implied the existence of greater knowledge or more public-spirited or patriotic sentiment, or any kind of superior virtue, some reason might be urged for their existence, although even in that case it would be better that the electors should be permitted to act upon their own judgment of such attainments, but the fact that a candidate is rated at £20, or £50, or £100 a year, or owns property to a certain amount in a certain place, affords not the smallest test of his capacity or fitness to be a member of a town council, or of a county or parochial board.

Thirdly. The provisions, which require one-third of the Town Councillors,[1] and of the members of the District[2] and Metropolitan Board of Works,[3] to go out of office annually, are inconvenient and unnecessary. It was probably thought that if the entire body were dissolved like the House of Commons, at one time, a change of political feeling in the locality might have the effect of preventing the re-election of any of them, and the public interests and business of the town might be suddenly placed in new hands, uninstructed,

—perhaps regardless of, perhaps hostile to, the proceedings of their predecessors, and more desirous of proving their incompetency than of fairly executing their designs. Against this mischief, these provisions of the statutes are supposed or intended to guard. It is evident that they are directed to meet an evil peculiar to a system which places the choice of the council or board solely in the hands of the majority. If a scheme had been considered on which every voter or ratepayer might be certain of being represented, the framers of the Municipal Corporation Act would have had no reason to fear that, however the numbers of the majority or the minority might vibrate, there would still be at all times more than sufficient voters whose opinions had not been changed,—to re-elect such a number of the old members as would prevent, even more effectually than a triennial vacating of office can do, the evils of any sudden reversal of system or any instability of purpose.

Fourthly. No provision is made for the direct representation of the owners of property. The method adopted on the election of poor-law guardians, of giving a plurality of votes, based on the amount at which the voter is rated, is no real security for the due representation of the owners, while it gives an undue weight to a certain, and perhaps not always the most enlightened or public-spirited of the middle-class electors, who occupying places of business or otherwise, are yet tenants for no more than short terms. It was well that such a delusive attempt to give weight to property was not introduced into the Municipal Acts. A representation founded on status only, as by justices of the peace, would be still more unsatisfactory, and would be a perpetual source of jealousy and distrust, but the absence of any distinct representation whatever of the proprietary body is clearly a defect. It is not enough to say that some of the occupiers will be owners, or will no doubt be influenced by owners. The power should rest upon reality and not mere hypothesis, and be

exercised according to legitimate influences only. The Report
of the Select Committee of the House of Lords in 1859 on
the Municipal Franchise mentions one ward in a corporate
town in which the minority of voters represents property of
the value of £26,000 a year, and the majority property of
£4,000 a year; and another in which 302 voters, rated in the
whole at £661, are able to control the elections, where the
entire rating of the ward is £16,000. In a northern town
the Report says, of 5,300 voters, 1,000 pay on £27,000, and
the remaining 4,300 on no more than £7,000. It is possible,
in fact, that there may not be a single owner of property
beyond a tenant from year to year, or at will, in the local
constituency. In the evidence given before the Commons
Committee on Metropolitan Local Government, in 1866, a
witness from Rotherhithe remarked that there was no representative of the great proprietors of wharfs and other valuable
property there; and of St. George's in the East it was
observed that the London Dock Company paid nearly half
the rates, and yet had no voice in the local government.

The author in his evidence before the same Committee
referred also to the fact that there are not only great proprietors in the metropolis, as the Marquis of Westminster, the
Duke of Bedford, Lord Portman, and others, but also corporate bodies, city companies, and other institutions holding
estates for ecclesiastical, municipal, and charitable purposes,
whose representatives should properly be heard in matters
especially relating to the locality. The proprietary votes in
such cases might be given by the various governing or
directing bodies: those in respect of property held for educational purposes might be given by the School Boards; of
eleemosynary estates,—if for medical charities, by the College
of Physicians, and College of Surgeons, or some recognized
professional authority. It was suggested that of 150 councillors for London, 50 might be chosen by the owners, and
100 by the inhabitants. Thus if proprietors of property of
the aggregate annual value of £5,000,000 were to vote, the

votes of owners to the extent of £100,000 a year, would elect one member. The number of members to be allotted respectively to property and to persons, is the question for consideration. The former might compose a third, a fourth, or a fifth of the municipal or governing board. They should be present for discussion and for mediation, but not to outvote or overrule. The definite proportions of the proprietary and the personal members being fixed, every proprietary vote would have a weight exactly proportioned to the annual value at which the estate is rated. A single registry office may be established in every local government district, for the proprietary voters within it. A small fee for each estate would be sufficient to meet the charges of such an establishment. The voting papers [1] could be received at the same

---

[1] The subjoined form of voting paper is borrowed from the Schedule of the Public Lands and Commons Bill (No. 63), Session 1872. It is a form suitable, for example, to the election of proprietary representatives on the Lincoln County Board.

COUNTY OF LINCOLN.—OWNER'S VOTING PAPER.

Name of Owners.	Description of Property.	Gross Annual Value.	Names of Candidates voted for, in the order of preference.	
The Master Warden and Assistants of the Guild or Fraternity of the Holy Trinity and St. Clement, of Deptford Strond, in the county of Kent.	House, farm buildings, and lands, in the parish of Goshill, Lincolnshire.	£545	1	Abraham Carter.
			2	John Jones.
			3	William Mills.
			4	Frederick Stanhope.
			5	James Brenton.
			6	George Wilkinson.
			7	Henry Brown.
			8	Thomas Isaacson.
			9	
			10	
			11	
			12	
			&c.	

This vote is to be counted for the candidate first named; and for the other candidates respectively, in the order of preference indicated, only in case the first or prior candidate, or candidates, has, or have, enough votes in value for his, or their, election without this vote; or, in case he, or they, have not enough votes in value to be elected. The surplus value of the vote, where a portion only is appropriated, to be transferred in the like order of preference.

Signature of Owner, or Seal of Corporation, &c.

office, to which they might be transmitted by post or other-wise, without inconvenience. The secret form of ballot would not be required for the proprietary body. The personal votes would be given by the secret ballot, as provided for parlia-mentary elections,[1] but extending over a narrower area would be more readily counted.

Fifthly. The system of indirect election introduced into the constitution of the Metropolitan Board of Works is in-compatible with its immediate responsibility to the community at large.[2] That constitution is founded on the Report of the Commissioners on the Corporation of London, in 1854. The reason for recommending it seems to have been an apprehen-sion of the power which must be conferred on a single body of councillors, and which the Commissioners thought would be in some way diluted or diminished if divided between bodies of a primary and a second degree, the second being a kind of federation of the first. The Commissioners say,—

"If the precedent of the Municipal Corporations Act were followed absolutely, it would be necessary not only to alter the constitution of the corporation, but to advance the boun-daries of the City until they surround the entire metropolis —a process by which 723 acres would be converted into an area of 78,029 acres, and an assessment of £935,000 into an assessment of £9,964,000. A change of this magnitude would, as it seems to us, defeat the main purpose of municipal institutions. London in its full extent is a province covered with houses; its diameter from north to south and east to west is so great, that persons living at its farthest extremities have few interests in common; its area is so large that each inhabitant is in general acquainted only with his own quarter, and has no minute knowledge of other parts of the town. Hence the two first conditions for municipal government, minute local knowledge and community of interests, would be

---

[1] See Chap. VII., pp. 124, 125.　　　　[2] Pp. 267–270, *ante*.

wanting. The enormous numbers of the population, and the vast magnitude of the interests which would be under the care of the municipal body, would likewise render its administration a work of great difficulty."

Upon this it may be remarked that the corporate body elected by the people connected with each parish and district would naturally form committees to whom the business of the locality with which they were specially acquainted would be referred, and in action upon their reports the aggregate body would have the benefit both of local and general knowledge aided by paid functionaries wherever necessary.

In the labours of a great Metropolitan Council scope might be found for the employment of all the varied talents and genius of a large body of public-spirited men, in which the acquirements of science, of study, and of travel, and the knowledge and experience of practical life, may be enlisted and employed in promoting the public welfare. Such a Council would be an admirable school of preparation for the business of the Imperial Legislature. It cannot be hoped for, under a system which partitions and divides it into small bodies and sections.

It is not, however, the magnitude alone of the metropolis which is the supposed objection to its consolidation. The Commissioners have other reasons both of a special and a general kind. They say:

"That the bisection of London by the Thames furnishes an additional reason for not placing the whole town under a single municipal corporation. All roads, streets, sewers, gas-pipes, and water-pipes, in short, all means of superficial or subterraneous communication which run in continuous lines from north to south, are necessarily stopped by the river. Many of these are, directly or indirectly, the subject of municipal control; and therefore a municipal body which governed the metropolis both north and south of the Thames would find that the continuity of its operations was, in many respects, broken off by natural circumstances."

It is not easy to see why operations on one bank of the river may not cease, and be resumed or not as occasion shall require on the other bank, without forming any obstacle to the vesting of powers in the same body to deal with both sides of the stream. The government of Paris is not impeded by the Seine, nor that of Lyons by the Rhône and Saône. But the Commissioners, however, conclude:—

"These observations appear to us decisive against the expediency of placing the whole of the metropolis under a single municipal corporation, without adverting to those more general questions of public policy which naturally suggest themselves in connection with the subject."

This is a statecraft which it is not easy to comprehend. When any great object is to be accomplished there seems no better means than to confer upon those to whom its performance is committed the most ample scope and power for the exercise of their judgment and discretion, and to strengthen that judgment and discretion by every practical means. This applies alike to the individual, to the local corporation, and the Imperial Government. Let the individual have the most unlimited and unfettered choice of his representatives, and a sense of personal responsibility in its exercise; the municipal body, the widest and most unimpeded power of action, which, by its capacity for good, shall attract and include the best and most public-spirited mind of the locality; and let the national Legislature be a concentration of the result of the intellect and moral as well as the material force of the kingdom.

> Deliver not the tasks of might
> To weakness.

Instead of frittering away the municipal constitution by a multitude of elections for detached and exceptional purposes, in many of which little interest is severally taken,—an incorporation of the whole metropolis under a great council, chosen by a perfect representative organization, would invest every

branch of its administration and its offices and dignities with
a weight and value calculated to make them just objects of
ambition for its most distinguished citizens. There are no
obstacles in the way of such an union and incorporation which
a powerful government might not overcome,—nor probably
any which all the more enlightened citizens would not rejoice
at having overcome. It has been conceived by many of the
inhabitants of the metropolis, that the difficulties in the way
of placing the entire city under one municipal constitution are
rather found in objections arising with the Imperial Government than with the people. It is thought, whether correctly
or not, that the successive governments have entertained a
jealousy of a body, so powerful as the municipal council of the
metropolis would be, if it concentrated the suffrage of three
millions of people, surrounding the offices of the state. In such
a constitution the dignity of the mayor of the City would be
restored to its ancient, or more than its ancient splendour.
History does not record the existence of any provincial or
municipal officer having jurisdiction over a community of equal
extent, wealth, or intelligence. It might be very possible,
therefore, that governments, feeble in parliamentary force,
would shrink from creating at their doors a rival power of such
magnitude. If the time should come, in which these fears
cease to operate,—if a government should exist not tottering
on the crutches of party, but strong in the sympathies and
affections of the people, and of a parliament their faithful
exponent, it may yet be that the City of London,—instead of
being confined within the narrow boundaries, and decked with
the antique trappings of its early and comparatively infantile
existence,—will assume the position which it has attained
amongst cities, and open its arms to embrace the vast population which has gathered around its ancient walls. It is not
by a servile crawling in the paths of our ancestors, but by
following in the spirit of their institutions, that we most fully
show our respect for antiquity.

U

A prospect of London and our other great cities, as well as extensive rural districts, governed by municipal and local councils which, in the manner of their formation, shall everywhere evoke the highest intelligence and public spirit, and, possessing the public confidence, shall be powerful agents in all works of social amelioration; and the still larger prospect of the representative institutions of the kingdom aiding in the improvement of individual character, and in the elevation of the whole tone of popular life, may appear Utopian. "I believe," observes a living master of our language and of art, "the quiet admission which we are all of us so ready to make, that because things have been long wrong it is impossible they should ever be right, is one of the most fatal sources of misery and crime from which this world suffers. Cast the word Utopian out of your dictionary altogether. There is no need for it. Things are either possible or impossible—you can easily determine which in any given state of human science. If the thing is impossible, you need not trouble yourself about it; if possible, try for it. The Utopianism is not our business, —the *work* is." I may conclude with the same counsel from the mouth of the philosophical statesman, so often cited in these pages,—Mr. Burke,—who, in his speech on economical reform, said,—"I know it is common for men to say that such and such things are perfectly right—very desirable, but that, unfortunately, they are not practicable. No sir, no. Those things which are not practicable are not desirable. There is nothing in the world really beneficial that does not lie within the reach of an informed understanding and a well-directed pursuit. There is nothing that God has judged good for us that He has not given us the means to accomplish, both in the natural and the moral world. If we cry, like children, for the moon, like children we must cry on."

APPENDICES.

Appendix A.

SWITZERLAND.—THE ASSOCIATION RÉFORMISTE OF GENEVA.

It is either in republican countries, or in states in which efforts, more or less earnest, are made to carry out the principles of national self-government in their integrity, that the system of proportional and preferential representation has been most enthusiastically received. In no nation has the labour of propagating a knowledge of the method, and of the results which may reasonably be expected from it, been more vigorously and intelligently undertaken and pursued than in Switzerland. The Association Réformiste, devoted to this object, was inaugurated in 1865, with an address from M. Ernest Naville.[1] This was followed by several productions by the same eminent writer, by MM. Roget and Morin, and by the establishment of a journal 'The Réformiste,' especially directed to the purpose of making known and advocating a just electoral system. This journal continued in circulation until shortly before the commencement of the late Continental war, when most domestic discussions were for the time absorbed, and the journal was merged in the 'Indépendence Suisse.' A collected statement of the proceedings of the Society was published in the last year,[2] from which the progress of thought on this subject nearly in every part of Europe and America will be gathered. An extract from the 'Réformiste' of the 4th of May, 1869, reviewing the results of the general election of this kingdom in 1868, concludes with the following warning, "pour les hommes qui veulent s'instruire à la grande école de l'expérience."

1°. La lutte exclusive de deux partis, qui résulte forcément du principe des majorités, fausse la représentation du peuple anglais, et ne permet pas aux divers éléments de la vie nationale de se manifester.

2°. La mesure adoptée pour la représentation des minorités (dont on ne saurait trop louer l'intention) est en elle-même un palliatif insuffisant qui ne saurait tenir lieu d'une vraie réforme, même dans le cas où la mesure serait généralisée.

3°. Si l'Angleterre n'adopte pas et ne réalise pas sérieusement le principe de la représentation vraie, elle dérivera de plus en plus vers les écueils trop connus de cette fausse démocratie qui abaisse les parlements et les peuples.

The Report presented by M. Ernest Naville to the Association Ré-

---

[1] La Patrie et les Partis. Genève, 1865.

[2] Travaux de l'Association Réformiste de Genève, 1865–1871. Recueillis par Ernest Naville. Genève et Bâle, H. Georg, Libraire-Editeur.

formiste, in March, 1871,[1] introduces the question by a review and logical analysis of the various amendments which were proposed in the rude electoral machinery of earlier times. Their differences and several results are thus accurately described :—

"La revue générale du mouvement réformiste dans le monde fait reconnaître, à des signes manifestes, les progrès rapides de notre cause. Cette revue a, de plus, l'avantage de signaler les voies diverses qui se sont offertes à la pensée des publicistes et des législateurs pour réaliser le principe de la représentation vraie. Le nombre des travaux a été si grand que toutes les voies possibles paraissent avoir été signalées et explorées ; et nous avons à recueillir, pour les mettre à profit, les résultats d'une étude faite dans toutes les parties du globe par des hommes de toutes les opinions.

"Les plans de réforme proposés supposent tous des collèges élisant plusieurs députés, parce que pour une élection unique la loi de la majorité est nécessairement maintenue. Ces plans forment un nombre considérable de procédés divers, mais plusieurs de ces *procédés* sont de simples variantes d'un même *système*, parce qu'ils réalisent, avec quelques modifications de détail, le même principe fondamental.

"Les systèmes peuvent être réunis en deux classes, celle des *systèmes empiriques* et celle des systèmes rationnels.

"*Systèmes empiriques.*

"Les systèmes empiriques cherchent à établir la représentation des minorités, sans se préoccuper du caractère proportionnel de cette représentation. Ils sont au nombre de trois :—

"*Pluralité simple.*—L'électeur dépose dans l'urne le nom d'un seul candidat. Sont élus, dans le nombre voulu, les candidats qui ont obtenu le plus grand nombre de suffrages. Un minimum peut être fixé. Ce système a été proposé en France depuis longtemps par M. Emile de Girardin, et en dernier lieu, par M. le Baron de Layre.

"*Vote limité.*—L'électeur inscrit sur son bulletin un nombre de candidats moindre que celui des députés à élire, les deux tiers ou les trois quarts par exemple. Les candidats qui obtiennent le plus grand nombre de suffrages sont élus. Un minimum peut être fixé. Ce système a été établi et pratiqué en Angleterre pour les collèges nommant trois députés.

"*Vote Cumulatif.*—L'électeur dispose d'un nombre de suffrages égal à celui des députés à élire. Il peut *cumuler* tous ses suffrages sur un seul candidat, ou les répartir, à son gré, sur un nombre de candidats quelconque et dans la proportion qui lui convient. Les candidats qui ont réuni le plus de suffrages sont élus. Un minimum peut être fixé. Ce système a été adopté en Illinois pour la représentation politique, et pratiqué en Angleterre pour l'élection des Conseils d'Ecole.

---

[1] Travaux, &c. Appendix, p. 703.

" *Systèmes Rationnels.*

" Les systèmes rationnels ne cherchent pas seulement à accorder une représentation aux minorités, mais à établir, d'une manière proportionelle, qui est la seule représentation vraie. Ils sont au nombre de trois :—

" *Représentation personnelle des électeurs.*—L'électeur désigne sur son bulletin le candidat qu'il désire en première ligne, puis celui qu'il désire en seconde ligne, si le premier est élu déjà, et ainsi de suite, en joignant à son premier et principal suffrage une série de suffrages éventuels. Le nombre des bulletins divisé par le nombre des candidats à élire détermine le nombre de suffrages nécessaires pour l'élection (quotient électoral). Un candidat est élu dès qu'il a réuni le quotient électoral. Chaque bulletin ne compte que pour un seul candidat, pour le premier d'abord, pour le second si le premier est élu déjà, et ainsi de suite.

" *Représentation proportionelle des partis.*—Divers partis librement formés, et en nombre indéterminé, présentent leurs listes de candidats. Les électeurs choisissent le parti auquel ils se rangent, et chaque parti obtient un nombre de députés proportionnel au nombre de suffrages qu'il a réunis.[1]

" *Suffrage Uninominal.*—Chaque candidat publie une liste indiquant, selon l'ordre de sa préférence, les autres candidats auxquels il veut transmettre les suffrages superflus ou insuffisants qu'il pourra obtenir. L'électeur désigne le nom d'un seul candidat. Les suffrages superflus (ceux qui dépassent le quotient électoral), puis les suffrages insuffisants (ceux dont le nombre est inférieur au quotient), sont transférés selon les listes d'indication que les candidats ont déposées. Le résultat de l'opération est qu'on obtient le nombre voulu de députés qui ont tous, directement ou par suite de transfert, un nombre de suffrages égal au quotient électoral."

" Telle est la classification générale des divers plans de réforme. Je crois que tous les procédés proposés, soit en Europe, soit en Amérique, se rattachent à l'un des six systèmes indiqués. La pluralité simple, le vote limité et le vote cumulatif forment la classe empirique des projets de réforme ; la représentation personnelle, la représentation proportionuelle et le suffrage uninominal en forment la classe rationnelle.

" L'adoption des systèmes empiriques constitue un succès réel pour l'œuvre de la réforme, non-seulement parce qu'ils rompent avec le principe de la majorité, mais parce que leurs défenseurs proclament hautement les principes de la représentation vraie. Mais ces systèmes restent fort loin du but qu'il faut atteindre, et en vue duquel on les recommande et les adopte. En effet, ils offrent tous les caractères suivants :

---

[1] M. Naville adds that he regards " le système de la valeur décroissante des suffrages," proposed by Messrs. Burnitz and Warentrapp (Appendix B, p. 298, *infra*), as merely a variety of this class. The same may be said of a former suggestion of the author. (Appendix C, p. 301.)

" Les suffrages qui s'accumulent sur un candidat au-delà du quotient électoral, et les suffrages qui restent au-dessous de ce nombre, peuvent être sans influence sur le résultat de l'opération électorale ; ce sont des suffrages perdus.

" L'existence de suffrages perdus est cause que le résultat de l'élection n'est pas nécessairement proportionnel. Les minorités que l'on cherche à faire représenter, sans le faire d'une manière rationnelle, peuvent obtenir trop ou trop peu de députés. La certitude de la justice fait défaut."

M. Naville then proceeds to show the necessity of an implicit submission to party leaders and party management in designating the candidates who are to be put forward and supported, in order to avoid these consequences.

The Report, after stating that the Association had at first " indiqué le système de la représentation personnelle, en modifiant les plans de MM. Andræ et Hare par l'idée émise de M. Rivoire, mais le journalisme génevois l'avait signalé comme une nouveauté étrange, très-éloignée de nos mœurs politiques ;" and they therefore recommended *la liste libre*, taking as the basis the following method proposed by M. Morin (author of *Précis de l'Histoire Politique de la Suisse*) in 1862 :—

" *Système électoral proportionnel simplifié.*

"Art. 1er. La proportionnalité est admise comme base de l'élection au Grand Conseil.

"Art. 2. Les listes de candidats remises au bureau central, avant la distribution des bulletins, ont seules droit à la réparation proportionnelle des députés.

"Art. 3. Cette répartition s'opère de la manière suivante :

" *A*. Immédiatement après le dépouillement du scrutin, le bureau arrête, d'après le nombre des bulletins valables, celui des suffrages indispensables pour l'élection d'un représentant. Ce dernier nombre, déterminé par le chiffre des députés à élire dans chaque collège, est $1/44^e$ des bulletins valables dans l'arrondissement de Genève ; $1/38^e$ dans celui de la Rive gauche ; $1/14^e$ dans celui de la Rive droite.

" *B*. L'importance des listes en concurrence est donnée par le chiffre des bulletins compactes qu'elles ont réunis, et l'ordre des noms dans ces listes est déterminé par le nombre des suffrages qu'ils ont obtenus, en tenant compte des bulletins égrenés ou panachés.

" *C*. Chacune des listes a droit à autant de députés qu'elle renferme de fois le nombre de voix nécessaire pour l'élection d'un représentant.

" *D*. Les noms portés sur plusieurs listes, ayant droit à la répartition, sont élus d'emblée Le surplus leur est réparti proportionnellement à leur force, sans que la part revenant à d'autres groupes soit réduite ou augmentée par ce fait.

" *E*. Les fractions ne comptent pas.

" Art. 4. Si, après la répartition entre les listes du nombre de députés auquel elles ont droit, il en reste à nommer, ceux-ci sont élus à la majorité relative, à condition toutefois qu'elle ne soit pas inférieure au minimum indispensable pour l'élection d'un député."

Observations sur le système simplifié.

L'exemple suivant, qui présente au premier coup d'œil une objection très-spécieuse au système proportionnel, contribuera à mettre en relief la facilité avec laquelle ce mécanisme résout les questions en apparence les plus embarrassantes.

Supposons 1000 bulletins valables et 20 députés à élire. Le minimum indispensable pour l'élection d'un député est $^{1000}/_{20}$, soit 50. Deux listes, A et B, sont en concurrence.

A réunit 400 bulletins compacts et, par le fait de suffrages égrenés, le nom qui est en tête a 700 voix.

B compte 600 bulletins pour 19 de ses candidats, mais le 20° n'en a que 300.

Comme suit:

Candidats.	Liste A.		Candidats.	Liste B.	
1	700 suffrages.		1	600 suffrages.	
2	400	,,	2	600	,,
3	400	,,	3	600	.,
4	400	,,	4	600	,,
5	400	,,	5	600	,,
6	400	,,	6	600	,,
7	400	,,	7	600	,,
8	400	,,	8	600	,,
9	400	,,	9	600	,,
10	400	,,	10	600	,,
11	400	,,	11	600	,,
12	400	,,	12	600	,,
13	400	,,	13	600	,,
14	400	,,	14	600	,,
15	400	,,	15	600	,,
16	400	,,	16	600	,,
17	400	,,	17	600	,,
18	400	,,	18	600	,,
19	400	,,	19	600	,,
20	400	,,	20	300	,,
	8300			11,700	

8300+11,700 font 20,000 voix. Donc les 1000 électeurs ont voté. Les 400 de la liste A ont voté d'une manière compacte. Entre les votants de la liste B, 300 se sont séparés des autres, pour un seul nom, et ont porté leurs voix sur l'un des candidats de la liste A.

L'importance de celle-ci étant représentée par 400 bulletins compactes, celle de la liste B est réduite à 300, puisque 300 électeurs seulement l'ont portée sans y faire de changement.

D'après l'article 3, lettre C du système simplifié, le nombre de députés qui doit être attribué à la liste A est $400/_{50}$, soit 8, et à la liste B $300/_{50}$, soit 6. Donc la liste B, comptant 11,700 votes, aura moins de députés que la liste A, qui n'en réunit que 8,300. Il y a là une inconséquence, mais elle n'est qu'apparente.

D'abord les 300 électeurs qui ont abandonné un nom de la liste B, pour porter leurs voix sur un candidat de la liste A, ont eu probablement la précaution de remettre au bureau une liste modifiée d'après leurs sympathies. Cette 3me liste étant entrée en concurrence, elle a droit à la répartition. Celle-ci doit s'opérer comme suit :

1 nom commun à la liste A et à la 3me, élu d'emblée.

8 appartenant à la liste A.

11 communs à B et à la 3me liste, élus d'emblée.

Total 20

La scission entre les votants de la liste B a donc pour résultat d'écarter le candidat qui en était l'objet, mais il donne un député de plus à la liste A.

Dans le cas où les électeurs, abandonnant la liste B pour un candidat, négligeraient de remettre au bureau une 3me liste, voici ce qui se passerait :

La liste A aurait droit à 8 députés,

    „ B   „   „   6   „

Les 6 noms qui auraient réuni le plus de voix, après les 14 élus, seraient nommés dans l'ordre de la majorité et pris dans la liste B qui compte le plus de suffrages.

A aurait donc   8 députés.

et B   „   12   „

Total 20

résultat un peu plus favorable à B et qui rétablirait la répartition entre les listes, comme si tous les noms de B comptaient 600 voix et tous ceux de A 400.

Le système proportionnel simplifié pourvoit donc, par l'addition de l'article 4, à l'objection soulevée dans l'exemple proposé.

Après avoir réparti entre les diverses opinions qui se sont fait représenter par des listes, le nombre de députés qui leur revient, le reste appartient évidemment aux électeurs indépendants, et la majorité peut seule décider entre eux. C'est ce motif qui nous a porté à introduire la disposition contenue dans l'article 4, au moyen de laquelle les intérêts des électeurs indépendants se trouvent complétement sauvegardés.—Pp. 25-29.

APPENDIX B.

EXTRACT from *Methode bei jeder Art von Wahlen sowohl der Mehrheit als den Minderherten die ihrer Stärke entsprechende Zahl von Vertretern zu sichern.* Dargestellt von Dr. Gustav Burnitz und Dr. Georg Varrentrapp. Frankfurt a. M., 1863.

Wir nehmen an, es sei 1 Vertreter zu wählen und es stehen sich drei Parteien gegenüber, deren die eine über 1500, die zweite über 900, die dritte über 600 Stimmen gebietet. Hier ist der mit 1500 Stimmen bedachte Candidat der ersten Partei als der Höchstbestimmte, als der, welchem das gröszte Masz von Zustimmung zu Theil ward, der Gewählte und zwar der mit Recht Gewählte. Ist dann eine zweite Wahl vorzunehmen, so wird, bei geschlossenen Parteiverhältnissen und bei abermals 1500, 900 und 600 für die verschiedenen Parteicandidaten abgegebenen Stimmen, wiederum der Candidat der ersten, relativ stärksten Partei der Gewählte sein, und ebenso in ferneren Wahlgängen, wenn noch weitere Vertreter zu wählen sind. Ganz dasselbe Ergebnisz wird erzielt, wenn 3, 6, 10 oder mehr Vertreter in *einem* Wahlgange ernannt werden; es werden nur die Candidaten der stärksten Partei aus der Urne hervorgehen ; die Minorität wird, gleichviel ob gröszer oder kleiner, stets und gänzlich unvertreten bleiben.

Es ereignet sich dies, weil man nur die abgegebene Stimmenzahl, nicht aber die Rangordnung, welche die Partei ihren verschiedenen Candidaten gibt, im Verhältnisz zur relativen Stärke der einzelnen Parteien beachtet. Je nachdem ein oder mehrere Vertreter zu wählen sind, gestaltet sich das Verhältnisz verschieden.

1. Bei jeder durch eine Anzahl von Personen vorzunehmenden Wahl eines oder mehrerer Vertreter findet bewuszt oder unbewuszt, auch innerhalb derselben Partei, eine Werthschätzung der zur Wahl Empfohlenen, sei es im Allgemeinen, sei es unter Berücksichtigung eines speciellen zu erreichenden Zweckes, statt. Diese Werthschätzung tritt bei der Wahl in zweierlei Weise zu Tage : *a)* durch die Zahl der dem einzelnen Bewerber zufallenden Stimmen : *b)* durch die Rangordnung, welche demselben Seitens seiner Wähler im Verhältnisz zu den anderen von derselben Partei aufgestellten Bewerbern zugewiesen wird ; diese Rangordnung drückt das Masz des Werthes aus, welcher dem einen Candidaten vor den anderen derselben Partei zufällt, das Masz der Glücksaussicht, welches die Partei dem einen ihrer Candidaten vor den anderen zu gewähren wünscht.

Nur bei der Wahl eines einzigen Vertreters fallen beide Werthschätzungen zusammen in *einer* Wahlziffer.

2. Wo mehrere Vertreter zu wählen sind und mehrere Parteien von verschiedener Stärke sich gegenüber stehen, gilt es einerseits, die Stärke der einzelnen Parteien (also die Zahl der den einzelnen Bewerbern von ihnen zugewendeten Stimmen), andererseits den verschiedenen Werth, welchen die einzelnen Parteien ihren verschiedenen Candidaten beimessen, klar darzulegen und in einem richtigen Verhältnisz einander gegenüber zu stellen. Dies geschieht durch die Wahlziffer, welche sich ergibt, wenn man die absolute, einem Bewerber zugefallene *Stimmenzahl* durch die relative (d. h. durch die ihm auf den verschiedenen Stimmzetteln zu Theil gewordene) *Rangzahl* dividirt.

Wird dieses Gesetz zur Geltung gebracht, so wird die Mehrheit der Wähler jedesmal die entsprechende Mehrheit der Vertreter ernennen, aber auch der Minderheit wird die ihrer Stärke genau entsprechende Zahl von Vertretern zufallen.

Es möge dies aus etlichen Beispielen erhellen, welche die verschiedenen vorkommenden Parteiverhältnisse darstellen und an deren Spitze wir das bereits oben erwähnte Beispiel setzen. Drei Parteien mit je 1500, 900 und 600 Stimmen treten zur Wahlurne und es ergeben sich folgende Resultate:

	BISHERIGE ZÄHLUNGSWEISE.			WAHLZIFFER NACH RANGORDNUNG.		
	Partei A.	Partei B.	Partei C.	Partei A.	Partei B.	Partei C.
1r B.	1500	900	600	$\frac{1500}{1}=1500$	$\frac{900}{1}=900$	$\frac{600}{1}=600$
2r „	1500	900	600	$\frac{1500}{2}=750$	$\frac{900}{2}=$	$\frac{600}{2}=300$
3r „	1500	900	600	$\frac{1500}{3}=500$	$\frac{900}{3}=300$	$\frac{600}{3}=200$
4r „	1500	900	600	$\frac{1500}{4}=375$	$\frac{900}{4}=225$	$\frac{600}{4}=150$
5r „	1500	900	600	$\frac{1500}{5}=300$	$\frac{900}{5}=180$	$\frac{600}{5}=120$
6r „	1500	900	600	$\frac{1500}{6}=250$	$\frac{900}{6}=150$	$\frac{600}{6}=100$
7r „	1500	900	600	$\frac{1500}{7}=214$	$\frac{900}{7}=128$	$\frac{600}{7}=85$
8r „	1500	900	600	$\frac{1500}{8}=187$	$\frac{900}{8}=112$	$\frac{600}{8}=75$
9r „	1500	900	600	$\frac{1500}{9}=166$	$\frac{900}{9}=100$.	$\frac{600}{9}=66$
10r „	1500	900	600	$\frac{1500}{10}=150$	$\frac{900}{10}=90$	$\frac{600}{10}=60$

u. s. w.   u. s. w.

Es würden hiernach

bei der Wahl	nach der bisherigen Zählungsweise			nach der Wahlziffer		
	der Partei A.	der Partei B.	der Partei C.	der Partei A.	der Partei B.	der Partei C.
von 6 Vertretern.	6	—	—	3	2	1
„ 10 „	10	—	—	5	3	2
„ 12 „	12	—	—	6	4	2
„ 16 „	16	—	—	8	5	3
„ 20 „	20	—	—	10	6	4
„ 25 „	25	—	—	13	7	5

zufallen, Schon für den zweiten Vertreter ergeben die 900 Stimmen, welche von der zweiten Partei ihrem ersten Candidaten gegeben wurden, eine höhere Wahlziffer, als die von der ersten Partei ihrem zweiten Candidaten gegebenen, d. h. 900 ist mehr als $\frac{1500}{2}$; ebenso ist 600 stärker als $\frac{1500}{3}$.

Stehen sich nur zwei Parteien gegenüber mit z. B. 60 und 38 Stimmen Stärke, so zeigt sich folgendes Verhältnisz nach den beiden Systemen:

BISHERIGE ZÄHLUNGSWEISE.		WAHLZIFFER.	
Partei A.	Partei B.	Partei A.	Partei B.
1r Vertreter 60	38	$\frac{60}{1} = 60$	$\frac{38}{1} = 38$
2r „ 60	38	$\frac{60}{2} = 30$	$\frac{38}{2} = 19$
3r „ 60	38	$\frac{60}{3} = 20$	$\frac{38}{3} = 12{\cdot}5$
4r „ 60	38	$\frac{60}{4} = 15$	$\frac{38}{4} = 9{\cdot}5$
5r „ 60	38	$\frac{60}{5} = 12$	$\frac{38}{5} = 7{\cdot}6$
6r „ 60	38	$\frac{60}{6} = 10$	$\frac{38}{6} = 6{\cdot}3$
7r „ 60	38	$\frac{60}{7} = 8{\cdot}5$	$\frac{38}{7} = 5{\cdot}4$
8r „ 60	38	$\frac{60}{8} = 7{\cdot}5$	$\frac{38}{8} = 4{\cdot}7$
9r „ 60	38	$\frac{60}{9} = 6{\cdot}6$	$\frac{38}{9} = 4{\cdot}2$
10r „ 60	38	$\frac{60}{10} = 6$	$\frac{38}{10} = 3{\cdot}8$

Nach der ersten Stimmenzählung bleibt also die zweite Partei vollkommen unvertreten; nach dem System der Wahlziffernberechnung erhält sie dagegen bei der Wahl von 3 Vertretern einen, bei 5 Vertretern 2 gegen 3, bei 8 Vertretern 3 gegen 5, bei 10 Vertretern 4 gegen 6, bei 13 Vertretern 5 gegen 8.—Pp. 5-8.

The above examples are followed by others showing the operation of the system if parties were more numerous, and also exhibiting the effect in the cases of specific elections referred to.

APPENDIX C.

A METHOD proposed for ascribing to every vote a weight, or value, for every candidate named, according to the order in which the name stands upon the voting-paper. It was subsequently abandoned, for the reasons mentioned in page 187. It will be understood by the following example, extracted from page 55 of " The Machinery of Representation," by Thomas Hare. Maxwell, Bell Yard, 1857. 2nd ed.

" The first table exhibits a supposed number of actual and possible votes for candidates A, B, and C (counting the first uncancelled votes as the first possible votes, the second as the second, and so on), and the second table contains their relative value. The actual and possible votes of C, as it will be seen, amount in the aggregate to less than those of B and A, and the name of C would, therefore, be first cancelled. Some of the votes for C would, perhaps, by the voting papers, be next given to A or B, and the computation would then be made again, and the lowest on the poll again struck off, until the process can be no longer continued, and effect is given to every vote, so far as the elector has enabled that to be done.

Candidates.	1st Votes.	2nd Possible Votes.	3rd Possible Votes.	4th Possible Votes.	5th Possible Votes.
A	1760	1527	1654	1364	844 !
B	1620	1816	1022	1230	965
C	1786	1249	1452	726	483

A	B	C
1st —— 1760	1st —— 1620	1st —— 1786
2nd $\dfrac{1527}{2} = 763\frac{1}{2}$	2nd $\dfrac{1816}{2} = 908\,\cdot$	2nd $\dfrac{1249}{2} = 624\frac{1}{2}$
3rd $\dfrac{1654}{3} = 551\frac{1}{3}$	3rd $\dfrac{1022}{3} = 340\frac{2}{3}$	3rd $\dfrac{1452}{3} = 484$
4th $\dfrac{1364}{4} = 341$	4th $\dfrac{1230}{4} = 307\frac{1}{2}$	4th $\dfrac{726}{4} = 181\frac{1}{2}$
5th $\dfrac{844}{5} = 168\frac{4}{5}$	5th $\dfrac{965}{5} = 193$	5th $\dfrac{483}{5} = 96\frac{3}{5}$
$3584\frac{19}{30}$	$3369\frac{1}{6}$	$3172\frac{3}{5}$

Appendix D.

In the Report of Mr. Lytton, Her Majesty's Secretary of Legation at Copenhagen, on the Election of Representatives for the Rigsraad (Reports of Secretaries of Embassy, &c., No. 7, presented by command to both Houses of Parliament, 1864, Parl. Paper), an objection is stated to have been made to the Danish Electoral Law, that it affords no guarantee for the representation of majorities and minorities in just and adequate proportion, in proof of which the following problem had been triumphantly put forward. If, it was said, three members were to be elected by 600 voters, and there are five candidates, A, B, C, D, and E, for whom votes are given as follows :—

For A ⎫ 299
    B ⎬ votes.
    D ⎭

For A ⎫ 200
    C ⎬ votes.
    B ⎭

For A ⎫ 101
    C ⎬ votes.
    E ⎭

The quotient of the 600 votes, divided by 3, being 200, it follows that A, who has 299 votes, will be elected, and 99, the surplus, then appropriated to B, whose name stands next on all those papers. A's name being next cancelled on the 200 papers in which he is coupled with C and B, those 200 votes are then appropriated to C, whose name stands next on all those papers, and C, having attained the quota, is thereupon elected. Both the names of A and C, the elected members, are next cancelled on the 101 papers on which C and E appear, and those 101 votes are given to E, who is then elected under the 24th section of the Danish Electoral Law, as he would be under Clause XXV. of the law proposed in this treatise. It is objected that this result is unjust, because B, who was second in the choice of 299 voters, and third in the choice of 200, is excluded, and E, who was only third in the choice of 101, is elected.

Mr. Lytton has shown by his own argument that the combination supposed is politically preposterous, and, by a calculation made by M. Andræ, abstractedly, having regard only to probabilities, next to impossible.

I am willing, however, to accept the problem as it is stated by the opponents of the system, and adopt the result, which I believe is perfectly reconcilable with the principle which is at the foundation of this method of voting, and also reconcilable with justice.

The object is to give the elector the means of voting for the candidate who most perfectly attains his ideal of what a legislator should be, but it does not contemplate giving him the choice of more than one. The simple operation of the principle is seen when it is applied to an election *vivâ voce*, without voting papers, as is suggested for municipal elections (pp. 282-3). A and C would there have polled quotas, and E the comparative majority. The primary purpose of giving the voter the opportunity of adding to his paper the second, third, or other names for one of whom his vote is to be taken on the contingency of the name at the head not requiring it, is not to add greater weight to his vote, but to prevent it from being thrown away or lost owing to a greater number of voters than is necessary placing the same popular candidate at the head of their papers. The purpose is, in fact, to prevent what would have happened in the case supposed, if provision had not been made for the contingency, for the result of the above disposition of the votes would then have been that A alone could have been elected. Keeping in view this main purpose, to which all other objects are secondary, and comparatively unimportant, it is immaterial in what order the votes are counted. I should have stated the problem thus,—600 votes are found to have been given for A, 200 of these only are appropriated to him. A further number of 200 votes are next appropriated either to C or to B, depending on the order in which the voting papers bearing A's name at the head have been liberated by his return, and which depends again, in Denmark, upon the order in which the votes issue from the urn, and in the system here proposed, on the localities or particular constituencies for which A happened to be a candidate, and which govern the rule of appropriation. (See Clauses XVIII., XIX., and XXIV.) In whatever order or manner the votes have been taken, there will remain a majority, or, as I have named it, a comparative majority, and a minority of 101, or 99. If B has succeeded in obtaining the quota of 200 in the process, C will have the majority of 101,—if C has succeeded in obtaining that quota, as in the case put by Mr. Lytton, B is in the unlucky predicament of having the votes of his friends exhausted in their successful efforts to elect A and C, and he is left with the minority of 99,—E being supported by 101 voters, who have given no vote to B. The first 200 voters, whose voting papers are appropriated to A, have no ground of complaint, for their votes have been attended with entire success, namely, the return of their candidate to the representative assembly, with all the moral weight of the emphatic expression of esteem shown by the proffered votes of the whole constituency of 600. Still less have the second 200 voters, whose votes were appropriated to C, any reason to complain, for they also have not only elected a favourite candidate of their own, but, equally with the first 200, they are gratified by the triumphant success of A. The 99 voters for B have also the latter satisfaction, and if they have failed to return their next favourite candidate, it is simply because 101 are more than 99.

The complaint of injustice is no doubt made rather in the interest of the candidate than in that of the electors. Instead of a struggle for mastery in which 301 may overpower, set at defiance, and extinguish the voices of 299, this method of election promises that each 200 shall be free to choose the exponent of their opinions; but it does not promise that any vote, taken singly, shall aid in the return of more than one candidate. In the supposed Danish case, the candidate might certainly complain of the ill-fortune which had brought out of the urn the voting papers of his friends in an order so wonderfully adverse to his success that, according to the computation of M. Andræ, it would not happen in one election out of some millions. If such a case had occurred under the method proposed in this treatise, B's only ground of complaint would have been that A and C had offered themselves as candidates to constituencies in which they happened to be more popular than himself, and in which, unluckily for him, his only supporters also chiefly dwelt; and the votes of these constituencies having been appropriated to A and C, that appropriation had exhausted the votes which, but for their prior possession, would have come to him, B. The law of appropriation by locality, in fact, redresses any fortuitous injustice or hardship which a resort to chance or lot may occasion, for although the circumstances supposed are obstacles to the political success of B, as every interposition of a superior or more favoured competitor must be, yet it is no fair ground of complaint.

There is no doubt that if the system of valuation of votes, according to the position of the candidates on the voting papers were adopted, as in the Frankfort proposal, Appendix B, and as in Appendix C, pp. 209–302, that the result would be very different. The supposed poll would then stand thus :—

$$ \text{A} \ \frac{600}{1} = \qquad 600 $$

$$ \text{B} \ \frac{299}{2} + \frac{200}{3} = 216\tfrac{1}{2} $$

$$ \text{C} \ \frac{200}{2} + \frac{101}{2} = 150\tfrac{1}{2} $$

$$ \text{D} \ \frac{299}{3} = \qquad 99\tfrac{2}{3} $$

$$ \text{E} \ \frac{101}{3} = \qquad 33\tfrac{1}{3} $$

It is certain, however, that such a method would open a door for party organisation and party action of a most formidable kind, by the means of settled and printed lists, giving an increased amount of influence to mere numbers acting together, which under the simpler system of regarding only the first, or first uncancelled name, and of appropriation according to localities, no party ticket could secure, but which, on the contrary, any such ticket would rather impair.

It will be interesting, however, to refer to the different result of this case, as it would be determined if the improved rule for obtaining the quota, examined in Appendix E, were applied. The last example there put (p. 307) shows that B would be returned with A and C, without any of the dangerous consequences of giving overwhelming power to numbers, which might be feared from the foregoing method of valuation.

Appendix E.

Among those,—Earl Russell, Mr. Andriæ, Mr, James Garth Marshall, Earl Grey, and others, who within the last ten years have sought a remedy for the defects in representative institutions which have made them the creatures of a number of dispersed majorities,—must be included the name of Mr. Droop, of Lincoln's Inn, and late Fellow of Trinity College, Cambridge. Mr. Droop, " on observing the rather peculiar phenomena of the general election in 1857, directed his attention to the problem how representatives might be elected who should best represent the whole constituency, and not merely the majority." Perceiving that I had introduced contingent voting, which was also a part of his scheme, he has kindly communicated to me his method of appropriation of every vote to the candidate for whom it is successively designed, and of arriving at a quota which should be exactly the number of votes that ought to be retained for each successful candidate in order to ensure his election. The accurate determination of this quota, Mr. Droop remarks, would require the solution of an algebraical equation of a high degree, but there is no difficulty in approximating to it to any required degree of accuracy. One step of this process may be adopted with great advantage. It is the result of an observation that the quota proposed to be adopted cannot be greater than the quotient produced by dividing the aggregate number of votes polled for the number of candidates to be elected, who stand highest on the poll, by such last-mentioned number. Thus, if there were 2,000 candidates, all polling more or less votes, of whom only 654 can be elected, it is not necessary to take as the dividend the whole number of votes polled by the 2,000, but it is sufficient to take the number of votes polled by the 654 who stand highest on the poll. The quotient thus obtained, which will be necessarily far smaller in number than that obtained by the process prescribed in the text (Clause I., page 25), is termed the "first-trial" quota. The excess votes of the candidates having more than the quota will then be reapportioned among the successive names, and a dividend composed of the numbers attributed to the [654] highest again divided, and a "second-trial" quota obtained, and the same process of appropriating the excess votes, and again computing the successive quotas, repeated, until the uniform quota can be no further reduced. This is explained in the following example :—Take the case of 7 candidates, of whom 5 are to be elected by 200 electors. A receives 37 first votes, B 14, C 31, D 45, E 24, F 19, G 30. To obtain the first-trial quota, the 5 highest, which are D 45, A 37, C 31, G 30, and E 24, are added together, and the result, 167, divided by 5 = 33, which is the first-trial quota. As D's number therefore exceeds the quota by 12 (45—33) these 12 votes are then distributed to the candidates whose names follow his on the voting papers. C is supposed to stand next on 3 of the papers, E on 6, G on 3 ; these votes are added to those already given to those candidates, and if A's 4 surplus votes (37—33) being set free belong to B, and C's last vote (34—33) also to B, the 5 highest will now be found to be, D 33, A 33, C 33, G 33, E 30 : these numbers must again be added together, and the result, 162, divided by 5 = 32, which is the second-trial quota. The same process must now be repeated, D's surplus vote (33—32) given to G, whose name stands next on the voting paper, A's surplus vote to B, C's to B, G's two last votes (one received from D) to F, the 5 highest are now, D 32, A 32, C 32, G 32, E 30, added together = 158 ÷ 5 = 31, which is the third-trial quota. D's surplus vote must now be set free, and E's name following on the voting paper, is given to E, A's to B, C's to B, G's to E, which gives E one surplus vote,—supposing this vote when set free to belong to F, we have now, D 31, A 31, C 31, G 31, E 31 ; these five candidates are therefore elected, with a quota of 31.

In adopting this reduced quota a succession of trials is indispensable ; for the reappropriation of the papers after settling the first-trial quota, may displace some of the candidates who were at first within the number to be elected, and bring up in their stead some of the candidates lower on the poll. Those originally higher will therefore be entitled to require that the same process shall be continued until the quota is fixed at its lowest point, and no further substitution can occur. There is really nothing complicated in this process. It only repeats several times what it was at first proposed to do once for all. The alteration of a few lines in the Electoral Law would sufficiently prescribe the course to be taken. A larger number, or perhaps the whole, of the voting papers would, when arranged, be required to be transmitted to the Registrars, and the declaration of the ultimate result would probably have to be deferred a day or two longer.

A very striking illustration of the effect of this mode of computation is found upon its application to the Danish problem, objected to the system of Mr. Andriæ (Appendix D, p. 302). It would in that case place B in a position equal to A and C, by bringing more contingent votes into operation, without the dangerous consequence of giving greatly increased weight to mere numbers. Thus:—

First trial:—Votes polled $\frac{600}{3} = 200$.

First appropriation,—A, 200; B, 99; C, 200; E, 101.

Second trial,—A, 200+C, 200+E, 101 = $\frac{501}{3}$ = 167. B, 99.

$200-167 = 33.$

Second appropriation,—A, 167; C, 167; B, 99+33+33 = 165. E, 101.

Third trial,—A, 167 + C, 167 + B, 165 = $\frac{499}{3}$ = 166⅓. E, 101.

Third appropriation,—A, 166⅓ + C, 166⅓ + B, 166⅓. E, 101.

The result is, that A, C, and B, are elected by an equal quota of votes. It will be seen, however, that this has been effected at the expense of increasing the minority having no influence on the election, from 99 (as it stood in the example in Appendix D) to 101.

Appendix F.

Parliament of New South Wales.

THE earliest suggestions which are found, for the adoption of personal representation in this colony, are contained in the *Sydney Morning Herald,* of the 26th November and 4th December, 1861, on the proposal to make the Upper House of the Colonial Parliament elective, instead of nominative, as theretofore. Early in the session of 1862 a Bill was brought into the Legislative Council, adapting the principle to the election of the Upper House. This Bill was, on the 18th June, 1862, referred to a Select Committee, of which Mr. Wentworth was chairman. The Committee made its Report on the 21st of August, 1862. The following passages relate to this system :—

" As respects the mode of voting, your Committee have given much consideration to the plan now commonly known as that of Mr. Hare, and which has lately attracted considerable notice among leading political writers in Europe.

It has been urged on the attention of your Committee, not only by the intrinsic merits of the scheme, but from the circumstance that it admits of being applied to the formation of a Colonial Legislative Council in a much simpler form than it presents in the original scheme of the author, as intended for application to the British House of Commons. The mere fact of its tending to increase the distinctness of character between the two Houses has been felt to be a strong recommendation. Your Committee are not disposed to shrink from its adoption merely because it is new and experimental.

" The leading feature of the plan is the representation of *all* the electors, in the proportion of the numbers of their respective parties and sections, instead of the representation merely of the majorities prevailing in each local electorate, while leaving the defeated minorities wholly without representation. Under the usual system, if one interest or prejudice be prevalent in a majority of the electors in twenty constituencies, twenty members may be elected to represent those majorities, although the minorities may collectively amount to a number not far short of the successful majorities. A difference of one vote in each electorate might determine the election, and twenty votes might thus determine the fate of twenty elections, leaving thousands of electors, forming the minorities, without a single representative. This is doubtless an extreme supposition; but the merits of any system may be fairly illustrated by showing to what it tends when carried to its utmost length.

"The system of Mr. Hare provides a remedy; but while it renders this injustice to minorities impossible, it equally maintains all the just rights of majorities. It establishes a true representation of the whole society, with its various interests and opinions represented in due proportion ; and the manner in which this is effected is, when fully explained and understood, extremely simple. Supposing the number of voters to be 30,000, and the number of members to be thirty, each 1000 voters (called a quota) is considered entitled to be represented by one member. Instead of a local electorate, inhabited by 1000 electors of divided opinion, and comprising a minority, which, if out-voted in that particular electorate, is left wholly without representation in the legislature, each member's constituency will consist of 1000 electors, coinciding in their choice of a representative, irrespective of their places of residence. For this purpose, the whole colony will form a *single electorate*, the electoral districts of the Assembly being adopted solely for the purpose of more conveniently making up the roll and polling the votes, but not for the purpose of restricting the votes of the electors to any special local candidates. This term " single electorate " will, however, be apt to lead to a serious misapprehension, unless care be taken to observe that under Mr. Hare's system the effect of a consolidation of many electorates into one is quite the reverse of that which would result under the present system of voting. Under the present system, it would merely give the aggregate majority the power of defeating the aggregate minority on a wider field, and of sending into the Council a preponderating number of members to represent one party to the exclusion of the other. The sub-division of electorates under the present system thus increases the chance of the occasional prevalence of a weaker party in one or more local electorates, but it affords a mere chance, uncertain and capricious, whereas Mr. Hare's system insures, without any subdivision whatever, the due and proportionate representation of each party. Thus, while the colony forms a single electorate as regards territory, each quota of electors, agreeing in the choice of a member, forms a separate electorate as regards persons.

"Each elector can thus ensure the return of at least one candidate, by associating himself with a sufficient number of fellow-electors, wheresoever resident, to form a *quota*. But if the vote of each were limited to the naming of the one candidate he prefers above all the others, it is evident that more than the quota would often concur in the choice of a popular candidate, and thus lead to the throwing away of the votes given in excess. To prevent this, each voter is entitled to name several candidates in the order of preference, so that if the vote be not required for the first, it may be used for the second, if not for the second, then for the third, and so on, to ensure its being made ultimately contributory to the election of some candidate of his choice. He cannot fail of his object so long as he does not fail to name on his list some one candidate in whose election he and the required proportion of other voters concur. Whether the first or last on his list be the recipient of his vote, his intentions are equally fulfilled. More so, indeed, if it be the last, for it can only descend to that candidate when all those higher on his list, and therefore of his earlier preference, have been already elected by other votes. Nor is this justice to individuals purchased at the expense of any injustice towards leading parties and majorities. Whatever number of quotas are comprised in the ranks of any party, they can so vote as to obtain a corresponding number of members, and thus maintain their legitimate proportion of influence in legislation. The *ideal* of representative government in the writings of statesmen has long been the representation of classes and interests in due proportion, so as to render the legislature a true epitome of the political opinions of society. Hitherto nothing but an approximation to this *ideal* has appeared possible. Mr. Hare's system, for the first time, proposes to make it a *reality.*"—[*Ordered to be printed*, 21 *August*, 1862; *Sydney. J. Richards, Government Printer.*]

The Committee amended, agreed to, and reported, the Bill. It was read a first time in the Legislative Council, and on the 4th September, 1862, on the order of the day for the second reading,

Mr. HOLDEN said that on account of the share he had taken in preparing the amended Bill, and his identification with one of the chief principles of the measure, he had yielded to the desire of several members of the committee to bring forward the measure. His ambition was limited to securing the result he desired; and if that result—the passing of a safe and wise measure—could be obtained by the silent expression of his secret will, he would gladly relinquish to others the prominent share in the steps taken to accomplish it. He had been uniformly a supporter of the elective principle, and had advocated it ten years ago in this Chamber. He had, however, felt its difficulties; and perhaps the delay which had taken place had not been without its advantages. He believed that the enunciation, in the mean time, of Mr. Hare's system, had thrown a new light on the subject, and had rendered it possible to do now what it was impossible to do then. When that system was first brought to his attention it struck on his mind exactly as it struck on the mind of John Stuart Mill; and he was not ashamed to identify his own feelings and ideas with those of that great man. He (Mr. Holden) could have written and thought and felt exactly in the words in which he (Mr. Mill) said (referring to Mr. Hare's system of representation) that "it solved the difficulty of representation, and by so doing raised up the cloud which hung over the future of representative government, and therefore of civilization." For he felt that the civilization of mankind was identified with the success of true, wise, well-constituted representative government, and that that species of government never had existed yet on the face of the earth. But he trusted that it would, and might, and should exist; and he trusted that the first specimen of it might be exhibited in this country. And the only fear he had about it was, that it might not be so effectual as it would otherwise be (supposing that this Bill should pass), because of the system being confined to one House of Legislature, and not being extended to the other. The hon. member then stated that his measure, though alleged to be in a spirit of conservatism, was yet truly in accordance with liberal principles, and showed that his views of the necessity, function, and qualification of a Senate, were those expressed by the founders of the American Republic—by Madison and Hamilton, in the *Federalist;* by Calhoun, by Sir James Mackintosh, and also by Lord John Russell. The want of a proper negative power in the constitution of a country compelled the Legislative power, when established on too wide a basis, to concentrate itself by degrees into a single Executive. This occurred as an inevitable consequence if the struggle for place and power between the two parties of the State was more and more developed, until at length all power was virtually concentrated in political leaders—ruling as absolutely as any aristocracy. The evil was augmented instead of lessened, as the community advanced in prosperity. By rendering the representation more equitable as regarded the interests of opposing parties, it was made more possible to have universal suffrage without the dangers which might be apprehended to arise therefrom, and the division of power secured by such a division of power, promoted a harmoni-

ons action between co-existing interests which would not be likely otherwise
to take place, or to continue uninterrupted. Speaking of the mode of voting
adopted in this Bill, Mr. Mill, in his work on Representative Government,
said, " Of all modes in which a national representation can possibly be constituted, this one affords the best security for the intellectual qualifications
desirable in the representatives. At present, by universal admission, it is
becoming more and more difficult for any one who has only talents and
character to gain admission into the House of Commons. The only persons
who can get elected are those who possess local influence, or make their
way by lavish expenditure, and who, on the invitation of three or four
tradesmen or attorneys, are sent down by one of the two great parties from
their London clubs as men whose votes the party can depend on under all
circumstances. On Mr. Hare's system, those who did not like the local candidates would have the power to fill up their voting papers by a selection
from all the persons of national reputation on the list of candidates, with
whose general political principles they were in sympathy. Almost every
person, therefore, who had made himself in any way honourably distinguished, though devoid of local influence, and having sworn allegiance
to no political party, would have a fair chance of making up the quota ; and
with this encouragement such persons might be expected to offer themselves
hitherto undreamt of. Hundreds of able men of independent thought, who
would have no chance whatever of being chosen by the majority of any
existing constituency, have by their writings or their exertions in some field
of public usefulness made themselves known and approved by a few persons
in almost every district of the kingdom; and if every vote that should be
given for them in every place should be counted for their election, they might
be able to complete the number of the quota. In no other way which i
seems possible to suggest would Parliament be so certain of containing the
very *elite* of the country. Not solely through the votes of minorities would
this system of election raise the intellectual standard of the House of Commons. Majorities would be compelled to look out for members of a much
higher calibre. When the individuals composing the majorities would no
longer be reduced to Hobson's choice, of either voting for the person brought
forward by their local leaders, or not voting at all ; when the nominee of the
leaders would have to encounter the competition not solely of the candidate
of the minority, but of all the men of established reputation in the country
who were willing to serve ; it would be impossible any longer to foist upon the
electors the first person who presents himself with the catch-words of the
party in his mouth, and three or four thousand pounds in his pocket. The
majority would insist upon having a candidate worthy of their choice, or they
would carry their votes somewhere else, and the minority would prevail.
The slavery of the majority to the least estimable portion of their number
would be at an end. Had a plan like Mr. Hare's by good fortune suggested
itself to the enlightened and patriotic founders of the American Republic, the
Federal and State Assemblies would have contained many of those dis-

tinguished men, and democracy would have been spared its greatest reproach, and one of its most formidable evils. When the Democracy is supreme there is no One or Few strong enough for dissentient opinions, and injured or menaced interests to lean upon. The great difficulty of democratic government has hitherto seemed to be, how to provide in a democratic society, what circumstances have provided hitherto in all the societies which have maintained themselves ahead of others—a social support—a *point d'appui*, for individual resistance to the tendencies of the ruling power; a protection, a rallying point for opinions and interests which the ascendant public opinion views with disfavour. For want of such a *point d'appui*, the older societies, and all but a few of the modern ones, either fell into dissolution or became stationary (which means slow deterioration), through the exclusive predominance of a part only of the conditions of social and mental well-being. The only quarter in which to look for a supplement or completing corrective to the instincts of a democratic majority is the instructed minority, but in the ordinary mode of constituting democracy this minority has no organ; Mr. Hare's system provides one. The representatives who would be returned to Parliament by the aggregate of minorities would afford that organ in its greatest perfection. A separate organization of the instructed classes, even if practicable, would be invidious, and could only escape from being offensive by being totally without influence. But if the *elite* of these classes formed part of the Parliament by the same title as any other of its members, by representing the same number of citizens, the same numerical fraction of the national will, their presence could give umbrage to nobody, while they would be in the position of highest vantage both for making their opinions and counsels heard on all important subjects, and for taking an active part in public business. Their abilities would probably draw to them more than their numerical share of the actual administration of Government, as the Athenians did not confide responsible public functions to Cleon or Hyperbolus (the employment of Cleon at Pylus and Amphipolis was purely exceptional) but Niceas and Theramenes and Alcibiades were in constant employment, both at home and abroad, though known to sympathise more with oligarchy than with democracy. The instructed minority would in the actual voting count only for their numbers, but as a moral power they would count for much more in virtue of their knowledge and of the influence it would give them over the rest. An arrangement better adapted to keep popular opinion within reason and justice, and to guard it from the various deteriorating influences which assail the weak side of democracy, could scarcely by human ingenuity be devised. A democratic people would in this way be provided with what in any other way it would almost certainly miss—leaders of a grade of intellect and character better than itself. Modern democracy would have its occasional Pericles, and its habitual group of superior and guiding minds. With all this array of reasons of the most fundamental character on the affirmative side of the question, what is there on the negative? Nothing that will sustain examination when people can once be induced to bestow any real examination upon a new thing. Those, indeed, if any such there be, who under pretence of equal justice aim only at substituting the class ascendancy of the poor for that of the rich, will, of course, be unfavourable to a scheme which places both on a level." The hon. member addressed himself to the question of the suffrage for the Council roll. He had been asked why they did not adopt the ballot? He had been anxious for something of the kind in first drafting his Bill; but it might be said in reply that Mr. Hare's system was itself so superior that it would not conform to the ballot, to secret voting in its essence; but still there was so much of the ballot that there could be no violence, no influence used at the time of voting, which the ballot sought to avoid. He moved that the Bill be read a second time.

Mr. PLUNKETT seconded the motion; and after some observations by Mr. Mitchell, Mr. Merewether, Mr. Brown Russell, and the Attorney-General, the debate was adjourned.

The above report, omitting the argument on the other portions of the Bill, is taken from the *Sydney Morning Herald* for Thursday the 4th September, 1862. The report of the discussion on the next day has not come to hand, which is the more to be regretted, as the Bill appears to have been opposed by one member, Captain Ward, who would seem from the subsequent report to have addressed himself especially to this method of election, and to have contended, 1, that it would not be a guarantee for the representation of majorities and minorities in just and equal proportion, putting forward in support of that argument, substantially the problem suggested in Denmark, in which E with 101 third votes is elected, while B, with 299 second and 200 third votes, fails (See Appendix D, p. 302); 2, that mere single voting would be a better method without the contingent vote; and 3, that the loss of votes, owing to a large number of electors polling for the favourite candidates, might be obviated by publication of the state of the poll from time to time.

Wednesday, 17th September, 1862. The debate was resumed by Mr. MEREWETHER. He did not admit that popular election of an Upper Chamber was better than a selection by the ministers of the Crown, with proper restrictions, to prevent a creation of members to carry particular measures. If the Lower House was the people's Chamber, the Upper should be the

Chamber of statesmen, composed of public men who had passed through great political offices and employments. Addressing himself to the election clauses, &c., he could not refrain from referring to the manner in which his hon. friend Mr. Butler had misunderstood both Mr. Hare and Mr. Mill on this subject. The hon. member had complained that the committee had mutilated Hare's scheme by rejecting manhood suffrage. But Mr. Hare's scheme had nothing to do with manhood suffrage; it was, in fact, devised for England, where, happily, manhood suffrage did not exist. But Mr. Hare's scheme was nothing more than a mode of voting applicable alike to any constituency. He had weighed the Bill under a deep sense of their responsibility to the future, and he supported it not as a perfect measure, but as one which it would be wise in them to pass, and as one which they might pass without prejudice to the future policy of the country.

After discussion on other parts of the Bill,—

Mr. HOLDEN replied.—The first objection of Captain Ward arose from a misapprehension of the principle and object of the contingent votes. Their entry on the voting paper was apt to be misunderstood as a departure from the system of single voting, whereas it was merely an expedient to prevent the single vote from being thrown away on a candidate who did not require it. It merely indicated for whom the elector would desire to give his vote, if on his coming to the poll he were told, "Mr. A., for whom you intend to vote, is already elected by a full quota, and you are therefore at liberty to aid in the election of another." It was not a second vote, and should be regarded as if it were non-existent, or written in invisible ink, until effect was given to it in consequence of the primary vote not being required. Then it has all the effect of a primary vote. Such being the case, it was evident that no candidate whose name was second on any voting paper has any claim whatever to consideration on this account if the first-named candidate received the vote as a part of his quota. It was a mere indication that the elector would have voted for him if he had not used his vote for another in preference. A vote given by an elector to B, because his greater favourite A did not require it, was as good a vote as the vote of another elector, who esteemed B as superior to A. Now if these two considerations were borne in mind, all the objections raised by his hon. friend Captain Ward to the method of allotting contingent votes, on the ground of supposed injustice to candidates, fell to the ground. It was wholly the concern of the voter, and if he had secured the privilege of rendering his vote—his one vote—effectual for some one candidate of his choice, no other candidate was entitled to complain. Surely nothing could be more ridiculous than that a candidate should complain of it as a hardship that he is not allowed to derive any advantage from the votes of electors whose votes had returned another, because they would have voted for him if they had not voted for that other person. But although no candidate had any greater right than another to influence the selection of the voting papers which were to be taken as the surplus beyond any candidate's quota, general policy required some rules, and these have been applied. The first rule was to select those on which the greatest number of contingent votes were entered. The reason of this was obvious. The greater the number of names entered, the less likely was the vote to be lost in the election. After this rule had been applied, Mr. Hare had introduced a great number of complicated rules, which he had rejected for the sake of greater simplicity. All that appeared necessary to him was, to provide some rule which should preclude any selection of papers by the registrar, through personal or political motives. A political motive could, indeed, hardly apply, because the question would not be (as now, in ordinary elections) between candidates of different parties, but those of a second choice of two electors of the same party, which of two voters for A should have a second choice, because A did not require both votes. An equality of chance was the only impartial course to be adopted, and the most convenient mode of accomplishing this seemed to be the taking the votes in the order in which they happened to stand on the roll; and, notwithstanding it was characterised by the hon. and learned Attorney-General as absurd and ridiculous, he would venture to abide by it until some wiser and better plan were suggested; when that were done, he was perfectly ready to consider and adopt it. The hon. member (Captain Ward) said that under this system A might be returned and B rejected by a course which had no greater merit than the system of tossing up. This was a very narrow and fallacious view of the case. The *system* was a matter altogether distinct from the tossing up. True, it might be that in the working of the system, as in that of any other, a state of facts might result in which there might be a tie, or two or more parties might have equal claim to that which all could not by the nature of the case obtain. A resort to some plan equivalent to tossing up was in such case the only way out of the difficulty. But the hon. member (Captain Ward) had not been content with criticising the system of Mr. Hare. He has declared his preference for another. The system of single voting without quotas and without contingent voting appears to him preferable. It will, he says, protect minorities better. Possibly it might do so; but in what manner and at what expense of confusion and injustice towards majorities it might be worth while first to consider. Taking his friend Captain Ward's illustrations in order, he would answer his objections *seriatim*. In his first example, he complained that if 1, 2, 3 were taken to make A's quota, A and C would be returned, whereas if 4, 5, and 6 be taken, A and B would be returned. He (Mr. Holden) denied that this was any objection, unless either B had some claim superior to A, or A superior to B. This not being shown, some form of decision by lot was the just and proper course. If instead of an election by contingent voting the votes had been taken by 1, 2, and 3 going to the poll first, and 4, 5, and 6—knowing how they had voted—going to the poll afterwards, and voting for the candidates of their respective second choice, in consequence of such knowledge, the candidate whose election was defeated by his not receiving the vote of 1, 2, or 3 would have no ground of complaint, because he would have received it had they voted last in order. With regard to the second example, in which a greater claim was maintained on behalf of the excluded candidate, on account of his having more primary votes, the fallacy of the objection was equal, though of another kind. It was forgotten that when the contingent votes were used, they had the same force as primary votes. The fact that an elector would have voted for A, if A had wanted his vote, did not render his vote for B less valid, if it were not used for A. Thus, the return of C, in example two, by contingent votes in excess of B's primary votes, is quite legitimate. It was not because the vote was called contingent when placed on the voting paper that it was contingent or inferior when used. It has then become absolute, and of equal power with the primary vote. It was the actual vote of one elector. The third example turned upon the converse fallacy. Here contingent votes were taken into account which had never taken effect. The objection assumed that B was entitled to reckon, as influencing his claim to consideration, contingent votes on voting papers actually used for a preceding candidate. These were only votes which would have been given for B, but have not been given in fact. They should be, therefore, considered as non-existent for the purpose of the computation, and the objection would then utterly vanish. This system of single voting, without the protection of Hare's adjuncts, was that proposed in the Bill of the Forster Ministry; but as it was never fully discussed, public attention was not attracted to the objections to which it was open, although they at that time very clearly presented themselves to his mind, and he was thereby more prepared to welcome Mr. Hare's discovery as an escape from them. And his friend Captain Ward hinted that some better plan than Mr. Hare's contingent voting might answer all the purpose of this cumbrous system,—this better plan being, as he understood, a public statement of the number of votes already polled for candidates. If his honourable friend had said at once that he proposed to supersede the necessity of a cumbrous system by a system of voting through the electric telegraph, he could hardly have more astonished him. If he would show in what manner his suggestion could be practically carried out, he was willing to relinquish the field to him. The only merit he claimed for Hare's system was that of doing in the most practicable way which has hitherto been propounded. But what did the publication proposed involve? First, that by some miracle of intuition all the polling-officers in the colony were to be aware of the instant at which any candidate had acquired a sufficient number of votes in the aggregate to effect his return. Secondly, that the polling be then simultaneously stopped, and the fact published, the machinery of election being suspended until all the electors are duly apprised. When, on this being effected, the election recommenced, it could only go on until another candidate were elected, when the polling would again stop, and the same proceedings would be repeated until the electors were tired of travelling backwards and forwards to the poll. If it were practicable to prevent votes being thrown away at elections by any such publication as his hon. friend suggested, it would surely have been long ago introduced in connection with the existing system. It was no part of the avowed policy of the electoral law that votes should be thrown away. It had only been tolerated, as an evil supposed to be unavoidable, until Mr. Hare's invention had, for the first time, supplied a remedy.

The second reading was carried by a majority of 11 to 4. It was passed by the Legislative Council, and read a first time in the Legislative Assembly. In that House, on the 13th November, 1862, on the order of the day for the second reading,—

Mr. Wilson, after addressing himself to the other questions, said he had heard no one who had risen to speak attempt to defend the principle of one electorate only, and the only question was, would it be at all tolerable even under Hare's system?—though it was scarcely to be dreamt of that that should be adopted here. He believed it to be too complicated for any person to understand it; so much so, that he did not think there were ten members in this House and the other who thoroughly understood it. [An hon. member: "It is very simple."] Possibly it might be; but they had the declaration of the Master of the Mint, who was no mean authority in mathematical matters, that it was directly the reverse. For himself, he would confess that he had not understood much of it when it was first introduced into the Bill, but afterwards the explanations of the hon. gentleman who had proposed it had so mystified him, that he now knew less of it than before.

Mr. Morris, after adverting to the franchise and other subjects, added, the principle, however, most important in this Bill, whatever franchise might be adopted, was the principle known as Hare's system—a system of election by quotas. There had been great prejudices against this system, and it had been frequently observed by hon. members that they could not understand the practical working of it. He would explain to the House in a few minutes that there was no mystery in connection with the practical application of this principle. Hare's system was the only one by which representation according to numbers could possibly be secured. Under that system a man carried his rights with him, and could exercise his power of voting in whatever part of the colony he might be at the time of an election. If the Upper House be composed of members returned for large districts, it would, after all, be a mere reflex of the majority of the community; and consequently, out of a community of 100,000 people, it might so happen that 49,000 were not represented at all. But such a state of things could not possibly arise under Mr. Hare's system. He wanted to know why these 49,000 persons were not to be represented? No reason had yet been given why the majority of the people should have the whole of the representation. This principle — which many hon. members were fond of exalting — of taxation and law-making by representatives, was practically ignored by the system at present adopted; the majority alone of the community made the laws and taxed the people.

Mr. LOVE did not think there would be any necessity for discussing Hare's system, because the country was so thoroughly against it; and it was so imperfectly understood, that every one believed it would never become the law of the land. He considered it to be a system that would never work well in this country; it might look well in theory, but would be impracticable. Too much power would be left in the hands of the Registrar-General, who could almost return what members he pleased.

Mr. DALGLEISH, among other observations, said: As to the principles of this Bill, he disagreed with them all, except the one pertaining to Hare's system. He believed that no system of representation was so perfect, or so capable of fully eliciting the will of the people as this which was called Hare's. It was impossible to define it fully in a speech, but any hon. member who carefully examined it would see the truth of what he stated. The hon. member (Mr. Harpur) had struck the only objection that he saw to the system, in the suggestion as to two candidates having equal votes. The effect of this would be to throw the election virtually into the hands of one person. But the present and any other system was open to the same objection. Such an occurrence would, however, happen only very rarely. He did not agree with the drawing by lot as proposed, but would prefer to have the decision left to some impartial person, uninfluenced by personal considerations, as a returning officer should at all times be. Hare's system, he repeated, was the only true way of obtaining the will of the people, and by having the whole colony formed into one great electorate, and all the elections taking place on the one day, every one could vote, while no person could possibly vote in more than one electorate. He could not understand how members of that House could say they preferred the present nominee Chamber to an elective House under the Hare system. He was told, when he asked how it was that hon. members could possibly express such an opinion, that they justified the preference indicated on the ground that, in the present state of things, there was the "swamping power" to fall back upon. He could not understand the force of such an argument as that. Was it to be supposed, if a ministry, to insure a majority, should suddenly create a number of new members, that an immediately-succeeding government would be disposed to accept such a set of nominations? And if they should not accept them, what was to be done? Was it not clear that their only course in such a case would be to increase the number of members of Council to a very large and indefinite extent, so that the influence of such a Chamber might be practically nullified.

Mr. W. FORSTER, after explaining what had been proposed by a former ministry, and discussing the general question of the construction of an Upper Chamber, observed that representation of the average opinions of the country was assumed to be arrived at under our present system. But how was it proposed to produce that effect when there was only one electorate returning six or seven members ? [Mr. Harpur: By the progress of truth.] Whatever faith the hon. member might have in the operation of truth (or perhaps Providence was meant), it was their duty, as legislators, to have in their institutions as little liability to error as possible, to prevent injurious and unjust results. It was a palpable injustice when, in proposing to give the whole country representation, a small majority of a constituency was given the power of returning the whole of the members. That was a result we should endeavour to guard against. He thought a majority of the House would agree with him that this would be unfair, and not a representative in principle at all—only one section was represented, having, it might be, only a majority of three or four, to the entire disfranchisement of the other, at any rate, for a certain period. He thought a result like that which must arise in many instances ought to be guarded against by the institution they were now endeavouring to perfect. He thought he had demonstrated that if the principle of large electorates were admitted, they must alter the system of voting. It was the fear that he and others entertained of this result which led him to make, in the measure his administration introduced, a provision by which an elector was allowed to vote for only one candidate. He admitted that that was an imperfect attempt, and he conceived that Hare's system, so much spoken of in the present debate, went in the same direction, but did the thing aimed at in a far more effective and just manner. They had heard all sorts of denunciations, but not a single argument against that system. Was it a reason that the House should reject this system, which had obtained the attention and approval of thoughtful men, including one honourable member well known to be extreme in his democratic notions, because certain hon. members informed the House that they did not understand it? Or did it follow that because hon. members did not understand it the public would not understand it? It was called a conservative measure. Now, according to his mind, it was one of the most democratic measures ever proposed; it was a complete innovation upon old established principles. It was conservative in the sense in which every reform was conservative, because it seemed to him to conserve justice, being allied with truth and equity, and thus conserving the very best interests for the people. That it was conservative in the sense of obstruction, in the sense of the word "tory," or the maintenance of obsolete, oligarchical, or anti-democratic notions, he denied; and no one who thoroughly considered its operations could entertain such an opinion for a moment. They were told that it was unpopular—that the people out of doors were against it. But the people out of doors had not considered it; there had been no discussion or expression of opinion on the part of the public to entitle any hon. member to come to that conclusion. He thought it was a popular belief in the widest sense, though not in the superficial sense of being approved of by the people, because they had given no opinion upon it. But it was popular as being thoroughly democratic in its theory, and would prove democratic in its practice. It seemed to be the idea of population carried out in principle; the principle of proportion applied to numbers. In brief, he might say that at its roots were the axiom that equal numbers should have equal representation. [Mr. Harpur: Not as embodied in the Bill.] He admitted that the details were imperfect; he was speaking of the principles of the system. So far as equality could be attained, the system proposed that each equal portion of electors should have an equal representation; and could the equity of the system be better shown? How was it possible to find fault with a system that told off the community into different sections, giving each a representative in proportion to its numbers? [Mr. Harpur: Stereotyping faction.] This 're-mark contained no argument. Anything might be termed faction. Majorities in the House, and even the Government themselves, had been termed a faction, until people were tired of hearing it. This system was a mere mechanical provision, if anything like faction could be involved in that. He believed he had been able to understand the system, after giving it a considerable amount of attention, and he would endeavour to explain to the House some of the features he had remarked in it, and which he thought were in its favour. One objection he had heard against the system would show the manner in which it was treated by honourable members. It was said, suppose a case in which 20,000 electors were to return ten members, and supposing there were forty candidates, each having an equal number of votes — why, such a thing was simply impossible; or if possible it was provided for by this system. The easiest way of putting the question was, by supposing a case of one electorate where there was but one returning officer. Supposing there were 10,000 votes to be given and ten members to be returned. The quota was arrived at by a simple sum in division, the number of electors being divided by the number of persons to be elected. Thereby was obtained what was called a quota. It was not arbitrary, but a definite proportion of the electors to the elected. [A voice: How if *less than the quota* voted?] And here he took exception to the phraseology of the Bill—the expressions "primary" and "contingent" not being at all connected with the Hare system of voting. Strictly speaking, there was but one vote. He was supposing a case where the electorate was sufficiently limited to admit of one returning officer officiating. Say there is a certain number of candidates to be elected—ten, for instance—and there are 10,000 electors. In such case the quota will be 1000 votes. Well, the returning officer receives votes up to 1000 for A and B. After that, if any electors wish to vote for A and B, they are told the votes are not required, and they then vote for C and D, or, if these candidates have also obtained the quota, they are carried to E and F, or any others that the electors approve of. [Mr. Harpur: But the votes are given on paper.] It is not at all necessary. In this way, in a small electorate, the whole number to be returned may be elected without the necessity of any great expense, and without the need of much official machinery. But, of course, when you came to apply the principle to extensive electorates, then this official machinery became necessary, just as it was necessary at present. It was not more liable to abuse than any other system. In all cases you must necessarily depend on the integrity of individuals, and if they could not repose confidence to this extent in their officials, the sooner we obtained a despotism the better. But he (Mr. Forster) had no doubt on this score, and he saw no difficulty whatever in applying this system, which embraced the best possible means of securing a representation of opinions. It was argued that persons might combine to secure the election of particular candidates. But was there anything improper or undemocratic in that? Suppose the Wesleyans, or the Roman Catholics, or any other body, desired to elect one of their own number to represent them, was there anything wrong in their combining in order to secure that end? He maintained there was not. On the contrary, he contended it was quite in accordance with the true theory of representation, which regarded the candidate as the representative of opinions, and not of mere numbers. The more he considered the Hare system, the more he admired it as calculated to secure democratic freedom. He might be told that it destroyed responsibility. It destroyed responsibility to local opinion, perhaps; but it held the representative amenable to the general opinion of the country; for the holding of his position must depend on his having gained the confidence and the respect of the commonwealth of which he formed part. He (Mr. Forster) said, therefore, he had no hesitation in giving in his adherence to the Hare system—a system admirable for its simplicity, and one that did honour to its contriver in the mother-country, and for the introduction of which the honourable gentleman who had brought it so prominently under notice here was entitled to great credit.

Mr. Hoskins would accept the single electorate, in combination with Hare's system, which had the advantage of giving effect to every vote. The provision for giving five votes to each elector was no part of Hare's system, and should not have his support.

Mr. Lucas was in favour of trying Hare's system; and, in so far as he could understand it, he regarded it as being as simple and easy as the present system. Nor did he think there was any possibility of a vote being lost, as had been stated by one hon. member; for every man who voted must tell for one member at all events; and if he put one name only on the paper, then it would be the duty of the returning officer to first select those papers which had one name only on them, so that the vote should not be lost. The present bill differed somewhat from Hare's system, but he believed that difference to be an improvement. Under the system the returning officer collects the number of votes registered, and from that forms his quota. Thus, if there were 30,000 electors and thirty to be returned, he formed his quota by dividing the one by the other; but if only 8000 electors voted, the probability would be that the matter could not be worked out, inasmuch as no one member would get a quota. According to the bill, however, the returning officer took the number of votes actually recorded, and divided them by the number of members to be returned, in order to obtain his quota. In that way every man would have his vote used, without the possibility of loss. He believed the system to be a good one, and he would like to see it tried; and as there was a bill to amend the Municipalities Act now before the House, he thought a good opportunity was afforded of testing the working of the system. He would be willing enough to apply it to the Council elections if the bill were such a one that he could support.

Mr. R. Forster would remove from the bill the part relating to Hare's system, for the simple reason that he did not understand it. It appeared to be a very ingenious theory, but one that had never been brought into operation. The Government were bound to see that the bill, with the alterations proposed, was passed by the Upper House, and was not again sent back to us.

Mr. Holt thought that the hon. member for New England (Mr. R. Forster) might, if he would only take the pains, easily understand Mr. Hare's system of representation. He would try to explain the matter to the hon. member. The system would give every elector the opportunity of voting just as if he knew the state of the poll. He would suppose that there were twelve hundred electors, and that there were three vacancies; the quota in that case would be four hundred. He would also suppose that the four Ministers were the candidates. First of all, the electors would vote for Mr. Cowper, who ought to be returned on account of his long services. Well, when the number for Mr. Cowper was made up the elector would give his vote for the Minister for Lands; and on Mr. Robertson's number being made up he would give his vote for Mr. Arnold. Every elector had the opportunity of doing what he would do if the polling booths had glass windows. Although the clauses were drawn up in legal phraseology, they were when examined easily intelligible. The instructions to the scrutineers were very complete and explicit. He looked upon this bill as merely a skeleton measure, and in voting for the second reading it was with an anxious desire to get this important matter settled. He did not, however, commit himself to any of the details. If he thought any bill could be so altered as to make it a satisfactory measure, as he thought was the case with this bill, he would support it. There was a good deal in the bill of which he quite approved, and more especially that clause which contained Hare's invention, as it might be termed.

Mr. Stewart said that, as to Hare's system, he must admit, from the opportunities he had had of judging, it was his impression that nineteen-twentieths of the community did not and would not, if it was passed, know how to carry it into effect. He thought the present system, which enabled the electors at the close of the poll to know which was the successful candidate,

was the best that we could adopt, and with the ballot the elections had been
the most satisfactory that had taken place in the colony.

Mr. DANGAR and Mr. DICK addressed the House, and on a division the
second reading was carried by a majority of 24 against 20.—*Sydney Morning
Herald*, Friday, November 14th, 1862.

Soon after the debate the Ministry resigned, and the
measure proceeded no further.

APPENDIX G.

Parliament of Victoria, Wednesday, 4th March, 1863.

IN a Bill for the Amendment of the Electoral Law of the
Colony, it was proposed to allow any voter of a constituency entitled to elect more than two members, to vote
for all the candidates which the constituency could elect,
or cumulate such votes on one or more of the candidates.
The discussion on this clause is fully reported in the
(*Melbourne*) *Argus*, Thursday, March 5, 1863, and somewhat more briefly in the (*Melbourne*) *Age* of the same day.

Mr. FRANCIS, to raise the discussion on the question, moved an amendment rejecting the clause for cumulative voting, but without therefore
pledging himself to vote against it. He thought that if the clause passed, as
it stood, it would be an instance of too rapid legislation in so young a colony.
He should like to see the principle first accepted elsewhere. He had not heard
of its introduction into the elections of members of the House of Commons.
The proposal of Lord John Russell had not been adopted. It was scarcely
adapted to a constituency returning less than three members, and was inapplicable to a constituency returning only one. In such a constituency the
successful candidate might receive 1,100 votes, and the next on the poll
might have 1,095. Where, under this clause, would these 1,095 voters find
representation? This led him to think that the clause did not go far enough,
or, that it failed to provide a perfect mode of representing minorities. . . .
He should be glad to hear arguments which would justify the Parliament of
Victoria in being the pioneer in such a legislative experiment.

The ATTORNEY-GENERAL said the question had been left an open one by
the Government. When he introduced the bill the matter had not been
fully considered. Hare's book, with the commentaries upon it, had arrived
in the colony while the bill was being draughted. In the legislature of New

South Wales, a bill had already been introduced by Mr. Wentworth, giving effect to Hare's system. . . . . He thought it desirable that minorities should be represented. Take a constituency with 2,100 voters. It seemed very hard that a moiety of the constituency with one or two votes over should have the power to send into Parliament a member to represent the whole of the constituency, when nearly one half of them would not be represented. It was said that it was wrong to make the experiment now, when it had not been adopted by the Imperial Parliament. He had great respect for the House of Commons, but, if the principle was a philosophical one, the fact of its not being introduced at home was no reason why it should not be tried here. It was also urged that it was not a perfect principle, but it was useless to aim at perfection, for some fraction of the minority must always be unrepresented.

Mr. HEALES objected to the attempted application of the principle to particular districts only. There was no class of the community to whom he would give advantages which others could not enjoy. If the power of concentrating their votes should be given to the voters of certain districts it would be unjust, and give one set of voters an unfair advantage over others. He was opposed, moreover, to the principle of the representation of minorities.

Mr. J. T. SMITH opposed the clause. In the district which he represented three members were returned, and the effect of the clause would be injurious to it. Were it divided into three portions, and each part allowed a member, it might be represented as a whole; but to give an inconsiderable minority, perhaps not numbering one-twelfth of the whole body of electors, the privilege of returning a member who would vote in opposition to the other two, was practically to reduce the representation of the district to a single member.

Mr. WOOD said that if the Legislature once laid down a correct principle that was a very important thing, even though it were attended with no great practical results. He was not affected by the argument that this was a small experiment, applying to four constituencies only. It was for the political philosopher to lay down a great scheme, and it was for the practical man to test that scheme. The hon. member for East Bourke had said that minorities did occasionally return representatives, even under the existing system, by what was commonly called plumping. This was, however, a mere matter of chance; it could only happen where the majority was divided. The same hon. member had also told the committee that under the present system there was a representation of a variety of opinions; that the colony was divided into various interests—mining, agricultural, and town interests; but the hon. member seemed to have overlooked the fact that the same class might be predominant in every instance—that the majority, in every instance, might hold the same set of political opinions. To take the question of protection, for example. There might, probably, be a majority in the towns in favour of protection; and they all knew that in the agricultural constituencies, the farmers, and probably the labourers, were also in favour of protection. In the mining districts, no doubt, there was a majority against protection. It was clear, however, that even on the question of protection there would be a majority in favour of protection in two classes of constituencies, although those two classes might seem, at first sight, to have no connexion whatever. The result of the present electoral system had been, that there was a representation of interests, but not a representation of opinions. He did not think that interests ought to be represented at all. What, after all, was the representation of interests but the representation of selfishness? Men's "interests," in the common meaning of the word, implied that a certain number of persons belonging to the same sphere or the same branch of industry thought their selfish interests would be advanced by a certain course of legislation being pursued. That was not what ought to be obtained in the selection of representatives; but if, as was the case, it was found that the people of the colony held very different opinions, the object ought to be to get as many as possible of those opinions represented. How was the truth to be elicited but by hearing different opinions expressed by those who were best able to put them forth in the Legislature? Every interest in the colony might be represented, and yet nothing like a majority, or even a fair proportion, of the opinions of the colony be represented. It had been asked what practical advantages would follow the adoption of the principle of the clause? Great advantages would follow it, if it were carried out systematically. All classes of opinions, or, at all events, all those opinions which commanded the assent of any considerable portion of the colony, would be represented in that House, and all sides of any question would be heard. Whatever Ministry had been in office, he believed that it had not represented, in any degree, opinions, and the consequence had been to degrade the politics of the colony. Instead of being supported on the ground of its opinions, the Ministry had always been supported on personal grounds or interests; and either a Ministry or an Opposition, supported on those grounds, did not tend to raise the character of the Legislature. In the constituencies of Collingwood and St. Kilda, large minorities were defeated on every contest. The result of all elections had been that the minority was politically annihilated. This was calculated to lead to political inaction. The minority, feeling themselves powerless, would decline to take any part in future elections. This was not a desirable state of things. It was not to the interest of the colony that a large body of men should be led to feel that it was useless for them to take any part in political contests. A gentleman sitting behind him said, "Divide the constituencies."↕[No doubt, in some cases, one class of political opinions was predominant in one part of a district, and another class of opinions was predominant in another part of the district. This, however, was a mere accident; it was one which was not likely to continue, and above all, it was one upon which no stable system of legislation ought to be based. The Legislature ought to endeavour to give the minority a fair share of the representation in every locality. It had been said that the four constituencies ought to be consulted by their representatives before the change. If it were proposed to place them under some disability, it might be reasonable to ask their opinion, but he really could not see what ground they had for being consulted, when it was proposed to confer on them a privilege not extended to other constituencies. Moreover, it was contrary to the very principle to consult the constituencies, for it was the opinion of the majority which would have to be asked, while the principle of the clause was the representation of the minority. He could refer to subjects which had been agitated from time to time in the colony; and, without disrespect to any members, he would say that candidates had been driven of necessity occasionally to conceal their opinions, or, at all events, to put a gloss upon them. ("Oh !") No doubt there might be a class of persons who had not been driven to that—who, having no opinions of their own, merely endeavoured to ascertain the opinions of a majority, in order to subscribe to those opinions; and he admitted that that class of persons had had no violence done to their opinions. (Laughter.) From time to time a few active persons banded themselves together to agitate for certain changes in the law. When the Constitution was inaugurated, many persons were anxious for the repeal of the clause which authorised a grant of £50,000 a year for religious purposes; and in almost every constituency where these persons had been at all successful candidates were driven to say either that they would vote for the immediate abolition of state aid to religion, or that they would not oppose the principle, although they thought the grant ought to be continued for some years longer; and yet all this time there was a very large minority entirely opposed to the theory. (Hear.) Then, with regard to the land question, there had been from time to time a vast amount of agitation, and persons had been obliged to give up the opinions they entertained, or, at all events, simulate opinions which they did not hold, in order to be returned. But it would have conduced more to the character of the Legislature if these persons had been able to come honestly and openly forward, and say—"We are opposed to the prevailing theories on the land question; we admit we are unable, in consequence, to command the support of the majority, but we appeal to the minority of the constituencies, who, we are sure, agree with us." (Hear.) Electors would not be driven to take advantage of the clause unless they pleased. (Hear.) Theoretically speaking, the chief objection to the clause was, that it did not apply to the whole colony—that it was limited to four constituencies. But, if the system worked well, it could be extended. Constituencies now returning two members could be so enlarged as to return three; and constituencies at present returning only one member each could be amalgamated, so that the united electoral district should have three representatives. In all countries where legislation had been really progressive, it had been tentative. An experiment was tried on a small scale, and when found to work well the principle was extended. (Hear.)

Mr. Higinbotham, after dealing with the objection that the clause would give the power of combined action to particular sects of politicians, and the argument as to the possibility of representing all opinions, expressed himself hostile to the proposed measure. *If the government had proposed Hare's system in its entirety, he would gladly have assented to the proposition; but for other and far more important reasons than the representation of minorities;* but it merely suggested the adoption in a mangled form of one feature of the system applied to four particular constituencies, and for which he had heard nothing urged which had any weight on his mind.

Mr. DUFFY said that the present clause was copied from the bill previously introduced by the member for Portland, to whom Mr. Mill had written to express his gratification that a representation of minorities was to be attempted. The principle of such a representation was the result of the best and most philosophical opinions. He adverted to Lord John Russell's proposal in the bill of 1854, and the interruption to the progress of reform caused by the Crimean War, and addressed himself especially to the arguments with regard to the force which might be acquired by the professors of religious or political opinions.

Mr. WOODS, admitting that, theoretically, it was correct that minorities should be represented, said the bill did not carry the principle out. It was possible that some opinions might not be represented in the House, but this was an evil which could not be obviated : they must stop somewhere, or else a minority of one intelligent voter might demand to be represented.

Mr. O'SHANASSY appealed to members, in considering this question on the high ground from which it deserved to be reviewed, to discard from their minds all thoughts of the effect of the clause upon local political parties. If they did so, whatever the present conclusion might be, the discussion could not be fruitless, for it would tend to educate the community. After replying to arguments of preceding speakers, he expressed his belief that the more the question was discussed and examined the more likely it was that at a future day a full system of representation would be brought forward by some government possessing the confidence of the country. He did not know any country in the world in which such a system could be more judiciously tried than in Victoria, a colony accustomed from its infancy to the exercise of political privileges. He hoped to see the day when public opinion would be so enlightened that, no longer seen through the narrow medium of local or sectarian jealousies, this most equitable scheme would be adopted with the full approbation of all thinking and right-minded persons.

Mr. BERRY opposed the clause. If the question of minorities were to be dealt with, it should be considered in all its bearings, and not upon a clause by which the principle was introduced in a mangled form. Hare's proposition was not before the House.

Captain M'MAHON regarded the representation of minorities as opposed to the great principle of constitutional government—the rule of the majority.

Mr. L. L. SMITH predicted that the adoption of such a clause would lead to anarchy, like that in America.

Mr. COHEN and Mr. ORR also opposed it in its principle.

Mr. FRANCIS, having referred to Hare's book, quoted the observations it contained on the minority clause in the English bill of 1854. (Pp. 14, 15.)

Mr. LEVI supported, and Mr. McLELLAN, Mr. RAMSAY, and Mr. HOUSTON, opposed the clause.

The ATTORNEY-GENERAL replied.

The clause was ultimately negatived.

APPENDIX H.

THIS system was discussed in Frankfort in 1861, 1863, and 1864. See *Die Zeit,* 10th December, 1861 ; *Frankfurter Reform,* 15th May, 20th May, 24th May, and 31st May, 1863. The *Frankfurter Reform* of the 29th January, 1864, contains the following article by Dr. Gustav Getz, on the application of the system to the elections to the Legislative body (Gesetzgebenden Versammlung) of the City of Frankfort.

Zum Wahlgesetz.

Wenn das Dach unseres Hauses in Brand steht, sind wir wenig geneigt, an die zweckmässigste Einrichtung unseres Wohnzimmers zu denken; wenn die Geschicke des Gesammt-Vaterlandes einer verhängnissvollen Entscheidung entgegeneilen, fühlen wir wenig Stimmung für Beschäftigung mit Localfragen. Dennoch rückt der Zeitpunkt immer näher, an welchem die Verfassungsfrage und mit ihr ein neues Wahlgesetz auf die Tagesordnung unserer gesetzgebenden Versammlung kommen werden. Im Hinblick hierauf haben gerade jetzt die Herren Drs. Varrentrapp und Burnitz eine Methode veröffentlicht, durch welche sowohl der Mehrheit als der Minderheit eine ihrer Stärke entsprechende Zahl von Vertretern gesichert werden soll. Es ist hier nicht der Ort, in mathematische Erörterungen einzugehen. Von einer kundigeren Feder soll anderwärts nachgewiesen werden, dass die am Schlusse des Schriftchens aufgestellten mathematischen Formeln auf willkürlichen, nur in seltenen Fällen zutreffenden Annahmen beruhen, dass jedoch in manchen Fällen diese Methode, nicht wie die beiden Verfasser annahmen, ein mathematisch exactes, aber ein *approximativ* befriedigendes Resultat ergibt. Uebrigens beruht es auf einem Irrthum, wenn diese Methode sich als eine neue ankündigt. Dieselbe findet sich bereits in dem von den Verfassern citirten Hare'schen Werke *pag.* 212 erwähnt (*thus, the vote at the head of the paper as* 1 *should be equal to* 2 *second votes,* 5 *fifth votes, and so on*); freilich ist sie daselbst verworfen, als den Zwecken, die Hare ins Auge gefaszt hatte und die weit über die blosse Vertretung der Minorität hinausreichen, nicht entsprechend. Wenn die Verfasser sich dennoch zur Aufstellung ihrer Methode veranlasst sehen und dabei bemerken, das Hare'sche System habe bisher mehr Gegner als Vertheidiger gefunden, so ist uns unklar, was so einsichtige Männer mit einer solchen Aeuszerung bezwecken? Ist unter den Gegnern etwa die grosse Masse derer, welche alles Neue anzweifeln, verstanden? Auf diese werden sie gewiss keinen Werth legen. Wollen sie die Stimmen aber wägen und nicht zählen, so hat vor Allem ein deutscher Staatsmann, dessen Autorität ihnen hochsteht, R, v. Mohl, das Hare'sche System bald nach seinem Erscheinen geradezu mit dem Ei des Columbus verglichen. Englische Staatsmänner haben es thatsächlich gebilligt und fast ganz unverändert in den Colonien, wo die Verhältnisse einer Neugestaltung günstig waren, einzuführen gesucht. [*The article here adverts to the Bills introduced into the Parliaments of Sydney and Melbourne.*]

Wir wollen den Leser nicht durch andere Beweise ermüden ; wir freuen uns zu sehr, diese beiden Männer nach demselben Ziele hinstreben zu sehen, als dass wir eine nutzlose Polemik zu provociren gewillt sein könnten. Für Frankfurt wird ebenso wenig die Einführung ihrer Methode, als die unabgeänderte Einführung des Hare'schen Systems in's Auge gefasst werden; aus dem einfachen Grunde, weil sowohl nach ihrer Methode, als auch bei der Hare'schen, eine verhältnissmässig allzukleine Anzahl von Personen einen Vertreter ernennen könnte. Bei 3600 Stimmenden und 90 zu wählenden, könnten nach beiden Wahlarten je 40 Mann, die zu einer Partei vereinigt wären, einen Vertreter durchsetzen. Bei dieser Sachlage bedarf es der Modificationen, und solche lassen sich sehr leicht in schützender Weise treffen, wenn man die Gesetzentwürfe nachahmt, welche in Genf sowohl vom Advokaten Charles Bellamy, als von Hrn. A. Morin (*De la Représentation des Minorités, par A. Morin.* Genève, chez Jules Fick, 1862) vorgeschlagen worden sind. Mit den für Frankfurt anzubringenden Abänderungen hätte das Wahlgesetz, falls man die Zahl der städtischen Mitglieder des gesetzgebenden Körpers auf 90 festgesetzt, zu bestimmen :

1. Jedem Wähler steht frei, bei der Wahl für den gesetzgebenden Körper einen Wahlzettel, auf welchem 90 wählbare Bürger verzeichnet sind, in die verschlossene Stimmurne zu werfen und ist es gestattet, sich sowohl gedruckter als geschriebener Wahlzettel zu bedienen.

2. Jeder Partei oder Vereinigung von Gesinnungsgenossen steht das Recht zu, mindestens 3 Tage vor der Wahl einen Wahlzettel, auf welchem 90 wählbare Bürger verzeichnet sind, als Wahlvorschlag bei der Stadtkanzlei einzureichen.

Nur also eingereichte Wahlzettel (für welche bei der alsbald erfolgenden

Wahlhandlung von wenigstens 200 Wählern gestimmt worden ist*), haben Anspruch auf eine dem Zahlenverhältniss aller Abstimmenden entsprechende Zahl von Vertretern.

3. Diese Zahl wird ermittelt wie folgt :

a) Nachdem alle Stimmzettel abgegeben worden sind, setzt das Bureau die Stimmenzahl fest, welche für die Zutheilung eines Vertreters erforderlich ist. Diese Normalzahl ist ein 90tel ($^1/_{90}$) aller Stimmenden. Brüche werden nicht gerechnet.

b) So oft die Normalzahl in der Zahl der für einen Wahlvorschlag unabgeändert abgegebenen Stimmzettel enthalten ist, so viele Vertreter werden diesem Wahlzettel zugetheilt. Die Zutheilung erfolgt nach der Reihenfolge, in welcher die Namen der zu Wählenden auf den Wahlzetteln verzeichnet sind.

c) Namen, welche auf mehreren Wahlvorschlägen verzeichnet sind, gelten als von selbst gewählt, ohne dass dies die verhältnissmässige Vertretung der Listen, auf welchen sie stehen, beeinträchtigte.

4. Bleiben nach dieser verhältnissmässigen Zutheilung noch Mitglieder zu wählen, so werden diese nach der relativen Majorität aller abgegebenen Stimmen erwählt.

Ein solches Gesetz würde sich an die bisherige Uebung anschliessen, und nur rechtlich organisiren, was bisher stets thatsächlich stattgefunden hat ; dass nämlich die Mehrzahl mit Parteizetteln, aber immer auch viele Bürger mit selbst verfassten Zetteln stimmen.

Es gäbe aber nicht jeder kleinen Colonie, vielmehr nur solchen Vereinigungen ein Recht auf verhältnissmässige Vertretung, welche wenigstens 200 Bürger für sich hätten. Es lässt keine Stimme verloren gehen, wahrt vielmehr denen, welche keiner Vereinigung angehören, dasselbe Recht, welches sie bisher besessen haben. Würden z. B. 3600 Bürger stimmen : die Partei A hätte einen Wahlvorschlag eingereicht, die Partei B gleichfalls. Für A hätten 1800, für B hätten 900 Wähler gestimmt und 900 sog. wilde Stimmzettel fänden sich in der Wahlurne : so wäre die Normalzahl 3600 dividirt durch 90 also 40. Die Partei A erhielte ihre 45 erstverzeichneten, die Partei B ihre 22 erstverzeichneten Vertreter, und die übrigen Vertreter, sowie die Supplcanten, würden wie bisher nach der relativen Majorität aller abgegebenen Stimmen erwählt. Auch an diesem Vorschlag mag noch manches zu ändern und zu bessern sein. Doch erscheint er uns als praktisch in Vermeidung aller bisher gerügten Misslichkeiten. Wir empfehlen ihn desshalb der Prüfung unserer Mitbürger. G. G.

---

* Die Zahl 200 ist willkürlich gegriffen. Die eingeschaltete Bestimmung fehlt in den Genfer Entwürfen, ist hier aber aus dem oben angeführten Grund als Cautel nothwendig.

Extracts from the *Bericht des 'Ausshusses zur Berathung über Abänderungen der Verfassung*, Friday, February 12, 1864.

Die Wahlart ist die directe. Die Stadt und Sachsenhausen bilden einen Wahlbezirk. Jeder Wähler gibt einen Zettel mit 84 Stimmen ab. Gewählt ist, wer 350 Stimmen erhält. Auf jedem Zettel gelten nur drei Namen und zwar zunächst die drei obersten, dann die folgenden der Reihe nach, wenn die vorhergehenden bereits 3500 Stimmen auf sich vereinigt haben. — Die Wähler geben ferner in eine zweite Urne einen weiteren Zettel mit je 60 Namen für die Suppleanten. Diese werden nach relativer Stimmenmehrheit sämmtlicher Abstimmenden erwählt und zwar der meistbestimmte als erster Suppleant u. s. w. — Werden bei der ersten Abstimmung nicht sämmtliche 84 Mitglieder für den gesetzgebenden Körper erwählt, so treten die meistbestimmten Suppleanten als wirkliche Mitglieder in den gesetzgebenden Körper ein.   DR. E. PASSAVANT.

Friday, March 25, 1864.

M. MAY. Die wichtigste Frage, welche wir zu entscheiden haben, ist diese : ob die gesammte Bürgerschaft, oder nur eine geschickt operirende Minderheit hier vertreten sein soll. Hr. Dr. Passavant hat einen Modus vorgeschlagen, der auch den Minderheiten eine verhältnissmässige Vertretung sichern will, und diesem Princip stimme ich vollständig bei, wenn ich auch die Modalitäten der Ausführung noch dahin gestellt sein lasse. Vorerst aber handelt es sich überhaupt nur um die Entscheidung über das Princip, und ich stelle daher den Antrag :

Bei der Stimmenzählung ist so zu verfahren, dass die Minderheit eine Vertretung nach der Anzahl ihrer Stimmen im Verhältniss zur Gesammtzahl der abgegebenen Stimmen finde.

Die Versammlung soll der möglichst treue Ausdruck der Bürgerschaft sein, und dazu ist es erforderlich, dass die verschiedenen in der Bürgerschaft waltenden Ansichten ihren Ausdruck auch in der Versammlung finden. Die indirekte Wahl läszt nur die Ansicht *einer* Partei zur Geltung kommen, und das ist der Hauptgrund der geringen Betheiligung an den Wahlen, denn wer der bekannten Majorität nicht angehört, enthält sich lieber ganz der Wahl, da er doch nichts erzielen kann.

Dr. KUGLER. Es hat sich eine entschiedene Abneigung gegen die indirekten Wahlen gebildet, und ihre Miss-stände sind auch nicht zu verkennen. Nun aber frägt es sich, welche Art der direkten Wahlen den Vorzug verdient. Es gibt hier drei Wege: 1) nur *einen* Wahlbezirk—da wären die indirekten Wahlen noch vorzuziehen; 2) geographisch abgesteckte Wahlbezirke—was schon besser ist; und endlich 3) freiwillige Wahlbezirke, das heisst, es wird bestimmt, dass wenn so und so viel Bürger sich zur Wahl eines Mitgliedes vereinigen, ist es gewählt. Dieser

Modus allein entspricht der Billigkeit und sichert der Minderheit die ihr gebührende Vertretung.

Dr. Fuld ist gleichfalls für diese freiwilligen Wahlbezirke oder die verhältnissmässige Vertretung der Bürgerschaft. Wozu haben wir eine Mehrzahl von Vertretern, wenn es nicht ist, um die verschiedenen, in der Bürgerschaft waltenden Ansichten zum Ausdruck zu bringen? Hätte nur die Majorität das Recht auf Vertretung, dann genügte es zu diesem Zweck vollkommen, nur *Einen* zu schicken. Es gibt ebenso eine Tyrannei der Majorität, wie eine Tyrannei der Despoten. Jedes Wahlsystem, welches nur eine Vertretung der Majorität zulässt, ist eine solche Tyrannei. Der Ausspruch der Bürgerschaft, das Vorherrschen der wirklichen Majorität der Bürgerschaft in der Versammlung, und die Vertretung auch der Minderheitsansichten, das sind die Bedingungen eines guten Wahlgesetzes. Diesen Anforderungen entspricht mit Ausnahme des von Dr. Passavant gestellten Antrags, keiner der Vorschläge, am wenigsten aber das indirecte Wahlsystem; ebenso gut könnte man sagen, drei Männer sollen sämmtliche Abgeordneten wählen. Es ist ein Misstrauensvotum gegen die Bürgerschaft. Dr. Müller's Vorschlag geht hiervon ab, behält aber die Tyrannei der Majorität bei und verhindert sogar, dass auch nur, wie bei den indirekten Wahlen, durch die Gnade der herrschenden Partei Andersdenkende hereinkämen. Dr. Neukirchs Vorschlag strebt schon darnach, die Minorität zum Ausdruck zu bringen, allein die Abgränzung von Wahlbezirken ist ganz wohl ausführbar in einem grösseren Lande, nicht so aber in einer Stadt. Ferner ist nicht zu übersehen, dass bei den einfachen Bezirkswahlen die Majorität in der ganzen Bürgerschaft der Minorität unterliegen kann. Nur Eins ist sicher und gerecht: ein Wahlmodus, welcher den verschiedenen Ansichten eine proportionnelle Vertretung gewährt.

Dr. Passavant. Hier ist das Volk souverän, wir leben in einer demokratischen Republik. Der Grundzug derselben ist, dass das Volk selbst seine Angelegenheiten führt. So war es in Griechenland, so ist es noch in den Urkantonen der Schweiz. Nachdem dies unausführbar geworden, hat man zur Vertretung gegriffen; diese aber soll den Grundgedanken möglichst wiedergeben, sie soll ein Abbild der Landgemeinde im Kleinen sein. Lässt man nun blos die Majorität zu, so verschliesst man allen Andern den Mund, die ehedem, in der allgemeinen Volksversammlung, ihre Meinung geltend machen konnten, und dazu hat man kein Recht. Es ist dies aber nicht nur ungerecht, sondern auch unklug, denn es fordert die Unterdrückten heraus, sich auf anderem Wege die ihnen zukommende Geltung zu verschaffen und bedroht daher fortwährend die Sicherheit des Staates. Bisher war die Majorität, den Mangel des Wahlgesetzes fühlend, so vorsichtig gewesen, immer selbst einige Anhänger der Minorität in die Versammlung zu berufen; bei der directen Wahl in nur einem Bezirt wird auch das unmöglich, und der Minorität bleibt gar keine Vertretung. Die von mir aufgestellten Zahlen sind nicht wesentlich, es handelt sich zunächst nur um das Princip, dass der Minderheit eine verhältnissmässige Vertretung zuerkannt werde.

Dr. Müller. In der Landgemeinde würde immer die Majorität den Ausschlag geben; da nun aber die Landgemeinde nicht zusammen kommen kann und eine Vertretung wählen muss, so ist es ganz in der Ordnung, dass auch die Majorität diese beruft. Die Minorität kann auch in der Landgemeinde nicht mehr als ihre Ansicht aussprechen, dazu ist ihr jetzt in der freien Presse das Mittel geboten. Das Hare'sche System der Minderheitsvertretung ist so complicirt und künstlich, dass die Wähler es nicht verstehen werden. Sie sollen 84 Namen aufschreiben, von denen doch nur 3 zählen; das dürften nur Wenige begreifen. Die directe Wahl in Einem Wahlbezirk ist das Einfachste und unsern Verhältnissen Entsprechendste.

Dr. Neukirch. Die indirekte Wahl scheint selbst von Denen aufgegeben, die sie in der Commission mit aller Energie vertheidigten. Sie gehört nur in das Arsenal der Reaktion, die auch stets das direkte Wahlsystem durch das indirekte verdrängt hat. Obwohl ich dieser Hauptfrage gegenüber auf die von mir beantragten Wahlbezirke nur einen sekundären Werth lege, so glaube ich doch, dass durch diese Dasjenige, was von anderer Seite erstrebt wird, am kürzesten zu erreichen sei. Die Erfahrung anderwärts hat gezeigt, dass nie *eine* Partei in allen Wahlbezirken durchdringt, und so würden wir auch hier durch solche Abtheilungen den einflussreicheren Minderheiten eine Vertretung ermöglichen. Bei nur einem Wahlbezirk würde die Majorität Alles beherrschen.

Dr. Med. Friedleben. Es liegt der eigenthümliche Fall vor, dass ein sogenanntes Majoritätsgutachten eingebracht ist, dessen Vaterschaft von Allen verläugnet wird. Es hat heute gar keinen Vertheidiger gefunden. Ein zweiter Vorschlag geht dahin, dass die Minorität in der Bürgerschaft auch ihre Vertretung finden solle. Wo aber ist diese Minorität? Die Minorität kann nur so weit eine Vertretung verlangen, als ihre Candidaten mehr Stimmen haben, als gewisse Candidaten der Majorität. Man sagt: sie müsse doch auch gehört werden. Nun wohl, die Vertreter der Minderheit in der Constituante haben einzig nur intriguirt, und die jetzigen Vertreter der Minderheit in dieser Versammlung haben während der ganzen Debatten über die so wichtige Verfassungsfrage noch kein Wort gesprochen. Warum geben sie ihre Ansicht nicht kund? Das Bestreben der Minderheit kann immer nur sein, die Mehrheit zu werden. Wir haben uns jetzt nur über das Princip auszusprechen. Mit der Annahme des Princips der direkten Wahlart ist Alles geschehen, was jetzt zu geschehen hat, und ich beantrage, dass die Bestimmung über die näheren Modalitäten der Wahl einem besonderen Gesetz vorbehalten bleibe, denn diese Modalitäten werden den wechselnden Bedürfnissen und Ansichten gemäss Veränderungen erleiden, und es ist daher nicht gut, sie in die Verfassung selbst mit aufzunehmen.

Dr. Brannfels. Ich stimme dem ganz bei. Der Antrag des Hrn. Dr. Passavant ist ebensowohl unpraktisch, als unrichtig. Es erleidet keinen Zweifel, dass wir direkte Wahlen bekommen werden. Wenn nun unser Staat aus mehreren Provinzen oder Städten bestände, würde es wohl Niemand in den

Sinn kommen, das Hare'sche System vorzuschlagen. Bis jetzt hat es nur bei den Antipoden, in Australien und am Cap der guten Hoffnung Eingang gefunden. In einem grossen Staate ist es gar nicht durchzuführen. Ueberhaupt, bis wohin soll sich [denn die Vertretung der Minorität erstrecken? Es kann doch nur Diejenige Anspruch darauf haben, welche sich geltend macht. Die jetzige Majorität in dieser Versammlung ist auch einmal die Minorität gewesen; sie war aber darum keineswegs mundtodt; sie hat sich gerührt, die Bürgerschaft überzeugt, und ist schliesslich die Majorität geworden. Das ist der einzig richtige Weg. Durch die vorgeschlagenen Versuche werden Sie nicht sowohl zur Vertretung von Parteien, als nur von Cliquen kommen. Einflussreiche Leute, die eine Anzahl Stimmen beherrschen, werden ihre Vertreter hereinschicken. Unbedeutende Minoritäten haben keinen Anspruch auf Vertretung, grössere allerdings sollten berücksichtigt werden. Man hat zu diesem Zweck Bezirkswahlen vorgeschlagen, und in der That lehrt auch die Erfahrung, dass in den verschiedenen Bezirken die verschiedenen Meinungen leicht die Majorität erlangen können. Allerdings gibt es für die Bezirke keine natürliche Abgränzung, diese wird immer willkürlich gezogen sein, allein die ganze Einrichtung hat grosse Vorzüge. Eine allgemeine Bürgerversammlung lässt sich nicht ausführen, wohl aber sind Bezirksversammlungen leicht einzuberufen, und vor diesen kann der Candidat seine Ansichten darlegen. Man hat zu Gunsten des Hare'schen Systems noch hervorgehoben, dass es eine regere Theilnahme der Bürgerschaft an den Wahlen mit sich bringen würde; das ist mir aber sehr zweifelhaft, denn es begünstigt die Bildung im Geheimen werbender Cotterien, während bei den Bezirkswahlen, wo die Meinungen sich offen gegen einander aussprechen können, die Theilnahme am meisten angeregt wird. Ich schliesse mich ganz dem Antrag des Hrn. Dr. Med. Friedleben an, dass für jetzt nur beschlossen werden möge: die Wahl erfolgt durch unmittelbare Abstimmung in mehreren Bezirken, über das Nähere bestimmt das Gesetz.

Da noch viele Redner zum Wort angemeldet sind, wird wegen vorgerückter Stunde die weitere Discussion vertagt.

Friday, April 1st, 1864.

Dr. ENYRIM schlieszt sich dem Antrag des Hrn. Dr. Passavant an. Wenn der Grundsatz aufgestellt wurde, dass nur die Majorität ein Recht auf Vertretung habe, so beruht das auf einer Verwechselung der Beschlüsse, welche von der Vertretung zu fassen sind, mit dieser selbst, welche nur die Landgemeinde darstellen soll. Unser altes Wahlgesetz war ein verspäteter Ausläufer des ständigen Princips und dieses ging von der Voraussetzung aus, dass die Interessen und Anschauungen in den verschiedenen Ständen andere seien und alle auf eine gleichmässige Vertretung Anspruch haben. Diese Voraussetzungen treffen heute nicht mehr zu, allein das früher so sorgsam gewahrte Recht auf Vertretung der verschiedenen Interessen und Ansichten besteht auch heute noch und muss seinen Ausdruck in dem neuen Wahlgesetz finden, wie es ihn in dem alten gefunden hatte. Das nun sucht das Hare'sche System zu bewirken, und es ist nach dieser Seite hin das Ei des Columbus. Um sich gegen die befürchtete Bildung kleiner Coterien zu schützen, braucht man nur die zu einer Wahl erforderliche Stimmenzahl etwas höher anzusetzen, etwa auf 4—500. Man tadelt, dass dies System so komplicirt, ein Rechenexempel sei : die Gerechtigkeit ist aber nie einfach, und je mehr unsere Gesetze der Gerechtigkeit nach allen Seiten zu entsprechen suchen, umso komplicirter werden sie. Es kommt auch gar nicht darauf an, dass die grosse Masse genau verstehe, was hinter den Thüren der Wahlcommission vorgeht. Ein etwas schwieriges Wahlsystem wäre übrigens auch nur ein ganz gutes politisches Erziehungsmittel für den Bürger.

Hr. DIETZ ist der Ansicht, dass nach Durchführung der Verfassungsreform die Parteifragen sich vermindern werden. Es gibt überhaupt nur noch zwei Parteien, die Fortschritts und die Stillstandspartei. Auch schon bei den früheren Wahlen hat es sich stets mehr um die Person als um die Partei gehandelt. Der Redner erklärt sich zunächst für das Hare'sche System, in zweiter Linie für die Bezirkswahlen und in dritter für den Antrag des Hrn. Vogtherr.

Dr. FULD. Ich habe gefunden, dass Diejenigen, welche sich bisher gegen die proportionellen Wahlen ausgesprochen, ihre Berechtigung eigentlich anerkannt haben. Zuerst Herr Dr. Braunfels, der sich am eingehensten und behaglichsten darüber ausgelassen hat. Er hat geltend gemacht, dass dies System in einem grossen Staate nicht ausführbar sei, womit aber seine Ausführbarkeit in einem kleinen Staate, wie der unserige, indirect zugestanden ist. Ferner machte er es ihm zum Vorwurf, dass es noch nirgends eingeführt sei ; allein alles Neue war vorher noch nicht da, und es kann uns gewiss nur lieb sein, wenn auch wir einmal mit etwas Gutem zuerst kommen. Man sagt, es würden sich Coterien bilden. Wenn man die Grenze zwischen Coterie und Partei scharf zu ziehen weiss, so bestimme man die zu einer Wahl erforderliche Stimmenzahl darnach. Man erkennt an, dass es Minoritäten gibt, deren Berücksichtigung seitens der Majorität von der Klugheit und Billigkeit geboten ist,—dann muss man aber diesen Minoritäten auch ein *Recht* zugestehen und sie nicht von der blossen Gnade der Majorität abhängig machen. Durch die Bezirkswahlen wird die Vertretung der Minorität, wie selbst der Majorität, dem blossen Zufall anheimgegeben. Wenn es der Zweck einer Vertretung ist, nicht blos Beschlüsse zu fassen, sondern die verschiedenen Ansichten zu hören und zu prüfen, so bleibt kein anderer Weg, als das Hare'sche System, mit denjenigen Modificationen, welche die zu ernennende Commission daran zu machen findet.

Dr. Jur. FRIEDLEBEN. Wenn ich mich dem Antrag auf directe Wahlen angeschlossen, so geschah es nicht aus dem Grunde, weil ich diese Frage für eine principielle halte. Die Beispiele von Preussen, Hessen, Nassau einerseits und von Frankreich anderseits beweisen, dass indirecte Wahlen eine weit unabhängigere und freisinnigere Vertretung ergeben können, als die directen. Die Wahl in nur einem Bezirk braucht durchaus nicht, wie man befürchtet, ein exclusives Ergebniss zu liefern. Wir haben hier zugleich eine politische und eine Gemeinde-Vertretung. Wenn die Erstere die Partien scheidet, führt sie die Letztere wieder zusammen, denn sie bedingt die Berufung von Männern verschiedener Fähigkeiten. Die politischen Minoritäten haben als solche gar kein Recht auf Vertretung, denn die Repräsentation soll nur die öffentliche Meinung zum Ausdruck bringen, und diese ist in der Majorität gegeben. Wenn man der Mehrheit Abgeordnete der Minderheit aufdrängt, gründet man eine Tyrannei der Minorität. In Bezirkswahlen müsste man noch viel exclusiver verfahren, als bei der Aufstellung einer Wahlliste für nur einen Bezirk. Die Zahl unserer Mitglieder könnte allerdings vermindert werden, 60 wären ganz ausreichend. Den Landgemeinden wird die Zusammenlegung in einen Bezirk nur gut thun, zumal sie fortan das Recht haben werden, ihre Vertreter aus dem ganzen Staatsgebiet, nicht nur aus ihrer Gemeinde zu nehmen. Meiner Ansicht nach ist das Hare'sche System unrichtig im Princip und ungerecht in der Anwendung. Unrichtig, weil es *à priori* einen Satz aufstellt, der dem konstitutionellen Staatsrecht widerspricht, welches der Mehrheit die Leitung der öffentlichen Angelegenheiten zuweist. Der Volkswille soll entscheiden, das ist aber nicht der Wille der Minorität. Mit diesem System würden wir einen Rückschritt noch hinter das Drei-Klassensystem machen; es trägt die Gefahr in sich, die Bürgerschaft in ganz kleine Coterien zu zerreissen. Wir würden den traurigsten Missgriff machen, wenn wir dies principlose Princip hier in Frankfurt annähmen.

Hr. Rütten macht darauf aufmerksam, dass, wie hoch oder niedrig man auch bei dem Hare'schen System die zu einer Wahl erforderliche Stimmenzahl ansetzen möge, es bei geringerer Betheiligung an den Wahlen doch geschehen könne, dass die vorgeschriebene Anzahl von Abgeordneten gar nicht zusammenkomme.

Dr. Stern erklärt sich ebenfalls gegen das Hare'sche System. Es beruht auf dem Missverständniss einer Verwechselung der Minorität mit den Minoritäten. Der Minorität allerdings muss die Gelegenheit gegeben sein, sich geltend zu machen, aber sie darf sich nicht in Minoritäten auflösen. Wir würden bei den letzteren keine Gesammtvertretung haben, sondern nur eine Vertretung von lauter unbedeutenden Fraktionen. Solcher kleiner Gruppen können sich möglicherweise 84 bilden, und wir haben dann gar keine Vertreter der Gesammtheit mehr. Es ist überhaupt ein System zu verwerfen, welches die Wahl von einer freien That zu einer Manipulation macht. Die Bezirkswahlen haben den Vorzug, dass sie die Bürgerschaft zu einer lebhaften Betheiligung an den öffentlichen Angelegenheiten heranziehen. Sie sind die politischen Bildungsschulen in Preussen. Die Wahl in nur einem Wahlbezirk ist eine Täuschung. Die 84 Abgeordneten können nicht freigewählt, noch weniger discutirt werden.

ʹ Dr. VARRENTRAPP. Wenn es etwas Illiberales gibt, so ist es die Behauptung, die Minderheit besitze gar kein Recht, bis sie nicht die Mehrheit geworden ist. Es ist eben so unhistorisch als unmoralisch, dass eine Ansicht nicht eher gehört werden solle, als bis sie die Anerkennung der Mehrheit gefunden hat. Man schneidet damit aller Fortentwickelung, aller Belehrung eines Besseren den Weg ab. Wenn man ein Solches Princip durchführt, dann spreche man nur nicht mehr von Freiheit. Ursprünglich kamen die Menschen in der Familie, in der Landgemeinde zusammen und tauschten ihre Ansichten aus. Als nun dies in Folge ihrer Vermehrung und Ausbreitung nicht mehr thunlich war, sandten sie Vertreter, und nun will man sagen: bisher habt ihr das Recht gehabt mitzureden, mitzustimmen, von heute an hört dies auf und ihr habt nur noch das Recht zu wählen. Die Vertretung verdient nur dann diesen Namen, wenn sie ein möglichst treues Bild der Vertretenen selbst ist. Das bezweckt das Hare'sche System, in dessen Einzelheiten einzugehen überflüssig erscheint, sobald man das Princip selbst verwirft. Die Zulassung von Vertretern der Minoritätsansicht aus blosser Gunst, ist ignobel für beide Theile. Ich erkläre mich für die Beibehaltung der zwei ersten Theile des Passavant'-schen Antrags und wünsche, dass statt des dritten einfach gesagt werde: das Gesetz bestimmt den Wahlmodus auf Grund des Hare'schen Systems.

Dr. BRAUNFELS. Das Hare'sche System beruht darin, dass man die wirklich Wählenden durch die zu Wählenden dividirt und darnach die zur Wahl erforderliche Stimmenzahl festsetzt. Nun gibt man von vorne herein zu, dass dies nicht angehe, dass man eine willkürliche höhere Zahl annehmen müsse, und fällt damit gleich selbst wieder von dem Princip ab. Wir dagegen sagen, eine Meinung hat nur dann das Recht auf Vertretung, wenn sie die Mehrheit, sei es im Staate oder in dem Bezirk, besitzt, und haben dabei die Praxis aller Länder für uns. Wenn aber, wie es das Hare'sche System erstrebt, alle Meinungen vertreten sein sollen, so führte das zu einer höchst verderblichen Zersplitterung, während doch das Ziel sein muss, die Ansichten möglichst zu koncentriren. Dr. Varrentrapp nannte es ignobel für beide Theile, wenn die Majorität freiwillig die Minorität berücksichtigt; ich finde darin vielmehr einen Beweis des Vertrauens, der beide Theile ehrt. Die Bezirkswahlen bieten nicht nur die Möglichkeit, sondern sogar die Wahrscheinlichkeit, dass jede namhaftere Minoritätsansicht da oder dort zur Geltung kommt.

Dr. KUGLER. Es ist von den Vertheidigern des einen Wahlbezirks geltend gemacht worden: die Majorität allein habe zu entscheiden, mit der Wahl sei Alles abgeschlossen, von da ab habe die Minorität nur noch zu schweigen. Dadurch würde die Vertretung selbst nur noch zu einer Abstimmungs-maschine. Ich bin anderer Ansicht. Die Bürgerschaft schickt deshalb viele Vertreter, damit sich hier die verschiedenen Ansichten aussprechen, dass darüber deliberirt und nicht nur abgestimmt werde. Jede einigermassen bedeutende, redliche Minorität muss demnach hier ihren Ausdruck finden. Eine räumliche Bezirksabgränzung bietet nicht die entfernteste Sicherheit für ein solches Resultat der Wahlen, diese ist nur in den freiwilligen Wahlbezirken des Hare'schen Systems zu finden.

Dr. REINGANUM. Um gleich den Beweis zu geben, dass ich mich nicht als blosse Wahlmaschine betrachte, erkläre ich, dass mich die ganze Discussion von meiner ersten Ansicht, nach welcher ein indirectes Wahlsystem für uns am zuträglichstem wäre, noch nicht abgebracht hat. Alle die andern vorgeschlagenen Systeme führen dahin, dass die Wahlzettel von Parteiausschüssen gemacht, von den Parteigenossen angenommen werden. Ob ich aber Andere den Wahlzettel entwerfen lasse, oder Vertrauensmännern die Wahl selbst übertrage, ist ganz dasselbe. In Kurhessen hat das wiedergewonnene directe Wahlrecht nur einen Democraten, Trabert, in die Kammer gebracht, während die indirecten Wahlen in Preussen ein ganz anderes Resultat ergeben haben. Das Hare'sche System will intellektuelle Bezirke. Wenn darnach in Bornheim eine Anzahl Kinder Gottes sich zusammenthun, haben sie das Recht, das Kind Gottes zu wählen. Dieses System stiehlt der Majorität ihre Stimmen, um sie der Minorität zu geben. Wenn Lord Palmerston 20,000 Stimmen hat, worin der Regierung ein werthvolles Vertrauen ausgesprochen ist, kommt Mr. Hare und sagt: du branchst nur 1000 Stimmen, die übrigen 19,000 gebe ich Anderen.[1] Dies System treibt die Zersplitterung zum Excess. Wie soll es anderseits mit den Bezirken hier werden? Um eine verhältnissmässige Zahl Bezirke herzustellen, müszte man nicht mehr Quartierwahlen, sondern Gassenwahlen einführen. Man hofft, die Wähler und Candidaten werden zusammen kommen und sich gegenseitig Kopf und Nieren prüfen. Ich glaube das nicht; wir haben sehr viele tüchtige Männer, die doch nicht hintreten und in vorhinein versprechen möchten, wie sie in jeder möglichen Frage stimmen würden. Dr. Varrentrapp nannte es ignobel, wenn die Majorität Männer der Minorität freiwillig beruft. Als seine Partei am Ruder war, hatte sie mehrere Jahre ganz exclusiv gewählt, dann aber zuerst drei Demokraten mit aufgestellt. Wir sind auch gekommen, und weder sie noch wir haben das ignobel gefunden. Eine Verminderung der Mitgliederzahl wäre sehr wünschenswerth, soll dies aber nicht sein, so möchte ich, um aus allen den Quälereien herauszukommen, vorschlagen, dass man in drei Wahlgängen jedesmal 28 Mitglieder wählen lasse.

Wegen vorgerückter Zeit wurde die Discussion hier abgebrochen und auf die nächste Sitzung vertagt.

---

[1] Dr. Reinganum overlooks the fact that Lord Palmerston would, from the public declaration of the votes polled, acquire all the moral weight of the proffer of 20,000 votes, while the appropriation of 19,000 of them to the other candidates named lower on the papers, so far from lessening that weight, will probably contribute to the election of *nineteen* of his supporters, and add therefore greatly to his power in the representative body. See, on this point, p. 255, n.

Friday, April 8, 1864.

Die Versammlung geht nunmehr an die Fortsetzung der Verhandlung über das Wahlgesetz.

Nach einer persönlichen Bemerkung des Hrn. Dietz ergreift Hr. May das Wort zur Vertheidigung des Hare'schen Systems. Dem Prinzip, dass der Minorität eine entsprechende Vertretung zukommt, muss Jeder beistimmen, mag er sich auch mit den Vorschlägen zur Ausführung desselben nicht einverstanden erklären. Zu den Lasten des Staates, zu den Steuern, zur Conscription u. s. w. zieht man die Minorität heran, da ist sie gleichmässig *verpflichtet*, aber von der Berathung will man sie ausschliessen, gleich *berechtigt* soll sie nicht sein. Es wird so grosses Gewicht darauf gelegt, viele Stimmen zu bekommen; damit geht es aber doch manchmal eigen zu. Bei den Wahlen zur Gewerbekammer hatten wir einen Namen auf unserer Liste, der sich auch auf der Liste unserer Gegner befand, und dieser Einzige wurde demnach einstimmig gewählt. Ein besonderes Zeichen des Vertrauens hierin zu sehen, wäre vielleicht sehr unbedacht. Mein Antrag geht dahin, dass man zuvor alle Namen, die nicht wenigstens 200 Stimmen auf sich vereinigen, als zersplitterte Wahlen ausscheide, und den andern Parteien die auf sie entfallende Abgeordnetenzahl nach Verhältniss ihrer Stärke zuschreibe.

Dr. Leykauf erklärt sich ebenfalls für das Hare'sche System. Nach dem Axiom der Gegner derselben hat nur die Majorität das Recht zu herrschen und demnach auch allein Vertreter in die Versammlung zu senden. Das Erste ist richtig, das Zweite aber falsch. Die Majorität hat nicht das Recht, der Minorität das Wort zu verwehren. Das wichtigste Recht des Bürgers, das Recht des freien Wortes von der Tribüne will man von der Gnade oder Politik der jeweilig herrschenden Partei abhängig machen. Das Hare'sche System wird die Theilnahme der Bürgerschaft an den Wahlen, die so beständig abgenommen hat, aufs Neue beleben.

Dr. Sauerländer. Die Frage, ob direkte oder indirekte Wahlen, scheint entschieden, es handelt sich also nur um die näheren Bestimmungen. Die Wahl in nur einem Bezirk führt zu einer Tyrannei der Majorität. Die ganze Vertretung wird zu einem blossen Parteiorgan. Die schwächeren Parteien ziehen sich, um einer sicheren Niederlage auszuweichen, von den Wahlen zurück, und so erkaltet die Theilnahme für das wichtigste politische Recht der Bürgerschaft. Auch im Hare'schen System gebietet die Parteidisciplin die Annahme von Wahllisten, auf denen sich Namen befinden mögen, die man nicht frei wählen würde. Die Bezirkswahlen empfehlen sich am meisten. Hier ist die Möglichkeit eines lebhaften politischen Ringens geboten und die Minorität in dem einen hat die Aussicht des Sieges in dem andern.

Hr. J. Rütten stellt den Antrag, dass die Zahl der städtischen Abgeordneten auf 72 vermindert werde, doch wird dieser Antrag bis zur Berathung des betreffenden Gesetzes vertagt.

Nachdem noch die Hrn. Dr. Neukirch und Dr. Reinganum ihre respectiven Anträge vertheidigt, wird zunächst der von Hrn. Dr. Kugler formulirte Antrag auf Einführung des Hare'schen Systems, dass nämlich Jeder als gewählt betrachtet werden solle, der eine näher zu bestimmende Zahl der von sämmtlichen Wählenden abgegebenen Stimmen erhalten hat, zur Abstimmung gebracht und abgelehnt. Sodann wird der allgemeine Grundsatz: Die Wahlart ist die direkte, mit grosser Stimmenmehrheit angenommen, und nach Ablehnung der Anträge des Hrn. Dr. Med. Friedleben, dass über die Art der Ausführung das Gesetz bestimme, und des Hrn. Dr. Braunfels, dass die Abstimmung in mindestens 3 Bezirken stattfinde, über das Weitere aber das Gesetz bestimme, der Antrag der Hrn. Dr. Neukirch und G. Hoffmann, dass die Stadt in *acht* Wahlbezirke getheilt werde, mit 35 gegen 27 Stimmen *genehmigt*.

Ferner noch erklärt sich die Versammlung dafür, dass jede der sieben Landgemeinden einen Wahlkreis für sich bilde, und dass die Abstimmung in der Stadt wie auf dem Lande eine geheime sein solle, während die Fragen, ob absolute oder relative Majorität zur Wahl erforderlich sei und ob Suppleanten gewählt werden sollen, vorerst ausgesetzt bleiben.

APPENDIX I.

THE following extract is from an article from the pen of M. Louis Blanc, which has had a wide circulation, and excited much attention in France :—

Le peuple, ce n'est pas la *pluralité*, c'est l'*universalité* des citoyens : d'où vient donc qu'on parle toujours de la souveraineté du peuple, comme si le PEUPLE était un être simple, unique, immuable, dont on puisse dire ce qu'on dirait d'un individu : IL veut ceci, IL ne veut pas cela ?

Quant à la souveraineté, il serait temps de s'entendre. S'il est vrai que d'après Hobbes, d'après Rousseau, d'après tous les publicistes qui ont écrit sur la matière, d'après le dictionnaire, d'après l'usage, elle soit le pouvoir suprême, celui dont tout relève, il est clair que son essence est d'être absolue.

Mais si, étant absolu, un pareil pouvoir n'était pas incontestablement juste et regardé avec raison comme infaillible, loin d'être légitime, loin de constituer un droit, il aurait l'odieux caractère d'un fait écrasant, et la souveraineté serait infâme. Qu'une iniquité soit commise au nom du souverain, fût-ce à l'égard d'un seul homme, la souveraineté disparaît comme principe, et ne subsiste plus que comme force. Et, n'est-il pas certain, n'est-il pas historiquement prouvé qu'un seul homme peut, à un moment donné, sur une question donnée, avoir raison contre cent mille hommes, contre un million d'hommes, contre tous les hommes, moins lui ?

Ainsi donc, pour que la souveraineté, dans le sens absolu qu'on attache à ce mot, fût autre chose qu'une pure abstraction au point de vue du droit, il faudrait qu'elle répondît en fait à l'idée d'*universalité*; qu'il y eût unanimité d'idées, de sentiment ; que toute pression du plus grand nombre sur le plus petit pût être écartée par la communauté des intérêts et l'harmonie des volontés. Touchons-nous à la réalisation de ce rêve d'or ? Il est sans fond l'abîme qui nous en sépare.

Que faites-vous donc, vous qui prétendez investir du caractère qui conviendrait au *gouvernement du peuple par lui-même* ce qui n'est, et ne saurait être que le *gouvernement d'une partie du peuple par une autre partie?* Vous faussez la notion du droit ; vous transportez à la *pluralité*, qui est exposée au malheur d'être injuste, le pouvoir de l'*universalité*, qui ne peut pas être injuste, parce qu'on ne l'est pas envers soi-même ; vous mettez le *relatif* à la place de l'*absolu ;* vous mutilez le souverain, et en lui dérobant son nom pour le donner à ce qui n'est pas lui, vous courez le risque de consacrer la tyrannie !

Il faut quelque chose qui empêche le droit des plus nombreux de trop ressembler au droit des plus forts ; quelque chose qui serve à distinguer avantageusement l'état de société, où l'on se compte, de l'état de nature, où l'on se bat ; quelque chose qui protége la liberté contre la substitution possible du pouvoir d'un chiffre à celui d'un coup de massue ; quelque chose enfin qui fasse que la démocratie cesse d'être un régime de privilége en faveur du nombre. La majorité doit avoir plus de représentants que la minorité, fort bien ; mais s'ensuit-il, comme dit M. John Stuart Mill, que la minorité n'en doive pas avoir du tout ? Eh bien, c'est pourtant ce qui arrive sous l'empire du système qui ne permet aux électeurs de voter que pour le candidat qui se présente dans le district électoral auquel ils appartiennent. Le représentant élu pour le district est celui de la majorité, et le vote de la minorité se trouve n'avoir pas plus de valeur, l'élection faite, que si la minorité n'existait pas.

Cela est-il équitable? cela est-il conforme à l'intérêt, bien entendu, de la société et au principe de l'égalité démocratique ? Il y a là manifestement un mal qui appelle un remède. La conviction que ce mal est considérable, que ce remède est nécessaire, me fait un devoir de vous exposer le système au moyen duquel M. Hare a cherché à atteindre ce but important, et éminemment démocratique : LA REPRÉSENTATION PROPORTIONNELLE DES MINORITÉS.

An explanation of the method then follows.

Le mécanisme en est beaucoup moins compliqué qu'on ne serait tenté de le croire, au premier abord. En réalité, l'opération sur laquelle il repose n'a rien de plus difficile que le triage des lettres à la grande poste.

Quant à sa portée politique et philosophique, elle doit vous frapper.

Là où il n'y a pas égalité de représentation, on peut poser hardiment en fait qu'il n'y a pas de démocratie. L'essence de la démocratie, c'est l'égalité ; et partout où les minorités risquent d'être étouffées, que dis-je ?

partout où elles n'ont pas leur influence proportionnelle sur la direction des
affaires publiques, le gouvernement n'est au fond qu'un gouvernement de
privilége, au profit du plus grand nombre. Contre ce mal, le système de
M. Hare fournit un remède.

On répondra peut-être que, dans le mode d'organisation adopté jusqu'à
ce jour, la minorité ne reste jamais sans représentants, parce qu'il arrive que
le parti en minorité dans un collége est en majorité dans un autre, ce qui
tend à rétablir la balance.

Mais une pareille compensation, outre qu'elle n'a rien de certain et rien
d'exact, est évidemment contraire à tous les principes du régime représentatif. L'étouffement de la minorité ici ne cessera pas d'être regrettable
parce qu'il y aura eu étouffement de la minorité ailleurs en sens inverse.
Un mal donné pour correctif à un autre mal ne saurait tenir lieu de remède.
Ce qui importe, c'est que la voix de chaque électeur compte à l'homme de
son choix, du moins autant que possible. Quoi ! je nomme Pierre à Paris, et
je dois me tenir pour bien et dûment représenté si Paul est nommé à Bor-
deaux ! Passe encore, si le pays n'était divisé qu'entre deux grands partis
se disputant le pouvoir, et en présence dans chaque collége ! Mais en
dehors de ces deux partis, je puis appartenir à une opinion dont il me
plairait fort de préparer l'avenir ; je puis faire partie d'une minorité éparse
dans le pays, et qui, bien que trop faible pour l'emporter dans un collége
quelconque, serait cependant assez forte pour former une section du corps
électoral, si les membres qui la composent votaient ensemble ; je puis enfin
vouloir pour mandataire, d'accord en ceci avec beaucoup d'électeurs
répandus çà et là, un homme sans influence locale, sans relation avec les
partis en vue, sans engagement avec les opinions du jour, mais d'un caractère
élevé et d'un esprit aussi supérieur qu'indépendant. Dans ce cas, je le
demande, à quoi me servira ma qualité d'électeur ? Il faudra, ou que je
donne ma voix à un homme qui ne représente mon opinion que très impar-
faitement, et alors mon vote est à moitié perdu, ou que je m'abstienne, et
alors, il est perdu tout à fait.

Il est vrai que le système de M. Hare est loin d'assurer aux minorités
une garantie complète, en ce sens qu'il laisse sans organe parlementaire
toute minorité qui n'atteint pas le nombre minimum de votants requis pour
l'élection d'un député. Ainsi en supposant que la Chambre se compose de
650 membres, et qu'il y ait 6,500,000 électeurs, ce système n'empêcherait
pas toute minorité au dessous du chiffre de 10,000 d'être sans organe dans
la législature. Mais c'est là un malheur inhérent à la nature des choses.
Le nombre des sections électorales est fatalement déterminé par le nombre
des députés à élire. Et, d'autre part, il est assez naturel qu'une opinion ne
pèse dans la balance des destinées publiques, que lorsqu'elle se trouve
avoir acquis un suffisant degré d'importance numérique.

Au reste, je n'entends pas dire que le système de M. Hare soit parfait ;
mais ce qui est sûr, c'est qu'il offre des avantages nombreux, et de l'ordre le
plus élevé.

Il assurerait la représentation, proportionnellement au nombre de chaque section du corps électoral. Toute minorité serait représentée, pourvu qu'elle se composât d'autant de citoyens qu'il en faudrait pour faire un député, eu égard au nombre des membres à élire.

Chaque minorité locale pouvant s'unir par ses votes à d'autres minorités locales éparses dans tout le royaume, et atteindre de la sorte le chiffre voulu pour l'élection d'un représentant, nulle opinion de quelque importance numérique ne risquerait d'être réduite au silence, ou désarmée.

Les électeurs n'étant plus forcés, ou de voter pour un candidat de la localité, alors même qu'ils ne voudraient pas de lui, ou de s'abstenir, et pouvant donner leur voix aux hommes d'une réputation nationale dont ils partagent les principes, une place parmi les représentants du peuple serait réservée aux grands esprits, aux citoyens vraiment illustres, aux caractères indépendants : il ne serait plus indispensable, pour être élu, de se faire l'instrument d'une coterie influente ou l'esclave d'un parti.

Chaque vote aurait toute la valeur qu'il doit et peut avoir.

Chaque membre de la Chambre représenterait un corps électoral, disséminé peut-être, mais unanime.

Par cela même, le représentant et le représenté seraient identifiés l'un à l'autre.

Ce qui serait représenté à la Chambre, ce serait, non plus des pierres, mais des hommes.

Et toutefois, le principe de la représentation locale serait respecté dans une juste mesure, puisque dans tout collège où la majorité des votants égalerait ou dépasserait le chiffre requis pour l'élection d'un député, il ne tiendrait qu'à elle d'avoir un représentant local.

Dans chaque collège électoral, la majorité serait nécessairement amenée à fixer son choix sur le plus digne, parce que son candidat préféré aurait à soutenir la concurrence, non plus seulement du candidat de la minorité, mais de tous les hommes distingués sur toute la surface du pays.

Dans la Chambre, les représentants de la majorité ayant devant eux les organes les plus distingués de chaque ordre d'idées, seraient contraints, pour les combattre, d'étudier les questions sérieusement et de penser, ce qui élèverait le niveau de l'intelligence générale.

Enfin, la majorité prévaudrait, la démocratie règnerait; mais en même temps une issue serait ouverte à chaque opinion dissidente, et un point d'appui ménagé au droit des minorités : droit non moins respectable dans sa sphère que celui des majorités dans la sienne, droit sacré, lui aussi, et qu'un membre fameux de la Convention revendiquait en ces termes, le 28 décembre 1792, aux applaudissements du peuple qui remplissait les tribunes : " Sidney, mort pour le peuple, était de la minorité. Socrate était de la minorité quand il avala la ciguë, et Caton quand il se déchira les entrailles."

See, also, note to p. 161, 3rd ed. of *Mill's Considerations on Representative Government*, on the opinions by other continental writers.

Appendix K.

Discussions in Holland and Belgium.

The question at the head of the Amsterdam programme of the International Congress for the Promotion of Social Science, in 1864, was, "*Quels sont les moyens les plus pratiques, dans un gouvernement représentatif, pour assurer la liberté des élections et la sincérité des votes.*"

This method was brought before the Congress by M. Rolin-Jacquemyns, who thus states the result:—

"Pour parler franchement, il lui parut que la première impression produite par son exposé, sur les esprits non prévenus, était un étonnement mêlé de défiance, et une assez vive tentation de rejeter d'emblée tout le système, comme entaché d'une nouveauté excessive. Bientôt cependant on discuta. Peu à peu la discussion, de dédaigneuse qu'elle était, devint sérieuse et approfondie. Des défenseurs chaleureux et convaincus se présentèrent. Bref, on finit par trouver que la chose valait au moins la peine d'être examinée, et l'on nomma une commission chargée de faire un rapport, en général, sur les solutions proposées ou à proposer en réponse à la première question du programme, et en particulier sur le mérite du système Hare."

M. Rolin-Jacquemyns has since published a work (*De la Réforme électorale*, Muquardt, Bruxelles, 1865), the third chapter of which contains an able synopsis of this system, and a summary of its advantages (pp. 115-119). The following are extracts from the latter :—

"1. Diminution des tentations de fraude et de corruption chez les candidats. 2. Une fois l'élection soustraite aux vicissitudes d'une popularité de clocher, on ne verrait plus, comme de nos jours, les hommes qui représentent le plus fidèlement, dignement une grande opinion, exclus du parlement par une petite majorité locale. 3. Les déclarations de principe, habilement équivoques, où l'on exagère la partie de ses opinions qui est de nature à plaire au grand nombre, où l'on dissimule le reste, ces promesses que l'on sait impossibles, ces imputations que l'on sait téméraires à l'égard du candidat opposé,—toute cette mise en scène deviendrait inutile si, au lieu de s'adresser à un public restreint, on s'adressait aux partisans inconnus qu'une opinion, franchement avouée, éloquemment défendue, ne peut manquer de concilier dans le pays entier. 4. Le choix des électeurs ne serait plus restreint entre deux nuances de candidats, qui souvent leur sont personnellement inconnus, ou qui leur déplaisent également. Mais ils seraient appelés à se prononcer avec discernement, entre tous les candidats possibles, à les classer dans un certain ordre de préférence, et ils seraient presque assurés que chacune de leurs désignations aurait une valeur réelle. 5. En même temps que le sentiment de la responsabilité et de la dignité individuelle augmenterait chez l'électeur, il serait entraîné à faire un usage de plus en plus grand du principe de l'association en matière politique. L'influence de l'individu cesserait de s'arrêter aux limites, parfaitement arbitraires, d'une circonscription électorale. Du moment qu'une idée, un principe ou un intérêt sérieux voudraient trouver place au parlement, il leur suffirait de recruter des adhérents indistinctement parmi toute la masse du corps électoral. Prenons pour exemple la question du libre-échange. Combien de temps n'a-t-elle pas tardé à se faire jour ! Partout, dans les arrondissements les plus riches, les plus populeux, elle rencontrait une coalition aveugle de toutes les industries. Partout les instincts conservateurs conspiraient pour étouffer à leur naissance des minorités encore imperceptibles. Il a fallu des années de persévérante énergie pour amener la thèse du libre-échange à être soutenue à la tribune. Avec le système de M. Hare, cette thèse eût probablement trouvé, dès le début, un défenseur officiel et convaincu. Il eu est et il en sera de même de toutes les vérités nouvelles, économiques ou autres."

Referring to the work of M. Morin (p. 16, n., and Appendix A, p. 295) M. Rolin Jaequemyns says :—" Il est permis de croire que son idée, si elle avait pu être suivie, aurait épargné à sa patrie la sanglante échauffourée de septembre. Car le système a précisément pour but d'éviter la situation qui, à Genève, a produit les troubles, savoir : le défaut d'homogénéité entre le groupe des représentants et le groupe des représentés."—(P. 9.)

In his first chapter M. Rolin-Jaequemyns discusses the " Projet de loi sur les fraudes en matière électorale, présenté le 15 novembre 1864, par le Gouvernement Belge aux Chambres Législatives," and amongst other things combats the suggestion which had found some advocates at the Amsterdam Congress, that it should be made compulsory on every elector to vote. Such a proposal had also been maintained by M. Eugène Delattre, an advocate of Paris, in his *Devoirs du Suffrage Universel ;* and by M. Albert Gloss, as an amendment of the Constitution of the United States (*Das Leben in den Vereinigten Staaten.* Leipsig, 1864), which he compares with the Athenian law (p. 30, and see *ante,* pp. 251-2). The second chapter examines the question of the suffrage in a manner in which it has been rarely treated (pp. 50-73), and a section treats of the political education of the electors :— " Des efforts permanents à exercer sur l'électeur pour le mettre à même de comprendre sa mission " (p. 87). The same chapter discusses the provisions necessary for secret voting, which the author seems to think desirable (pp. 77-82).

I have stated elsewhere (pp. 139-147) some of the grounds on which I deprecate the introduction of the ballot. There would be nothing absolutely irreconcilable with the ballot in this method of election, and with little alteration of the proposed rules, secret votes might be admitted ; but I confess I have no disposition to undertake the adaptation. The aim is to elevate the moral and intellectual character of the voter, and I think that it is personally degrading to him to be obliged to shrink from the performance of this great act of national sovereignty except under a cover, and in darkness. *The workman is of infinitely more value than the work ;* and if it cannot be

done except under such conditions, it is better that he should not be required
to do it. I have, however, shown that the act of voting can be performed
under conditions which will give it a moral value of so high and sacred a
character that the general opinion of society will as surely protect a voter in
its independent exercise, as it would at this moment guard the sanctity and
virtue of his home from violation by any one, however powerful; even
meteing its indignation by the height of the rank or of the greatness of the
power which is so attempted to be abused. Instead of contriving how we
can best conceal weakness and palliate infirmity, let us rather turn to the
remedy which promises strength.

One part of the new Belgian *Projet de Loi* is curious. It enacts that the
voter on his way to the bureau is to pass through a passage of six mètres
(about 6½ yards) in length, closed in by a door at each end, and two
mètres (about 2½ yards) in height: that no voter is to approach the table
where the bureau is situated, before his name is called, and that he shall
retire directly he has placed his bulletin in the box.

On this provision, M. Rolin-Jaequemyns remarks,—(p. 82) "Qui croirait
que la mesure proposée en Belgique, en l'an de grâce 1865, pour protéger
les abords du scrutin, était connue et appliquée sous l'ancienne république
romaine? Les savants les plus autorisés (Becker, Rœm. Alt. t. ii. pp. 3, 102;
—Rein das Criminalrecht der Römer, pp. 709 et ss.) nous apprennent, textes
en mains, qu'aux abords de chaque centurie, c'est-à-dire, de chaque section
électorale, on avait eu l'idée, précisément pour sauvegarder la liberté du
votant, de construire un pont (pons) ou avenue spéciale, cloisonnée de part
et d'autre, c'est-à-dire un véritable couloir. Ces avenues s'étant trouvées
trop larges, de façon que plusieurs électeurs s'y pressaient à la fois, Marius
les fit rétrécir. Mais il paraît que cette mesure ne fut pas encore suffisante
pour empêcher la violence et la corruption. Car Plutarque nous apprend
que les adversaires de Caton d'Utique, voulant empêcher son élection
comme préteur, se mirent les uns à distribuer de l'argent, les autres à
entraver la remise des votes. Du reste, toute la législation sur les délits et
crimes électoraux chez les Romains est des plus curieuses et, il faut bien
l'ajouter, des plus tristes. Nous y voyons la décadence des mœurs renchérir
sans cesse sur la sévérité impuissante du législateur, depuis les beaux jours
de la République, où l'on se bornait à défendre aux candidats, comme un
acte contraire à leur dignité, d'aller quêter des suffrages sur les marchés et
dans les réunions, jusqu'à l'époque où César établissait, en plein Champ de
Mars, des comptoirs où l'on payait les votants et où Pompée, *suarum legum
auctor idem ac subversor* (Tac. *Ann.* t. iii. p. 28), profitait de sa toute-puis-
sance pour faire contre ses adversaires des lois qu'il violait lui-même."

The great lesson surely is, that no penal laws,—no protective machinery,
—no negative contrivances, which may threaten or surround the voter, are
sufficient to inspire or to maintain such a patriotic feeling, or ruling sentiment of regard for the public good, as shall be sufficient to overcome the
sinister efforts of influential individuals or classes to convert the powers of

government into means of personal aggrandisement or profit. It can only be accomplished by the operation of a new, a positive, and an active principle of a higher nature implanted in the mind of the individual voter himself. Instead of giving mechanical aid, to secure the uncontrolled performance of an act which is reduced to one of small importance to himself, let the act be made as interesting and important as it can be, and give the voter a scope and freedom which shall awaken the emotions and call into exercise all the efforts of his moral and intellectual being. I can conceive nothing with so great a tendency to produce this result, as to place in competition before the voter, not merely one or two mediocrities, but every quality and talent existing among his contemporaries calculated to win his respect or excite his admiration.

Appendix L.

United States of America.

The earliest notice of this system in America appeared in the *Philadelphia Inquirer* in 1860, in which the plan is thus introduced :—

" Its leading feature is, that a *unanimous* constituency is necessary to the election of a representative. Nor is this unattainable, as at first sight it appears to be. It is rendered feasible by simply taking away the restraint which at present limits a voter to a choice between the two local candidates.

" Let us suppose, for the sake of illustration, that there is to be held an election of Congressmen for this State. There are twenty-five members to be elected, and half a million of votes will be cast ; the quotient, twenty thousand, shows the number of votes necessary to elect a member. If every voter is at liberty to select according to his preference from all the candidates in the State, there can be no doubt that the prominent candidates of either party will secure the requisite twenty thousand votes. In all probability they will receive more than that number : and this surplus would be thrown away, were it not for the provision that each vote should be a list of the members desired by the voter, and in the order of his preference for them. Thus, if the first member on his list already has the requisite number, that name should be stricken from the list, and the vote will then count for the second in order, who is the next choice of the voter, and so on. The admirable simplicity which characterizes this plan is likely to make us ignore the wonderful results that would flow from its adoption. Let us consider what would be gained by its introduction.

" First, it starts out with the fundamental idea, now almost lost sight of in the abuse of the system, that the representative body should reflect exactly tho feelings and opinions of the community which it *represents*. Under this plan every opinion is represented, and that, too, just in proportion to the generality with which it is entertained. Tho only limitation is, that those holding a given opinion should be sufficiently numerous to entitle them to at least one representative. That is, in the case of a Congressional election, twenty thousand in the whole State should be agreed in that opinion. The majority thus has all the influence which it is strictly entitled to have, but it cannot exercise the undisputed sway which has hitherto given it the character of a tyrant. Every measure which it proposed would be contested inch by inch, and though it would be ultimately carried, it would only be after it was shorn of all its most obnoxious features, in consequence of the thorough exposure which it had received.

"Thoughtful men have at all times endeavoured to secure a due share of influence to the minority. John C. Calhoun devoted himself to this subject, and has left a treatise upon it, to explain the mode in which such a scheme could be realized. But the plan which he proposed is wholly impracticable, and is now looked upon only as a monument of his patience and ingenuity. Every one feels the hardship of a minority, whose voice is not heard, and whose wishes go for nothing. We have submitted to the inconvenience because we have not heretofore seen any practical plan suggested for avoiding it. Our ready philosophy has taught us that it would be better to be poorly represented than not to be represented at all. Fully aware of the injustice of our condition we have endeavoured to make the best of it, hoping, with labour and time, to become, in our turn, the majority.

"The grand recommendation of this plan is, however, the tendency it would have to bring forward distinguished men as candidates. An individual of any note soon becomes known throughout the State, and he will be voted for in preference to the unheard-of nominee of some petty local convention. The same reason which induces the bringing forward of men of reputation also operates to keep them in the position which they have shown themselves qualified to occupy. At present the reverse is true. The moment a man becomes prominent by displaying his ability or integrity, he makes himself obnoxious to those who rather desire tools to carry out their sinister designs, than men of character who will obstruct them. Hence, an intrigue is set on foot to defeat such a man, and always with success. Those in the community who would sanction his conduct, in case an opportunity was given them to express their opinion, have no influence whatever. It is all settled in the primary meetings, where delegates to the convention are chosen, hostile to him. We all know how these matters are managed. Some greedy aspirant scours up his confederates to aid him to elect, in the ward meetings, his favourites to the convention. They are successful, because respectable citizens will not degrade themselves by frequenting such dens. When in convention, they nominate a candidate who professes the political principles of a party, and its members must either vote for him or throw their vote away. In such an alternative they give him their vote rather than his opponent, who is probably no better, and professes the opposite principles."—*Philadelphia Inquirer*, 22nd Oct., 1860.

Since the termination of the civil war in the States, the subject has rapidly become more and more prominent throughout the Union. See the Report of the Constitutional Convention of the State of New York on Personal Representation, 1867. Suggestions on the Revision of the Constitution of New York, by David Dudley Field, 1867. It was not long before the agitation assumed a practical form.

In January, 1869, a Bill was introduced in the Senate for the amendment of the representation of the people in Congress, and was referred to a Committee, which, in April, 1869, presented their report, setting out at length the reasons on which they unanimously and strenuously adopted what is called the cumulative vote. The report dismisses the minority clause adopted in England, calling it "a rude contrivance which cannot have extensive application." Speaking of the preferential method the language of the report is remarkable. It says that it "may be put aside from the present discussion, because it is comparatively intricate in plan and cumbrous in detail, *because it assails party organization*, and because some of its most important effects cannot be distinctly foreseen. It is so radical in character, so revolutionary in its probable effects, that prudence will dictate that it should be very deliberately considered, and be subjected to local experiment and trial, before it shall be proposed for adoption upon a grand scale by the Government of the United States." The Committee proposed the following law, for the amendment of the electoral constitution :—" That in elections for the choice of representatives to the Congress of the United States, whenever more than one representative is to be chosen from a State, each elector of such State shall be entitled to a number of votes equal to the number of representatives to be chosen from the State, and may give all such votes to one candidate, or may distribute them equally or unequally among a greater number of candidates, and the candidates highest in vote upon the return shall be declared elected." This step in electoral improvement, though not yet extended to the entire Union, has, however, been adopted by the State of Illinois. The new constitution of that State divides it into 51 electoral districts, every one having one senator and three representatives. In electing three representatives, every elector may cumulate his three votes on one or more of the candidates. The New York journal, *The Nation* (14th July, 1870), describes this as "the first serious attempt made by a democracy to amend its legislative machinery, and perhaps for that reason, and in consideration of the magnitude of the evils it is intended to correct, the most important political reform effected since Parliament first met." The legislature of the State of Pennsylvania has, by recent Acts, authorized the application of cumulative voting to the municipal elections of Councillors in the towns of Bloomsburg and Berwick. The *Chicago Times*, of the 21st April, 1870, after giving an account of the election of the Town Councillors of Bloomsburg, in Pennsylvania, contains

2 A

the following passage:—" Such was the eminently satisfactory result of the first election ever held in America according to the free vote. By that election the practicability of this great and beneficent reform is proven, its justice and fairness illustrated. It is the small beginning of the most valuable political reform that has ever been advocated on this continent. It is the beginning of an electoral reformation, that is as certain to be made general in all our elections, federal as well as State and municipal, as that ours will continue to be a popular form of government." The Alumni of Harvard College, Massachusetts, under a resolution of the 30th April, 1870, adopted proportional voting, in its most perfect contingent and preferential form, for the nomination of ten candidates for their Board of Overseers. The importance and value of this experiment, as well as of the preparation for it in the Technological Institute at Boston, is shown in Appendix M on the " Preferential Vote."

Mr. Simon Sterne, of New York, published in 1871 his work *On Representative Government and Personal Representation* (Hippencot and Co., Philadelphia). The subsequent labours of Mr. Sterne, and his coadjutors in the committee of seventy, in their endeavours to form a new charter for the city of New York, would alone form a valuable contribution to the history of the present movement. Those labours are rendered unavailing for the present, owing to the proposed Act having, after passing the State Legislature, been vetoed by Governor Hoffman. The reasons he has assigned for thus rejecting a measure for applying the cumulative system to the election of the aldermen of New York city, are, so far as they are practical and intelligible, entirely based on the special defects of that system, as hitherto framed (see Appendix N), and do not apply to a method under which every one would be independent of party managers. They are set out in p. 159 of a valuable work just published, *Minority or Proportional Representation, its nature, aims, history, processes, and practical operation,* by Salem Dutcher, New York, U.S., Pub. Co., 411, Broome-st., 1872. It is a condensed repertory of the public manifestations on the subject in the United States. The author may be permitted here to repeat that he has always looked forward to the reception of this electoral system by the American people with an anxious hope. It may be a less grateful task to struggle against effete traditions and implacable prejudices in Europe, but an appeal to the patriotism of a people who shrink from no sacrifice in pursuit of their ideal of national greatness, can hardly be in vain. It is to the American Republic that the eyes of the Old World will turn for a spectacle of what self-government can accomplish. Its unexampled progress is the marvel of these modern ages. The rich imagination of Burke, warmed with the theme, recalled to the view of his hearers the " little speck scarcely visible,—a seminal principle rather than a formed body," which had grown within the life of one man, into populous and wealthy provinces. If that statesman could have been gifted with a forward prescience, even his eloquence might well have failed to picture in appropriate language the mighty federation of the century then to come. Surpassing all other people in the arts of Peace, as they minister to the universal comfort and well-being,—attaining a not less distinguished though unhappy eminence in the art of War,—a nobler work remains to them,—that, rising like a strong man in his strength, they shake off the parasites that prey on the credulity and folly, and pander to the vices, of the public,—and become the leaders of mankind in the far greater art of government. It is said to nations as to men, "Better is he that ruleth his spirit than he that taketh a city."

APPENDIX M.

THE PREFERENTIAL VOTE.

The Board of Overseers of Harvard College, Massachusetts, was first established by an Act of the General Court in 1642; its constitution underwent variations in 1780, 1810, 1814, 1861, and 1865; in 1869 it was resolved to nominate the overseers by this method. The first nomination was, at the instance of Mr. W. R. Ware, the secretary of the Standing Committee of Electors, preceded by a literary exercise in the Technological Institute of Boston, calculated to prepare the way for the application of this system. The manner in which this experiment was carried out shows how greatly the fulfilment of the political duties of the people may be facilitated, during their school instruction, and how desirable it is that the state should realize the importance of introducing into the educational course of its youth, exercises and studies that will assist them in after life in this essential part of the work of a self-governing community. The following extracts from the letter of Mr. Ware (1st March, 1871) explain the exercise and its results:—

"In order to avoid, so far as might be, the awkwardness and errors that were likely to attend a first performance of their duties, and to gain an experience that would furnish rules of procedure to guide them in counting the ballots, the committee subjected the scheme to the test of a preliminary experiment. My own connection with the Institute of Technology afforded the desired opportunity for conducting a mock election, on a scale sufficiently large for the purpose in hand. A

Preference.	Please add to this list of authors any other names you may prefer, and then indicate your preference among them all by writing the figure 1 against your first choice, 2 against your second choice, and so on.	
.	1.	BACON.
.	2.	SHAKESPEARE.
.	3.	SCOTT.
.	4.	BYRON.
.	5.	BURNS.
.	6.	MACAULAY.
.	7.	TENNYSON.
.	8.	THACKERAY.
.	9.	
.	10.	
.	11.	

ballot was accordingly prepared in the annexed form, and the students in the School of the Institute, nearly two hundred in number, were invited to express their preferences among certain English authors who were nominated as candidates (of whom four were to be selected according to the principles of Mr. Hare's scheme).

In the casting of the votes three things were noticeable. In the first place, although no instructions or explanations whatever were given to the young men beyond those printed at the head of the ballot itself, very few votes had to be rejected on the score of informality. Out of 150 votes, 144 were correctly made out. In the second place, what errors were committed were all of one kind, consisting in the indication of two or three names as the voters' first choice, two or three as second choice, and so on. In the third place, a large number availed themselves of the permission to add to their list names not regularly in nomination, the followers of Mr. Dickens especially rallying handsomely to his support.

The experiment perfectly answered its purpose. The following table exhibits the application of these principles to the case in hand. It is a copy of the Tally, or Register of the Votes cast at the Institute of Technology.

TALLY. 144 Votes. Four to be Elected. Quota, 36.	First Count.	Shakespeare elected. Shakespeare's surplus redistributed.	Second Count. No election.	Twenty-six scattering votes redistributed.	Third Count. Scott elected.	Milton's votes redistributed.	Fourth Count. No election.	Bacon's and Thackeray's votes redistributed.	Fifth Count. No election.	Byron's votes redistributed.	Sixth Count. No election.	Macaulay's votes redistributed.	Seventh Count. No election.	Dickens' votes redistributed.	Eighth Count. Tennyson elected.	Tennyson's surplus redistributed.	Ninth Count. Burns elected.
	I.		II.		III.		IV.		V.		VI.		VII.		VIII.		IX.
Bacon	4	..	4	..	4	..	4	[4]	..	..	..	..	.	..	..	..	..
Shakespeare	48	[12]	=	=	=	=	=	=	=	=	=	=	=	=	=	=	36
Scott	22	5	27	9	36	=	=	=	=	=	=	=	=	=	=	=	36
Byron	6	2	8	2	10	..	10	..	10	[10]	..	..	..	..	..	..	..
Burns	9	2	11	5	16	..	16	..	16	4	20	2	22	8	30	2	32
Macaulay	6	..	6	3	9	..	9	2	11	1	12	[12]	..	..	..	..	..
Tennyson	8	..	8	4	12	..	12	5	17	4	21	7	28	10	38	[2]	36
Thackeray	4	..	4	..	4	..	4	[4]	..	..	..	..	..	..	..	..	..
Dickens	11	2	13	..	13	1	14	..	15	1	16	2	18	[18]	..	..	..
Milton	..	1	1	1	2	[2]	..	..	..	..	..	..	..	..	..	..	..
Scattering	26	..	26	[26]	..	..	..	..	..	..	..	..	..	..	..	..	..
Lost	..	..	..	2	2	1	3	..	3	..	3	1	4	..	4	..	4
	144	12	144	26	144	2	144	8	144	10	144	12	144	18	144	2	144

It will be observed that the alternate columns, showing the successive counts, all add up 144, as they should do, counting the double lines as representing 36. The sum of the figures in the intermediate columns is equal, as it should be, to the number of the votes redistributed. Facility for checking and verifying the accuracy of the work is thus afforded at every stage of the election.

The ballots marked *Lost* are those which proved on redistribution, not to contain the names of any of the remaining candidates. The *scattering* are those who stood first on one ballot only.

In counting off the quota in order to redistribute the votes of the elected candidates, the committee counted the votes in the order they were received. This is a natural and convenient rule, though arbitrary in its nature. Its effect upon the result is, however, very slight, the destination of only 14 votes being affected by it. Even this number might, of course, if selected under a different rule, materially change the result of the election, and it is true that the necessity of adopting an arbitrary rule in counting off the quotas, introduces an arbitrary and fortuitous element into the scheme. But it is to be observed that although counting off the votes in a different order might elect one candidate rather than another, it would not be the candidate of a different party, but another candidate of the same party. The element of chance, in fact, though seriously affecting the fortunes of the candidates, has no terrors for the electors, who are sure in any case to secure an acceptable representative, and it is to be remembered that it is in the interests of the electors, not of the candidates, that elections are carried on.

The objection has been brought against this method of voting, as well as against the Limited and the Cumulative vote, that it makes no provision for the filling of vacancies. A vacancy should, under any scheme, be filled by the action of the special constituency whose candidate retires. But where this constituency is scattered through the whole body of electors a special appeal to them is of course impracticable. The experience of the committee, however, enables us to show that if the original ballots are preserved, a vacancy can be filled without holding a new election. By taking the ballots assigned to the retiring candidate as his quota, and putting with them those set down as *lost*, representing the whole number of electors who are now without a personal representative, a new count can be taken, which will result in the election of a candidate acceptable to as large a proportion of the electors as could probably be brought to unite upon any one."

[Here follows a table showing the redistribution of Shakespeare's ballots (supposing him to be the retiring candidate) together with the *lost* ballots, resulting in the selection of Macaulay.]

"Considering that the favourite candidates are already elected, and that Macaulay narrowly missed election before, this may be regarded as a felicitous result. The same experiment being tried with the ballots for overseers, resulted also in the election of the most conspicuous of the defeated candidates. This last experiment shows, moreover, that, contrary to the generally received opinion, the system of preferential voting is applicable to the choice of a single candidate. In such case it enables the party of the minority to select between two candidates of the majority, preventing a mere majority of the majority from dictating the result.

The advantages claimed for this method of voting may, accordingly, now be counted up as follows:—

1. It protects the minority from the tyranny of the majority.

2. It protects the minorities and majorities alike from the tyranny of party chiefs.

3. It permits the utmost freedom of individual action.

4. It secures the most perfect co-operation and organization.

5. It gives every elector a representative after his own heart, whom he has actually helped to elect.

6. It gives every representative a constituency who are unanimous in his support.

7. It gives the representative a certain security in the tenure of his place.

8. It affords a natural and reasonable method of rotation in office.

9. It makes it for the interest of every party to put forward its best men.

10. It makes it worth while for good men to become candidates.

11. It is equally efficient whether one candidate is to be chosen, or a dozen.

12. It is available in the filling of vacancies as well as in general elections.

13. It is easy for the elector to cast his vote intelligently.

14. It is not difficult to count the votes with precision and promptness.

15. Hardly a ballot is ultimately thrown away.

16. Every ballot is assigned just as the voter who casts it desires.

It is not easy to say how practicable this scheme would prove in public affairs. But it would probably work perfectly well in the election of members of Congress, for instance, though for convenience the larger States would probably have to be divided in two. The ballots would of course all have to be counted at a central bureau. But the first sorting and counting could be done where they were cast. The labour at the central office would be great, but not greater than is performed any day in counting or sorting letters in a large post-office. But these considerations belong rather to the general discussion of the question, than to the special experiment you have asked me to relate.

It is sufficient to say, in conclusion, that although the amicable character of the contest prevented the Cambridge experiment from testing the scheme in all these particulars, it was satisfactory as far as it went. An excellent list of names was presented, representing every class among the Alumni, one or two of them, at least, giving expression to the wishes of considerable numbers of persons who on another system of voting would have been simply outvoted and silenced. The scheme seemed also to have been successful in effecting a perfect freedom of action on the part of the electors. They evidently voted with a view to express their real wishes, without any *arrière pensée* as to what other people were likely to do. To those whose duty it was to inspect the ballots the frankness and sincerity with which the electors had voted was most striking. Each ballot, differing from every other, was the exact expression of the personality of the elector who had cast it. The counting of the votes proved unexpectedly easy, taking only two or three hours, not nearly so much time as it had taken the committee the previous year to count the same number of votes under the old system, that of the Limited Vote, in which each elector sent in five names.

I am, etc.,

WILLIAM R. WARE."

Report on the Nomination of Overseers of Harvard College.

In compliance with a resolution adopted by the Alumni Association last Commencement Day, requesting the Standing Committee of the Electors to prepare and distribute among the Alumni a detailed statement of the methods and results of the systems of nominations for the Board of Overseers which have now for two years been in use, together with a copy of their tally, or register of votes, the committee beg to present the following report:—[After stating historically the constitution of the Board, it proceeds]:—In 1869 the present committee were appointed, a chief part of the first committee having resigned on becoming members of the Board of Overseers. At the same time a resolution was adopted "that the Standing Committee be requested to investigate the system of voting devised by Mr. Thomas Hare; and, if in their opinion it offers substantial advantages, to adopt it in the nomination of Overseers." This the committee, being of opinion that it offered advantages the practical value of which could be determined only by experiment, thought fit to do. The system in question was adopted in 1870, and, by a renewal of the resolution, in 1871. Last year the resolution directing a third trial of the scheme the present year was accompanied by the resolution cited above, asking for this Report.

It was claimed for this method of nominations that it would retain all the advantages of that in use the two previous years, with others of its own. It would retain the nomination of a double list of candidates, which had worked admirably well, and had rendered the election on Commencement Day a *bonâ fide* exercise of the elector's will, not a mere indorsement of a foregone conclusion. It would also retain the system of nominations through the post-office, which had served to put the Alumni at a distance from Boston into active relations with the College. At the same time it proposed to give the elector more independence of action and a greater range of choice in the nominations, and to ensure a list, or double list, more truly representing the variety of opinions and interests to be found among the electors. This last point seemed of special importance, since, if an official nomination list is to be prepared at all, it should plainly be a representative one, so variously composed as to afford to every elector at least one candidate whom he can heartily support. It is the distinctive peculiarity of Mr. Hare's method of voting that it claims to secure for every interest or party a representation exactly proportioned to its numerical strength.*

The results both last year and in 1870 were such as, on the whole, to justify these pretensions. The system, in working, fairly fulfilled its promise, and met the expectations of its friends. The first year there were about three hundred and sixty ballots received, and each name finally reported by the committee was the unanimous choice of one-tenth of that constituency, each candidate being nominated by about thirty-six votes. Among these names were several which were generally recognized as representing opinions and interests that under another system of nomination might not have obtained recognition.

---

¹ In order to effect proportional representation, Mr. Hare's scheme proposes first to establish a quota, or number of voters entitled to a representative, and then to divide up the constituency into a number of such quotas, each unanimously, in favour of a particular candidate. The number of such quotas must of course equal the number of persons to be elected, and the size of each, or number requisite for a choice, is obviously to be ascertained by dividing the number of voters by that of the places to be filled.

To effect this division of the constituency into as many equal parts as there are men to be chosen, without any external constraint, so that every voter shall find himself in the group he best likes to be in, is the object of Mr. Hare's system of voting. It is accomplished by a process of balloting exactly imitating what would happen if all the electors and all the candidates were collected in a room together. The quota being ascertained, the electors would "rally" around the candidates of their first choice. Some candidates would have a large following, some a small one. The most popular would be elected at once, having a full quota, and more. The surplus—the latest comers—would then seek each the candidate of his second choice, and this might probably suffice to elect some of those to whom allegiance was thus transferred. The rest of the candidates would have their own supporters, many or few, but all less than enough. If now the candidates having the fewest votes, say those with only a single follower, should withdraw, and then the candidates with two votes, and so on, their followers would naturally transfer their support to more pro-

The counting of the votes, which the committee had feared might be vexatious and laborious, proved unexpectedly easy; not more time being consumed than in counting the same number of ballots under the other system the previous year. The success of the scheme in favouring the independence of the electors was also conspicuous. Each vote, differing from every other, seemed exactly to reflect the mind of the elector who cast it.

The same experience was repeated the next year. The results of this second trial, and the methods by which they were reached, are, in accordance with the request of the Alumni Association, given in detail below.

This is given in a tabular form, as before (p. 352). The following is an abstract :—

There were 30 candidates who polled more than one vote each, and 20 others who had only one vote apiece. The ballots cast were altogether 355, which, divided by 12 (the number to be nominated), gave a quotient of 29, being the quota which was therefore sufficient. There were eleven successive counts.

I. On the first count, three (*Russel, Hilliard*, and *Salisbury*) were nominated, and their surplus votes, beyond the quota of 29, were distributed.

II. On the second count, none of the candidates had a quota, and the votes of the 20 candidates who had single votes were then distributed.

-----

minent men, who would thus gradually collect enough supporters to elect them. Their quotas would fill up. In this way there would presently remain in the field only just enough candidates to fill the places, all of whom would have a full quota and be duly elected. The division of the constituency into equal groups, differing widely in opinion but each unanimous in support of its own man, would have been accomplished.

This system the committee endeavoured to embody in the following rules, according to which, as they advertised, the ballots for the nomination of overseers would be sorted and counted :—

I. Every candidate who receives one-twelfth of the whole number of ballots cast is entitled to a nomination.

II. Each elector may send in the names of any number of candidates, all on one ballot, and shall indicate his preference among them by writing the figure 1 against the name of his first choice, 2 against that of his second choice, and so on.

III. Each ballot will be counted for the first choice indicated upon it, alone ; the other names being considered as substitutes, to be resorted to, in the order of the preference indicated, only in case (I.) the person named as the first choice has enough votes to nominate him without it, or (II.) in case he has not enough votes to entitle him to a nomination.

IV. The ballots will be counted in the order in which they are received.

III. *Hill* attained the quota and was nominated. The votes of candidates who had polled no more than 3 were then distributed.

IV. V. counts. No election. Votes of candidates having no more than 9, distributed.

VI. *Dana* and *Shattuck* elected by quota. Their surplus together with the votes of candidates having 10, distributed.

VII. VIII. No quota. The votes of candidates having no more than 13, distributed.

IX. A quota for *Lowell*. Votes, where no more than 16, distributed.

X. A quota for *Lawrence*. The votes of all candidates having no more than 20 were then distributed.

XI. The eleventh and last count terminated in the nominating of the four overseers remaining to be chosen : *Bacon* (28), *Sanborn* (27), *Saltonstall* (26), and *Phillips* (22). All these were chosen by less than the quota, there remaining no more ballots to distribute : the 20 that were left not being given for any of the remaining candidates.

The report then, after discussing the probability of the system ever being sufficiently understood for public use, adverts to its operation by transmitting the ballot papers through the post-office. This part of the report is of much value and importance, having regard to the means, and the system could in this manner afford for securing the representation on the councils of learned bodies of the members who dwell in various parts of the kingdom, as, for example, councils of the medical, the legal, or the scholastic professions. After mentioning the plan by which the election strikes off all the names of candidates beyond a certain number as under the limited ballot, the report proceeds to observe that " it seems a little simpler, but it is likely to involve a great inequality of votes, the favourite candidates getting many more votes than they need, while the ninth and tenth, perhaps, have but a handful. This was the case in our own experience of this system in 1868 and 1869. Mr. Hare's preferential plan is more elaborate, but it makes sure that nobody shall be nominated without a certain following, and that as few votes as possible shall be thrown away.

"Variations of these methods might be suggested, but without gaining any substantial advantage. In indicating preferences among the candidates, for instance, instead of marking the order of choice, as in Mr. Hare's plan, the Cumulative method might be used, and the votes at the disposal of the elector be all heaped upon the man of his first choice, or be divided among several candidates, in equal or varying proportions, as he might see fit. This is, perhaps, not so hard to understand as the other, but it is certainly more vexatious to the voter. He would find it easier to say which man he preferred than to say how much he preferred him ; a qualitative analysis of such sentiments being simpler than a quantitative one.

" Under the rules of the Limited Ballot, also the electors might be limited to four votes in place of five, or to two, to three, or to one. Those who are fond of arithmetical puzzles may find in the investigation of these different cases some curious phenomena. The last case, that in which each elector casts but a single ballot, is the same as Mr. Hare's scheme, without the provision for the transfer of surplus votes. In the absence of such a provision, great inequality and injustice must, under any system, result. In Illinois, for example, where the Cumulative Vote is now on trial, an agitation for the introduction of some method of transferring votes from candidates who have too many to those of the same party who have too few, is already begun.

"The only other method likely to be mentioned in this connection is the Swiss scheme of the Free List, or the Registered Ballot. But this method, however admirably adapted to party politics, has no application to cases like our own, where organized parties are not in existence."

(Signed)

> WILLIAM M. PRICHARD,
> WILLIAM R. WARE,
> HORACE H. COOLIDGE,
> WILLIAM E. PERKINS,
> STEPHEN SALISBURY, JR.,
> *Standing Committee of the Electors.*

BOSTON, May 10, 1872.

APPENDIX N.

MEMORANDUM OF THE HISTORY, WORKING, AND RESULTS OF CUMULATIVE VOTING.

Some foreign governments, through their ministers in this country, having applied to the Secretary of State for Foreign Affairs for information as to the history, working, and results of Cumulative Voting, a memorandum was prepared under the above title, to supply the particulars thus sought. This paper, showing the relation which the Cumulative system bears to, and its results in comparison with, the other methods that have been proposed, is, with some omissions of detail, here given. It is treated under the following heads:—

1. Single majority representation.

2. Majority representation and the election of representatives for separate districts.

3. The original proposal of the Cumulative Vote.

4. Its numerical effect.

5. The restricted vote in what are called the three-cornered constituencies, and its numerical effect.

6. The discussion on both systems, and the adoption and maintenance of the restricted vote in the British Parliament in 1869 and 1870.

7. The legislative adoption of the Cumulative Vote.

8. The cause of the greater popularity and readier adoption of the Cumulative Vote than of any other improvement in the frame of the constituency.

9. Cause of popular dissatisfaction with it in practice.

10. Comparison of the numerical effect of the Cumulative Vote and the Single Vote.

11. Effect of the Cumulative Vote in Birmingham on the representation of the School Board of the more numerous party.

12. Effect in Marylebone, Finsbury, Lambeth, and Sheffield.

13. Complaints of the operation of the Cumulative Vote in the School Board election, viz.:—

(A.) Nullity or mischief of permitting minorities to be represented.

(B.) The power it confers on intense or earnest opinion or feeling on public matters, as opposed to "common sense," acquiescence, or comparative indifference, and its consequent susceptibility of active organization.

(C.) That it operates not to elicit, but to suppress public opinion.

(D.) That it creates an inducement for too great a number of candidates to offer themselves, whereby votes are wasted and lost.

14. The loss of votes, together with the necessity for, and the power acquired by, party organization in the present rude method of applying the Cumulative system.

And pointed out as amendments:—

15. (I.) Rendering individual voters independent of party organization, if they desire to be so, and making such organization, where adopted, purely beneficial.

16. (II.) Preventing the loss of the surplus votes polled for the more popular candidates.

17. (III.) Preventing the loss of votes polled for unsuccessful candidates.

18, and lastly. The value of the electoral principle which is the basis of the Cumulative Vote.

[The substance of the memorandum, relating to the first six of the foregoing heads, will be found in the first chapter of this work.]

7.—*The Legislative Adoption of the Cumulative Vote.*

The first adoption of the Cumulative Vote for the election of representative, administrative, or governing bodies in England was, by the passing o the Elementary Education Act, whereby, touching the election of the School Boards, it is enacted that "At every such election every voter shall be entitled to a number of votes equal to the number of the members of the School Board to be elected, and may give all such votes to one candidate, or may so distribute them among the candidates as he thinks fit."[1]

---

[1] Stat. 33 & 34 Vict., c. 75, sec. 29.

8.—*Cause of the Readier Adoption of the Cumulative Vote.*

The reason of the greater popularity of the Cumulative Vote than that either of the Restricted Vote or of the Single Vote, which has been elsewhere proposed, is that it seems to give more power to the elector than he has heretofore had, whereas the other methods appear nominally to diminish that power. The Cumulative rule, expressing: "That every elector shall be entitled to a number of votes equal to the number of the members to be chosen, and may give all such votes to one, or distribute them among the candidates as he thinks fit," is favourably contrasted with the law of 1867, which enacts that, at a contested election for a constituency represented by three members, no person shall vote for more than two candidates. The latter gave an opportunity for the somewhat grandiloquent preamble of the bill introduced to repeal that restriction, which begins, " Whereas it is expedient to restore to the electors those rights which by the ancient law and custom of the realm belonged to them, of voting for so many persons as there are members to be returned," etc.

9.—*Cause of Popular Dissatisfaction with it in Practice.*

Against the foregoing plausible but really valueless distinction in favour of the Cumulative Vote, should be set the grounds of dissatisfaction produced by its results, when, as in the examples that are hereafter given, the candidates having the support of a large number of electors fail, while those supported by a small number succeed. This seeming injustice is entirely due to the cumulative method of computation, and would disappear if no one could vote for more than a single candidate. It is, in truth, explained and justified by the perfect fairness of the intention and result of the system; but popular ignorance and party prejudice are too often impatient of argument in defence of that which, to a superficial view, may be made to appear as a hardship. When it is seen that the votes of 3,000 electors have been successful where votes of 13,000 fail (see Section 11), it may, in the present state of education, be hopeless to expect that the apologists of the fact will satisfy the defeated party by showing them that it is due to the greater intensity and force which the 3,000 threw into their electoral effort (by the concentration of their votes), as compared with the smaller amount of power which the 13,000 exercised in favour of any single candidate (by dividing it among many), and that they have the means of correcting the inequality in their own hands.

10.—*Comparison of the Numerical Effect of Cumulative and Single Voting.*

If 100 electors, forming one constituency, have 10 votes apiece, it is obvious that singly and relatively they have the same power, one with the other—their weight is the same relatively, for the purpose of the election, as if they had but one vote each. The aggregate number of votes given is more, and the computation is more laborious, but the result is the same.

Thus, suppose there were five candidates, and three to be elected members, and the votes stood :—

	Single Votes.	Cumulative Votes.
A.	40	120
B.	37	111
C.	16	48
D.	4	12
E.	3	9
	100	300

The preferences of every elector and the degree of his preference being, of course, for the purposes of the above comparison, assumed to be in all cases precisely the same, it is plain that the amount of electoral power possessed and exercised by every one is also the same.

The practical question in applying either the Cumulative or the Single Vote for the purpose of averting the exclusive government of mere disciplined majorities, is first to consider whether the illusion that the Cumulative Vote gives the greater power is so ineradicable that it must be accepted as the preliminary method of reform, or whether it is not possible, by calling the popular attention to the two methods, and their real effect, to make the simpler process of the Single Vote equally acceptable, and thus get rid of the feeling of dissatisfaction which is produced by the corresponding illusion that the lesser number of voters has overpowered the greater. It is believed that the equality of the two systems in point of justice might be made popularly intelligible, and that the greater simplicity of the Single Vote, and the obvious fairness of its results at the poll, would give it the preponderance in the public favour.

11.—*Effect of the Cumulative Vote in Birmingham on the Representation of the Popular Party.*

The effect of the Cumulative Vote on the large Liberal party in Birmingham, which for the most part gave its support to fifteen selected candidates on the late School Board election, was to secure the return of no more than six of such candidates. The supporters of the fifteen polled altogether 220,638 votes, of which 96,427 were effectual in electing the candidates for whom they were given, while a majority of such votes, or no less than 124,211, were ineffectual, having no operation whatever, owing to their having been distributed among nine candidates, none of whom had sufficient votes to be returned. On the other hand, smaller parties, or minorities of the constituency, by the concentration of their votes on one, two, or three candidates, succeeded in electing them.

The complete and admirable directions issued by the Education Department, with reference to the method of computation of votes, and the form in which the results might be returned, directions which were generally followed by the returning officers, afford the means of considering the operation of this electoral system in nearly every conceivable point of view. The following is a copy of the return made by Mr. Hayes, the Town Clerk of Birmingham, of the election there:—

	Ones.	Twos.	Threes.	Fifteens.	Total Votes.
Baker	13,037	244	55	7	14,101
Burges	1,190	7,785	500	45	21,925
Chamberlain	13,200	439	100	8	15,090
Collings	13,165	201	39	5	13,873
Cooper	12,778	234	71	9	13,873
Crosskey	12,706	154	25	5	13,314
F. S. Dale	1,340	7,125	152	29	17,465
R. W. Dale	13,229	760	210	6	16,387
Dawson	13,023	643	232	33	17,103
Dixon	13,197	735	214	5	16,897
Elkington	1,366	6,508	68	..	14,925
Evans	475	942	207	34	5,351
Gough	1,864	6,013	167	69	17,481
Holland	12,484	216	73	17	14,359
Hopkins	1,516	6,559	189	8	15,696
Kirkwood	315	123	69	339	7,095
G. B. Lloyd	12,850	978	115	8	14,642
S. S. Lloyd	1,289	7,315	744	237	30,709
Melson	978	564	230	328	11,017
Middlemore	13,007	280	79	13	14,332
O'Sullivan	506	140	100	2,143	35,120
Radford	12,146	94	25	1	12,515
Raffles	325	52	16	80	2,050
Sandford	12,526	199	37	1	13,202
Sargant	2,197	5,973	221	18	15,683
Vince	13,119	652	196	5	15,843
Wilkinson	1,424	7,259	500	23	19,829
Wright	12,880	416	114	11	15,007
	208,132	62,003	4,748	4,387	..
Multiplied by	1	2	3	15	
	208,132	124,006	14,224	52,305	..

In fours, 6,114 votes were given; in fives, 14,110; sixes, 2,250; sevens, 4,711; eights, 4,776; nines, 486; tens, 2,920; elevens, 77; twelves, 408; thirteens, 312; and fourteen, 182; making altogether 435,083.

It is impossible to say that there was any injustice in this result. The whole number of voters was 29,183. There were 15 candidates to be elected, and certainly the 2,113 electors who concentrated all their votes on Canon O'Sullivan (to say nothing of the other 1,028), being much more than a fifteenth of the electors, were sufficient in number to be entitled to one of the fifteen representatives.

12.—*Effect of the Cumulative Vote in Marylebone, Finsbury, Lambeth, and Sheffield.*

In the Marylebone election three candidates, for whom from 3,287 to 4,298 electors voted, were excluded, while another candidate, for whom only 1,857 persons voted, was successful. This was effected by 1,043 voters having given him all their votes, no other candidate, except one, having half that number of exclusive supporters. The 4 highest and the 7 lowest of 22 candidates occupy the same position on the poll in both the tables of Voters and of Votes, but there is much diversity in the position in the two tables of the 11 candidates who occupy the middle place in the return. The Marylebone return is chiefly remarkable as exhibiting the consequence of an exceptional interest prevailing in favour of a particular candidate in causing a surplus of votes. Miss Garrett polled 47,858 votes, being between three or four times the number of any other candidate.

The return of Mr. Greenwell, the Deputy Returning Officer, states that in Marylebone, 23,619 voting papers were admitted, and estimates the number of ratepayers at 58,000. In the following table the names of the 7 successful candidates are in italics :—

Candidates.	Ones.	Twos.	Threes.	Fours.	Fives.	Sixes.	Sevens.	Total.
Garrett	1,444	3,348	8,061	7,116	1,700	450	25,739	47,858
Huxley	852	3,118	3,240	3,060	325	204	2,695	13,494
Thorold	2,698	2,124	2,223	1,952	235	84	2,870	12,186
Angus	3,001	2,304	2,079	1,784	240	90	1,974	11,472
Hutchins	286	364	480	516	180	126	7,301	9,253
Dixon	839	1,832	1,800	1,292	255	72	2,891	9,031
Watson	2,535	1,198	1,257	858	160	90	2,177	8,355
Mills	2,620	1,414	1,482	1,184	95	12	1,120	7,927
Powell	2,485	1,428	1,404	1,096	110	48	1,281	7,852
Whelpton	258	474	720	592	170	108	3,437	5,759
Waterlow	664	996	1,062	692	105	54	1,421	4,994
Garvey	2,495	822	585	324	55	36	616	4,933
Marshall	2,395	532	441	384	115	24	777	4,668
Guedella	425	762	633	460	150	84	2,121	4,635
Cremer	548	1,240	1,248	692	85	36	553	4,402
Edmunds	221	506	567	556	95	54	1,974	3,973
Verey	80	166	258	284	65	24	1,253	2,130
Stanford	110	176	198	164	35	12	791	1,486
Wyld	36	40	54	29	10	12	154	334
Dunn	37	18	60	44	10	12	77	258
Brewer	23	26	15	28	..	..	21	103
Beare	14	10	15	16	..	..	7	62
	24,066	22,938	27,912	23,152	4,215	1,632	61,250	165,165

Sheffield and Lambeth are to be noticed as examples of the vast losses of votes expended on unsuccessful candidates, whereby several who were known to be desirable representatives of classes greatly interested in the business of the School Boards, were excluded.

THE SHEFFIELD SCHOOL BOARD.

1	Ellison, Michael J., Roman Catholic	17,057
2	Wilson, Henry, Churchman	12,489
3	Wardlow, Charles, U. M. Free Church	11,464
4	Cobby, William, Wesleyan	11,372
5	Moore, Thomas, Churchman	10,823
6	Firth, Mark, New Connection	10.316
7	Cole, Skelton, Wesleyan	10,315
8	Doncaster, Chas., Society of Friends	9,762
9	Fisher, William, Unitarian	9,756
10	Brown, Sir John, Churchman	9,344
11	Holden, R. W., Primitive Methodist	9,303
12	Fairburn, John, Wesleyan	8,310
13	Crossland, James, Churchman	7,215
14	Allott, Alfred, Independent	6,947
15	Eadon, Robert Thomas, Unitarian	6,624

UNSUCCESSFUL CANDIDATES.

16	Sissons, William..	6,426
17	Rowbotham, Thomas	6,220
18	Langley, Batty	5,941
19	Peace, Wm. Kirkby	5,680
20	Wilson, John	5,540
21	Bragge, William..	4,924
22	Hibberd, Emmanuel	4,734
23	Penton, Thomas	3,358
24	Bacon, Stephen	3,114
25	Robertson, Alexander	3,049
26	Collier, John	2,721
27	Robertshaw, Jeremiah	2,712
28	Jackson, Alfred	2,664
29	Hallam, Reuben	2,605
30	Hime, Thos. Whiteside	2,373
31	Pye-Smith, John William	2,326
32	Nadin, Alfred Cutler	1,870
33	Jones, Benjamin	1,752
34	Griffiths, Francis	1,645
35	Orton, Thomas	1,200
36	Knox, George Walter	1,106
37	Burns, John Wild	869
38	Aitchison, David Alexander	858
39	Unwin, John	837
40	Dronfield, William	752
41	Lester, William Henry	642
42	Tasker, John	638
43	Adams, John Edward	581
44	Emsley, Samuel	574
45	Parkes, David	509

UNSUCCESSFUL CANDIDATES—*continued.*

46	Foster, Thomas ..	..	..	..	..	..	490
47	Gillott, James ..	..	..	..	..	..	349
48	Birch, William ..	..	..	..	..	..	348
49	Dearden, Henry ..	..	..	..	..	..	342
50	Godson, Thomas..	..	..	..	..	..	322
51	Cropper, George..	..	..	..	..	..	214
52	Hall, Frederick William		..	..	..	..	174
53	Goodlad, James ..	..	..	..	..	..	158
54	Prideaux, Thomas	..	..	..	..	..	95

The Sheffield return, by Mr. Yeomans, the Town Clerk, was made with especial accuracy of detail. The above statement of the result is taken from the *Sheffield and Rotherham Independent.*

LAMBETH DIVISION.

Candidates.	Ones.	Twos.	Threes.	Fours.	Fives.	Totals.	No. of Voters.
Stiff.. ..	1,093	3,342	3,852	236	13,555	22,078	6,818
Tresidder	885	2,674	2,751	296	10,050	16,656	5,223
Tilson ..	710	4,176	5,856	152	3,680	14,574	5,524
McArthur	1,073	2,538	1,848	204	6,300	11,963	4,269
Few.. ..	532	4,134	3,444	188	2,210	10,508	4,236
Murphy.. ..	692	2,124	1,791	180	3,615	8,402	3,119
Tugwell ..	423	1,010	1,107	148	5,140	7,828	2,362
Applegarth ..	486	1,274	1,470	172	4,280	7,682	2,512
Kavanagh ..	72	124	108	40	4,380	4,724	1,056
White	309	716	534	72	2,345	3,976	1,332
Selway	580	1,204	807	68	760	3,419	1,620
Mottershead ..	211	456	360	36	2,000	3,463	968
Gibbons.. ..	62	166	126	4	1,115	1,073	411
Shaen	101	192	123	12	490	918	339
	7,229	24,130	24,177	1,808	59,920	117,264	..

(Stiff, Tresidder, Tilson, McArthur, Few — Elected.)

13.—*Complaints of the Effects of the Cumulative Vote.*

The National Education League has issued a pamphlet,[1] which may be regarded as its summary of objections. These may be considered under four heads:—

A.—First, it is argued that the principle on which the Cumulative Vote rests is fallacious: that minority representation is either a nullity or a mis-

---

[1] *The Cumulative Method of Voting: its Nature, Operation, and Effects, as exhibited in the late School Board Elections.* London: Simpkin, Marshall, and Co. Birmingham: Alex. Day.

chief: If only proportionate in numbers, the minority will always be out-voted: That the national policy of recent years, such as freedom of trade and other great innovations and improvements, would have been frustrated if Parliament had been elected in batches of nine, eleven, or fifteen. It insists, in fact, that minorities, though admitted to preliminary discussion, should be altogether driven from the field of action. It does not admit that the election is for the choice of a deliberative body, the necessary presence of whose members, supplied by the best materials for judgment at the place of legislation, together with their concentrated attention and individual responsibility, are to be relied on for dealing wisely with the great and novel problems that constantly arise in the changing conditions of modern life. It assumes that the constitution of tribunals, the boundaries of the civil rights of person and property, the system of national defence, all internal organization for public instruction, national and local taxation, and the treatment of pauperism, and the conditions of colonial and foreign intercourse, are all to be finally determined by the votes at the hustings, the person chosen being no more than the bearer of the decree to the house of delegates. If this be so, the election is an idle ceremony. Appointing messengers, called representatives, is a clumsy and unnecessary contrivance maintained at a useless cost. All that is wanted is a clerk at every hustings to register the decision, and send it by post or telegraph to the central bureau.

B.—Secondly, that it increases the power of party organizations, giving scope to intensity of feeling or fanaticism, whether of the elector himself or those who influence him, his power being in the proportion of his personal earnestness or docility. That it has thus led to voting according to prepared lists, without any proper discrimination by the public of the individual merit of those for whom they vote. On the complaint it must be observed that it was the larger party in Birmingham—the 14,000 who adhered together—which exhibited the most complete example of voting according to a list, if that be any reproach. It may fairly be inquired whether the true ground of this complaint is, not that organization and its consequent influence have been employed, but that the pre-existing organization has been partially overpowered. Under the exclusive majority-system, organization is indispensable to the selection of the party candidates, and their restriction to the necessary number, unless it can be supposed that, by some miracle of intuition, the whole party is at once led to adopt, without any differences, the favourite candidates, and that all other than the favourite list acquiesce and waive their pretensions. The grievance felt by the opponents of the Cumulative Vote rather is, that it has introduced new and different organizations not of the whole party, but of sections and classes of opinion. Of the two consequences, it may be fairly contended that the organization brought into play by the Cumulative Vote is, in the view of those who really believe that the people are to be trusted, and the public opinion should be in truth consulted, far preferable, inasmuch as it gives more scope to individuality of thought, and the free representation of individual opinion. The vote is given with greater sincerity, and the aggregate result in moderating or graduating political action is free from the danger to which order and government are exposed by efforts to give exaggerated force to enlarge majorities. Dependence on electoral organization, though not more chargeable to the Cumulative Vote than to the majority system, is in itself an evil to be encountered by other remedies.

C.—Thirdly, it is to suppress rather than elicit public opinion. The fact that nearly half the constituencies abstained from voting at the School Board elections is attributed apparently to two causes, the greater length of the list of candidates, and the intricacies of the voting paper; the primary cause of both being, it is said, the form of vote. These combined causes raised, it is said, insuperable difficulties in the way of the election of working men, although they did not prevent a candidate in Birmingham, alleged to be supported by a community mainly composed of Irish labourers (p. 20), from arriving at the head of the poll. It cannot be meant to be implied that others were too stupid to understand and too obstinate to be taught, but rather that they did not care to take the pains. It is a matter of serious regret that of five candidates of the artisan class in London only one was elected. Members in a different sphere of life may be well able to construct and organize a scheme for establishing the necessary Elementary Schools, but the teaching of experience has never led them to realise the difficulty of inducing or enabling the poor, in their present condition, thoroughly to appreciate, and still less to prolong, the education of their children; and it may be long before the means are devised, by the use of endowments or otherwise, of bridging over the chasm of apathy and ignorance left by ages of neglect. It is, however, more probable than otherwise that, without the Cumulative Vote, even the solitary member of that class would have been excluded. There is no evidence that any voters were kept from the poll by the form of vote. If it gave expression to every diversity of opinion, it is hard to see how it could render the electors more apathetic, and the greater choice of candidates is surely calculated to excite rather than repress effort to promote the election of one or more of them. Looking forward to the future, any apparent intricacy in filling up the paper would be better met by some arrangement to instruct the voters where necessary, than by impairing the intelligent result of the vote.

D.—Fourthly, that it creates an inducement for too many candidates to offer themselves, whereby votes are wasted and lost.

The Cumulative method, in common with any other method that encourages the development of more varied thought, by giving more perfect representation to majorities as well as to minorities, necessarily presents inducements for candidates to come forward who, without that encouragement, would not have appeared. In a multitude of cases these, either from attraction or aversion, provoke the activity of electors who would not otherwise have taken the pains to vote. To the extent in which the supernumerary candidates attract voters who ordinarily unite with any of the greater political parties, they must withdraw so much from the force of the latter, and add to that of smaller sections of the people. It is true, also, that the accumulative power thus given to minorities is increased by the disposition of electors, who are thereby more encouraged to "plump," or give their entire voting power, for particular and favourite candidates, lest they should otherwise be defeated. The application of the proportional system in a more perfect form is needed, not a lessening of the number of candidates. The widening of the electoral choice must be desirable, if the object be true representation.

14.—*The Loss of Votes, together with the Necessity for, and the Power acquired by, Party Organization in the School Board Elections, and how far such evils are attributable to the Cumulative Vote.*

The double mischief here complained of, and of which examples have been given, are not created by or peculiar to, although they, perhaps, are more prominently shown by, Cumulative Voting. They exist, if not in a more aggravated shape, yet in one which it is more difficult to encounter, under the prevailing majority system.

First, in regard to the loss of votes, the Cumulative system, as hitherto applied, is open to the same objections as the majority system, that both the surplus votes given to candidates who may be highly popular, and the ineffectual votes given to candidates who fail, are thrown away. The former, the loss of surplus votes, may, in open voting, be more or less avoided, by ascertaining and making known at the shortest possible intervals the number of votes polled for every candidate; but the utmost care would scarcely prevent considerable loss, and it may afford an opportunity for trickery and party manœuvres; and in secret voting it is irremediable, except in a manner hereafter explained (Section 16). The latter infirmity, the loss of votes from the candidates for whom they are given being unsuccessful, cannot, under the method in use, be recovered, although this loss, it will be seen (Section 17), is also susceptible of a remedy.

The Cumulative system does, however, offer the means of preventing a loss of votes, of which its opponents take no account, that is, the votes of all those who, disagreeing with the majority in their electoral district, are now, in Parliamentary elections, outvoted and left without representatives, a number which cannot ordinarily be taken at less than two-fifths of the whole electoral body, or 400,000 out of 1,000,000 votes. It is therefore, even in the rude form in which it has been adopted, a vast economy of electoral power.

Secondly, as to party organization. The utmost which the Cumulative system has done is to preserve it, and that, as it has been already said, in an ameliorated form,—one better suited to the character of mankind, and the diversities of sentiment and opinion. Instead of being called "minority" representation, a truer appellation would be "the better representation of majorities."

REMEDIES.

15.—Rendering Individual Voters independent of Party Organization if they desire it, and making such Organization, where adopted, more purely beneficial.

The system of proportional and preferential voting, practically accomplishes the foregoing objects. (Its operation is shown as applied to the nomination of the Overseers of Harvard College, Cambridge, Massachusetts; set out fully in Appendix M, *ante*, pp. 351, 355.)

16.—*Secondly. Preventing the Loss of the Surplus Votes Polled for the more Popular Candidates.*

This is effected by adopting the principle of the quotient explained in the last section; that is, taking either the number of the registered electors in the constituency, or the number who actually vote at the election, and dividing it by the number of members to be chosen. Suppose, for example, that at Birmingham there had been 45,000 electors or persons entitled to vote, and 15 members to be elected, the quotient would be 3,000. If, then, it were provided that, when 3,000 voters had polled for any candidate, all additional votes given for that candidate should be passed on to the next candidate named in the voting paper who had not already made up his quotient, the elector would have the means of preserving his votes from being practically without effect. Instead of taking the number of registered electors as the number to be divided for the purpose of ascertaining the electoral quotient or quota, a better plan is—even at the expense of two or three hours' delay—to ascertain the number who actually vote at the election, and divide it by the number of members. The quotient is then smaller, and thus more votes are saved. Thus, at Birmingham, where only 30,000 voted, the quotient would not have been more than 2,000, and the number of effectual votes would have been vastly increased. This calculation is made for the sake of simplicity, on the hypothesis that every elector has one vote for one candidate, and no more. Applying it to the Cumulative form, the figures only differ. For the total of 45,000 electors substitute 675,000 votes, for the quotient of 3,000 voters 4,500 votes, for the total of 30,000 electors substitute 450,000 votes, and for the quotient of 2,000 substitute a quotient of 30,000 votes.

17.—*Thirdly. Preventing the Loss of Votes Polled for Unsuccessful Candidates.*

The growth of opinion will inevitably bring forward candidates for legislative and administrative bodies appealing to principles not hitherto known or recognized, and whom it will be neither possible nor desirable to exclude. The degree of support given to such candidates will be the most trustworthy indication that can be had of the course of popular thought. The more numerous parties—those who form the great Liberal or Conservative majorities—would have no reason to apprehend a reduction of influence by votes being withdrawn from them, nor would the voter have cause to fear that his vote will be thrown away by an independent expression of opinion, if, when the state of the poll is ascertained, and all the candidates are known for whom votes enough have not been given, the names of those lower on the poll, beginning at the lowest, be then cancelled on the voting papers appropriated to them, and the voting paper passed on to the next candidate the elector has named upon it, who has not already obtained the quotient. Any voter who wished to prevent his vote from being transferred would avoid it by inserting no other name than that of the sole person whom he desires to see elected. Applying this rule to the Sheffield election, the 95 votes given by 54 voters for Prideaux would be first redistributed ; next, the 158 votes of 95 voters for Goodlad ; next, the 174 votes of 89 voters for Hall ; next, the 214 votes of 94 voters for Cropper ; and so on, until all the voting papers on which the electors had indicated such desire had been redistributed, and only the fifteen candidates who, in the result proved to be successful, would remain. In Marylebone the process of redistribution of unsuccessful votes would have begun with the 62, then the 103, then the 258, then the 334, and so on until there were seven left. In Lambeth this redistribution would no doubt have had the effect of returning one of the working-class candidates, by combining their 7,682 and 3,062 votes. In all these cases the state of the poll being affected by every new distribution of votes, the order of every succeeding distribution may also be affected.

18.—*Lastly. The Value of the Electoral Principle of the Cumulative Vote.*

The objections to the operation of the system, when examined and understood, are so many testimonies in favour of its principle. To the just complaint of the loss of the votes, from being too many or too few, of those who go to the poll, are added the charges that it has induced multitudes to abstain from voting, and enabled ignorance to overpower knowledge.

The design of the Cumulative Vote, as well as its true principle, is to obviate those very evils ; and corrected in detail, as it is capable of being, the application of the principle will be found an effectual means of accomplishing that design. With arrangements broad enough to afford a sufficiently extensive choice of candidates, it will enable every voter to be reasonably certain that his vote shall not be given in vain, or be without a distinct and appreciable effect on the result of the election. It would thus be a direct and powerful appeal to the conscience of every one who has any care for the community in which he lives, not to neglect this public duty. The universal sense that there is a constitutional outlet for every political aspiration is the true safeguard against unlawful or violent courses. It would evoke, and give its due measure to the expression of every sincere and earnest opinion, formed by any considerable number of the people, on the measures calculated to promote their moral and material well-being.

And in the struggle of knowledge against ignorance it recovers the forces that are wasted and lost under the local majority system. All unselfish, patriotic, and noble motives are invited and encouraged to enter into the great moral conflict. The advocates of the exclusive rule of majorities try to reconcile themselves to it by the figment that it matters not how many electors are extinguished in one place, because it may happen that some others who think the same as they do, may succeed in silencing another body of electors who think differently, in another place. They strike an imaginary balance of ignorance in one constituency against intelligence in another. They forget that this is no exchange or substitution of one value for another, and every exclusion is pure waste. The aggregate intellectual power of the nation is no more than that of the individuals who compose it. No identity either in thought or in opportunity of action is found to compensate in one locality for what is thrown away in another. The local majority system tends to create governing bodies dependent in a great measure on hazard or accident, and in the formation of which the deliberate judgment of half the people is powerless. Yet, if the election pretends, as it does, to be an intellectual process, appealing to the knowledge and discretion of the electors, the appeal should be in no case a mockery. The state owes to every one of its members the best assistance and encouragement it can give him in the performance of his electoral duty, and the assurance that the labour shall not be fruitless. In a work spread over the whole country, that of gathering several hundred parts or members to constitute the great machine of government, in which it is the business of all to weigh and sift, with keen and logical scrutiny, a multitude of competing elements—to recognize and detect imposture—it is not too much to say that nothing should be left to chance that can be made certain; that none should be shut out who can bring to the task the result of study, experience, or knowledge; and that no portion of the intellect of the nation should be paralyzed.

THOS. HARE.

Athenæum, 24th May, 1871.

APPENDIX O.

PROGRESS OF THE STUDY OF THE REPRESENTATIVE PRINCIPLE.

It is not right to pass without notice the fact that there are many who view with much distrust, if not hostility, all attempts to perfect representative institutions by making them real instead of merely virtual or nominal. Of these some are utterly dissatisfied with representative government; and others, accepting it in the shape which it has commonly assumed, either find it effectual for all the purposes which they consider important, or apprehend that any measure which would render it more perfectly expressive of the general will would be for the worse.

The former class includes those who would return to popular legislation. *Direct Legislation by the People*, versus *Representative Government, translated from the original Swiss pamphlets, by Eugene Oswald*. London, 1869. Practical effect has been given to opinions of this nature in Zurich, where a new constitution has recently been adopted, providing not only that all laws and all important money grants shall be submitted to the vote of the whole people—the referendum—but also enabling the same popular assembly to initiate and make new laws without the intervention of their representative body. The referendum has also been introduced in other cantons, but not including, as in this, the power of independent legislation by the popular vote. Among the former must also be classed those who repudiate all appeal to the popular voice, whether directly or through representatives. "It has long been a cardinal doctrine of the Positivist system that government by the suffrage, the election of the superior by the inferior, the basing of authority on the nomination of the majority, is inherently vicious."—*Revolution of the Commune*, by Frederick Harrison, *Fortnightly Review*, May, 1871, p. 571.

The opponents of real representation who fall within the latter of the two divisions consist; I. of those whose objections to Cumulative voting have been considered (see Appendix N, Sec. 13), and who think it not only right, but an advantage favourable to good government, that the minorities in every electoral district should have no voice in the election; II. those who, not enamoured with the results of representative government and household suffrage, consider that the chances which the restrictions and anomalies of our existing system offer to the possessors of wealth and power, to be better safeguards than any accurate expression of popular thought could be; that in fact the higher order of political intelligence in the electoral body would be overwhelmed and swept away by the numbers, stupidity, and corruption arrayed against it; and, III., there are others who, with Lord Russell, look back on two centuries of parliamentary government, under great Whig and Tory leaders, as having brought it to the utmost perfection that can be achieved, and conclude that " it is difficult to believe in this age of the world that there are models of government, still untried, promising a cup of felicity and of freedom which England has not yet tasted."—*Essay on the English Government and Constitution*, by Earl Russell. 1865. Introduction, p. 51.

Against such conclusions all the labours recorded in this work are of course a protest. It will be enough to leave them to the consideration of the students of this subject, who will perhaps find in such counter-theories an explanation of the efforts or courses of political action, whether positive or negative, to which they lead.

In addition to the progress, both legislative and literary, referred to in the foregoing pages as having been made in Europe and America in the last seven years towards the attainment of a just system of electing representative and governing bodies, the remarkable degree of interest which the subject has created in Italy, requires especial notice. Some of the first works published in that country were—

Del Potere Elettorale negli Stati Liberi, Luigi Palma. Milan, 1869.

Teoria della Elezione Politica, Guido Padebetti: Mémoire couronné en Janvier, 1868, par l'Académie des Sciences Morales et Politiques de Naples, imprimé en 1870.

La Representanza delle Minoranze nel Parlemento, Ferrario Carlo. Turin, 1870.

Il Suffragio Universale in Italia, par Sidney Sonnino. Firenze, 1870.

Libertà e Democrazia, studi sulla rappresentanza delle minorità, Attilio Brunialti. Milano, 1871.

Della Libertà e Equivalenza dei Suffragi nelle Elezionè ovvero della Proporzionale Rappresentanza delle Maggioranze e Minoranze. Studio Critico Del 'Avv Francesco Genala. Milano, 1871. This work contains a tabular enumeration of all the publications on the subject heretofore issued, under the heads of the several countries in which they had appeared : exhibiting the intelligence and the vast industry which the author had brought to the task.

Degli Inconvenienti e dei Pericoli degli attuali sistemi eletorali. Discorso del Socio Dott Attelio Brunialti. Tipografia Nazionali Paroni, Vicenza, 1871.

In the month of May last, there was founded at Rome the " Associazione per lo Studio della Rappresentanza Proporzionale." The first meeting was held on the 10th May, 1872, and attended by the Signori Bonghi, Broglio, Lazatti, Mumiani, Mancini, Messedaglia, Minghetta, and Perazzi, members of the Italian Parliament; and Signori Brunialti, Genala, Paddelletti, Saredo, and Allessandro Spada. The programme of the society was issued in the month of June. *Bollettino* 1°, Roma, 1872, Stabiliment Cevelli. Foro Trajano, 37.

Other publications have followed *Della Rappresentanza Proporzionale in Italià*, par Sidney Sonnino. Firenze, 1872.

Among the recent works in this country, which have not been mentioned, or have been but cursorily referred to in the foregoing pages,—are

Speech of J. Stuart Mill, M.P., in the House of Commons, 29th May, 1867.
On Methods of Electing Representatives, by H. R. Droop. London, 1868.
Representative Reform. Report of Committee of Reform League and others in Mr. Hare's Scheme of Representation. February and March, 1868.
Proportional Representation applied to the Election of Local Governing Bodies, by H. R. Droop. London, Wildy, 1871.
A Modification of Mr. Hare's Scheme for the Election of Representatives, by James Thornton Hoskins, B.A., London, Vic. Press, 1871. Second edition.
General Representation, on a complete readjustment and modification of Mr. Hare's plan, by Archibald E. Dobbs, M.A. London: Longman, 1872. Second edition.
Proportional Representation in Large Constituencies, by Walter Baily. London: Ridgway, 1872.
Sovereignty: Royal and Representative. Westminster Review, July, 1872, p. 1; *Redistribution of Political Power,* by E. H. Knatchbull Hugessen, M.P. Macmillan's Magazine, November, 1872, p. 67.

The press of other Continental nations has also contributed to the discussion and propagation of the proposed amendments:—

Representation för minoriteterna genom Val-Lag. Upsala, Kongl. Akad. Boktryckeriet, 1866.
Die Wahlreform en Europa und Amerika. Zürich, D. Bürkh. 1868.
Unparteiishe Worte zur Zurcherishen Bewegung. Zürich, 1868.
Les Minorités et le Suffrage Universel, par le Baron de Layre. Paris, 1868. And besides the numerous and valuable works of M. Ernest Naville, referred to in Appendix A, we must not omit to mention his recent pamphlet,
La Reform Electorale in France. Paris; Didier, 1871.

Since the foregoing pages have been in the press, intelligence has been received, not only of new efforts in the study and propagation of the principles on which representative government must be constituted, if it is to be true and just, but also of the actual experience which has been gained of the application of a system of proportional representation in the election of the House of Representatives in the State of Illinois.

A conference of the Associazione per lo Studio della Rappresentanza Proporzionale was held in the Accademia dei Georgofili di Firenze, and was continued by adjournment on the 29th and 30th of June, 1872. A full report of the discussion—in which the system of exclusive majority representation, as especially necessary to be preserved in Italy, having regard to the respective positions of the Church and State, and to the other circumstances of the kingdom, was maintained in argument by Il. Prof. Luchini against Signori Genala, Pareto, Fontanelli, Brunialti, Ferraris, Sidney Sonnino, Franchetti, and others, who urged the advantages of the proportional methods—will be found in the Bollettino 2° of the Associazione. Firenze, co i tipi di M. Cellini. E. C. alla Galileiana, 1872.

Subsequent conferences were announced : " L'una a Venezia presso l'Ateueo Veneto nella sera del Dicembre prossimo ; L'altra a Genova per cura della Società di pubbliche letture, nella sera del 5 Gennai, 1873."

Far more instructive than any speculative argument can be, is the report of the working of even an imperfect proportional system in a populous state of the Union. The seventh section of the fourth article of the amended constitution of the State of Illinois provides that " in all elections to the House of Representatives, each qualified voter may cast as many votes for one candidate as there are representatives to be elected (viz. three in each Senatorial district), or may distribute the same, or equal parts thereof, among the candidates as he shall see fit, and the candidates highest in votes shall be declared elected." (See p. 349, *ante*.) This law came into operation for the first time at the recent election. The comparative strength of parties was shown in the late Presidential contest. The number of representatives to be elected was 153. If each party were to be properly represented in the House, there would be 85 for the majority, and 68 for the minority. The Republicans carried 33 districts, and would have had, under the old system of representation, 99 representatives. The Democrats carried only 18 districts, and would have had but 54 representatives under the old system.

The Hon. J. Medill, in a letter to the *Cincinnati Commercial* (2 Dec., 1872), thus describes the actual result :—" For the first time in the history of political organizations, each party is represented from every portion of the State, and the aggregate representation is exactly in proportion to the numerical strength of each party. Thus the Republicans have elected 86 members of the House, and the Democrats 67. The Republican vote of the State was 240,837 ; the Democratic vote (including O'Conor's) was 187,250. This would give an average of 2,800 Republican votes cast for each Republican member, and 2,790 Democratic votes cast for each member of that persuasion.

" What could be more equal or mathematically exact ? The majority party have complete control, but the minority party have just the representation they are entitled to on principles of equality. Had the House been elected on the 'grab-all' method, it would stand, Republican 99, Democrat 54. We elected our Senate by single districts, and the Republicans carried 33 districts and the Democrats but 18. Divide the total Republican vote by the number of senators elected, and the quotient is about 7,300 votes to each. Divide the Democratic vote by their senators elected, and their quotient is 10,400. Thus you perceive the Democrats are not nearly represented in the Senate in proportion to their strength ; but in the House, which was elected on the minority representation plan, they have secured precisely the number of members they should have on principles of right and justice.

" The practical working of the two systems, viz. the 'grab-all' and the

proportional, was strikingly exemplified in this county, which is divided
into seven senatorial districts. The Republicans carried 6 of them and the
Democrats only 1 ; but for the other House, the Democrats elected 8 and the
Republicans 13 members, and that is exactly the number of members each
party was entitled to in proportion to its strength at the polls in this county.

"For the first time for many years will the Democrats of this city be represented in the General Assembly by men of their choice and sentiments ;
and for the first time since the Republican party was organized in Illinois
(in 1854) have the Democrats secured a representation from Northern or the
Republicans from Southern Illinois, with rare exceptions. The strongest
and bitterest Democratic districts down in 'Egypt' have now, for the first
time in the history of existing parties, elected Republicans to the General
Assembly.

"I send you a list of the members elect from all the districts—beginning
with Chicago and ending with Cairo. Mark the number of Republicans
who have been chosen to the House from the Thirty-third to the Fifty-first
District inclusive. These, with two or three exceptions, have heretofore
constituted the Democratic strongholds of our State. Also note the number
of Democrats who have been returned in the districts from the First to the
Twenty-third. (This territory is called 'Canaan' in contradistinction to
'Egypt,' at the opposite end of the State.) From this 'Canaan's fair and
happy land,' Democratic members have, therefore, been as scarce as white
blackbirds.

"Some of the politicians, before the election, predicted that Cumulative
voting would cause so much confusion and mischief that it would have to
be abolished right away. The people, they said, would never comprehend
it, or know how to vote by that method ; and the judges of the election,
they predicted, would be unable to count up the votes and make correct
returns. But none of their evil prognostications came to pass. The people
seemed to understand their new power of Cumulative voting, and exercised
it freely. In some instances they elected two Republicans in a Democratic
district, or two Democrats in a Republican district. This was done by
'plumping' for favourite candidates or transferring a part of a vote to a
political opponent on account of his personal merits or popularity. But the
general result did not change the proportional representation of parties."

The *Chicago Times* (28th November, 1872) contrasts the result of this
election of representatives, with other elections, especially that of senators,
in which the majority, or as it terms it, the "jug-handle" method has been
retained. Adverting to the statement of Mr. Medill, it observes that, clear
as it is, it still "fails to exhibit with due precision and force the most
remarkable contrast between the new proportional system and the old
'grab-all' system. The *Times* yesterday directed attention to the fact that
in the new Illinois Congressional delegation, only 250,181 of the 434,252
citizens who sought to gain representation are actually represented, while

no less than 184,071 of the number seeking representation are actually unrepresented or misrepresented. The like fact appears no less conspicuously in the election of our State senators. In the seven senatorial districts in Cook County, 50,355 voters sought to gain representation in the State senate. Of this number, only 31,935 will be actually represented; leaving no less than 18,420 wholly unrepresented or misrepresented. The table of votes, showing the represented and unrepresented voters in each of the seven senatorial districts, is as follows:—

Districts.	Represented.	Unrepresented.
First	3,342 ..	.. 2,263
Second	6,740 ..	.. 3,077
Third	3,995 ..	.. 4,109
Fourth	4,304 ..	.. 3,886
Fifth	6,175 ..	.. 1,167
Sixth	2,663 ..	.. 2,634
Seventh	4,716 ..	.. 1,284
Total	31,935	18,420

"Seven senators to be chosen by 50,355 voters gives 7,193 as the representative quota. From the table it will be seen that there were two full quotas of voters, and a surplus of 4,034, making in fact three senatorial quotas who were unable to choose a single senator, while no more than four quotas (justly entitled to four senators, but no more) elected all seven of the senators; taking to themselves a monopoly of the whole senatorial delegation. And this is what 'free and intelligent' American citizens are told by the professional office-begging politicians is popular representation!

"Some critics of the free vote have expressed fears that it might result in a great 'waste of votes.' By 'waste votes' they mean votes that fail to elect anybody. The 18,420 unrepresented voters shown in the foregoing table would be described by them as citizens who wasted, or threw away, their votes. They 'threw away their votes' because the law arbitrarily excluded them from the right of representation, and conferred upon four representative quotas all the representatives (senators) to which seven quotas were entitled. They 'threw away their votes' because the law in order to give a monopoly of the representation to a part of the constituency disfranchised them in the Senate of Illinois.

"But how was it in the choice of representatives, by the same voters, for the other branch of the Legislature, in which choice the free or cumulative vote prevailed? How many voters in the seven Cook County districts 'threw away their votes,' or failed to gain representation, under the operation of the new system? The following table shows the number of represented and (apparently) unrepresented voters, in each of the same districts, under a free vote:—

Districts.	Represented.	Unrepresented.
First	4,448	993
Second	7,906	1,799
Third	6,798	204
Fourth	7,491	1,018
Fifth	4,945	1,109
Sixth	3,870	1,520
Seventh	4,927	834
Total	40,385	7,477

"This table shows that the whole number of voters in the seven Cook County districts, who sought to be represented in the Lower House of the Legislature, was 47,862, of which number 40,385 actually gained a representative or representatives of their choice. In reality, the number who actually gained representation was much more than that, and the number who failed to gain representation much less than 7,477. The column 'unrepresented' in this table is reduced from all the votes given to candidates that were not elected, and is therefore largely made up of voters who gave only a portion of their three votes to the defeated candidate and the rest to a successful candidate. All such are, therefore, not unrepresented, but are actually represented by one representative of their choice. The actual number of unrepresented would, of course, be only those voters who gave all their votes to a defeated candidate. It is impossible to ascertain the exact number of such, without an examination of the ballots. It may, however, be fairly presumed that the actual number of voters in the seven districts who failed to gain representation would exclude a few more than those who, in the Third, Sixth, and Seventh Districts, voted 'plumpers' for Mr. Lowe (204), Mr. Buckingham (600), and Mr. Plowe (324). Assuming this to be the fact, the total number of voters in an aggregate of 47,862, who, by the use of the free or cumulative vote, failed to gain representation, was only 1,128.

"The comparison, then, of the results of the old and new system, operating side by side in these seven districts, at the same election, is as follows:—

	Voters Represented.	Voters Unrepresented.
Old system	31,935	18,420
New system	46,734	1,128

"These facts are recommended to the thoughtful consideration of all men who believe in popular representative government."

The evident fairness and justice of this distribution of political power between the great parties in the State would seem to have awakened a patriotic enthusiasm in the press in favour of proportional representation. Adverting elsewhere to the results of the election of the Lower House, the *Chicago Times* (Nov. 20, 1872) says:—"Such are some of the more than gratifying results of the 'free vote' upon its first trial in Illinois. Such practical demonstrations of the eminent justice of proportional representation in its actual results speak more convincingly in its favour than whole volumes of argument would do. Indeed, the happy results of the first trial of the proportional system upon so extensive a scale render further argument in its support almost needless. By its results in actual operation, the proportional system has already established its superior merits beyond the reach of cavil or doubt."

The *Chicago Daily Tribune* (Nov. 21, 1872), summing up the same results, concludes—" There are a number of defeated candidates who declare minority representation a humbug, and demand its repeal at the earliest possible time; but, on the whole, it has worked admirably; it has secured the great end sought, and has enabled the people, in many instances, to defeat the objectionable candidates by the election of better men. The principle of minority representation has been fully vindicated by the results."

The *World* adds—" If the work of this 'reformed' House of Representatives makes good the promise given by the nearly equally balanced state of parties and the defeat of objectionable candidates at the polls, we may expect to see the principle which has brought about these results incorporated into the various State constitutions."